LIFE AGAINST DEMENTIA
Essays, Reviews, Interviews 1975 - 2011

~

JOE CARDUCCI

REDOUBT PRESS
Centennial, Wyoming

Life Against Dementia
Essays, Reviews, Interviews 1975 - 2011

Joe Carducci

First Edition

Life Against Dementia
©2005, 2012 D. Joseph Carducci
All rights reserved.

Cover painting by Joseph F. Carducci (1936-2009)
Book design by Snowy Range Graphics

ISBN 0-9627612-2-2
ISBN 978-0-9627612-2-5

Redoubt Press
Centennial, Wyoming

Guy Debord talks of radical subjectivity, but never addresses the impact of music. It wasn't just American provenance that made Debord ignore Hendrix and Coltrane, it was also his failure to admit impulses below the level of verbal communication, his Lukácsian rationalism. What is missing in Debord is any hint of what fires Theodor Adorno, Nick Tosches and Joe Carducci – any understanding of the social subjectivity of abstract art, a subjectivity whose last refuge is music... This is not to imply that Adorno, Tosches and Carducci are wonderful examples of happy socialisation. Far from it. It is precisely their sociopath choler that allows them to perceive things denied the media-sycophan[ts].... Tosches and Carducci love rock'n'roll as much as Adorno hated it, but despite this, and despite the fact that Carducci is a redneck, they also grasp the social critique embedded in musical form, the incapacity of bourgeois market relations to deal with the musical object.

Ben Watson / Conference on the Situationist International

Contents

Acknowledgements	
Foreword	10
Introduction:	
Life Against Dementia	16
Film:	
Charles Bronson – Dark Buddha	53
Acting Methods, Alive or Dead	58
Acting Lessen	63
Clint the First	76
D.W. Griffith and the Biograph Shorts	79
Sword of Doom – New Vulgate	82
Sword of Doom – Damage	85
Nosferatu the Vampyre	86
Violence and the New Movie	88
Music:	
David Lightbourne and Outlaw Folk in 1970s Oregon	92
Rock Against Concrete	115
Arguing with the Fishes – The Minutemen	121
Minutemen Were Reactionaries	124
Armando and Saint Vitus	127
The Obsessed, Mk II	135
The Algorithm of Radio's Death Spiral	139
Frank Navetta and The Descendents	143
Radio Programmer Tip – 3 Tunes, 2 Segues, 1 Story	151
Renaissance, Systematic, and Rough Trade	156
Drink the Repulse Kava	163
Cheese: How Much Can Money Buy?	168
Peanuts... Jellybeans... MET-Rx Protein Bars...	177
Baroque Is Dead	182
Music Killers in the Pop Mausoleum	189
Meat Puppets II	197
Folk and the Pop Narcotic	201
Breakdown Lowdown 2004	204
Breakdown Lowdown 2005	206

Breakdown Lowdown 2006	208
Breakdown Lowdown on the Eights	211
The Last Upland Breakdown Lowdown, 2010	214
From the Northwest Desk	217
The Nig-Heist	219
Declassified Records, Dear Audio Buff	223
The New Wave	224
Sadistic Mika Band	228
Tangerine Dream – "Sorcerer"	230

Books:

End Times for the Hero – The Batman and Frank Miller	234
American Culture From and Against the Rest	242
Misrepresentational Art	247
The New York Times Criterion	251
Paul Nelson – First You Dream Then You Die	255
The Grate Game: Tibet	269
Real Impolitik – Pat Buchanan in the Crossfire	273
Rage to Serve – Hillaryland 10514	279
The Complete Jack the Ripper by Donald Rumblelow	293
Sergei Eisenstein – A Life in Conflict	296
Warren Oates – A Wild Life	299

Media:

Bring Me the Head of Lee Abrams	302
The New Vulgate: Blog as Fanzine	309
Rolling Stone, June 10 & 24, 1999	313
MTV's Adults-Only Juvenilia	316
Letter to the Editor, San Francisco Bay Guardian	321
Time – The Antagonist Obituary of the Year honoree	323
New Yorker Than Thou	325
Wired – The Geek Looks Up	328

World:

Brave New Class	332
Kalifornia unter Alles	344
Two Wisconsins	352
America in the Old Worlds	357
Arab Explanationalism	372
Egypt, and Step on It!	376
The Tea Party vs. The Metagaming of the System	382
The Framers vs. The Farmers – Bust the Corn Trust!	387

The American Alloy – Model, Export, Ideal...	390
The Metaphysics of Boomer Materialism: Death Panel Redux	397
Hipterama Heterodox	401
Racism as Set-aside for White Americans	406
Clinton Legacy Found!	412
So.Viet-nam	417
Pinochet in Winter – Last Act for the Hero	421

Sports:

Dad's Pirates vs. The Yankees, Game 7, 1960	428
Chicago Blackhawks, Stanley Cup 2010	434
Winter Sports Wrap, 1997-98	443

Songs:

Jesus and Tequila	448
Better to Die	449
Chinese Firedrill	450

Cartoons:

The Oregon Organism	452

Interviews:

Brazil site, by Eduardo Ramos, Feb. 2008	458
Alarm, by Andrew Williams, late 2002	461
Throat Culture, by Rob O'Connor, 1992	465
Non-Stop Banter, by Kevin Unsell, March 1986	469

ACKNOWLEDGEMENTS

Jay Babcock, Steve Beeho, Budd Boetticher (1916-2001), D. Boon (1958-1985), Jack Brewer, Bart Bull, Joseph F. Carducci (1936-2009), Maya Carducci, Philomena Carducci, Secondo Carducci (1899-1980), Henry Carlsen, Nina Carlsen, Lauren Chapman, Benoit Chaput, Jim Chasse (1964-2006), Byron Coley, Chris Collins, Lenny Diener, Bill DeLeonardis, Chris D., Ray Farrell, Jon Fine, Jonathan Formula, James Fotopoulos, Glen E. Friedman, Randy Gelling, Mike Vann Gray, Jason Gross, Jack Hammond, Loretta Hartlaub (1892-1988), Craig Ibarra, Bruce Kalberg (1949-2011), Drew Katsikas, Curt Kirkwood, Grace Krilanovich, Brad Lapin, David Lightbourne (1942-2010), Michael Lightbourne, Dave Markey, Keven McAlester, Thurston Moore, Brendan Mullen (1949-2009), Marie Navetta, Kara Nicks, Rob O'Connor, James Parker, Archie Patterson, Chris Petersen, Naomi Petersen (1964-2003), Raymond Pettibon, Joe Pope, Eduardo Ramos, Simon Reynolds, Henry Rollins, Jane Schuman, Ben Schwartz, Jordan Schwartz, Doug Sheppard, Paul Sommerstein, Spot, Bill Stevenson, Roger Trilling, Kevin Unsell, Mike Watt, Scott Weinrich, Mike Whittaker, Andrew Williams, Fred Woodworth, Mom, Dad, the kids and the grandkids.

FOREWORD

This collection came together when, in the course of gearing up for a website that never debuted, I wrote a number of essays and book reviews. They joined a couple commissioned pieces done in the wake of my first book, *Rock and the Pop Narcotic*. This attracted odds and ends I had written and sometimes got published going back to 1975. Then I threw in other stuff until I heard the distinctive -clunk- of the kitchen sink. I started *The New Vulgate* weekly blog in late 2009 with Chris Collins and David Lightbourne and pieces re-worked from those postings allowed me to extract that sink. Still I've kept some juvenilia in for laughs and seventies color. I've tagged those with a "Posterity Alert."

    I don't pretend there is any measurable demand that these pieces be made available. That's not how it works. Editors and Publishers don't know much since the seventies when the punk era was sidetracked by a class of sixties music entrepreneurs. The withholding of oxygen from this country's music culture retarded our literature as well since these have been twinned since Twain, or the Jazz Age at least. In the U.K. punk occurred in a completely different context, and for that narrative to be switched for ours by the know-nothings is twice a lie. Even after a refined version of punk surfaced fifteen years late the arrival of the web meant the Publishing world would never catch up to that past. I suppose conventional, competent material gets ignored as well, but there's a surplus of that and, hell, these baby boomers are going to make the *"60 Minutes"* geriatric ward look like a day-care center. So let's stipulate that the true engine behind the proliferation of self-publishing, web-mags, and blogs is that mainline publishing in Manhattan and elsewhere lost the American beat. It tried to replace the musical heartbeat of the age with stand-up, talk-radio, comedy... words.

    Lee Harris' post-9/11 debut in *Policy Review*, later amplified in his book, *Civilization and Its Enemies*, is the only important exception I can think of since Camille Paglia's *Sexual Personae* showed up on a university press in 1990. Other distinctive voices are either creatures of the web (David P. Goldman, Glenn Reynolds...) or have somehow survived tunneling up from political journalism (Christopher Caldwell, Christopher Hitchens, Paul Berman...) or culture media (Bart Bull, James Bowman, Russ

Smith, John Strausbaugh...) without losing their way. None but Hitchens really took it to television, which made his recent slow decline and death-by-cancer quite a phenomenal and touching media sidebar for anything concerning a mere writer. Nominally new voices like the neo-litterateurs are more often decadent end-points of a zombie culture that encourages the playing at assorted fantasies of being a writer or artist. They don't know what they're missing, except to fend it off when it actually threatens the fantasy.

In contemporary letters, editors mal-adapted, preferring to mis-assign good writers to marketing campaign trivia and then misunderstand, de-tune and un-write what they turned in. The repression by insider entrepreneurs which left the best art beyond mass concern was thereby defended by editors. Unwilling to "make" writers or artists they settled for fabrications. The greater American culture apparatus in the seventies and eighties was spared having to acclimate to the contemporary analogues to Elvis Presley, The Beatles, or Jimi Hendrix and so decadence and its agents were ushered in to the best seats. M.C. Ed Sullivan was a master at acclimation to whatever the backwoods of Tennessee or Rumania could throw at him. He would've booked The Ramones; the much hipper Lorne Michaels of "*Saturday Night Live*" never did.

The blizzard of small press activity is better than nothing, only there's no such thing as nothing. The free weeklies, and the fanzines, and the webzines and blogs, though they have forced the air out of the former mass media, like a blustery Thanksgiving Day might the overblown but quite fragile Parade balloons, they did not replace them scoop-for-scoop, scandal-for-scandal, blow-for-blow. The *Chicago Reader* once ran a nice long feature on the making of a film by director Jim Sikora which I co-wrote and produced. Rex Benson, the late, great character-actor and all-around character who worked his way up from clip-joint Chicago to managing Lord Buckley and thence to Hollywood (*Hooper*, Mighty Carson Art-Players, "*Superboy*"), was in the cast and when he saw the piece exclaimed in old school cold-blooded appraisal: "This is a career-making article." Us pups perked up our ears at that, but no, not quite. The Press is more open as more folks have them so its power is diminished as press relations becomes less networking the few brokers and gatekeepers of yore, and becomes instead a front-loaded game of brinksmanship that only the established players can affect to the point of ubiquity in everything from the freebies to the dailies to video and radio and web and phone. They strive for hundreds of thousands, millions of "impressions" upon the impressionable for a successful mainstream release.

But the young have no memory of what it is that's been lost in this mass media meltdown, though they often appear to remain in thrall to those last popular artists. The rise of the second great independent record label economy in the late 1970s was a tacit indictment of the majors' disinterest in the music of the age. But the pretense that too often followed from this simple structural truth was allowed to harden into just another marketing handle (as the independent film market from the late 1980s did in just half the time). I regret my short-lived enthusiasm for this sterile trope in my pre-SST Records rec-biz career, and I'm astonished that those post-SST often turned our failure into a hollowed out ideology, while often selling many multiples of what we had managed.

The splintering of the formerly mass media which our punk rock ground-war accomplished has made it more difficult to put over such artists as deserve the spotlight wattage that could once be provided by network television's Steve Allen and Ed Sullivan, and AM radio's Alan Freed, Howard Miller, and Howard Hancock. Once, these mass media shuttled a mix of professionals, folk artists, and rank amateurs through their spotlights. Andy Warhol's famous dictum was true for at least two decades before he coined it as a prediction just as it ceased to be. What is allotted these days no longer meets the definition of fame as once understood; now it might more properly read: Today everyone serves as flitting minor irritant to everyone else periodically amongst the flotsam and jetsam of the feed.

We no longer even look up as the pop thrushes, cagers, wrestlers, skaters, strumpets, comedians, actors, rockers, *et. al.* dance through the dimming media lamps. Lester Bangs famously closed his Elvis obit, "I can guarantee you one thing: we will never again agree on anything as we agreed on Elvis. So I won't bother saying good-bye to his corpse. I will say good-bye to you." (*Village Voice*, August 29, 1977) The more recent weeklong funerals of Ronald Reagan and Pope John Paul II remind us that we are seeing the last personages that command such attention pass from the scene.

As Lightbourne put it in his intro essay to my *Wyoming Stories*, instead of Mass Media we now have massed-media. Where once three TV networks, five movie studios, six major labels, ten book publishers and a dozen radio networks bent over backwards trying to please everyone in a coherent, mostly working class society, there are now a handful of global multi-media corporations whose offices are so high up the skyscraper they can't see the street. And their programming outlets and formats are so specialized that all they have time for is market research and lying to Wall Street. The guerrilla marketing done by their street teams of intern conscripts is conducted like recon patrols through the foreign jungle our class structure has become to them.

These ten corps are no longer involved in truly mass media however. Even the films made by Hollywood, the top of the culture food-chain, are no longer the mass culture its founders built. "Number One!" is a relative term in today's box office, or Billboard chart, or ratings game; today it merely means some hardware-software conglomerate is keeping its chin above the pooling massed-media hemorrhage more successfully than the other congloms – its distribution network attenuation momentarily slowed.

The last labels and studios standing fret over the web's transformation of their loyal customer base into swarms of locusts; the news media obsess on the blog-writing masses – their closest readers – who now critique, check and supervise the professionals as in some chaos theory experiment run in reverse: Millions of agitated curs barking up thousands of the wrong Weyerhauser™ trees in the shadows of the last of the Redwoods as these rot out from the inside. Millions of chimps at millions of keyboards... Dime novels a-dime-a-dozen... And not a journal or editor or critic to sort through it. There's thousands of them but they're busy with some sort of myopic posture maintenance as the ships of the state of American arts founder.

And the great public institutions resisted everything new as if surrounded by a cordon sanitaire against the plague. Could one not say, in fact, that things have got better since then? ...New movements are constantly being started; everybody attends both the academic and the avant-garde shows, and even the avant-garde of the avant-garde; the family magazines have bobbed their hair; politicians like to sound off on the cultural arts, and newspapers make literary history. So what has been lost?

Robert Musil / *The Man Without Qualities*

Introduction.

~

Life Against Dementia

I was working on this in summer 2002 without an idea of what I might do with it when Jay Babcock wrote to say he would launch a magazine called Arthur. *I sent it to him and he ran it in No. 1. It's updated and about three times as long here.*

Anyone familiar with the roiling currents and tidal motion of American culture knows that the film and music industries are delivering less than ever – less heat and less cool. Across the twentieth century in American film and music it's hard to isolate any valleys among the peaks, in fact it is more correct to say there were only rivulets along the folds of a single massive peak. To illustrate this by decade in admittedly criminal shorthand here's a list of masters driving American culture and its industries (you can add your own but you may not subtract):

1900s
W.K.L. Dickson, Edwin S. Porter, Scott Joplin, Jelly Roll Morton, Buddy Bolden...

1910s
D.W. Griffith, Thomas Ince, Francis Ford, William S. Hart, Harry Carey, John Ford, Fatty Arbuckle, Mabel Normand, Mary Pickford, Henry King, King Oliver, Rogers & Hart, Irving Berlin...

1920s
Buster Keaton, Clyde Bruckman, Max & Dave Fleischer, Walt Disney, Robert Flaherty, Lillian Gish, W.C. Fields, Louis Armstrong, Charley Patton, Tommy Johnson, Jimmie Rogers, Bing Crosby...

1930s
Laurel & Hardy, Rowland Brown, Howard Hawks, Gene Autry, Duke Ellington, Count Basie, Thomas Dorsey...

1940s
Val Lewton, Orson Welles, Hank Williams, Woody Guthrie, John Lee Hooker...

1950s
Anthony Mann, Don Siegel, Philip Yordan, B.B. King, Elvis Presley, Link Wray, Muddy Waters, the Rock 'n Roll Trio...

1960s
Sam Peckinpah, Francis Ford Coppola, Dick Dale, Albert King, Jimi Hendrix...

1970s
Michael Ritchie, Clint Eastwood, Jeff Bridges, Terrence Malick, Neil Young, Stooges, ZZ Top, Ramones, Black Flag...

Anyway, we know that compared to the recent past, never mind the twenties, the wheels have come off. Since 1980 one could count The Descendents, The Minutemen, maybe Flipper as having ranked musically and loads more just a bit beneath them, but who in film? The independent film boom threw up a generation of poseurs and one-trick ponies. There are dozens of "Red Hot Chili Peppers" directing films, but is there a single "Minutemen" filmmaker? Steven Soderbergh works a lot at different things but is he working up to something worth all that middling stuff? Better to study the films of John Flynn and hope Eastwood lives as long as his mother.

The action film fell of its own overblown weight; it's hard to remember that it grew from such lean, tightly-scripted productions as *Dirty Harry* (1971), *Death Wish* (1974), *Rocky* (1976), *Alien* (1979), *First Blood* (1982), and *Terminator* (1984) – all their damn sequels saw to that. And whereas *Jaws* (1975) remade film marketing, *Titanic* (1997) threatened to remake the summer action blockbuster itself – fusing the disaster film with the woman's film takes an additional hundred million dollars and another hour in running time. The resulting summer behemoths trod the marketplace with such strong-arming confidence that the studios practically demand they be made without costly stars so as to pack in more fx and advertising.

The music industry's problems have been visible for decades. The autogenic rise of the web was clear enough in the record industry's peripheral vision, if only as a parade of hot NASDAQ listings through the late nineties. But the record biz is notoriously poor at adding things up and was too busy chasing or chewing ass to read the entrails. Late Hippie traveled full circle and met Nerd in the form of seventies west coast computer culture, at first yielding but a word processor, a fancy term for a fancy typewriter, until Netscape's browser let the unwashed hordes onto DARPA's internet, begetting the web, file-sharing, streaming, burning, and itching....

Introduction

Hard to blame the typical coke-head Buddhist perverts of the record business for missing the signs, I suppose.

The President and CEO of the National Association of Recording Arts and Sciences (NARAS), Michael Greene, was too busy counting his money, kvetching about Republicans and grabbing after the foxes in his hen-house to trouble his mind over THE END OF THE WHOLE GODDAMNED RECORDING ARTS & SCIENCES SHEBANG! On the February 2002 Grammys telecast he infamously declared war on file-sharing. Then resigned two months later after Jack Palladino (a.k.a., the People's Private Eye – you know, peeble like Bill Clinton and Mariah Carey) turned in his dick-work on a NARAS ex-execrutrix's charges of Clintonesque liberalism-with-the-hands on the part of said ex-Hampton Grease Band bass-plucker. Citing philosorfical differences Greene resigned in a settlement that cost NARAS 16% of its net assets. Not including the $650,000.00 settlement that went to she what got plucked. And the other two office charmettes held in reserve but never heard from must've got royalties against his advances too. Good thing NARAS's philanthropic wing, Musicares, pays out less than one dollar for every three donated for the poor, indigent, cancerous, gangrenous old bluesmen in their care or they never could've swung the deal closed.

In addition to the nameless internet horde, Recording Stars with Big Square Heads like Don Henley and Lars Ulrich were also threatening the gold and the goose. Stars were lobbying in Sacramento to void the record industry's exemption from the seven-year personal contract limit (an anti-slavery provision), and they wanted to own their own master recordings. (I say let 'em – no, wait, we may need those for evidence.) And over all the bogus Grammy proceedings loomed the specter of the computer-software-hardware-internet-broadband-4G-wireless juggernaut's paramount Holy Grail Killer App – FREE CHUNES!

*

So the questions became:

1) Have Radio, TV and Film so divided programming into blindered marketing niches that's they've cut the cords from today's pop to our rich musical and film traditions?

2) Has the music underground rejected all traditions but the line of nihilism diagrammed by Greil Marcus in *Lipstick Traces*, with the sole backstop of kitsch (such vicarious ex-pat pursuits as French

chanson, Brasiliana, Exotica, Canto-Pop, J-pop)?

3) Has the Organization Man of International Entertainment Corporate Culture proved incapable of recognizing and delivering music and film of the level that sundry Sammy Glicks and juke-box mobsters did for decades in their sleep?

4) Has the world market evolution of international Pop – its computer-generated virtual musics and virtual films – superseded the organic cultural motion within the once worldhistorical syncretisms of American music and film?

Sorry I asked...

We can't be sure whether the current thin gruel might not be the only possible art deduced from the slim pickings of the last three decades. Twenty year-olds in bands and thirty year-olds making films today have experienced pop culture of little depth or personality their entire small lives. Radio was formatted in the early seventies and so commercially ambitious recording artists quickly began to format themselves. But an entire generation of willful rock bands – Ramones through Flipper – refused to format themselves. These were the last bands to have grown up on the rich programming of pre-1974 radio and the television variety show music mix (not to mention the high grade of local "amateur" live music Americans of all ages once routinely encountered at county fairs, corn-boils, church socials, and school dances). But unformatted, these Punk bands were then, not programmed. To quote the reigning authority on such matters:

> "Contemporary rock bands spoke a musical lexicon derived from mass media America one generation on. But their preternatural media consciousness and its accompanying ease with rock music (and media) as plastic expression, though media-generated in this second generation ATV [after television] America, intimidated the same media. For it had been the media's autistic denial of depth and context itself which had bred the depths of sarcasm and absurdism in these bands and their audiences."
> (*Rock and the Pop Narcotic*)

Those bands that attempted to format themselves for hits (Talking Heads, Devo, X, Replacements...) ensured they would not be the bands to carry the musical torch of rock and roll forward; perversely, it would be the unprogrammed misses (Motörhead, Ramones, Avengers, Misfits, Bad Brains,

Introduction

Black Flag, Minutemen, Descendents, Saint Vitus...) that would launch a million bands. But since that last underground generation – 1974 to 1984 – even the best bands (Nirvana, Tool, Queens of the Stone Age, White Stripes...) seem more narrowly conceived, as if a young musician-to-be's input from today's constricted, utterly media-driven musical environment might in the end dry up the output of even bands that do not depend on hit radio and *MTV*.

Hollywood today, courtesy of marketing-science and Sammy Glick IV, offers CGI Potemkin villages and villagers for pulverizing in CGI thermidor for the boys, inspirational "making it" soaps or tearjerking emo-porn for girls, and hollow puzzle pictures for the sophistos. Generations of filmmakers have been destroyed by the *Star Wars* films, and as it's to be a trilogy of trilogies we can't expect relief until 2112 or so. Lucas intended to revive the Saturday afternoon serials which he did with the goofy, cheapo charm of the first film, but it earned so much money he decided the franchise must needs be profound and duly yea, sank the subsequent acts in pseud-Shakespearean tarpits; thank Darth he didn't do eight sequels to *American Graffiti* – Ron Howard would be playing a script-destroying producer-director by now. (In my unrequited meetings with film producers in L.A. and N.Y. the life-size star-trooper models in the office corners never relax their guard.) [*What, he's cancelled the third trilogy?! Well, we'll always have* Radar Men from the Moon, *and* Masterpiece Theatre.]

A recent issue of *Wired* magazine quoted George Lucas from Canadian television, "When I went to USC, I didn't know anything about movies, I watched television. I wasn't that interested in movies." He says that *American Graffiti* "derailed" him and then *Star Wars* "sidetracked" him. But as he moved his 1,500 employees into his Digital Arts Center at the former Presidio army base in San Francisco he promised, "I've earned the right to fail, which means making what I think are really great movies that no one wants to see." (*Wired*, May 2005) So six years later he rolls out *Red Tails* (2012) which he himself describes as old-fashioned and corny and for teenage boys! But lets assume there will be experimental films... Methinks Lucas will lose 0.002% of his capital (which certainly grows at a solid 5% annually, no?) on these "experimental" films-to come and be back to that third trilogy as if woken from a near-death experience – the *Howard the Duck* of his nightmares.

**

Recently passing on through the obit pages have been such American cultural figures as Peggy Lee, Herb Sargent, Ken Nelson, Budd Boetticher, Joey, Dee Dee, and Johnny Ramone, Dave Van Ronk, Pop Staples, Waylon

Jennings, Harlan Howard, John Lee Hooker, Richard Farnsworth, Bernard Klatzko, Carl Perkins, Ed Roth, Hilous Butrum, Otis Blackwell, John Fahey, Johnnie Johnson, Hunter S. Thompson, Katharine Hepburn, Robert Creeley, Johnny Cash, Bob Hope, Johnny Carson, Merle Kilgore, Stan Levey, Estelle Axton, Elmer Bernstein, Marlon Brando, Ray Charles, Ronald Reagan, Rodney Dangerfield, Skeeter Davis, Hunter Hancock, Rick James, Henry Townsend, Elvin Jones, Greg Garrison, Sam Phillips, Arthur Kane, Jackson Beck, Barney Kessel, Mercedes McCambridge, Robert Quine, Hubert Selby Jr., Greg Shaw, Frank Navetta, Jerry Byrd, Doris Troy, Fred Holstein, Terry Melcher, Son Seals, Johnny Paycheck, Charles Bronson, Artie Shaw, Paul Nelson, Jimmy Smith, J.F. Gourrier, Martin Denny, Jimmie Davis, Doug Sahm, Owen Bradley, Percy Heath, Don Pierce, Ed Cobb, Fritz Richmond, Bruce Conner....

Never mind the heftlessness of the obits in decades to come, Britney Spears may never die – I mean look at that forehead! Biotech nerds, not known for their ability to hear music are forging new frontiers in unintended consequences.

Our meta-sentient popular mechani-culture has foreshadowed this immortality. The explosion of cultural choices via cable and satellite has reached uncritical mass via the web – it's now become something different, a constant ambient hemorrhagic din. Kids watch *"Ozzie and Harriet"* and *"The Osbournes"*; Marshall Dillon rides again; Buster Keaton falls and springs up again; old game shows are replayed, and even the sword-and-sandal genre returns! We are either jacked by contemporary offerings or calmed by our immortal ghost culture (Lawrence Welk, Audie Murphy, *"Cheyenne," "Father Knows Best"*...). If little kids still have long, slow, endless summers, they will find this stuff as it is all over their TV dial, and what isn't there can be found at Netflix, and what's not there has surely been uploaded to *youtube*. The newly immortalized copyright laws ensure that the holders of these twentieth century culture collections will continue to push these properties in front of kids, not a bad thing at all. As the copyright laws stood ten years ago you or I could have written, drawn, inked, published and distributed our own Mickey Mouse comic book by now. In theory we must wait another decade, but in truth we know that as Mickey will never die, neither will Walt's copyright. It's the King's two bodies all over again – The rodent is dead, long live the rodent!

But might there appear a new character as durable as Mickey? While it is true that a musical/societal syncretism such as Elvis Presley can never be repeated, it is also true that there are no longer coherent folk cultures and pop structures which a given Elvis might be launched from and against. The Fifties pop consensus was bisected first by generation (Frank v. Elvis), then by gender (for men: Eastwood/Welch trumping Wayne/Mayo; for women: Redford/Streisand trumping Burton/Taylor), and then chopped into smaller and smaller fractiles (Russ Meyer, Roger Corman, speed-metal, adult comics, splatter films, death metal, lesbian romances, post-rock, the Olsen twins, nü-metal, abasement comedies, black metal...). These fractiles increasingly could only be enjoyed by one sex and by a small age group of said sex at that.

Instead of backwater geniuses being shuttled into the mass media spotlight for the benefit of a sincerely interested audience, the micro media now turns its spotlight onto itself in effect, for the amusement of a fallen, cynical audience. There was one Elvis; there are millions of Kim Fowleys. People lived vicariously through Elvis in that part of their grounded lives they reserved for dreams, a part which necessarily retreated once their adult lives began in their late teens or early twenties with marriage and kids. Today, Americans marry late and perhaps have a kid or two – these kids, often only-childs, are then that much more vulnerable to the virtual world. And once grown their work-lives generally require no physical labor. This new reality has loosed us to live in a veritable dreamland. And one can only laugh at a Kim Fowley as he chases his weightless dream whether in actual show business or in some reality-based version.

Conversely the sophistos, who ought to know better, retreat instead, entertaining only the guileless, even artless, atavist: Daniel Johnston, Wesley Willis, Roky Erickson, Gary Wilson, Wildman Fischer... A Henry Darger cannot disappoint, cannot turn on his fans who have, after all, invested their personal reputations for hip in him, or preferably in his memory. And today when the hip look to country or blues, they seem only able to appreciate that artist or song which might be appreciated as a token of some kind of melodramatic goth culture – Johnny Cash becomes merely The Man in Black/ex-con/bad-ass, when very little of his discography comports with that. The blues becomes merely Devil's Music. Lost is the party music. Lost is the beautifully intricate delta blues – a kind of one-man chamber music. Lost is Johnny Cash's gospel music. Lost is all of black gospel as the hipsters follow the communists and elide it from the blues as if they were not conjoined seven ways from Sunday usually in the same artists under a second name.

Gothic juvenilia in film manifests itself in the all-purpose Noir genre. The problem is that there never was such a genre prior to such imitations. *Noir* was a tag the French film critics of *Cahiers du Cinema* attached to war-time American films that were already ten years old by the time free-France got to see them. Whereas the American artist/writer Manny Farber would call the true B-films "termite art" for their makers' unpretentious m.o. within the major studios, he referenced camp, Damon Runyon, and "hucksterish flash" when writing contemporaneously about the merely arty, false-B of John Huston's *The Asphalt Jungle* (1950) – Farber tagged such as "white elephant" art. The French critics just saw black. They had their reasons, having just gotten their country back courtesy our red, white and blue. Still the term was first common in France in 1955 and exported by the later New Wave critic-directors to America by 1970 along with the auteur theory. The films this PR term is now applied to have origins in other true Hollywood genre-traditions and in any case had come and gone well before this naming.

Then-critic Francois Truffaut wrote in 1958,

> "One would have to say that the greatest film-makers are over fifty, but it is important to practice the cinema of one's own age and try, if one is twenty-five and admires Dreyer, to emulate *Vampyr* rather than *Ordet*." (*Cahiers du Cinema – The 1950s*)

Truffaut as a young filmmaker then made a couple of mature, humane pictures before going quite soft; he never made Dreyer and got further rather than nearer that ideal as he aged but didn't mature. But is *American Graffiti* Lucas' *400 Blows*? And just what is Spielberg's *Close Encounters of the Third Kind* (1977), wherein Truffaut plays a cross between Erich von Daniken and Jacques Cousteau? Is this an alien humanism? A whiz-bang lullaby? It's *Night for Day*, I would say. Perfectly misconceived – admittedly I have neglected to survey CE3K – *The Special Edition, The Network Television Edition*, or *The Collector's Edition* for this piece; I'm waiting for *The Holographic Homophobic Edition* where the alien Frenchman, a.k.a. l'Cineaste, shoves that mud-pile up Dreyfus' dump-hole while O.S. if you boost the volume you can just make out Spielberg sputtering, "Cut!" over and over again.

Italian philosopher-critic Mario Perniola claims we live now in an Egyptian moment,

> "...brought about neither by a return of the repressed nor by future shock, but by the enigma of their coincidence and the emergence of a condition in which the ancient past and the imaginable future are not merely similar – they can be confused."
> (*Enigmas – the Egyptian Moment in Society and Art*)

Naturally, he illustrates with a Spielberg film, *Jurassic Park* (1993), where "past and future are both collapsed into an ambiguous, supremely problematic present." (*Ibid*.) Actually that sounds like a better film. Malcolm McLaren thinks the world is "totally in love with its past and completely bored with its future." (*Literary Theory: An Anthology*)

Well, we know what works. It's been settled. It's the end of history. Now it is authorless systems maintenance of the semi-free marketplace regulated via some flavor of bourgeois democracy. The People's Republic of China confirms this from outside as each day it further builds up the institutions and actors to accomplish such self-regulation we in the West take for granted. Perhaps if society could still generate movements and trends in the arts and ideas one would attempt to jam this consensus, but it is a world-historical conclusion that sits atop a mound of corpses from the left revolutions, the right reactions, the world wars, the reformation, the Crusades, the religious wars, imperialism, Jihad, and the Hatfields and the McCoys. Might take more smarts and some decades to take that on.

***

The advertising industry runs on applied schizophrenia; its hacks work not to express themselves or even their clients, but to anticipate and produce what potential customers might respond to, all the while serving their clients' interests. It's this wheedling Madison Avenue energy, not just its money, which fuels the media and increasingly the art itself. There once was an ongoing garage rock revival wherein the Hives and others got commercial airplay, but why was it that we'd first heard that retro-garage-style in major ad campaigns for Target, the Gap, and Coors Light a full year earlier? Clearly there are sharper and more desperate minds in advertising and marketing departments than in music programming. This is the sped-up reverse of the old pattern of art-and-advertising.

A similarly desperate energy shoots prospective talismans of the *zeitgeist* such as mullet haircuts, *"Desperate Housewives,"* NASCAR, reality shows, or Twitter through an increasingly dim popular culture and before the even dumber cultures of media, politics and the academy whose leading cement-heads can always be counted on to belabor the slightest of trivia. We first saw the defensive nature of this reflex after Elvis' death when his name and image suddenly became rote punch-lines for middle-brow jokes – the jokers being those uncertain over just how many millimeters above the trucker from Tupelo and his fans they were perched on the American class ladder. Fans of Elvis the musician also often naively identified with his adventure in class transcendence; his necrophagites compulsively seek to convince themselves they are better than Elvis and his fans. They fear being caught naïve and uncool and get into quite a negative trip and Elvis abuse was one of the major calling cards of shock jock/morning zoo radio schtick as it arrived.

Related to this, I think, was the use by writers, poets and singers, of brand names in place of adjectives or nouns. I first noticed this at a reading in Portland by John Shirley in 1979. Shirley was singing for either The Monitors or Sado-nation, and had already written several novels of a style soon called cyber-punk. His intent in his poetry readings was clear, but it seemed a bad sign to me at the time, and sure enough over the years in lesser hands the brandishing of these corporate pronouns slipped easily into a false critique that masked a covert display of consumerist vanity.

Still, despite the derisive, corrupt energy leaking from Madison Avenue and its media, the gravitational pull of the marketplace and individual artistic consciousness tugs at notions from all cultural shards and seeks to remake of them the old A-film or hit record that once offered something for men and women, girls and boys, hipsters and squares. Then, this was attempted full-throatedly by artists such as John Ford, the Beach Boys, George Stevens, Neil Young; Now it's tried *sotto voce* by Steven Spielberg, No Doubt, Steven Soderbergh, Weezer. The *zeit* has no *geist*. The last mass phenotype in rock and roll was the Seattle look/sound, which in truth was the afterbirth of Punk, begun on major labels in New York, incubated at SST in Los Angeles, and returned to radio and the majors by the Northwest bands who exhibited neo-hippie heaviness with prog and freeform cut by the Punk reformation. A clutch of bands went platinum and forced changes in media and fashion at the moment Punk found its way back to 1974, only without the guitar- and drum-solos. The media culture did remember 1974, if dimly.

Since the mid-nineties trends have no such impact. Is a similar scene incubating occurring somewhere now in the independent label economy, or on the web? Not likely. Omaha artists were selling plenty of records when one showed up rather tentatively on the cover of the *New York Times Magazine* to zero effect. The straight media can no longer make a career but they can probably preclude a movement with their infectious unhipness. *NPR* seems to be moving music, but with rock and roll tamed for alterna-moms and dads there's nothing to alienate their still larger numbers of baby boomers. Nirvana's success even provided a new template for Christian rock, speaking of inalienable followers.

Refusal to grow up was very nearly the defining characteristic of the baby boom so it's no surprise they might refuse to die. Their pop culture likewise appears immutable. Kids and young adults – those born in the eighties or later – keep inherited styles like Hippie, Soul, Folkie, Radical, Beat and Bop alive. And the alternatives – Punk, Metal, Garage, Rap – date back to very nearly the same period. That these styles survive does not mean they stay vital. Each now exhibits the dementia of a played-out mind, no matter the condition of the body. And in youth-culture terms, when a style will not die, then the hollow posturing of the neo-neophytes within it forecloses the use of that style's original statements by any ambitious young musician seeking to create something new informed by the best of the past – this past the only possible source of ammunition against a sterile present. Hence while the hollowed styles thrive, vital young musicians are discouraged from rooting themselves in these traditions because their high school/college nemeses are camped out within them.

The slow organic rise of alt-country to the point that it has become a sturdy parallel economy augurs best for a musically rooted revolution today. Commercial C&W radio is as utterly irrelevant to this underground as commercial rock radio was to The Ramones thirty years ago, which can be a good thing if you're patient enough to wait for Nirvana. Who could be the shitkicker Messiah? Ryan Adams? Grandpa's Ghost? Cowboy Troy? No, no, and no I would hazard. That Kurt Cobain – boy sure was purty.

One false option that has sucked life and money from the roots-country economy is the "non-commercial" AAA format at *NPR*. Its provenance is probably the transformation of Rounder Records from the kind of label that would name itself after the Holy Modal Rounders to one that gave up on them, Michael Hurley and Jeffrey Fredericks under the sweet commercial pressure of their late seventies successes with George Thorogood and then Nancy Griffith. Bruce Cockburn was in the mix too with his slicked up folk-rock as was Richard Thompson. Then Steve Earle turned on Nashville under the influence of Springsteen and fell between the stools; he found a second or third life as a public radio folkie. As the public radio networks and stations begun to cater to the format whole careers have been made and labels launched or re-launched like Lost Highway, Nonesuch, Verve, Blue Note, and Vanguard, even in the teeth of record retailing's collapse.

The garage underground was far more reactionary than the country underground. It's an old scene that often cleaves to bad formless junk because it betrays no trace of pop, metal, punk or whatever gets their goat and so can't sell-out to anybody and embarrass them. Luckily it has a great, historically rooted fanzine voice in *Ugly Things*, and the scene's arbiters lost control of bands that deserved and almost got a wide audience.

The Fat Possum label roiled the well-oiled blues industry simply by trolling the delta for seventy and eighty year old delta bluesmen – the last of their genus, sadly. The city sophisticates of the blues business didn't immediately cotton to these rural eccentrics (R.L. Burnside, Junior Kimbrough, T-Model Ford...); that's how far from musical truth even music obsessives can drift when a subculture's weakness inspires defensiveness. Somehow *WXRT*'s poor but powerful taste in rock music has infected

Chicago's blues scene as well. Although the station has better taste in blues than rock it has retarded the white audience and that tells.

What seemed a promising development was that rash of young pop idols leaning on ex-rocker/songwriting-producer svengalis (John Shanks, the Matrix, Cliff Magness) to create a rock hit. In the changed environment such reverse sell-out rock-out can stand out as not so shabby. What was odd was that it was the girls (Avril Lavigne, Ashlee Simpson, Kelly Clarkson, Hilary Duff...) who wanted to rock or "rock" ("Losing Grip," "La-La," "Since U Been Gone," "The Math," respectively). Britney Spears and Christina Aguilera grew up and fixed their pop careers to the then ascendant hip hop/dance lexicon so it was progressive regress when a Disney kid like Duff cites Janis Joplin as her favorite and bothers to put a band behind her. Overseas pop-tarts like Kylie Minogue are in touch with neither style of carnal rhythm no matter how ostensibly sexy the view.

This stuff isn't Paul Revere and the Raiders because these singers are not parts of bands that grew up playing together before hitting Hollywood and getting the likes of Bruce Johnston and Terry Melcher to bring them into the industry without destroying them. Admittedly, these pop kids now are so *of-the-industry* they are all but indestructible. Still there are better tunes being written by and for young women generally, and their anxiety is proving more productive than whatever it is the boys are going through. Maybe it's as simple as that any boy who might have needed to sublimate via music or art are all on Paxil by the third grade and getting blowjobs by the eighth.

I might nominate "If Only Two" by Unida as the last great male vocal, powerfully expressive in both the writing and John Garcia's singing whereby the words prove inadequate and he trails syllables based on 'oh's and 'yeah's from verses and choruses. The metal screamers and emo wailers ought to listen here to what a male soul can project. Unida was Kyuss vocalist Garcia's highly anticipated follow-up band and they overspent. The band broke up soon after the album "Coping with the Urban Coyote" was released in 1999 and Man's Ruin folded thereafter. I'm also partial to Scott Weinrich's vocal performance on the Shine 45 version of "Lost Sun Dance" (1997) which was re-recorded less compellingly for the first Spirit Caravan album, though it's available on a 2xCD SC compilation.

Peter Aspden, the culture writer for the *Financial Times* wrote that "thanks to the most appalling set of circumstances" he found himself attending a Kylie Minogue show instead of the Cream reunion. He concludes,

> "A Kylie concert is just harmless fun, or, better, a victimless crime.

> It was a perfect night out for the under-12s, which hardly explains the number of 35-year-old (gay) men miming to every promise-laden word that came from her precarious, tiny frame. I imagined that Cream sounded precarious too... because they were playing this dated, hopelessly earnest music in front of a solemn audience that was trying to relive the days when each impromptu turn of a guitar solo was worthy of attention and loving analysis. I wished I was there, of course, but I was also happy to have this theoretical choice between portent and piffle, for who would want one without the other?" (*Financial Times*)

Well sure, except that Cream's audience wasn't that old either so they were not reliving anything but seeing such music for the first time as they no doubt fervently expected. Cream have at most a couple dozen more dates in them, whereas Kylie? Time is not on music's side, though perhaps above certain seats at the Royal Albert Hall one of those Beavis-type buzzing, unsteady light-bulbs struggled to light.

Bob Dylan (then 63) is quoted in his 2005 tour literature, "I wouldn't even think about playing music if I was born in these times." Adding to the codger gloom according to the *Financial Times* (Apr. 28, 2005), opening act Merle Haggard (then 68) announced at the New York stop, "We're probably the only band in the world that has nurses instead of roadies." But even in the late seventies Mick Jagger was doubting the Rolling Stones could have got signed. And twenty years ago I published a book to document the lost generation of bands from 1974 to 1990 and write them into the history of rock and roll. I was more optimistic then.

I'd suggest that teenage musicians listen to oldies, classic rock, classic country, and blues from the twenties to the sixties rather than their own contemporaries. This has gotten quite easy to do now with all the micro-formats on satellite and cable radio, and various internet and phone services. The first year of Dylan's satellite radio show, "Theme Time Radio," really let his themes cut their way through Tin Pan Alley, rock and roll, blues, jazz, gospel and country with an emphasis on the songwriter in a way even he could not maintain. But a young listener has to give music outside his ken time so the ear acclimates to the sound and he begins to understand the language like a native speaker. He must resist the impulse to screen it all through a contemporary goth or rock filter.

Learn these many American languages and whatever comes out when you put hands to guitar and open your mouth will be deeper and more expressive, re-grounded maybe. The great punk era bands of 1974-1984 were natural grand composites of everything after Elvis (or Bing for that matter); but for this very reason they are not enough to build something new from – they are too densely packed, as if historical punctuation. So young players must step back and then assemble for themselves a non-specialist mix. Unfortunately they must first create a rich musical environment for themselves – what was once simply in the air. They must do this immediately upon realizing that they are ambitious about music or they will fall into one narrow enthusiasm or another and at best flop from one to the next like a Bowie without an Iggy.

****

The movies' dilemma is different. Filmmaking is capital-intensive and it is art-by-committee of nominal adults. Four kids on a mission might make great music, but we probably don't want to see the film they might produce.

The old studio system was crippled by the Supreme Court's 1948 Paramount decision, which forced the divestiture of the studios' theater chains, and then it was destroyed by the growth of television whose production m.o. recapitulated the worst of the movie studios, their serials. Its history was then rewritten via the auteur theory, which re-evaluated low-budget programmers at the expense of prestige A-films. It took until the end of the sixties for a new production equilibrium to be reached. The unexpected successes of Sergio Leone's westerns (released in U.S., 1967-8), and *Easy Rider* (1969) woke Hollywood up and ended embarrassing studio attempts at youth films, most of which tried to fob off Manhattan hip for youth culture. But that youth culture's moment lasted less than a decade. Soon the small pulpy early/mid-seventies B/art film (*The Hired Hand, Two-Lane Blacktop, Bad Company, Badlands, Night Moves, Rancho Deluxe*...) was hammered into a comicy template by *Rocky, Jaws,* and *Star Wars.*

The commercial fiascos by the new directors – *The Sailor Who Fell from Grace with the Sea* (1976), *Buffalo Bill and the Indians or Sitting Bull's History Lesson* (1976), *New York, New York* (1977), *Sorcerer* (1977), *Heaven's Gate* (1980), *Hammett* (1983) – opened the door wide to the comic-populists whose sensibility was an easier fit with the teenage audience that remained as adult movie attendance declined. (The last true adults weren't interested in the new "adult films" with their swearing and grandiloquently casual sex and violence). And as the comic-populists weren't into drugs or high-flying muses they were more dependable with studio money. As John Lombardi wrote in 1988 as he contrasted sensible Bruce Springsteen to the comets Hendrix, Morrison, Joplin, *et. al.*,

Introduction

> "In a sales culture like ours, the fans invariably take over, preferring copies to originals because they're cheaper and last longer..." (*Esquire*)

According to Peter Biskind in his book, *Easy Riders Raging Bulls*, the Malibu druggies were eventually made paranoid by their friend Spielberg's efficient, straight politicking with the studios.

The pretentious continued a strategy of generational brinksmanship conceived against the last of the old studio heads in the sixties, but it was failing them. It ended when *Heaven's Gate* famously ended United Artists, the studio begun in 1919 as the original artist-owned studio by D.W. Griffith, Mary Pickford, Douglas Fairbanks, and Charlie Chaplin. It was to free the geniuses of the suits' ballast and the stars from the dead weight collateral of neophytes. U.A. quickly found out those newbies grinding through the genre formulas at a price for distribution through a company-owned theater chain were the locus of profit. But despite a rough path U.A. remained the more nimble studio in the sixties when Hollywood was confronted with the new youth culture, to its shareholders regret. (U.A. was known for mainstream fare like the James Bond series, British comedy, the Beatles films, Woody Allen, as well as insurgent mileposts like the Leone westerns, *2001*, *Alice's Restaurant*, *Midnight Cowboy*, *Shaft*, *Across 110th Street*, *Last Tango in Paris*, *One Flew Over the Cuckoo's Nest*, *Coming Home*, *Apocalypse Now*, *Raging Bull*, *Cruising*.)

Then-U.A. exec Steven Bach tells the *Heaven's Gate* story well in his book, *Final Cut*. He believed that aside from its vulgar budget what stirred antipathy to the Cimino film was

> "...[a] pervasive nihilism that runs through the film from its advertising slogan – 'What one loves in life are the things that fade' – to its climactic and violent reworking of history. That nostalgic-sounding slogan is finally reductive: It narrows the world instead of enlarging it. When it is pictorialized in the closing moments of the film, as Averill stands on the deck of his yacht and his eyes brim over with recollection of faded things, we feel untouched, and Averill's sorrow smacks of self-pity because only he can feel it." (*Final Cut*)

Remember, that the historical "Johnson County war" was typical late-nineteenth century brinksmanship between ranchers and nesters and but a single notorious rustler was killed by the "invasion"; however, coming out of the sixties/seventies, just as the Hollywood hip dreamed of getting the first true "blue" film greenlit, they also lusted over the idea that America was in a pre-revolutionary period. [See Warren Beatty: from *Shampoo* (1975) to *Reds* (1981).] So politically Cimino was likely channeling his immigrant grandfather's social resentment but trying to redeem it via some kind of Hobsbawmian wish fulfillment; Michael's copy of Eric's *Bandits* certainly sat next to his copy of A.S. Mercer's *The Banditti of the Plains*.

More important here, is Bach's general conclusion:

> "Perhaps there is something about the movie business itself... that mitigates against the kind of humanism that might have transformed *Heaven's Gate* from an essay in exploitation to what John Gardner called... 'moral' or 'generous' fiction. Perhaps the conditions in which careers are forged and films constructed partake so little of those qualities that we should not expect to find films imbued with them." (*Ibid.*)

Very true. In fact, the darkest, most paranoid political thrillers are less about America than they are about Hollywood itself. The political reflexes of the new Hollywood left can be seen as a kind of asserted redemption for their own whoring, about which their primary concern is to make it pay even better.

The human scale satisfactions offered in time-honored B genres have been replaced by formerly sub-B kiddie genres like adventure serials. Now however these are inflated with A budget whiz-bang to the point that 2nd unit directors, stunt coordinators and CGI-design platoons become crypto-auteurs (*Jurassic Park, Starship Troopers, Transformers*...), when in fact there need be no actual author of any script. Roger Corman tells Kenneth Bowser in his film version of *Easy Riders Raging Bulls* (2003) that he understood immediately that the studios were onto his exploitation game writ large as soon as he saw *Jaws*. *The Godfather* (1972) had opened unusually wide on four hundred screens; three years later *Jaws* opened on a record 1200. Corman's films often moved a few prints territory to territory so as to affordably work promotional opportunities. Bottom-feeding went uptown.

Stanley Kubrick may have been overrated but he was quite good with modest B material (*The Killing, Paths of Glory, Full Metal Jacket*), only that's not the Kubrick Spielberg was paying tribute to by taking over *A.I.* (2001) after Kubrick's death. Instead, in one of the more misbegotten features of recent years, Spielberg, who has also made great B films – *Duel* (1971), *Something Evil* (1972), both for TV, and *The Sugarland Express* (1974) – tries something he cannot do in tribute to what Kubrick did poorly – pretentious epics. And the industry makes everyone pay for arty expensive junk with more *Minority Reports* and less *sex, lies and videotapes*.

Introduction

Here too, it may be that such films offered for decades now, have corroded filmmakers' ability to deliver and audiences' to demand better work. In Wim Wenders' film, *Kings of the Road* (1976), which follows a projector repairman around small-town West Germany to a soundtrack of Creedence Clearwater Revival oldies, his lead says half-admiringly that "The Yanks have colonized our subconscious." Those were clearly Yanks with more pull. One wonders who or what colonized Spielberg's subconscious. Perhaps as with Lucas it was Sherwood Schwartz.

The Auteur theory and the seventies Hollywood cult seduced the nineties independent film world from the start. Here, where the screenwriter's contribution might've finally carried more weight, young directors succumbed to the false imperative to direct *and* write their films, a la Bergman. But without a writerly sense of tragedy or comedy or structure of any kind, these writer-directors (Tarantino, Rodriguez, Smith, Jonze) are left with little but their own fandom impulses and can only display personal cult *bona fides*. The vacant artiness of the worst of seventies pretension has been filled by the post-*Star Wars* comic book hordes; the attenuated thrall of *Heaven's Gate*'s faked screenplay for its own voluptuary's vision is quite like the faked screenplays of these reference-happy fan-boy quotation-machines. Cimino was snake-fascinated by world high cinema; Tarantino by world low cinema. Cimino wanted to bang Isabel Huppert; Tarantino Chiaki Kuriyama. Cimino's best film, *Thunderbolt and Lightfoot* (1974), contains 70% more fiber than Tarantino's total output. *Reservoir Dogs* (1992) is great cheap thrills in under a hundred minutes; *Pulp Fiction* (1994) at two-and-a-half hours starts the rot but recycling Has' *The Saragossa Manuscript* (1964) mobius narrative admittedly needed doing; *Jackie Brown* (1997) should've been his new *American* prototype but no Elmore Leonard story takes 154 minutes to tell. And then Tarantino went on a four hour spaghetti bender with the *Kill Bills*, wherein the western refs are all-Euro imports.

Ron Rosenbaum in the *New York Observer* (May 2, 2005) tried out several names for what he calls the *Kill Bill-Sin City* sensibility including "The Dumb Avant-Garde," and "The Cinema of Pretentious Stupidity," but he hits his bulls-eye with:

"The Bourgeois Avant-Garde."

The term is more aggressive than David Brooks' Bourgeous Bohemians, or Bo-Bos, though one provides the audience for the other. But it begs a question: Who is to be shocked by such an Avant-Garde, Gil Thorp? This phrase, and the trusty "fan-boy" bell these cats pretty well. Rosenbaum's tag by extension pushes the critique towards the entire American literary rebel tradition that legitimized this low pretense rising like radiation from the critical mass of a densening comic/game culture no longer left behind at puberty. The older lit-droogs corroded the narrative tradition for some high-low rationale that masked some true, mundane personal reason – they were gay, or Jewish, or drunks, or Euro-phobes or -philes or whatever, in a new post-war indulgent Americanist atmosphere, who insisted society give for their affliction rather than they trim their snapping sails by a single turn.

Several decades later and they are The Rebel Establishment. Their issues are dated and small, but as taught are helped along with bogus context about the horrors of the fifties. Jonathan Dee wrote about contemporary bad boy *littérateurs* (Neil LaBute, A.M. Holmes, Will Self, Chuck Palahniuk, Dennis Cooper) for *Harpers*:

> "Books that depend for their sense of opposition on the straw man of a presupposed bourgeois mentality outside the fiction itself – on shock value, in other words – are working in conditions of profound safety disguised as risk." (*Harpers*)

Dee concludes, "Artist, diagnose thyself." We still live with the sixties calumny of the fifties, though it's now the 'teens again! We know we know better, but it's so convenient because it keeps our parents in their assigned cultural place and ourselves young.

When a Robert Rodriguez (an ex-cartoonist, he brags) defers to a writer it is to comics auteur Frank Miller for *Sin City*. The film's PR narrative (so much more disciplined than the film's storyline) made much of Miller's alienation from Hollywood, perhaps due to the presumed sacrilegious mal-adaptation of James O'Barr's *The Crow* (1994) – a movie several times better than this one – and stressed how Rodriguez's Texas set-up allowed them to directly transfer framing and narrative from Miller's comics. Well then why is it less interesting than the ink on the page? All they really had to do is study the first four Dick Tracy feature adaptations which were directed by the forgotten pros William Berke, Gordon Douglas, and John Rawlins between the years 1945 and 1947.

Rodriguez and Miller had nothing to say of any interest to Terry Gross on *NPR* but the marketing blitz did succeed in dissuading her from challenging them as to the usual feminist complaints – the interview was cut to fifteen minutes. (Gross also gave R. Crumb a pass and even laughed along with his "misogyny" and rightly so as it is humane in its misanthropy and he is something more than a draftsman.) But Frank Miller told *Mean* magazine, "I can't stand seeing Luke Skywalker get that medal at the end of *Star Wars*." Lucas again is the sun in this system, but of course his wayward children would prefer Darth done in by a noir anti-hero rather than a boyscout. Kevin Smith, the ultimate fanboy-auteur [*Clerks, Dogma, Chasing Amy, Mallrats, Jay and Silent Bob Strike Back* – four of which deal with comic books], in his volunteered homage to the über-sell of the final *Star Wars* episode wrote,

> "[T]his Vader guy had me locked in his tractor beam, fueled by curiosity as to what would make a bad guy dress so obviously. Not unlike the white suburban youth of today, I was enamored with black culture, personified in Darth Vader." (*Rolling Stone*)

Whatever you say, boyo. They don't make negrophiles like they used to either. One of the film's advertising sub-campaigns featured Darth Vader under the question, Who's Your Daddy? Thankfully Smith has recently led the way in throwing in the towel, admitting that he really never had any idea how to make a movie.

Perhaps Frank Miller means only that Luke Skywalker should pull a Lone Ranger and be gone before any of the planet's folk are able to thank him. But laundered by a juvenile-style goth default-setting it all comes out Hobbes-for-kids, with the black hats and white hats switched. These boys are so enamored of their toys and the figments that proxy-play with them up on the screen that they no doubt believe their female leads actually came – this is one of the Trojan-tenets of what's been called boy-feminism. Uma Thurman and Rosario Dawson did their best acting in the PR phase of these films when they genuinely appeared thrilled to get the chance to play such "women." Everything I almost know about the female says this is not so.

A curious aspect of Rodriguez's greater pretense results in his contrived casting of Hispanics *apropos* nothing, unless what he is saying is that they are all coconuts, as utterly white-bread as any suburban *E.T.* geek, only, you know, *down* and *bad* as that Vader dude. Spike Lee is probably his inspiration here, but Lee has at least a few other things on his mind. Speaking of the white bread colonization of folks of color, M. Night Shyamalan, somehow managed to cartoon the comic as auteur-manqué for all these geeks. Before his subsequent soft-headed turkeys fully erased the reputation that *The Sixth Sense* (1999) made for him he managed to unintentionally undress himself by directing his own hagiobiography, *The Man Who Heard Voices: Or, How M. Night Shyamalan Risked His Career on a Fairy Tale*. Poor dude didn't actually intend to risk his career, he just thought it sounded cool and he could steal some of credit for that too as he tried to pander ever so fiercely to nerd-America. *The Sixth Sense* is good enough, again, like early TV-movie Spielberg, but the follow-up, *Unbreakable* (2000) is an unconscious striptease which reveals a shocking lack of soul or intelligence at work. Almost worth seeing for its fan-boy grand guignol self-seriousness, and the further use of Samuel L. Jackson by the white-Jewish-Asian nerd-realm as some new sort of Staggerlee-Uncle Tom quisling. Where's the N.A.A.C.P. when you need it?

Movie production being what it is today, no single person is to blame for such a catastrophe, and that's the worst of it. A couple hundred people read the script for *Unbreakable* and a handful of them might have stopped it. The film was a widely released bomb; nobody saw it. Except that you can smell its odor in the uniform marketing come-on for Netflix, Dish Network, DirecTV, *Starz*, *TCM*, videogames, *et. al.*, where fandom, playing, and spectatorship are dolled up with the promise that watching and playing are not decadent, nerdy, or evidence of an uncool sloth, but are rather the very promise of life. TCM, named for the man who was going to colorize *Citizen Kane*, is a rare cultural asset I use often, but look at their intro where folks look up from the street or out the window to see the fanfare that announces the next feature as if watching movies on television is like going out to the movies. It's quite a decadent come-on. The iPod silhouette ads are similarly false, painting the earphone experience of music as if it's the equivalent of listening to the radio or dancing in a crowd at a club, when it is the opposite.

During the recent Occupy demonstrations, one minor inane detail hardly seemed worth mentioning except that the image has become ubiquitous. The Guy Fawkes masks made from the design of the lead character in Alan Moore and David Lloyd's comic, *V for Vendetta*, which appeared in the film adaptation as well, seemed a perfect illustration of juvenile pretense. The design is from the comic and has been adopted by the Anonymous group of hacker-anarchists. Not that the demonstrations themselves weren't fairly disciplined, but that particular visage repeated as if an endlessly clever reference understood by a presumed hip cognoscenti is just sad. The sadder for the image itself's perfect unintended graphic realization of sealed-off self-satisfaction apparently blissfully unconscious of its own severe limitations. It also says something about the spell such kids come under as they watch or read such emaciated material. The material is so slight the audience must bring the spell with them. *Vendetta*'s masks seems a full rung lower than the old "Hayduke Lives" bumper stickers on the IQ scale. Hayduke, being the hero of the novel, *The Monkey Wrench Gang*, which inspired the Earth Liberation Front to start blowing things up or burning them down. You'd see those stickers in nominally pacifist environs, the kind of towns that have their own foreign policy. You'd feel embarrassed for the Edward Abbey who wrote *Desert Solitaire*.

Introduction

"Write what you know," so J.J. Abrams makes *Super 8* (2010), the product of yet another Spielberg-lobotomy satisfied customer. A specific problem with the Spielberg school is that set design is so meticulously unreal that every detail screams for attention and pulls apart the frame. High resolution and gratuitous set design always loses out to skilled *trompe l'oeil* marshalled to come in just under an expressively lit standard resolution. Most of the striking images in film history actually flirt with *not* deceiving the eye: the Cherokee Strip land rush in *Tumbleweeds* (1925), much of *Sunrise* (1927), much of *Vertigo* (1958), the slow, retreating close-up of Frank Sinatra driving with a rear projection of New York behind him in *The Detective* (1968), the continuity break at the shot that kills the lead character in *Madigan* (1968).... The eye can find more offense in decadent "white elephant" perfectionism than in skillful low budget corner-cutting.

Another contemporary false answer is puzzling up the narrative (*Mulholland Drive, Memento, Exotica!, Crash, Haywire...*), using alleged formal innovation to disguise lack of content and lack of storytelling chops. A.O. Scott has noted something like a nameless, gathering genre of films built upon coincidence and serendipity to force together characters across class or ethnic lines; his fellow-critic at the *New York Times* Neil Genzlinger refers to "the multiple-stories-that-interlock genre." This is hardly a new genre – no such thing. It's a high/low roundhouse train-wreck which, like the car accident that derails the Mexican feature, *Amores Perros* (2000), strains to fill two hours with dramatic sleight of hand. It's as if Eisenstein's theory of montage has spread to screenwriting. *Amores Perros*, which was an arthouse hit, begins with a first episode that strikes one as the original idea. The other two legs of the film debase that well-observed beginning by filling out to feature length with dashed-off clichéd melodrama dressed up as postmodern cinema. It only worked at all because that old-fashioned three-reeler segment showed us Mexico anew by placing surprising characters in an underground world of dog-fighting. The rest was dog-shite, actual and conceptual.

The strange compulsion of the filmmaker to trump his own material with a surfeit of perspective is the pseud-artist (here, Alejandro González Iñárritu) treading on God's prerogative. *La Ronde* (1950), *Rashomon* (1950) and late Buñuel pull off something akin to this, the integrating of anthology-like sections into a narrative feature film with a supra-human through-line. But the error goes back to Griffith's *Intolerance* (1916), where he was at pains to demonstrate his God-like perspective after being called a sectarian racist for *The Birth of a Nation* (1915). Directors who can't write *need* contrivance, and since such conveniences have long been legitimized in avant-garde literature and art by critics and aesthetes running riot in the resulting void, film writers and artists are often anxious to overshoot their own storytelling art.

Andrew Klavan sees a high-low parallel in *Sin City* in the Summer 2005 issue of *City Journal*:

> "The picture of mankind that emerges then – a picture being promulgated by our intellectual elite – is startlingly like the picture of womankind that emerges from the fantasies of the aforementioned 12-year-old boy. As an adolescent male thinks of girls, so these Academics think of all humans." (*City Journal*)

Except for themselves, I'd add – again, the appropriated perspective of God. And the Soviets loved Pavlov; treated the old man like royalty so to speak and adapted his ideas to film as quickly as possible. The materialist hollowness of such films today, the lack of human content necessary to animate the characters leaves it to the actors to fake what is not in the script; fake it like a pornstar. We could call this The Acteur Theory of film appreciation, the inadvertent wisdom of simple movie-star fandom. But the actors in such films struggle against their contrived scripts which move them around the set like so many props.

Watch the "serious" films. The ones the best actors take paycuts to be in. See the invention of the actors as they attempt to add what isn't there. Discern the backstories, written by the cast members to fill in their cipher-parts, to give them a grip in weightless empty space. See the cast fail to mesh in their cacophonous but near-Silent subtext. Still, that acting is where the action is; it's all that holds such films together. Thanks to HD video's astronomical shooting ratios, what the actors improvise from mere treatment can now be directed on the fly and then rewritten again in the editing in ways John Cassavetes never dreamed possible. Needless to say, such "writing" is inefficient and films run longer than the dramatic content can bear or the exhibitors and exhibitees desire. Were this era's writers and directors as good as our actors this'd be another Golden Age.

This is all part-and-parcel of the Performance Era we find ourselves in. Great work is no longer done by companies of artists and craftsmen producing movies, plays, or music. Rather the forms of expression seem to have broken down into just the performance aspect, and more often one in solo mode. When I was first serious enough about movies to start reading books about the subject, one of the first I bought was Leonard Maltin's 1970 book, *Movie Comedy Teams*. It covered the obvious ones that kids from my generation grew up watching on television, plus more obscure teams of the past up to Martin and Lewis. Maltin contrasts the complete characters that Laurel and Hardy had formed for themselves as they came

Introduction

up within movies with the more hollow patter-based personae of Abbott and Costello who came up as comics on vaudeville and burlesque stages:

> "Scenes like the one in *Pardon My Sarong* where Bud gives Lou a gun to shoot himself, so their stranded party will have one less mouth to feed, are indicative of misfire ideas that never would have been acceptable if Bud and Lou had created believable characters for themselves." (*Movie Comedy Teams*)

The Three Stooges were products of vaudeville and riverboat stages and though certainly harsher in appeal than Laurel and Hardy they had established an us-against-them brotherhood. A favorite gag from *Grips, Grunts and Groans* (1937) has wrestler Curly go berserk in the ring upon smelling Wild Hyacinth perfume and knocking out all comers including security. When he finally pauses and sees that he's also knocked out Moe and Larry, he panics and says, "Hey fellas, wait for me!" and then knocks himself out.

In the early 1970s I was also very interested in stand-up comics like Lenny Bruce, Woody Allen, Albert Brooks, Leonard Barr, Steve Martin, and others, but I did regret that my era produced no comedy teams or performers who invented characters and committed to them a la Chaplin, Keaton, Marx Brothers, Fields, etc.

Any number of today's leading actors are former monologists: stand-up comedians, rappers, singers, etc. In the days of the studio system it was more certain that such individuals would be fitted into the company on its terms. Today film sets are often *ad hoc* collections of service providers and these are more likely to indulge the soloist star and then neither the cast nor the crew become ensembles. A star catered to will unravel any script's sense as he or she begins to supersede the other parts which lose their fictional autonomy. This drains the drama or comedy of verisimilitude and relieves it of necessary dramatic and comedic tension.

The Renaissance launched an era of Painting and Sculpture and Music where these arts began to escape Church and Royal patronage. After the Reformation the West enters a Writing Era which in turn trades the subject of the exceptional historical hero for that of the everyman. The 20th century, then, became a uniquely productive battle royal over whether it would be a Writing Era or a Performance Era and in that long rocky transition it often seemed a Directing or Conducting or Adapting Era, where artists, writers, and performers might be marshaled into something greater by producers who were in the business of popular art. That *greater* was a kind of multimedia orchestration of high-art ambition as it collapsed down through the democratized class structure of America. The everyman was newly empowered within the inherited European metaphysical-mythological drama, and American art began to feedback into Europe where it was used to help break the grip of the class structure that fed the old high-art hierarchy that could be quite inhuman. Today perhaps that great structure has been fully leveled and artistic ambition resides in just that empowered individual. Everyone the star of his own one-man show; would that these were merely fifteen minutes long.

    The 21st-century film director is then a vestigial creature, operating technically as a stage manager but no longer with a disciplined artistic permit. Most pretenses hang on a minimalism that slights the human interior as it carefully lights and highlights his and her exteriors. The action is often determined by mere opposition to former genre convention; little else is on its creator's mind. The old studio lighting of actors for cameras was used to create a visual analog to the metaphysical-mythological story told of human beings against nature and their own nature. The images of actors then glowed with characters' life-forces in a pneuma of light within the black and white. All largely lost now, first to unstable color film stocks, now to digital video. This metaphysical aura is something precious few performers can conjure alone.

    The visceral drive of certain seventies action films like *Dirty Harry, Death Wish, Defiance* - what Orwell might have called Hundred Minute Hates - now look positively humane in their concern for getting a real, non-ironic rise out of an audience around issues of civilization, manhood, justice, freedom. Hollywood is a long, long way from Henry Hathaway, Henry King, John Ford, Jacques Tourneur, Joseph H. Lewis, Don Siegel, Anthony Mann, Budd Boetticher, *ad infinitum* it once seemed. We don't even got no Phil Karlsons or Gordon Douglases. It's like Lucas buggered Cimino and their shit-head litter have the run of the place. Shut that Star Gate, asshole!

*****

Well... what is there left in this culture that can be built upon? Who is there to build it? Must we rend the fabric of this era's time itself to defeat the present? Or is that what's happening?

    Kids are pushed into organized activities by boomer and post-boom parents who can't face letting them roam around in this world they demanded. Kids are likely siblingless and so the give and take of aggression and accommodation learned over years within a large family goes unlearned. The kids are touchier and so a casual detachment becomes the fragile ethos. What does a post-pube boy make of girls and women when he has no experience caring about/fighting with/making up with/worrying about sisters? Her existence is the one thing that might force him to consider the battle of the sexes from the other side before he goes nuclear. Girls are more other-obsessed by nature and by the age of five are already compensating mentally for this and the physical differential they must contend with in their playmates.

After WWII when the sexes got back together and everyone was having kids, American culture was kid-friendly and most of us had multiple brothers and sisters. In most towns you rode your bike anywhere you wanted so long as you got home by dinner. Other adults, parents themselves, would look out for you if you got near trouble. And the default setting for the arts was F-for-families, even if the storyline was grimly adult. Now with single parent or working parents, time is booked to keep kids occupied and supervised by professionals at institutions until evening. Individual sports are more common for boys, and even team-sports unravel into settings for individual showmanship. Conversely, girls are now pushed into team-sports courtesy the Title IX *diktat* where they are to learn teamwork to ready them for the workplace. The politicos and courts insist on its blind application so that volleyball scholarships for girls crowd out wrestling programs – *wrestling*, the last tie of academia to Greek classicism. Yet the social engineers of institutional feminism disallow competitive cheerleading from counting in their precious Title IX numbers game. Particularities aside, the former advantages of males in school, work and society generally, seem now more disadvantages and the former disadvantages of females seem flipped as well.

Still, the droning ideologues working their blind termite way through law and institutions, now seek to apply Title IX to the Sciences. They sense that those hard sciences threaten the soft sciences. In an average year we're told nearly a hundred million birth control prescriptions are written. Then we're told (Shirley Wang, *WSJ*, May 10, 2011) that a Pill side-effect encourages female interest in less masculine men. And further, masculine men are less responsive to women on the Pill. This is apparently a matter of smelling bacteria that is either there or it ain't. Smells like a way to breed out all those restless boys currently pathologized and drugged so they can sit still in female-normed public schools. Maybe we're even breeding homosexuals; now there's a breakthrough.

Other scientific counter-factuals include Katherine Ellison's book's look at neuroscience evidence that motherhood increases a woman's brainpower (*The Mommy Brain*); she duly notes the popular false factuals presuming the opposite. Feminists have been insinuating that pregnancy is a disease and childbirth a danger, when in fact rates of breast and other cancers begin to climb in a woman's late teens when she has not yet had a child. Cruel Darwinian anti-creationism seeks to shut down unproductive females. To defend that softest science, gender theory, it appears we will need the hard science of bio-engineering. Pharmacological science may not be enough.

****

The web and television and cell-phones are ubiquitous and merging, and the post-scarcity fastfood obesity apocalypse is accommodated by the skater/hip hop fashion world of XXL sizes and the faux-biker pseud-culture of tattooed tubboes with fu manchus. In early nineties NBA style, the older players hid balding pates by shaving their heads and bluffed even rookies into shaving off full heads of hair. The NBA young eventually turned the tables on hair and threads. There are always style options for a new youth culture, though even I hesitate to observe that short-shorts and Afros are the most obvious one for the NBA (sure enough, Madison Avenue's been there already). Music videos are likely to be fantasies of fat-faced rappin' chubblers, while MTV's reality shows are stocked with the ripped abs and bared midriffs of model American youth.

Boys skate, game or surf the web for porn; girls play soccer or politic among themselves. There's plenty of interest in music and film but it has been failing to develop beyond simple consumer response or artless careerism. The notional sex-roles that rise from skate culture, hip hop, girl-world, Maxim, Victoria's Secret, Abercrombie & Fitch, etc. are the Mook and the Model, the Player and Whore, the Pimp and the Dom. Girls may get something out of their end of these paired tropes, but at base they float the male fantasy that the dude-as-slob can get the hot chick-in-heels. This is culture, not life of course, no matter how many dipwads get their faces slapped trying to act it out. But it's also mob psychology, and is likely compensating for an opposite. The "player" is strangely passive and has easily bruised feelings, whereas his "whore" has a cold alpha-male in her peripheral sight whose child this "player" will find himself raising.

But where might a youth-style go from here? The rainbow tribe occupy the more naturally androgynous hippie option, the snobs are still wearing black, and even cheerleaders sport tattoos. There will be some new equilibrium that settles around the challenges from the web, mobile communications, corporate oversell and the reactionary localism that these provoke in McLuhanesque counter-formations, but it can't be seen yet. Unless this artless formlessness is it.

Female culture is still evolving under new pressures and opportunities, and there have been several generation gap-like breaks between female cohorts as feminism's ideas fall short in all this flux. Margaret Webb Pressler reports in the *Washington Post* (April 2, 2006) that children are moving

Introduction

through "play stages" more quickly:

> "This change is especially pronounced in girls. The result is that Barbie, which used to be a doll that 7- and 8-year-olds would play with for hours, is now the domain of 3-year-olds. Never mind that 3-year-olds don't have the fine motor skills needed to dress the 10-inch bombshell in her tiny outfits and teensy accessories. Playrooms across the country are littered with naked Barbies with missing arms and matted hair." (*Washington Post*)

Those eight-year-olds move on to Disney's airbrushed representations of teenage social, not-to-say sexual, melodrama which usually stars the normal high school girl who conducts a show biz career singing on the side. Actual teens are onto rude comedies and horror films.

When sex is culturally severed from reproduction as it has been since the Pill, then fashion ungrounded becomes an index of hysteria. This is why it is a domain of the homosexual. Such hysterical energy turned pretentious, often leads female artists to overshoot their mark yielding work that postures politically but can't or won't declare its art. It's as if Female runs too deep for a Pop this shallow to acknowledge.

Male culture seems to be either in denial about its nature (Emo, Pagan, Rave) or wallowing in it (the rest of 'em). The quiet tally of sex crimes at the recent "Occupy" demonstrations threatened the unnatural etiquette asked of young bucks at these long-running camp-outs. With young women going farther in college and finding better jobs, there is a canny unmacho young male style which postures cool-with-that – a kind of straight gayishness. The male board-sport culture seems to be most creative within this confusion. After the U.S. team swept the 2002 Olympic half-pipe event, silver medalist Danny Kass was prompted by *NBC* to describe what he expected from his moment on the podium and he responded with pitch-perfect new-male bravado, "I guess I'll try to cry." Interestingly, in a Winter Olympics women's snowboard event four years later Lindsey Jacobellis' fall which cost her gold was severely criticized as showboating by the straight sports media whereas boardsport sentiment encouraged her to defend herself with the insouciance you'd expect, "Snowboarding is fun; I was having fun."

There is no 'i' in team, but there sure is one in tennis. And so it shouldn't surprise that women's tennis has been something of an incubator for the new female athlete – her ego, her money, and her style. American men broke in the old British tennis etiquette and beginning with Jennifer Capriati and Martina Hingis the women's game burst into a new upgrade. The Williams sisters were plenty girlish, even as they unloaded a wild new power onto the game. Once Serena surpassed Venus it seemed no-one else would compete. But the game changed and women stayed with it. Some try to make a fashion statement but the demands of the game come first. The Belgians and Russians are less flamboyant and all business for this new game having been secured. (The soft-focus Kournikova game never arrived though the photogs still line-up for her rare appearances and quick exits.) Women's figure skating is too trapped inside its aestheticized erotic fantasy to break out into anything new (back-flips, etc., are illegal in competition). Michelle Kwan made a fine heroine but the sport doesn't really allow for the bad girl-style the television ponces marked out for Sasha Cohen. It's a wonder Tonya Harding ever took the sport up. The popularity of lone-wolf gamers like billiards champ Jeanette Lee and the distracting poker molls are new developments. And the young black women that have raged through MTV reality programming may signal more than Richter scale abuse or racist misogyny.

These young must do their culture work in and around a male dementia of beer ads, UFC, *ESPN*, Metal, emo, gangsta-rap, webporn, and horror films, and a female dementia of Oprah, Eve Ensler, Louise Erdrich, *Lifetime*, Le Tigre, "*Sex in the City.*" I'll be generous and say the jury is out on Miranda July, Kelly Reichart, Lana Del Rey, and Zooey Deschanel but then women are inclined more to comfort art rather than breathrough art. Video art seems mere research toward narrative film work to me, but if it is a stand-alone art then Laurel Nakadate may be more important than the filmmakers. Generally, girls' interest in their neo-vampire genre is promising too; it's certainly a fertile all-purpose metaphor for coming of age in this American neo-wilderness. I liked Grace Krilanovich's vampire-variant in her first novel, *The Orange Eats Creeps*; it has some of the ratty rock and roll at-large bravado that Kathryn Bigelow's best film, *Near Dark* (1987), possessed. Some woman somewhere is bound to cook up narrative art that no man might imagine that will nevertheless stand outside femme politesse. The pincher threats from feminism and Islam may force it out of her-with-the-skills.

Boys seem more at risk to their jack back-fire threat. Girls seem to locate their reality quicker now – they get through their pink/princess phase before kindergarten – but their dementia threat is laying for them in college and in a housewife culture brewed up in magazines and television.

So many attend college now that urban bohemias no longer collect idiosyncratic rule-breaking drop-outs so much as they endure annual graduating classes of operators who have already interned halfway up the bowels of the Man. The Portland Oregon I remember as a late seventies cultural afterthought with important things going on has become a lifestyle punchline. Recent American low-rent drop-out bohemias in Williamsburg, the lower eastside, Wicker Park, Silverlake, and the Mission were set upon and consumed by dotcom yuppies, starter execs, first-class immigrants, and trust-fund babies as if by swarms of locusts.

It's not that chances are not taken by these young, so much as they have not prepared themselves to know what bet to make. Chances are surely still taken in the military and maybe something will come of the returned G.I.s besides barfights. Those photos of PFC Lynndie England and SPC Sabrina Harmon posing with Abu Ghraib prisoners were powerful mostly for a completely unstated reason. Our newsmedia was only interested in the trouble they caused President Bush. The Western feminism that put these women in uniform had to be shielded from multicultural imperatives when dealing with Islam. But the shockwaves sent out to Muslims were primarily gender-based rather than um, Bush-based. (Can you picture the nightmarish wet dreams of young Arab men post-Ghraib? If so, you are as sick as they are, my friend.) For all the hubbub over it, anyone uncouth enough to try to parse those images for anything but an indictment of the war looked unhinged. There would be no close reading by supersophisticates, even at this late date.

Sad to say, since the sixties the new freedoms were grabbed by the elite with all their advantages. They demanded them in everyone's name but this was cover for what might as well have been a class war. The disciplining social track they objected to had been laid for, and by, generations of working class descendents of immigrants and slaves. Those tracks pulled up, this class has suffered. Another unplumbed zeitgeist-skyrocket was Cho Seung-hui, the Virginia Tech killer-suicide. These melodramatic American youth immolations, both female and male, may not yield the best raw material for fiction, but perhaps that's because we don't have a Dostoevsky. Instead of *Crime and Punishment* we get artless True Crime actualities. Lynndie England was in the Future Farmers of America as a girl; Cho Seung-hui grew up around his father's used book store.

***

So these kids today – what are they capable of? The unwitnessed death of music photographer Naomi Petersen forcefully brought home to me what I think is missing. Naomi was 17 when she drove from Simi Valley to the Cuckoo's Nest in Costa Mesa (60+ miles across Los Angeles) where Black Flag began to play gigs on release of the "Damaged" LP (the LAPD was still making L.A. gigs impossible). These Orange County shows were the first gigs featuring new vocalist Henry Rollins. I noticed Naomi as the stylish Asian-looking girl in the midst of the sullen, all-ages, but largely single-sex O.C. punk rabble – brave girl. One late night her father refused to let her back into the house. Left to Los Angeles at 3am she drove back south, slit her wrists somewhere, got scared and called the Black Flag/SST office from a payphone. She entered SST still bleeding – Chuck cleaned her up and calmed her down. He did a good job with her. Naomi didn't want to die; she wanted to live.

The next day Naomi became the SST photographer for the cost of her supplies – we were broke but she was excited to do it. Her first session was Saint Vitus under the powerlines behind the SST office on Phelan in Redondo. Next was Saccharine Trust at the Santa Monica Unicorn Records practice rooms. Her first gig-shoot was the Minutemen at Cathay de Grande. She shot Black Flag at SST and then at Global. Hüsker Dü and the Meat Puppets came through town soon after as well. For me this meant no more begging Glen Friedman or Ed Colver to cover our mini-bands for no money. Another problem solved! And it was nice to have girl around the place.

I left SST in 1986 and Naomi began to work in the SST office itself; I have letters from her in the late eighties where she described trying to get her SST hours down to fifty a week. Brave girl! She moved to the D.C. area. She promptly hired on to do accounts for the reggae label Ras and for the 9:30 Club, and was out shooting the best bands on the east coast – the Dischord bands, the Obsessed scene, *et. al.* – building the most thorough and only bi-coastal portfolio of the eighties rock underground. As the American music scene was so little covered after the first NYC bands were rejected by the media in the name of their audience, it seems inevitable that the world will come to know the decade through Naomi's camera.

Bill Stevenson and Mugger had been doing stuff around Black Flag/SST from their mid-teens, Henry joined the band at 20, Davo Claassen had quit college in his first year and became gofer, then driver, then sound-man-driver, and drummer for side-bands. Kira replaced Chuck on bass in Black Flag; she'd been in bands since age 14 or so. Jordan Schwartz threw in with the Global crew. Mugger remembered Kara Nicks from a Phoenix gig and when she turned up in L.A. he pulled her into SST and she was running the warehouse and distribution by the late eighties. These were the kids who dropped out of their cohort and threw in with Greg Ginn's vision and individually and together accomplished important things.

In 1995, Bill Stevenson had moved his All troop to Fort Collins and I moved to Laramie. He put together a label as his studio was recording great bands with no prospects for release. We thought our experiences at SST and elsewhere would allow us to get it together quickly. But everything had changed, from the kids up. We had four regimes of

Introduction

twenty-somethings doing the day-to-day in just six years before going dormant. We got great bands in front of so-so bands' audiences but the kids, assembled out of some conformist instinct by now, declined to be blown away. They didn't know and couldn't tell; it could've been Black Flag themselves in front of them, I expect....

The independent label economy by the end of the nineties was professionalized into a low-rent parody-played-straight of the majors. Fifteen years earlier only the worst of the small labels had had such a mindset. The whole of – was it generation x? y? z? – seemed unable to commit: the audience wanted tenth-hand O.C.-style punk that came at them from the center of what was now a conservative tradition; the bands needed to get on college radio and *MTV*; the label staff needed to get paid immediately – they had apartments, didn't sleep on the office floor. Anything less and they threw in the towel – went back to college, went to work and got married – unbelievable things in SST terms. Spot, Chuck, Greg, Raymond, Watt, Robo, Farrell, Whittaker and myself were then in our mid-to-late twenties and as sixties/seventies characters we were long gone from the straight world. I didn't fully appreciate then just what the kids who jumped in with us were made of. The last of the post-war drop-out bohemians I now think.

It seems that where once kids committed to living the music, they now merely try it on like some merch, or go through it like a phase or for credit, while keeping options open. Certainly, at times in the sixties and the nineties the underground bet has paid off well, but who bets everything anymore? The tats and piercings are the new camouflage of the bourgeois – rock and roll culture emptied out, minus the hassle of the shabby clubs, the crappy P.A.s, the drunken assholes, and the sad lost girls trying to create bright enough experiences to crowd out dark memories, and the angry restless boys daring themselves to have an impact. The well-adjusted young don't need any of it to play at rock and roll. The poseurs evolved quicker than the rockers. Their parents reproduced while we were burning off our young adulthood for art or action.

**

Norman O. Brown's 1959 book, *Life Against Death: The Psychoanalytical Meaning of History*, was his attempt to salvage the narrow protocols of Marxism and Philosophy by insisting they contend with Freud. Brown wrote it under the specter of an American culture unnaturally coherent due to the collective effects of the Depression and the War. Brown was a typical intellectual in that he'd supported Henry Wallace in 1948, but as something of a voluptuary he took the traditional conceptions of worthy external and internal areas of study – the socioeconomic and the philosophical – and forced contact with then more novel conceptions of external/internal: the psychological and a kind of neo-pagan sensuality that led to new age culture. This new framework was at first rejected as reactionary and decadent by progressives, but we see it now as one of the first intellectual sparks of the New Left and the cultural revolution on campuses. But in fact the real revolution had already begun on campuses though its foot soldiers weren't the expected heralds. The de-mobilization after WWII sent still young but now grown men to college on the G.I. Bill of 1944. These worldly, smoking, drinking, fucking and killing men come-to-learn began the destruction of *in loco parentis* discipline at colleges. And nationally the boom in suburban life and the drift westward, also accelerated by the war, slowly replaced the eastern-urban-ethnic-tribal pattern with more flexible modern ones.

Brown's book remains important, but today the subtext of his ulterior motive is of course dated. His End-of-Repression-that-frees-Life-to-become-as-Play, became co-ed Hillary's search for more ecstatic modes of living, and then Charles Manson's free-love/creepy crawl a long time ago. Today we stand in the ruins of real existing Liberation, where, as Brown "alumna" Camille Paglia has noted, regression rather than repression seems the greater threat. Post-war academic rebels took one last look at Stalin on Khrushchev's say-so and turned inward. Their focus lowered, they now dreamed of rationalizing and neutering sex so as to have a lot of it. A century after Gauguin, radicals still dreamt of an escape from Judeo-Christian moral pressure. They mostly laid groundwork for the thorough commercialization of a now de-contextualized sex in popular culture. And there was nothing, NOTHING!, Madison Avenue more desired than the cultural license to jack directly into the factory-wired Pavlovian sex drive of its subjects. Today the school nurse pushes safe sex on sixth graders with a perverse Puritanism that purports to be about hygiene and sterility.

The young remain victims of a dementia locked into our culture as well by the continuing demographic power of the baby boom. Brown was not entirely wrong, but his subtle turn was bested in the real world of the sixties boomers by scoundrels like Margaret Mead and Alfred Kinsey who were selling a sweeter wine. These two were unscrupulous in policing their own psychological motives and have recently been unmasked as having in the main, simply projected their own sexual self-loathing out onto the naturally occurring social equilibrium of the less pretentious – those de-mobed out of war into adulthood who raised the many children of this very baby boom out of a kind of inspired relief that the killing was over. Mead and Kinsey, *et. al.*, with their magic bag of data would catch the zeitgeist of those children – a new class, one insulated from the imperatives of war and privation, but lost in an accelerating virtual world of pop culture and pop philosophy. They took their golden post-war American reality as a naturally occurring given, to which the Protestant ethic, Catholic penance, and Jewish scholasticism contributed nothing but holding back the Millennium.

Much was wrecked, but not everything. America is best thought of as a process, one kept open to the marketplaces of ideas and capital by the Constitution's brake on the state's natural drift toward increasing its power. Law and Courts have been failing freedom for security and egalitarianism, but our dynamism has not yet slowed. Japan's accomplishment was great but it was narrow and fragile. China... we'll see. I was struck ten years ago when three Asia hands on the Hoover Institute's *"Uncommon Knowledge"* each called the long term for India over China; the deciding issue for them all was democratic dynamism and flexibility vs. top-down planning. It may be unfair to measure the race-nations of the world with our rolling migrant-fed bastard culture with its greater ease with flux, but they are following us with their own characteristic levels of trepidation, or they are surrendered to their oligarchic heirarchies.

The harshest critiques of America are not like the harshest critiques of the UK, Germany, China, Greece, or other places. Through the decades America is always a different country, moreso than the rest where critiques tend to hang in the air needing less amending and patching up. Since the collapse of the Soviet Union this has been the best age to assess what America is, and what we have accomplished, by studying the rest of the world as they struggle to find how much vertical and horizontal anarchy each can tolerate.

America will always tolerate more, so in terms of politics I'm optimistic. We just need to keep our mis-educated control-freak elite from making a federal case out of everything, or submitting our polity to the U.N. for approval. Culturally I'm somewhat less optimistic. In a richer musical culture teenagers in their garages cooked up amazing music. Today it's more likely to take twenty-somethings to have a shot. But that was the case twenty-five years ago with punk rock too, despite all the romantic talk of The Kids. When *Rolling Stone* mag and the radio formatters Burkhardt-Abrams stonewalled even the major label punk bands back in the seventies they didn't just defend and accelerate the pasteurization of rock and roll, they retarded American musical culture by breaking its rhythm. There's no fixing that, and there's no forgiving it. Talk-radio is the number one format today.

Film and television weren't as vulnerable to malefactors inside the business. But in serving the world Hollywood has retarded American movies as well. The low overhead of digital home computer post-production and the proliferation of cable and satellite outlets plus internet dispersion begs for a content renaissance. And digital video has already conquered the snobs at film festivals who were rejecting video productions out of hand only five years ago.

The Ramones began in the mid-seventies and they were churning out hit-worthy tunes all through the eighties. Now with Joey, Dee Dee, and Johnny safely underground, the performance fees from radio, TV, film, MLB, the NBA, and the NHL pour into Taco Tunes/Bleu Disque Music (ASCAP). Death rocks! Death lives! Sad, tragic, criminal, funny, rock and roll; "*Someone had to pay the price.*" Now paid, Life loses its context as Death retreats. What is Art when Life takes twice as long and drains slowly to dementia, rather that halts abruptly, unaccountably at Death?

*

Nirvana's popular breakthrough in 1991 was in no small part due to the arrival in Hollywood of Sony, BMG, and Matsushita – foreign capital and personnel from markets that had long made popular successes of American as well as British punk music. (Ironically their static pop cultures and class structures prompt them to defer to America for certain things.) The Germans and Japanese came to Hollywood and New York and showed up all of our fake record-men and company heads who'd blockaded the punk era for more than a decade and then clambered into the Rock and Roll Hall of Fame.

Still, Americans retain certain ambitions as restless creators of ideas, things and art. We may be fully middle class in some way that seems to trivialize anything we grab onto today, but the restlessness will move us past anything truly trivial rather quickly. That is not the case elsewhere, and I'm not sure I know why American intellectuals do not appreciate that. There's a kind of perverse expectation here that China will become the driver of global popular culture the way America has been since the Civil War. This is absurd, whatever the size of that audience and its gravitational pull on world pop. Despite the damage done to American film by the world market, that world of foreigners cannot generate the same kind of dramatic language whereby an ethnic scapegoat like the Irish quickly become the default everyman in American popular drama, only to be followed by a black everyman. Someday something one-tenth as potent might conceivably be possible in India, but it won't happen in China.

After decades of global corporate consolidation the market is saying we're due for a period of divestment if not actual trust-busting. (AOL bought Time-Warner in 2000 and in no time, separated out, AOL's market value was essentially zero; it is now again called Time Warner and *AOL* has been spun off.) If the markets and/or feds turn on these culture cartels (Time Warner, Vivendi Universal, Disney-*ABC*, Viacom-*CBS*, News Corp-Fox, Sony-BMG, Warner Music Group, and EMI) it won't be pretty, it'll be beautiful. Radio giant Clear Channel too has hit the wall and sold off the concert promotions side-line, which they bought to christen their arrival as behemoth; Chicago outfit Jam Productions beat the arm in court and others in Denver and elsewhere are pressing that fight over venues and market-by-market access.

The marketplace itself is squeezing waste from the bloated entertainment sector, and man, ain't there a lot of it! The music industry of 2010 was half the size it was in 2000. The squeeze is from all directions: from Shareholders to Pirates, from the Web to the War, from Artists demands to Audience rejection. The effects of format revolutions (CD, Video, DVD, cable, satellite, phone) and a mini-baby boom which juiced the teen pop and teen film markets led to outsized profit expectations which amplifies the present despair. DVD good news was box-office bad news; iPod good news was radio & records bad news. Power is devolving back to music publishers as in the beginning over a century ago when Tin Pan Alley was all about sheet music sales.

When there is no disc, and culture is by wire or wireless, all will be as either Nashville or Lawndale. The only issue will be whether virtual barriers will be contrived to replace the physical barriers that are dissolving. Nashville will push for barriers; Lawndale will dissolve them as they go up, at least for small subcultures. Brussels and Washington will determine the marketplace parameters for anybody making money enough that they smell it. And Beijing, as it hears from its own copyright and trademark holders in Shanghai and Hong Kong, will begin to close down the pirates and sail straight. Still, in the end these corporations will have to radically restructure themselves to cut the costs of developing, producing and delivering music and film. But they will be relieved of the physical demands and costs of product distribution.

The corporations that bought into Hollywood over the last twenty years have made half-hearted attempts before, but that was just about debt service after the purchase. Now it's about whether Wall Street judges the entertainment industry as something worth holding, and money moves faster than ever.

Bakunin's or Schumpeter's "creative destruction" never sounded more rockin'. Any resulting opening of the cultural market structures will beg for new musicians and filmmakers with better to offer. Only then we'll find out if we still have it in us.

Film.

~

CHARLES BRONSON; "*THE MAN WITH A CAMERA*" (1958-60).

Charles Bronson – Dark Buddha
I'd done enough research on Bronson for my forthcoming film book, so when he passed I asked the one publisher I knew, Jay Babcock, if he was interested in an appreciation. He said yes so I went and wrote one up for Arthur *magazine.*

Charles Buchinsky was following his brothers and father down the coalmine when WWII drafted him out from under the company town of Ehrenfeld, Pennsylvania. After the war he drifted and found pickup work to avoid getting locked down into the life of his family, and to protect and pursue his interest in painting. A job painting sets for a theater led to acting and marriage to actress Harriet Tendler. By 1949 he'd done bit parts on New York stages, and they moved to L.A. where he trained at the Pasadena Playhouse, which led to his first bit part in a Gary Cooper film, *You're in the Navy Now* (1951).

Buchinsky (often Buchinski), with his stocky thirties action-style body and toughguy face, was first just another uglyman character actor ~ not as mean as Neville Brand, not as nice as Ernest Borgnine. American film audiences after the war were no longer obsessed with pretty boy leads, but it was older actors who took advantage of this new appetite for realism ~ Robert Taylor, James Stewart, Gary Cooper, Henry Fonda ~ many of whom in fact had been those slim, unmarked romantic leads of twenty years earlier. Others who got the interesting B film leads were actors like Aldo Ray, Rod Steiger, Broderick Crawford; Buchinsky coveted these roles. He changed his name to Bronson in 1954 to sound less suspicious during the Hollywood red scare ~ his parents were both Lithuanian.

He was in the Hollywood system though not as a contract player with a studio. Still, he was soon getting third or fourth billed roles in westerns such as *Apache* (1954), *Drum Beat* (1954), *Jubal* (1956), and *Run of the Arrow* (1957). But he was ambitious and remained frustrated. He took lead roles in three great 1958 B-films, *Showdown at Boot Hill*, *Machine Gun Kelly*, and *Gang War*, did dozens of television one-off roles from 1953 to 1967, and starred in a cheapjack series, *Man with a Camera* (1958-60). 1960s A-films for Bronson meant playing in the action ensembles of *Never So Few* (1959), *The Magnificent Seven* (1960), *The Great Escape* (1963), and *The Dirty Dozen* (1967). It was progress, a career, but he'd expected more. Bronson was the eleventh of fifteen children of an immigrant who was dead of black lung disease by the time Charles was twelve. Several of his siblings died young. Once out of Ehrenfeld he'd been taken for an immigrant himself and he worked hard to leave his accent and naiveté behind. (Bronson used this accent for the character Velinski in *The Great Escape*.)

He bounced from agent to agent, divorced his wife, fell in love with his best friend's wife and found himself ready for lightning to strike. Bronson turned down a script from Italy called "The Magnificent Stranger." Richard Harrison, an American actor who had found work and fame in Europe, was busy and told Sergio Leone about Clint Eastwood. The idea was to have an American star in a German financed Italian directed western based on a Japanese film (*Yojimbo*) inspired by a Budd Boetticher/Randolph Scott western (*Buchanan Rides Alone*); it would be shot in Spain. Eastwood was younger, and had less to lose; he was looking forward to the end of the TV series *Rawhide* wherein he'd played a character he's referred to as 'trail flunky.' Eastwood simply threw out his character's and most of the others' dialogue and as luck had it Leone had an eye for the rest; the film became *A Fistful of Dollars* (1964). Bronson then rejected *For a Few Dollars More* (1965) and that part went to Lee Van Cleef, a marginal heavy in lots of westerns through the fifties. Van Cleef became an overseas star too; he looked great but never threw out enough of his dialogue. Bronson would have done *The Good, the Bad and the Ugly* because by then he'd seen *Fistful*, but he was committed to *The Dirty Dozen* (1967).

Meanwhile, Bronson was getting his own international action. He had married the English actress Jill Ireland after she'd divorced actor David McCallum. (It was apparently all very civilized and will someday make a nice little TV movie.) McCallum, who was quite a pop star due to his role in *The Man from U.N.C.L.E.*, had turned his agent Paul Kohner onto Bronson, and Ireland pushed him to France to do *Adieu L'Ami* (a.k.a., *Farewell Friend*, or *Honor Among Thieves*, 1968), and *Rider on the Rain* (1970). These arty messes were huge hits throughout Europe and Asia but are most interesting for being the first to really frame and linger on Bronson's potential for violence in its cool, calm potential phase. Following such stillness with his natural aptitude with guns and fists became his formula. Bronson made ten films in five years for European production companies. And Leone finally got Bronson for *Once Upon a Time in the West* (1969) where he played opposite Henry Fonda.

After five years dominating the overseas box office, Bronson returned to Hollywood, though by now the studios were mere distributors of the productions of smaller, hipper companies – companies who knew the value of Charles Bronson. Dino De Laurentiis Productions signed him for three pictures at a million dollars each. The third of these was *Death Wish*, a film that became the zeitgeist's skyrocket in the summer of 1974. And so, as the sixties youth culture crested and curdled in 1974, a deeply scarred fifty-two year old immigrant's son found himself the number one box office attraction in America, and the world.

Producer-Director Michael Winner who worked with Bronson in this period said, "He had a chance when he could have broken through, and I know the pictures he didn't do and it's a pity." But when the personal and professional pressures finally let up on Bronson, film had become to him merely a professional means to personal ends. He always knew his lines and hit his marks on the set. More often in Hollywood, actors were contemptuous of their craft and so drank or whored or subverted characterizations as written with a kind of performance striptease often hinting at closeted homosexuality. Bronson respected the work, but from hereon he considered himself a family man first, a painter second, and only then an actor. Bronson, the Dark Buddha, had reached his personal-professional goal or Dharma and it earned him the following or Sangha that further freed him.

He loved Jill Ireland; they were a Beauty and the Beast couple. She loved children as he did; more so perhaps for enduring repeated miscarriages to have them. His and her children from both previous marriages as well as their daughter were often together in the rural Vermont Bronson household and after *Death Wish*'s success Bronson and Ireland made films together. He gladly forced her on producers, and snubbed Hollywood by working primarily with Brit directors (Michael Winner, J. Lee Thompson, Peter Hunt). The best of these films are *Chato's Land* (1971), *Stone Killer* (1973), *Death Wish* (1974), *Death Hunt* (1981), and maybe even *Murphy's Law* (1986).

Three fortunate exceptions to this Brit preference are among the best films of Bronson in his prime: *Mr. Majestyk* (1974) directed by Hollywood veteran Richard Fleischer from a script by Elmore Leonard, *Breakout* (1975) directed by Tom Gries, and *Hard Times* (1975) Walter Hill's directorial debut. *Telefon* (1977), though directed by Don Siegel and written by Stirling Silliphant, is less than it ought to be (see Siegel's chapter on the film in his autobiography for details).

Late Bronson deteriorates but remains interesting. The *Death Wish* series (five in all; the last direct-to-video), *10 to Midnight* (1983), *The Evil That Men Do* (1984), and *Kinjite: Forbidden Subjects* (1989) are lurid collisions of an aging puritan-avenger Bronson with some of the sleaziest settings

Film

any box office champ ever got near. Here the sexual neuroses and Fleet Street cynicism of the Brits and Bronson's professional detachment yielded strikingly perverse films. Bronson's Beauty was dying of cancer through these years and when she succumbed in 1990 his career changed as well. He did one last great support role (fifth billed and without hairpiece) in Sean Penn's *The Indian Runner* (1991) and then moved to network television where he did some good wholesome work that was likely closer to his true taste: *Yes Virginia, There Is a Santa Claus* (1991), *The Sea Wolf* (1993),

ALAN LADD, CHARLES BRONSON; *DRUM BEAT* (1954).

Donato and Daughter (1993), and the three *Family of Cops* films (1995, 1997, 1999).

Today, Bronson's catalog has drifted off of the shelves of videostores with the phasing out of videotape, and interest hasn't yet demanded restocking in the DVD format. A failed career then, one might say, but surely a successful life – a complete kalpa. In Hollywood the reverse is more often true, though it's generally work from failed careers that endures. A Buchinsky autobiography is to be published.

Acting Methods, Alive or Dead

I've been working, with interruptions, on a film book since the rock book came out in 1991, so given cause it's easy to riff on films and filmmakers in The New Vulgate. Stone Male *will bookend nicely with* Rock and the Pop Narcotic. *But then what?*

David Thomson is a movie voluptuary of a type that is pretty rare today. Back in the high studio period (1935-1950 or so) closeted homosexuals often had similarly intense relationships with the screen, whether they wrote about it or not. But the attenuated emotional states of lush melodrama at its best never approached the intensity that silent films had for their viewers. That early audience was guilelessly open to the films and those films were made with a less cynical sense of storytelling – the earliest professional filmmakers (Francis Ford, Griffith, Ince, Dwan...) were dashing off one- and two-reelers two or three a week. The lack of naturalistic sound set the relationship of film and viewer deeper than the simpler vicarious one possible since then.

Originally, all were film voluptuaries when the earliest projectors' intermittent mechanisms showed darkness in the same ratio as the projected film frame (the mechanism moves to the next frame while the light is blocked). I can't resist quoting Terry Ramsaye's 1926 account of Thomas Armat's first successfully projected moving image:

> "This intermittent gear arrived about the middle of August, 1895.... They threaded up the machine with an Edison Kinetoscope film, and started the motor. Their hearts were in their mouths. In a second their fingers were in their ears.
>
> The thing worked. There was a living picture on the wall, probably the best motion picture that had ever appeared on a screen. But the noise was terrific. The picture, tearing madly, trying to reach a speed of forty-eight images a second, with the heavy three inch brass gear starting and stopping so often, lasted only a few seconds when the film ran out. They ran it over again and again. Very shortly the gear was battered out of shape by the intermittent stops.
>
> Pound for pound this was the noisiest piece of machinery in

the world. The art of the screen was born in boiler shop roar."
(*A Million and One Nights*)

Of course 48 frames-per-sec is twice the standard finally settled on. (The eye requires a minimum of 16 fps for persistence-of-vision to really kick in so 48 fps is extravagant.) Before the standard, flexible practices were allowed by the different cameras and projectors. The films projected in the late 1890s and into the new century then, created a stroboscopic hypnosis that left viewers uniquely open to the film's suggestion. This effect was then lost. The dark interstices were thereafter shortened and the image frames flashed twice to minimize flicker in a new standard. The speed of projection was still variable for effect until synchronized sound required the standard 24 frames per second we've known ever since.

It's important to remember the history of the motion picture's effect because the history of cinema otherwise is unmoored and becomes just a study of a critic's psychology, as if revealed under a still-existing hypnotic effect. Apparently Thomson's book, *Nicole Kidman*, is all that in spades. His *WSJ* article, "The Death of Method Acting", is poorly thought out as well, but editors value Thomson's unmoored movie star meditations. But in fact The Method is just a postwar Russophile pretense made of something that is as natural as the untrained or de-trained Hollywood approach to acting.

D.W. Griffith wrote, "We are forced to develop a new technique of acting before the camera. People who come to me from the theater use the quick broad gestures and movements which they have employed on the stage. I am trying to develop realism in pictures by teaching the value of deliberation and repose." Of course Griffith was making more than a film a week and learning by doing and pushing his cameraman Billy Bitzer and the Biograph partners to allow him to experiment, so one might wrongly reference Lillian Gish as Thomson does as totemic of "the histrionics of the years before 1920" if one's only seen the film *The Unseen Enemy* (1912), her and sister Dorothy's film debuts. It's one of six films Griffith made that July and it commenced immediately on their introduction to Griffith by Mary Pickford. Harry Carey is also in that film, though he was still playing sullen heavies rather than his soon-to-come low-key, witty western hero. For Griffith realism same year try *The Painted Lady* which stars Blanche Sweet. (Both are available on DVD; the youtube posts feature randomly applied music.)

The battle for realism in the theater is never-ending and predates Stanislavski. And it is a battle always lost. Though it is a never-ending battle in film too, there it is a battle often won, although always in films less celebrated. Whatever histrionics had come into film from theater at its beginnings, they were rooted out quickly by Griffith, Carey, Keaton and others before sound brought them all back in as the studios imported playwrights and thespians from New York all over again after sound came in big in 1928. This retarded film realism and Broadway Britishism suddenly reigned again in a flood of elocution.

At first in the sound era outdoor filming was suspended as sound studios were built, so westerns weren't made, and actorly film realism was sustained mostly in crime films and newspaper films, where recognizably American ethnic types would rattle off the colloquialisms that still echo through our lingo. But sound realism was different and tended to ground the spell a film might cast over an audience in a literalism best, though rarely, employed as throwaway. In Eileen Whitfield's book, *Pickford – The Woman Who Made Hollywood*, she references critic James Agate's idea that in the strange improvised moments in *The Jazz Singer* (1927) "the unrehearsed exchange had the aura of language overheard." But those moments stand out from the terrible rehearsed hamboning of the rest of the film. An early attempt at a sound western, *The Big Trail* (1930), directed by Raoul Walsh and starring John Wayne fails despite its widescreen epic budget mostly due to its poor use of sound; the acting and directing seem to have been undercut by the needs of sound equipment. At its best, what intimacy sound could provide was not as casually suggestive and metaphysical as the musical accompaniment had been as it treated the procession of images with nonliteral information. Synchronized sound recording can easily anchor an audience to the written wit alone, something better done with literature.

Properly used, sync sound can catch James Agee's "middle range of feeling" that comes of a cooler style of acting. Italian cinema never rebuilt their stages for sound recording; their production standard is for dialogue to be recorded later for dubbing in. In any dubbing process the voice doesn't match the body or the space, and the ear is much harder to fool than the eye. And so cultural differences aside, the Italian westerns become grotesques and hit the viewer-listener as circus-like cartoons. Even when the dubbing is in English by Clint Eastwood himself, the Man with No Name sounds like El Magnifico extranjero. The ear discounts here in a way similar to how the eye discounts when watching special effects.

Manny Farber on *Red River* (1948) refers to John Wayne's "clay-like acting" and Montgomery Clift's "one non-mush performance." Wayne worked his way into acting from crew and stunt work. Clift had been on Broadway as a juvenile lead and was a student of Lee Strasberg's Method. Wayne learned how to act by starring in serials and series westerns through the thirties. The films themselves are so bad it hardly mattered how good Wayne was. He got better though and John Ford gave him his re-entrance in *Stagecoach* (1939) but famously remarked after seeing *Red River*, "I didn't know the son of a bitch could act!" Ford had known Wayne for over twenty years at the time. Directed by Howard Hawks and written by Borden Chase, *Red River* is one of Wayne's best films; it's Clift's only good one, though he himself is often worth watching as he mushes through those white elephant productions, as Farber would call them.

Unlike Thomson, the painter-writer Manny Farber, whose complete film criticism has just been collected had an artist's concerns as he evaluated the movies he saw. He refers to the aging Wayne circa 1959 as still good at action but looking "nailed together" in repose, and a couple years later writes: "Wayne's acting is infected by a kind of hoboish spirit, sitting back on its haunches doing a bitter-amused counterpoint to the pale, neutral film life around him.... Wayne is a termite actor focusing only on a tiny present area, nibbling at it with engaging professionalism and a hipster sense of how to sit in a chair leaned against the wall, eye a flogging over-actor (Lee Marvin). As he moves along at the pace of a tapeworm, Wayne leaves a path that is only bits of shrewd intramural acting – a craggy face filled with bitterness, jealousy, a big body that idles luxuriantly, having long grown tired with roughhouse games played by old wrangler types like John Ford." That "middle range of feeling" again, that impresses an audience most in the drama's down-time when seemingly aimless in its observation goes about setting up the climax.

Marlon Brando, like Montgomery Clift was from Omaha and made his name on Broadway as they delivered some Method-measure of post-war realism to the theater. Brando avoided a direct contrast of himself with someone as stolid as Wayne, but he did make a number of rather goofy westerns. Brando is described in a recent biography as watching and absorbing everything he could from Ben Johnson on the set of *One-Eyed Jacks* (1961), which Brando also directed. But in the film Brando plays mostly against Karl Malden and the female leads.

Ben Johnson was the gold standard of movie acting, not really a star but more than a type; he came to acting from horse wrangling after a career in rodeo. He told Robert Pirosh in 1992, "As far as being an actor, that never did intrigue me a whole lot. Even after I started acting, I'd go out and wrangle or drive a truck or anything." No kind of movie star for David Thomson I suppose. His performance in a nondescript, generic western directed by John Rawlins called *Fort Defiance* (1951) is clear like mountain spring water – there is no affect. The other actors, Dane Clark and Peter Graves, burn hotter and they and the simple production value in an early cheapo two-color system, shot mostly outdoors, set off Johnson's movements and line readings perfectly, and there's none of the lesser

Ford hokum as in his cavalry pictures to get in the way. This too is movie magic.

Many elements go into a film, and the difficulty these impose accounts for the fact that a film's best moments are so often accidental motions of actors, or nature that are caught by the camera. It's also what offends when an A-budget production stamps out all such life and replaces all it can manage with the ersatz, a high polish set design that swamps any performance style attempted, any story told. But many prefer pure culture for its very inhuman processing because it takes us away from Life and Death. And the movies and star worship like other culture too often feed those appetites rather than the more time-honored human ones.

(original version posted at *The New Vulgate* No. 23)

Acting Lessen
More extrapolations from the coming film book, Stone Male – Requiem for the Living Picture. *This works pretty good as a précis for the book, though it will range over the rest of film history, process and effect too.*

The history of non-professional actors is right there alongside the accepted official history of hall-of-fame Great Thespian Portrayals in the films as they run on *TCM*, at MoMA, the Siskel, and the Cinematheque. But as a tradition it's invisible, completely swamped by Broadway gush about the Barrymores or Frank Langella, by Off-Broadway's counter-history of Brando and Dean, and by studio nostalgia in all flavors of corn: MGM's Clark Gable and James Stewart; Warner's James Cagney and Humphrey Bogart; 20th Century-Fox's Henry Fonda and Spencer Tracy; Paramount's William Powell and Randolph Scott; RKO's Cary Grant and Robert Mitchum.... At least the nostalgists know the work of the players I'm talking about.

As film critic Otis Ferguson put it in 1940:

> "The movies had the means and the press-agent flamboyance to screen-test anything that could get out of bed and walk. They didn't have to develop a school of acting. They accumulated, from all the fields of entertainment, including real life, a gallery of natural types such as was never seen on the face of the earth."
> *(The Film Criticism of Otis Ferguson)*

Each studio had its own gallery of types. Universal made their comedies and romances but their gallery included star Boris Karloff to play the monster or madman, against support type Maria Ouspenskaya whose job it was to play spooky old hags from the Carpathian Mountains. Fox didn't need one of those; they had Will Rogers so they needed Hattie McDaniel and Stepin Fetchit. Walter Brennan famously had one question when he was cast in a film, "With or without?" Brennan needed to know whether he was being cast with teeth or without teeth. Of course there was more to it – he set the standard playing helpless humanizing side-kicks to hardened heroes like Bogart in *To Have and Have Not* (1944) or James Stewart in *The Far Country* (1954), but he also excelled at playing frightening villains who drove the plot in films like *The Westerner* (1940), and *My Darling Clementine*

(1946). Not bad for silent era stuntman.

Walter Huston, a lead on Broadway who came to Hollywood with sound, played more interesting characters for possessing a harder, older look than typical. He slipped to support roles but nevertheless resisted his son John's entreaties to play the old prospector in *The Treasure of the Sierra Madre* (1948) without his false teeth. He finally agreed and the adaptation of B. Traven's novel was a great success. That bit of visual truth that changes the look of the face, the sound of the voice, that makes a character look and sound as if he's lived a life that's taken a toll, is not duplicable by mere method chops or make-up. Huston had played impressive, forbidding figures in excellent films like *The Virginian* (1929), *Abraham Lincoln* (1930), *The Criminal Code* (1931), *The Beast of the City* (1932), and *Dodsworth* (1936), but all it took was taking out the teeth and he's cackling away at the existential absurdity as it drives the younger characters (Bogart, Tim Holt, Bruce Bennett) mad.

I recently saw *The Bad Man* (1940) and its rogues gallery of types schtick their way through lines adapted to them and further polished by each actor: Wallace Beery as the bandido, Lionel Barrymore as the wheelchair-bound ranch owner, Henry Travers as the craven banker, Jack Conway as the swindler from the city, Laraine Day as the upstanding beauty, Nydia Westman as the homely ranchgirl who'd like nothing better than to be abducted to Mexico by Beery, Ronald Reagan as the man of the American southwest, Chill Wills as his trailhand, Chris-Pin Martin as the bandido's henchman, and Charles Stevens as his second. Of course it's not a real western, it's MGM and based on a Broadway hit. But the Porter Emerson Browne play, filmed twice before, gives the stock character hokum smart shape as Beery not only heads off both the banker's and the oil-man's swindles, he also repairs the various crossed lovers to their proper mates. And the players work it for all its worth. All director Richard Thorpe has to do is match the exteriors to the sets and connect the dots in rhythm. It ends with Beery racing on horseback to stop Travers from filing the mortgage, and hauling Barrymore in his wheelchair behind him across the desert. No masterpiece but no-one asked for a refund.

One of the best summary descriptions of silent era film production as nickelodeon novelties became feature films is the Allan Dwan interview that Peter Bogdanovich conducted in 1968. Here the question is about casting:

> "I remember the first actor I ever knew was a fellow named King Baggott. He was a good movie actor in his day – a very third-

OPPOSITE: RICHARD FARNSWORTH; *COMES A HORSEMAN* (1978).

rate actor in the theatre – but thoroughly ashamed of being in pictures. Yet he was a star and making good money. Finally he relaxed and said, 'I guess this is my forte,' and he stayed in. But our actors came from anywhere – we picked them up and trained them. They'd come to your gate in the morning to see if there was any work, and you'd bring them in. You'd ask one to do a little bit of business and he'd do it pretty well, and first thing you know there's a fellow who's intelligent, so you'd keep him in mind. He might turn into quite an actor. Girls were a natural. Children are great actors because they're always making believe. As a rule women could make-believe more readily than men. A man gets embarrassed. But they learn and if there's money in it, they'll try. And, of course, our cowboys were cowboys, and they were very natural, very real. Nearly 90 percent of the Western actors in all pictures are fellows who at one time or another were associated with cattle." (*Who the Devil Made It*)

Russian director-writer-actor-film theorist, Vsevolod Pudovkin, lectured cinematographers in 1933 on his use of "non-actors" and considered that unlike on the stage, in film their performances "at times can serve as an example to be followed by experienced actors." (*Film Technique & Film Acting*) The Soviet cinema had a cult for authenticity as well, at least until Stalin the cinephile stamped out formalist experiments for a "realism" that resurrected the hoariest stage-bound dramaturgy.

The writer Lillian Ross was a friend of John Huston's and grabbed the opportunity to cover the entire production of *The Red Badge of Courage* (1951), starting at the shoot on Huston's ranch in the San Fernando Valley, then to MGM in Culver City, and finally on to its parent company Loew's offices on Broadway. It's a fine book called *Picture* that was first a multi-part *New Yorker* essay titled "Production Number 1512" that ran in May and June of 1952. But the prime evidence of Huston's bold vision, his cast (Audie Murphy, Bill Mauldin, Royal Dano, John Dierkes, Arthur Hunnicutt, Andy Devine, Smith Ballew, Glenn Strange...) did not much interest her. Odd, given Ross' other book, *Player – A Profile of an Art*, is nothing but profiles of 56 actors, again spun from her work in the magazine. Those profiles are naturally come from a New Yorker's idea of actors – from the stage... song-and-dance men.... Had the film been one of the Huston-Bogart productions one imagines Ross would not have ignored the cast. Audie Murphy had no pretense that he was an actor; he wrote author Charles Whiting, "As an actor, I'd make a good stunt man." (*Hero*) But Murphy was inspired by John Huston here and later in *The Unforgiven*

(1960). Ross manages to catch Huston comparing Royal Dano to his father Walter (they'd just made *Treasure*), but her book's one bit of insight into Murphy, the most decorated soldier of WWII, then in the third year of his film career, occurs in the MGM commissary:

> "Drawing deeply on his cigarette, [Huston] looked down through the smoke at the table and brushed away some shreds of tobacco. Murphy fixed his gaze on the windows along the far wall. Huston looked at him. 'Excited, kid?' he asked. 'Seems as though nothing can get me excited any more – you know, enthused?' he said. 'Before the war, I'd get excited and enthused about a lot of things, but not any more.' 'I feel the same way, kid,' said Huston." (*Picture*)

Murphy grew up dirt poor in the large family of a drunk in east Texas; he rationed bullets by never missing the squirrels needed for dinner. He thence shot over two hundred fascists in Italy like they were squirrels. His boyish countenance was somehow convincing when claiming he'd never felt young, or when softly threatening a drunken, much larger Laurence Tierney at a party in Bel Air. In his book, *To Hell and Back*, he boiled his strategy down to "Destroy and survive." Fame hit him after he was incapable of excitement for deeds one doesn't dwell on. From his one letter home: "I like the army fine so far, they let you sleep till 5:30. On the farm I had to get up at 4." (*No Name on the Bullet*)

In Hollywood he slept with a gun under his pillow, and gambled away his money just slightly faster than he made it. His friend Budd Boetticher told me he didn't think Murphy's 1971 death was an accident. They had both recently finished what was to be the last film for each of them, *A Time for Dying* (1971), which was in part a deal-within-a-deal to make good on Murphy's debts; the film bombed, the plane crashed. Doesn't seem likely, but given Murphy's richness as a character himself, its testament to the need for this book, that Ross, even as a friend of Huston, did not understand there was anything to Murphy, or the rest of the cast. Instead her book details with New Yorker insouciance, the absurd world of the studio system already fretting about television. It is funny to hear the MGM-Loew's apparats and majordomos trying to make sense of this Americana art film that Nick Schenck had let Dore Shary allow John Huston to make over the objection of Louis B. Mayer. Si Seadler, Loew's eastern advertising manager is quoted,

> "The picture was beautiful but it was just a vignette. As soon as Mr. Schenck saw the picture, we knew it was a flop. Let's just say it was a flop d'estime. I guess that's the way Mr. Schenck would put it." (*Ibid.*)

And yet all male actors in the post-WWII era, when playing serious, somber, sober scenes are doing their best to channel the untrained authenticity of actors such as Carey, Wayne, Murphy...

Acting as metaphysical transcendence is easily overblown by voluptuaries like the Actor's Studio's James Lipton. CNN's Larry King and PBS's Charlie Rose fall off the deep end regularly too. TCM's Robert Osbourne seems intimidated to have an actor before him on the set though he is the better prepared. Public Radio's Terry Gross is impertinent enough to get more out of her interviews for all her ignorance. Still I prefer how one of Raymond Pettibon's screenplays channels or maybe tunnels the metaphysics of stardom. In the script, now the basis for a minor motion picture, a Cary Grant-type tells a young actor:

> "It felt funny, sitting there, front row center, getting studio-head head, while I'm watching myself from the screen. I was so nervous, it felt so eerie, that it took me forever to come, and when I did I left my body and entered the screen becoming my screen image, the stupid Canadian Mounties uniform and bright lipstick and all. I became him, it, myself... and with all my soul. I can still see myself up there, larger than life, and I can also see myself through those screen-eyes, pupils a foot in diameter, eyes perhaps... my best feature, but seeing eyes, too, and staring back into that screening room, lit by a projector I could feel my screen heart, a warm glow, like for one's own umbilical, found somehow, reclaimed from the scrapings and heapings and reattached, too, like a lost button, by some fawning Dr. Frankenstein and what I saw I saw clearly, which was myself, dripping and blushing as I stared back at myself self-consciously, embarrassed, to be sure, more than a little, no doubts about it." (*Untitled – Relax. Get In...*)

The power of film is metaphysical and it is the actors who most seem to give off this power. Often directorial touches and trademarks seem conceived in jealousy of the power actors possess. Flash concocted from behind the camera distracts the guileless audience, while pandering to those who watch films at a remove. One might learn a lot about film directing from *Citizen Kane* (1941), but really, whose need is pathological, the fictionalized William Randolph Hearst or the peripatetic Orson Welles behind the camera? Welles was a genius, but that is often a problem. However, Welles' tragedy was that he was smart enough to correct for *Kane* in artistic terms, but not in terms of Hollywood career politique: *The Magnificent Ambersons* (1942) as it survives gives evidence that Welles was immediately backing off of the busy fracturing of film space and attempting an organic if novelistic portrayal of characters in a place and time. But *Ambersons* was taken from him and re-cut and apparently cannot be put back together now for the profit of the destroyer's corporate descendents at TimeWarner. It was to be a dark, determinist tragedy, but the set up is too bright to be fully Marxian about it. You like the Ambersons and their turn-of-the-century Indianapolis more than it's possible to like anyone or anything in *Kane*.

The coldness of *Citizen Kane* is an imposition on the raw story material if you believe Louise Brooks' account of her time flitting in and out of various Hearst beach-houses and mansions with her friend Pepi Lederer, Marion Davies' niece. Brooks writes,

> "Mr. Hearst was not the ogre depicted by Marion. He did not devour pretty girl guests; he loved them. At San Simeon, I had run away from him twice – once when he came upon me drying my hair by the pool, and once when he found me looking at a rare edition of Dickens in the library – because his marked attention would result in banishment by Marion from the ranch and from Louella Parsons' powerful movie column." *(Lulu in Hollywood)*

It wasn't Kansas out there, but surely Brooks would've been among the last women to respect a home-wrecker's mansion on principle – her own Kansas eden had had a snake lurking in it. But it was as if Welles worked from Marion's worst nightmare – and she was basically a so-so comedienne whose tractionless career was juiced by Hearst's favors. The talented Welles then, took the P.O.V. of an actress's high suspicion of her own worthlessness in order to indict one of the more talented press barons of the age, presumably for his very dabbling in cinema. (If only he'd taken on pere Kennedy, another cinema dabbler, he might have done us all a favor.)

Welles' use of his "*Mercury Theater of the Air*" radio actors is another error of his early films. Radio actors were a special breed, largely forgotten now. An actor's voice coming over the radio worked best when it ladled inference onto ham. All the scenery-chewing of a Broadway blow-hard, only crooned into a microphone. Real bad. Something like a part being played by an announcer; any realism undercut at every syllable by unnaturally perfect timber and resonance of the voice. I guess this argues for just how good the singers who acted were since from Bing Crosby on, they all crooned into ribbon microphones, rather than keening to the rafters. And yet Bing, Dick, Frank, Dean and even Elvis did well in important films.

Film

Silent films are gone but thanks to the comedians Buster Keaton and Charlie Chaplin if no-one else, they'll never be fully forgotten. Far more forgotten are the sound-only radio dramas that were once so prominent. Often the original casts of Hollywood feature films re-recorded one-hour adaptations of their current films, but most radio dramas were unique productions and in their heyday before televisions were in every house, they were ubiquitous in homes. There is an intense collector fandom that has organized surviving radio dramas and production information but compared to film history it's a medium that seems to have just vanished from the pop culture memory.

Actors whose first starring roles were in radio dramas include Reed Hadley, William Conrad, and Jeff Chandler. Their too-fulsome, perfectly modulated Stradivariuses-of-a-voice could never quite convince as mere human in a drama no matter their talent. Tall thin Hadley might have had a more notable movie career but for that voice; in *Dark Corner* (1946) director Henry Hathaway actually seems to try to keep seventh-billed Hadley's face away from the camera in his scenes, though this was a step up from merely narrating Hathaway's *House on 92nd Street* (1945). Hadley played Zorro in the serial *Zorro's Fighting Legion* (1939) and then *"Red Ryder"* (1942-44) on radio – maybe his best acting though its total kidstuff. Hadley spent the fifties as a lead in television (*"Racket Squad"* 1950-53, *"Public Defender"* 1954-55), both shows naturally featuring his deep dulcet narration as well. He was notably Sam Fuller's idea of Jesse James in *I Shot Jesse James* (1948), though it's Bob Ford's story and Jesse gets back-shot at the twenty-five minute mark. Hadley also narrated Dept. of Defense films.

Wide-load Conrad had been able to play Matt Dillon on radio. For television the part required getting onto an actual horse without breaking the poor animal's spine, so James Arness got the part. (*"Gunsmoke"* ran on radio from 1952 to 61, overlapping the television series which ran 1955-75, then intermittent made-for-TV films.) Conrad did bits in well-known movies, guested on television dramas, skillfully narrated both the cartoon *"Rocky and his Friends"* (1959-61) as well as *"The Fugitive"* (1963-67) and even directed films and television, but he didn't become a star until the baroque phase of detective shows in the 1970s allowed him to play a fat detective in *"Cannon"* (1971-76) running from his car to pounce on bad guys in between fine dining experiences.

Jeff Chandler's voice got him into radio dramas, first under his real name, Ira Grossel, then as Tex Chandler in *"Frontier Town"* (1952-53). He looked good in a fit, swarthy, gray-haired, gleaming, nostril-flaring way but his career was cut short when back surgery later judged malpractice led to hemorrhaging, more surgery, transfusions and blood poisoning.

The point is, however, these guys with their howitzer voices destabilized any movie scene they were in. Especially in a police drama where the mundane patter of professionals going through their motions is supposed to impress the viewer with a world far more dramatic than, though as routine, as their own workaday reality. Strictly speaking, I'd argue that the same went for radio, but I suppose radio was more forgiving since the voices and a few sound effects had to carry the load. What radio drama I've heard could've used less in the way of effects as fight scene noise and other effects seem to break the spell the actors struggle to achieve with their voices. But radio drama conventions were developed quickly and they worked for a long time.

I think the ideal actor's voice for film is one that indicates a lack of self-consciousness by way of an "out-of-tune" delivery. You wouldn't say it was actually out-of-tune, unless you'd call Johnny Cash's voice out-of-tune as well, but the voice with a flat casual delivery is sure of itself and functional and not built up for dramatic effect. Not acted. And this helps the smart writer and director and sound engineer infer reality subtly by indirection. Actors who possessed ideal voices were Ben Johnson, Richard Farnsworth, Harry Carey, Jay Silverheels, Fess Parker, John Wayne and Charles Bronson. Just beneath them, slightly more tuneful, would be Jock Mahoney, Clint Walker, Jim Brown, Sam Elliott and others. Such voices can be heard as a special kind of music. Music is an encultured abstraction of speech over heartbeat. The speech of these men, over their even breath, communicates a certain frontier or rural, American ideal. I'm guessing the level speech patterns of the American Indians of the plains, mountains, and deserts might be the origin of this kind of flatted music, and that may be why it seems quintessentially American and works so well in westerns and other action-film settings.

In this country of immigrants there's a lot of remaking of personalities as kids look around and see more and different types – geographical, class and ethnic – as they grow up. Within America people move around a lot and so there are a number of ways a man might arrive at such a persona. Of that first list of actors I think John Wayne and Charles Bronson are so constructed, whereas the others are probably more naturally occurring. Wayne grew up in Los Angeles and gophered and extraed his way into acting, taking decades to get larger parts and star vehicles. Bronson grew up in a large family of Lithuanian immigrants in a company-owned mining town in Pennsylvania that was so isolated he had to shake an accent just to feel he could pass for American in his own country! He later used that accent in *The Great Escape* (1963).

Tom Milne, in his book on Carl Dreyer, writes of "the perfect harmony between actors, setting and narrative," which he judges Dreyer managed with *The Parson's Widow* (1920), *Mikaël* (1924), *Vampyr* (1932), *Gertrud* (1964) and others, but not with *The Passion of Jean d'Arc* (1927), *Day of Wrath* (1943) or *Ordet* (1954), where he believes "the narrative... takes the upper hand, dictating the somber texture of these films, and crushing the spectator into submission instead of winning him by persuasion." Milne means to defend Dreyer against his dour reputation based on these better known but more narrowly religious "narratives." It's interesting that for Milne it is the narrative, rather than the actors or the setting out of balance. Perhaps Dreyer has flushed out his critic's discomfort with religion generally, or maybe it's proof of an auteur that the story would be wrong while acting and setting were balanced. Dreyer began as a screenwriter in 1912.

Today only the directors believe they are auteurs. But it's usually an act designed to push back against producers and get things done easier. Film settings are as grande guignol as affordable. The scripts are unwritten though over-edited, as in polishing a turd. Surprisingly, it is often the actors holding today's films together. They make up their own backstories and walk through city streets and urban offices looking urgent and intense. As novelist and film writer Brian Garfield saw it in 1982:

> "Movies after the 1950s began to call upon actors with less and less experience and ability to do work of more and more demanding precision. The new fashion, influenced by the *Cahiers* attitude and the techniques of television commercials, required the sketchiest of screenplays with the emphasis on very brief scenes and rapid jump-cuts. Dialogue was minimized.... No longer is it used to reveal character; film becomes the medium of the meaningful silence, the pregnant pause, the 'beat.'" (*Western Films*)

Mere pretense, in other words. Garfield finished his book just after the release of *Heaven's Gate* (1980), that sprawling graveyard of the auteur theory and the counter-culture western. Those silences, written and directed by Michael Cimino, ended United Artists' independence (founded in 1925 as a quest for artistic autonomy and more money by D.W. Griffith, Charlie Chaplin, Mary Pickford, and Douglas Fairbanks) but they didn't kill arty emptiness, though these have subsequently been produced at a fraction of the cost.

Actors obsess on the wrong acting school but in the moment only the worst of them attempt to dominate the setting and story. And they aren't often to blame for the screenplays. Clint Eastwood will produce and direct *Mystic River* (2003), an acting nightmare that I guess he relates to as east coast ethnic realism which he is smart enough to keep himself out of. But that film's Industry prestige-style success helped set him up for the smaller stuff to come, most recently *Gran Torino* (2008) where Eastwood plays opposite a largely non-professional cast of Hmong immigrants, a film the old New York Film Critics Circle of, say, 1970 might've had aneurisms over trying to decide who can't act worse.

The problem with screenplays today is harder to see. I think the writer is treated no more contemptuously in Hollywood than before, but the studio-as-factory had a roster of writing talent braced against the cruel whimsy of studio-fate, but together getting some novel or play or first draft hammered into star-vehicle shape. The screenwriter Leonard Spigelgass discussed the thirties MGM m.o. at a 1971 AFI seminar:

> "[T]here were six of us writing Shearer, six of us writing Garbo, six of us writing Ruth Chatterton, six of us writing Robert Montgomery, and six of us writing Clark Gable. Which one would they choose? It was a great lottery." *(The Inquisition in Hollywood)*

The lottery was for who got the onscreen credit, important to them and to anyone trying to write about who made these films, but what's relevant here is Spigelgass' off-hand description of writers working the line in a gilt-edged Hollywood factory.

Today only the big summer event screenplays might have six or more contributors. Most scripts today have the author of the source novel, then two credited screenwriters, plus an uncredited script doctor or two. But still they don't often manage to contrive a dramatic center. They are merely polished voids. Nothing is wrong with them except there is no life in the writing.

One of my favorite films is *The Spirit of the Beehive* (1973). It plays like a spooky tone poem set in rural Spain after the civil war. It's about a young girl whose miscomprehension of things around her come to be shaped by seeing the movie *Frankenstein* (1931). I'd rather have bought just the film on DVD but given Criterion it was only available "complete" with the-making-of disc, so I ended up watching the extras with director Victor Erice, producer Elias Querejeta, writer Francisco Querejeta, and the actors and I was struck how inorganic and mechanical was their process of story construction. They really just hammered the elements together. The parade of images nevertheless has the intended effect on the viewer, perhaps in part because of the censorship of Franco's Spain that eliminated all overt righteous political intent. Censorship is not always an enemy of art, see Iranian and Chinese cinema as well. Or conversely, see today's Hollywood productions.

The void today is left for the actors, the music, the steadi-cam, the fifty-to-one shooting ratio, the cutting, the CGI to fill. The hope being that stray resonances to older, better movies will occur often enough to keep the viewer engaged. Writers can't direct and most of them know it. But the auteur theory leads directors to believe that their adaptive abilities qualify them to write, but they can only write around in the vicinity of a story. And their narrative sense, such as it is, develops in advertising, music videos or television. The producer has to throw the script at one of the handful of re-write men who have their hands on everything but credits on nothing. These are the best-paid writers, the ones whose credits ended years ago. Their number one job is to get the story told in under two hours – that is to lop an hour off the director's inefficient formless meanderings.

Cimino did great work with Eastwood and Jeff Bridges in *Thunderbolt and Lightfoot* (1974); he directed his own script for Eastwood's Malpaso company. And he earlier finished the script for *Magnum Force* (1973) when John Milius had to leave to direct *Dillinger* (1973), so Cimino had strangely enough been schooled in the Eastwood m.o., and Richard Schickel's biography, *Clint Eastwood*, recounts that production as a smooth one with no foreshadowing of trouble to come. But Cimino was no product of the depression. *The Deer Hunter* (1978) was bad enough in terms of being overblown and false, *Heaven's Gate* was ridiculous. Here's producer Steven Bach's description of the early casting ideas:

> "Cimino termed his casting 'extremely optimistic' but added 'not impossible.' John Wayne was suggested for the part eventually played by Kristofferson, Jeff Bridges for the Walken role, and as the female lead, Jane Fonda. The minor characters... included as mercenaries Henry Fonda, Burt Lancaster, James Stewart, Rod Steiger, Burt Reynolds, and James Caan. As immigrants, Cimino suggested Ingrid Bergman, Gene Hackman, George Kennedy, Richard Widmark, Jon Voight and Kirk Douglas, reserving the role of a U.S. Marshal for Joel McCrea, that of the governor of Wyoming for Randolph Scott, and that of a U.S. cavalry captain for William Holden..." *(Final Cut)*

Bach, was head of production and senior vice-president at UA but he was a cultured person and his involvement in and enabling of the disaster gave him perspective on it. Of course there are plenty of witnesses in Hollywood but there's rarely the honesty to tell the story; what books come are more often ass-covering whitewash re-writes. Everyone's Job #1 is to demonstrate fealty to any power believed to be now or in the future. But

Final Cut, like Lillian Ross' *Picture* is a classic study of the making of one film and the books stay in print.

I'm embarrassed to say I recognize half-baked post-sixties youth culture movie myopia when I see it. Cimino's playing fast and loose with the historical truth of Vietnam and the American west was done with an intent to counter Hollywood's own formula evasions and, these casting ideas suggest, redeem Hollywood. It was no simple arrogance, not if he expected to have the likes of John Wayne, Randolph Scott, and Joel McCrea participate. My dumb teen-age idea was to remodel Fritz Lang's M (1931), where the law and the underworld in Berlin unite to hunt down Peter Lorre's lone pedophile. I thought to have Eastwood the cop, Bronson the gang-boss, and the pedophile changed to a Weather Underground-type bomber played by somebody like Peter Fonda. There was a lot of penny-ante terrorism at the time and it was common then to think of them as fighting the good fight. I consider myself fortunate not to have been indulged.

Cimino was so indulged over *The Deer Hunter* at the Oscars that for his next groundless airy masterpiece, when history in the form of the 1894 eyewitness account, *The Banditti of the Plains – Or the Cattlemen's Invasion of Wyoming in 1892 (The Crowning Infamy of the Ages)*, by A.S. Mercer didn't provide a massacre of innocents – the invasion never actually occurred – he just made up his own calumny where dozens, hundreds, a thousand civilians are beautifully shot down by the cattlemen's hired guns in the magic hour just before dusk. (James Stewart was going to mow down farmers?! Rod Steiger, maybe...)

Anyway, the routine impugning of American businessmen, cops, soldiers, politicians, et. al., in the more seriously-intended movies is just displaced kvetching about Hollywood itself, made by people who know and care about little else. Oliver Stone's *JFK* (1991), *Nixon* (1995), and *W.* (2008), are not about their title characters at all. Shocking, I know....

(original version posted at The New Vulgate)

Clint, the First

As movie studios downsized in the fifties many actors settled for television as theatrical actors once had for films themselves. It could be difficult to get out of television and into movies even if one became a major star like Clint Walker. He was also one of the first stars to balk at the speed and cheapness of television production. This is more mining the upcoming film book for The New Vulgate.

For a good decade people heard the name Clint and they thought of Clint Walker. He'd been working at The Sands in Las Vegas as security one minute and after two bit parts – *Jungle Gents* (1954), *The Ten Commandments* (1956) – he became one of the biggest TV stars as the lead in *"Cheyenne"* (1955-62), which premiered the same week as *"Gunsmoke"* in Sept. 1955. It didn't have the run that *"Gunsmoke"* had but it made the bigger splash initially as it was an hour while *"Gunsmoke"* was a half-hour program for its first five seasons. *"Cheyenne"* was part of screwy rotating anthologies on ABC's schedule, first with *"Conflict"*, then with *"Shirley Temple's Storybook"*. Today the old show is available on complete season DVD collections, and runs daily on *Encore Westerns*. Currently the promo run on the channel for *"Cheyenne"* features a clip of guest-star juvie Dennis Hopper pointing his pistol at Walker and saying, "Hello dead man." Clint tells him to put his gun down and Hopper baits him to draw; he does and blows the gun from Dennis' hand. The juvenile delinquent made his retroactive appearance often in the west on the big and small screens through the fifties and into the sixties. They were played by young actors of that era like Hopper, Skip Homeier, Alex Nicol, Richard Jaeckel, James Best, Nick Adams, and even Jack Lord and John Cassavetes. These eye-popping ingrates made the stolid post-war hero projected west look even stolider.

The series was very cheaply made, and running an hour long it is often obvious they spent very little money on it. The many studio exterior sets look so bad it's a wonder they were produced by one of the great old movie studios. And the real location exteriors don't look much better. What's striking about the series is Walker himself, his untrained presence isn't faked, and in the first season his dry authority had the friendlier L.Q. Jones to play off of. Jones told Everett Aaker, "The director was the only human being in this business I couldn't get along with. I wouldn't spit in his mouth if his brains were on fire.... At my request they put me in a movie instead. That decision cost me three or four million dollars." (He's talking about either Richard L. Bare or Roy Huggins, methinks.)

Walker took his overnight success in stride and since the show was a Warner Bros. production and other TV actors at Warners got into some of their feature films, he walked off that threadbare set when they wouldn't allow it in his case. His agent Henry Willson, the connoisseur of beefcake (Rock Hudson, Rory Calhoun, Guy Madison, Guy Williams, Robert Fuller, John Smith, John Saxon, Mike Connors…) had a lot going on with Warners, especially their TV westerns, and *"Cheyenne"* was a huge hit so they caved and this first Clint returned to TV sets and got up onto the big screen too in 1958. Dave Kehr writes Sunday in the *New York Times*, "his place in film history hangs on the three modest western films he made with director Gordon Douglas." Kehr is writing on the occasion of Warners home video adding the second and third of these westerns to their burn-on-demand Warner Archive Collection.

These two films, *Yellowstone Kelly* (1959), and *Gold of the Seven Saints* (1961), are the lesser of the three though Kehr claims *Gold* is his favorite so I'll check it out again. It was written by Leigh Brackett for Howard Hawks according to Kehr. *Yellowstone Kelly* was written by Burt Kennedy though it is inferior to those scripts of his Budd Boetticher directed for Randolph

CLINT WALKER; *YELLOWSTONE KELLY* (1959).

Scott – *7 Men from Now* (1956), *The Tall T* (1957), *Ride Lonesome* (1959), and *Comanche Station* (1960). For one thing it is an historical bio-pic and reaches for A-film production values including color. What it does share with other Kennedy scripts is the carnal sense of sex that it took from fifties men's magazines and western pulp. In fact the whole of *Kelly* revolves around the Arapaho beauty played by blue-eyed Andra Martin, a captive of the Sioux, but able even while recuperating from a bullet in the back to split the tribe's leadership and threaten momentarily even the relationship between Kelly and his young apprentice trapper played by another *WB TV* star, Ed Byrnes. The set-up was sexy enough in the fifties but it doesn't carry a film today. Burt Kennedy told Jeremy Arnold, "*Yellowstone Kelly* I wrote for John Ford and John Wayne. Ford loved it and sent it to Duke, who was doing a terrible picture called *The Barbarian and the Geisha*.... It was really disappointing when you went from John Ford and John Wayne to Gordy Douglas and Clint Walker! And of course about five million dollars came out of the budget. I knew Gordy very well. I liked him, but his pacing on *Yellowstone Kelly* was atrocious."

It's the first film that Clint Walker starred in, *Fort Dobbs* (1958), that really ranks with the best westerns of the period. It has a Kennedy script as good as his best, and it's directed by an under-appreciated pro, Gordon Douglas, whose filmography is full of interesting movies (*Saps at Sea, The Falcon in Hollywood, Dick Tracy vs. Cueball, The Nevadan, Them!, In Like Flint, The Detective, Tony Rome, Skin Game, Slaughter's Big Rip-Off*), and it's got great support stars. It's got one of Virginia Mayo's best performances and that ain't nothing, and one is reminded what Brian Keith sold out when he let his career be destroyed in the sit-com, *"Family Affair"*. He makes another great villain in the Boetticher-Kennedy gallery, oilier than most. But *Fort Dobbs* works in the terse, grim way that it does because Clint Walker is such a low-key, wrong-foot actor that his hooded performance fleeing from a killing we see but don't understand until the end communicates realism in a way that the old studio style of Randolph Scott, or the Broadway musical style of Howard Keel, or the off-Broadway method style of Marlon Brando did not. Kehr notes that *Dobbs'* Monument Valley is "more desolate and sinister" than Ford's; the same can be said for the entire film up until its more-interesting-than-usual happy ending.

One exemplary shot, no doubt improvised, establishes a true moment on film of an actor and his part being one: Walker slide-surfing down a steep but soft wall of a dry wash as he flees the posse and descends into hostile Comanche territory. As Walker rides the earth down he reaches back to touch the wall behind him as a surfer might touch the curl of the wave for balance. He is in character.

(*original version posted at The New Vulgate No. 61*)

D.W. Griffith and the Biograph Shorts
Again, more riffing in the Vulgate *based on work done for* Stone Male.

There is a lot more to film history than even most film obsessives comprehend. The movie industry for all its short existence – movies were still just ten minutes long a hundred years ago – fairly jumped into existence, though firstly to provide novelty shorts, arcade loops less than a minute in length which debuted in 1895. These "actualities" were already wearing out their welcome after five years and were soon used in vaudeville programs to clear the house. True filmic story-telling began to evolve from this failing novelty. A new flood of storytelling cinema began at the turn of the century.

Terry Ramsaye's techno-cultural history of film was begun in 1920 for *Photoplay* magazine and published in book form in 1926. Even that early he called it *A Million And One Nights*. Ramsaye was able to interview most of the inventors and exhibitors from the days when it – the art, the business, the scam – briefly crawled before it walked, ran, flew. And it isn't until page 453 that Ramsaye reaches his Chapter 44, "Enter D. W. Griffith with Mss", and that's Griffith in 1907, still an actor.

The American Mutoscope Co. made a paper-based variant of the Edison Kinetoscope and they had the capital to invest in both film production and technical research. They hired W.K.L. Dickson when he left Edison in frustration over the quashing of his screen projection experiments. Thomas Edison did not believe in projection. He actually hadn't believed in the silent film either; his intent had always been to sync the image with his phonograph and have what were referred to as "living pictures" with sound. But the silent hand-cranked Kinetoscope "peep-shows" took off before he could perfect the synchronization. Ramsaye quotes an Edison memo, "[I]f we make this screen machine that you are asking for, it will spoil everything. We are making these peep show machines and selling a lot of them at a good profit. If we put out a screen machine there will be a use for maybe about ten of them in the whole United States."

American Mutoscope believed in projection because they listened to frustrated exhibitors – the single-viewer peep show was inefficient. They imagined projecting the living pictures before the audience at a vaudeville theater. The early movie studios that survived were creatures of these early exhibitors and their advantage was their truer sense of what their own audiences responded to. Dickson projected the living picture up on a screen with Mutoscope's backing. Mutoscope changed their name to The American Mutoscope & Biograph Company.

This company from the beginning brought more imagination to bear on their early filmed subjects; The Edison company's films were literal documents of stage performers or boxers – they were inventors and scientists rather than artists. (The earliest Edison films are available on DVD and some are worth seeing.) Ramsaye credits James White and Edwin S. Porter with creating the first "story picture" with their subject, *Life of an American Fireman* (1903), "Mark this: it was the grand staple situation of dire peril, with relief on the way, the formula that has made Griffith famous, or that Griffith has made famous, as you choose to view it. It was and is yet the greatest screen situation, of unfailing power."

Griffith came into New York from a stage tour. He made five dollars for appearing in the Edwin S. Porter film, *Rescued from an Eagles' Nest* (1908), but Porter was not interested in his subject ideas. The Biograph Studio was interested in Griffith's writing and he acted there as well at first. Mack Sennett showed up in this period too and the imaginative edge Mutoscope had over Edison widened.

D.W. Griffith began to make 1-to-2 reelers in 1908 and these films are well worth seeing. There are at least two different DVD collections of these mostly two reelers (14 to 20 minutes running time usually), and they are rentable from Netflix and available from Amazon and elsewhere. The Kino collection includes film historians with useful commentary tracks. It's worth seeing the earliest and the best of these films again with the audio commentary up.

A program of Griffith shorts are playing Sunday at the University of Chicago DOC Films: "D.W. Griffith at Biograph 1908-1913." The films show will be *The Guerrilla* (1908), *The Country Doctor* (1909), *A Corner in Wheat* (1909), *As It Is in Life* (1910), *Man's Genesis* (1912), *The Musketeers of Pig Alley* (1912), and *The Mothering Heart* (1913).

There are so many other great two- and three-reelers made at Biograph by Griffith that DOC should have programmed two or three weekends of these before moving on to his better known feature-length films. He made almost five hundred films at Biograph, first in New York and New Jersey and after 1910 increasingly in California; he left the company when he got resistance to his planned longer films. The second Sunday of this program features his first feature, *Judith of Bethulia* (1913) which was his last for Biograph, running about one hour. Subsequent Sundays run Griffith's more famous feature films, but these though well worth seeing can be wearying and reveal Griffith's weaknesses as a writer. Looking over his filmography it seems clear to me that his best work is found among his two-reelers – *Musketeers*, and *Mothering Heart* in this program, and, not on this program but on the DVDs: *The Painted Lady* (1912), *The Unchanging Sea* (1910), *The Girl and Her Trust* (1912), and *The Female of the Species* (1912).

These short story analogues really work in the then new medium and soon people were filling stand-alone movie theaters to see all-movie programs. The industry was no longer poaching on vaudeville, or game rooms. I've often thought movies since the fifties are too long. What people once expected was a couple short subjects, a programmer that might be 60 minutes in length and then the main feature that might run 90 minutes. When I went to repertory cinemas in the seventies and eighties the program was two feature films, often 90 to 110 minutes each. Almost nobody sits through a double feature anymore. But aside from certain gargantuan twenties productions by Griffith, Von Stroheim and others where two- to five-hour films were turned in, the feature length was fairly short until fifties A-films got bigger and longer and wider to compete with television. It really didn't work as a strategy because it's always about the mean storytelling ability of the industry as a whole that makes people go to films or stay home. Granted there is so much more at home that theatrical film exhibition will not boom again.

I've recently been watching a lot of half-hour TV dramas from the late 1950s and early 1960s, including the first four years of *"Gunsmoke"* (1955-59, CBS), *"Lawman"* (1958-62, ABC), *"Have Gun - Will Travel"* (1957-63, CBS), *"The Rifleman"* (1958-63, ABC), *"Wanted: Dead or Alive"* (1958-1961, CBS), *"The Westerner"* (1960, NBC), and *"Whispering Smith"* (1961, NBC). The half-hour television drama was history by the mid-sixties; drama was one hour (or longer), and sit-coms remained at 30 minutes. But in release on DVD or shown on the *Encore Western* channel, the now extinct short-drama are seen again, and now commercial-free they run 22 minutes long. They are two-reelers with sound, and though episodes are often clumsy, threadbare presentations, they are also routinely quite well-done by being wise about what can be accomplished within the limitations. Given skilled actors and the western sets the wise producer asked more of his writer than his director. And its easy to spot the quality that followed a writer's credit of Clair Huffaker, Sam Peckinpah, Dean Reisner, Burt Kennedy, Robert Thompson, Gene Roddenberry, and others in these programs. The half-hour drama disappeared from television but this time it was no Griffith-like genius who needed more minutes; not quite. As with feature films, most television dramas are a good fifteen minutes too long even without commercials.

(original version posted at The New Vulgate No. 65)

Sword of Doom

When The New Vulgate *was in a weekly rhythm I was able to post about revivals of films which had most impressed me over the years, whether the screenings were in New York, Chicago or Los Angeles.*

Japan Society, New York City
Kihachi Okamoto / Tatsuya Nakadai, Toshiro Mifune.

My simple answer to the question, What is my favorite film?, is this film, *Sword of Doom*. I'd rather have it be some American film since no national cinema compares to Hollywood, but there's just no other film so controlled and rich and always slightly out of reach no matter how many times you see it. It's based on a lengthy novel often adapted piecemeal for film and television in Japan called *Dai-bosatsu Toge: Great Bodhisattva Pass*, written by Kaizan Nakazato and published in 1929.

    I first saw the film at the PicFair theater in L.A. in 1977, part of a samurai series shown in a theater run by Iranians in a Jewish neighborhood. The real buzz for that series was Kurosawa's *The Hidden Fortress* (1958), which George Lucas had let on was in part the inspiration for his *Star Wars*, which was just then breaking records. I didn't think much of *Hidden Fortress* either, but *Sword of Doom* was so good that once I thought about it I got ticked off about the then-standard literature about Japanese film: How could Kihachi Okamoto or this film be absent?! Of course the art-film series that *WNET* put together for public television would not program an action film by a genre specialist; they stuck with *Rashomon*, and *Seven Samurai*, by Akira Kurosawa, and the even more classically styled films by Yasujiro Ozu and Kenji Mizoguchi. We didn't get to know about all that was happening in Japanese cinema until well after old-style "cinephilia" passed.

    Eventually one identifies the middle-brow fear that animates the milquetoasts who gravitate to culture reviewage, especially if you go on to run SST Records and watch who can be convinced, forced, or pushed out of the way when your bands headman a heretofore unsuspected twenty-year zeitgeist. In the late sixties reviewers looked around after seeing the Eastwood/Leone westerns and decided they better pretend to get the joke, but after *Dirty Harry* (1971) they decided they could use Eastwood back in

Amerika as whipping boy to demonstrate how much they despised Nixon's silent majority. Now Eastwood is considered the sage elder of classic American cinema, and by some of those same writers. But *Sword of Doom* is so well done technically, and so offhandedly masterful an action film that its absence from the literature must have come down to the specific fetishes of the Nihonophiles of the West. This film's dark truth about Japan is not the blossom they wished to contemplate.

I saw the film at every opportunity back in the repertory days before videotape; it tended to be shown in samurai film series, rather than included in more common art-film series as Kurosawa's *Seven Samurai*, or his excellent *Yojimbo* often were. I wrote a review of it for a punk mag in San Francisco called *Damage*, and for my current project, a film book, I focus on how skillfully Okamoto sets his actors, Tatsuya Nakadai as the increasingly bitter and paranoid evil swordsman, and Toshiro Mifune essentially playing the square-john archetype of the honorable samurai who tells his

TATSUYA NAKADAI; *SWORD OF DOOM* (1966).

students to study the soul. And that these light and dark poles do not meet... Perhaps they would have in part two, but here they do not and we accept this as an unfilm-like contrivance-evasion and that our anti-hero's dark unraveling explains all. Mifune is all barking rectitude, Nakadai is really doing something very un-Japanese I expect; he wrong-foots any action film mode for hero or anti-hero or villain.

This Sunday's *New York Times* featured a staffer's memory of how he and his friends saw *Sword of Doom*, and what it meant to them as rambunctious young action film connoisseurs. They may not have been reading Pauline Kael or Vincent Canby in any case, but with no reigning expertise filling you in on the original story, you can't guess as you stumble across the film that the dude doesn't die at the end and Okamoto expected to get to work on the second installment of the novel's plot as soon as its expected box-office success was certain. I had thought the freeze-frame end an indication of director Okamoto's falling in love with his character to the point that he refused to show his certain, promised doom. After all, the tradesman-smuggler-protector of the young woman orphaned by this lead villain's offhand cruelty years earlier, is waiting for him outside the burning, blood-stained brothel with a pistol – the image of which is a genre-shock that tolls the funeral gong on this dead-end island code, just as the A-bomb did next century for that iteration of the Emperor's code.

Okamoto explained to Chris D. in 1997:

> "At the last minute they [Toei Studio] had a premonition it wasn't going to do that well. Then it came out and did do mediocre business. So in a way they were right. But it was a very successful film overseas, especially the United States. When it first played New York, there were lines around the block."
> (*Outlaw Masters of Japanese Film*)

Okamoto looked slight and unassuming as he was introduced after the screening at Raleigh for the Directors Guild in Los Angeles. An interview was conducted through a translator, and Chris interviewed him for his book the next day. No real indication of genius per se, except for the film itself. The place was packed, but probably not with film directors unfortunately.

I've seen all of his samurai films which are occasionally programmed as genre exercises rather than on Okamoto's reputation, but Chris details Okamoto's early war films, plus there seem crime dramas and more mainstream productions which are also unseen and probably unseeable short of purchasing the DVDs from Japan. Donald Richie has a lot to answer for.

(*original version posted iat The New Vulgate, No. 85*)

Sword of Doom
Posterity Alert. This ran in 1981 in the San Francisco magazine, Damage.

Sword of Doom is the kind of film that pushes you towards all those fun but ridiculous exclamations such as "All other samurai films add up to a mere footnote in cinema history as the necessary preparation for *Sword of Doom*." Or how about this one: "*Sword of Doom* alone is sufficient justification for the existence of the Japanese people"? The point being, this film is the perfect realization of a complex and provocative plot, it is an awesome film and you want to communicate that to people.

Tatsuya Nakadai has played second man to Toshiro Mifune in most of the classic samurai films, and significantly, in *Sword of Doom*, this is reversed. Mifune plays the honorable samurai instructor. He has found one of the few legitimate niches in society for a samurai. Nakadai, of course, has not. His father, having taught him the silent form of swordplay, now frets from his deathbed that his son does not deserve to live. For you see, Nakadai is a cold – almost soulless – killer. We first see him when an old man and his granddaughter stop to rest on a hilltop. The girl goes for water and the old man kneels at a shrine bemoaning to his god his failure to die and ease the burden on his family. A sudden chill interrupts the old man's prayer and the camera glides left to reveal standing off behind the old man, a figure in black with his face hidden behind a straw helmet. The old man shakes with fear, for he knows he is in the presence of death.

This first scene sets the film's plot extremely well, for every character with critical impact on the plot is delineated in the first fifteen minutes. It is another facet of Okamoto's control of the film. The plotting, the black and white cinematography, the acting (very naturalistic for a samurai film), the music and the direction all contribute in this delicately drawn portrait of an incredible man and the hell he pulls down around himself.

What is finally most impressive about the film is the unflinching non-confrontation between Mifune the good and Nakadai the evil. It almost happens, but that would be too easy, and Okamoto knows that, instead, he plays the difficult game of making a genre film with both intelligence and guts. The bravado with which he attacks that challenge is thrilling.

Nosferatu the Vampyre

Posterity Alert: I remember the movie well. I play the Popol Vuh soundtrack often. But I forgot I'd reviewed it for the *Clinton St Quarterly* (Spring 1979) until I paged through a copy as I tore my house apart looking for my *Oregon Organism* cartoons.

Werner Herzog / Klaus Kinski, Isabelle Adjani, Bruno Ganz

Nosferatu, Werner Herzog's new film of the Dracula story has many things wrong with it. Though the idea of Herzog producing an adaptation of the classic vampire tale is certainly provocative. In films like Aguirre and Kaspar Hauser, Herzog examines the human situation with an awareness of the mysterious – mundane objects or events appear or occur out of context. The elusive truth, the grasp on reality is always just ahead of his characters.

The Dracula story, like many classic horror stories, uses a basic plot device – the attempt by those who know the horror's reality to convince the authorities (men of law and science) of that reality. The authorities live in cool conviction that they alone understand the nature of the world and they therefore deserve their positions of power.

In Kaspar Hauser, Herzog introduced an empty man – devoid of social, scientific, and even self-knowledge – into society. The man is aided by townspeople, but, upon coming to the attention of "real" society, he quickly becomes a novel entertainment. The man who understands nothing – not even how to conceal his ignorance to protect his ego – becomes an amusing caricature of human reality and is played with momentarily by the social class which, due to its own rapacious ego, has convinced itself that it knows, if not everything, at least enough to dictate what is best for all classes. These people quickly tire of Kaspar when his questions become focused and persistent.

In Nosferatu an equally primal aspect of our reality is explored. But where Kaspar Hauser is basically intraocular in its concern, Nosferatu is more concerned with us as a species and our uneasy pact with the cycle of life feeding off the rot of death. The Dracula myth is a powerful one because of this contradiction and the fear and guilt it provokes.

The film then should have been excellent. The plot of the original Stoker novel was streamlined to allow Herzog to work more in his style. He works subliminally, by mood rather than exposition and plot. Nosferatu fails at this because, despite all the ingredients for success, Herzog has allowed purely physical characteristics of the production itself to undermine everything.

One is suspicious from the beginning as the 20th Century Fox logo hits the screen. Then you read in the credits the words: "English dialogue by..." and you cringe and hope for the best. It doesn't come.

Klaus Kinski, Isabelle Adjani, and Bruno Ganz play the lead characters and they are fine actors but none of them know the English language. They nevertheless read their dialogue – translations from Herzog's German – in phonetic English which as might be guessed, totally subverts the art of acting. Inflections are out of place, words are mispronounced and more than once there are laughs where none should be. [The film was shot twice, once in German, once in English.]

It is all too clear that the politics of American distribution and its effect on whether production money would be forthcoming in the first place have ruined this film. It is all the more upsetting when you find that quite a lot of the film's images stick with you long after you've seen the film. It could have been the ultimate articulation of the Vampire myth.

Now, distributors being the venal people they are, the film may never see general distribution in America.

Violence and the New Movie

Posterity Alert. From the Sept. 1975 issue of The Match! *It was my first time in print; I was 19 when I wrote it and had just quit college and moved to Chicago. The Match! (b. 1969) paused around 1980 and when I happened on Sam Dolgoff I asked him if he knew why. He answered in his gruff shtetl-Bronx accent, "That guy has psychologic problems." If so Fred must've solved them because his little Tucson paper managed to keep going into this century.*

Violence in movies has come a long way. In the silent comedies guns were fired at rear ends and all it took was a little fierce rubbing to heal the wound. In drama, up until the sixties, bullets were invisible and left no scars on a body. There was no blood and no hole in the victim's suit. Today though, we even see organs blown out of people. Guns and knives are no longer the only murder weapons either; we can now witness such untidy killings as those done with chainsaws.

There are several possible reasons for this abrupt change. Two of them – that weapons have become infinitely more powerful, or that the human body falls apart much easier today – can safely be discarded. Technical improvements in film-making, such as lightweight cameras and color, have had an effect on violence as it appears on film, but these cannot be said to have caused it. It is reasonable to assume that people are what have changed – or more specifically the movie-going public has changed.

They've changed in two ways: First and of lesser importance is the change wrought by television's proliferation. This led to a smaller and younger movie audience, which was a change that spelled the end to Doris Day sex comedies and Tab Hunter-Rock Hudson type heroes, because the younger audiences couldn't enjoy them. Television also set up a competitive relationship with movies, leading film-makers to try to depict events that television could not because of its many technical and censorship restrictions. But even these cannot be main reasons for the excessive film violence of today, since television has been thriving for over twenty years, while film violence has become a problem only recently.

It was in the late sixties that film violence began to be profuse and realistic. However, unlike the bulk of violent movies today, the first onces to use explicit violence placed it in a realistic setting. *Bonnie and Clyde* and *Easy Rider* depended on violence to tell their story; today the story is violence. In a Charles Bronson or Sam Peckinpah film, characters are not developed and relationships are not explored. Instead the events are devised and manipulated to provide a maximum of "action" (read: violence).

What must be understood, though, is that these violent films, no matter how unrealistic in story, are realistic in attitude. They match the attitude of their audience perfectly and this is proven by the numbers that attend films like *Death Wish* and *Mandingo*.

This new attitude that allows people to enjoy films which are nothing but series of violent acts is the second and most important change the movie-going audience has gone through. It can only be explained in the context of the changes the American psyche has had to accept in the last decade. The catalyst for these changes was the Vietnam War.

THE MATCH!, SEPT. 1975.

Unlike World War II, the Vietnam War was a revolutionary war. When the Vietnamese communists attacked the French it was different from Germany attacking France. American leaders were convinced that they were the same, though, and proceeded to attack. Illustions eventually blow up in one's face and the Vietnam War did exactly that. As the war droned on protests became louder; these were suppressed until the general American populace made up its mind on the war. Then, in order to get out "with honor", Nixon made up with the Soviets and Chinese. Americans saw their president in Moscow and Peking praising what the communists had accomplished, and suddenly the Vietnam war looked as insane as it was.

In a more general sense Americans lost their self-righteousness. They found out that their soldiers were just as murderous as those of the other side (My Lai) and saw dissenters killed in the land of the free (at Kent State). Americans could no longer play the unqualified good guys sitting in judgment on the rest of the world. Add to this the new militancy of the Third World and the sudden economic problems and it becomes clear that the average, middle-of-the-road American has a lot of adjusting to do.

To escape this unfamiliar complexity of the world, people who attend movies look for simple, direct action; and nothing is simpler and easier to relate to than a knife in the gut. It requires no interpretation. In fact, in some films where there is no motivation behind the violence, there cannot be any interpretation. It is the isolated act, then, the knife in the gut, that is the sole attraction of the film. And the film makes money. In the mind of the American movie-goer, death has become the only certainly (and a comforting one) and murder the only unmistakable act. Ask questions later, or better yet forget the questions altogether.

Recently pressure has begun building from groups and individuals who wish to reduce the violence in movies (and on TV too). This is of course an admirable goal, but it is usually sought in an incorrect manner. Most film reformers would set up censorship, which suppresses rather than solves the problem. To solve the problem, the confusion that people feel when they confront the world their leaders have made must be eliminated, but this can only be done when people realize that their leaders are not serving them and can be done away with.

It would be possible to reduce people's feelings of confusion enough to soften movie violence if minimal reforms made government the least bit fathomable. But the problem will persist in some form until people take control of their destinies away from game-playing bureaucrats. Until this happens the only way movies can be hopeful and optimistic is under the cover of more illustions, which eventually would be destroyed anyway, leaving movies right where they are now.

MUSIC.

~

David Lightbourne & Outlaw Folk in '70s Oregon

This was posted at The New Vulgate *on July 28, 2010. I had written an earlier instant version in late May. The extra time allowed me to improve it but I could've written it so much better had Dave still been alive, but then I wouldn't have had to bother.*

Portland was once a nice, unpretentious, not to say sleepy, port town on the Columbia River that had had its big rock and roll moment when The Wailers, Paul Revere and the Raiders, The Sonics and others jumped from the Northwest's vibrant dancehall circuit to the national charts beginning in 1959 and lasting most of the sixties. That circuit started with Portland, Seattle, and Vancouver but for some bands included Spokane, Boise, and Reno. Important college towns included Eugene and Olympia. But as a whole the scene was isolated and often left off of national tours; this turned out an aesthetic advantage but a business handicap. The book that covers the fifties/sixties era in the Northwest in all its richness unknown to the *Billboard* charts or official oldies radio/*Rolling Stone* posterity is *Dance Halls, Armories and Teen Fairs*, by Don Rogers.

But whereas Portland and the Northwest helped lead the way post-Elvis/pre-Beatles, it began following the rest of the country, primarily San Francisco, by the end of the sixties, "In 1968... rumors spread that between 8,000 and 50,000 hippies were headed to the city" from suddenly drug-desiccated San Francisco, according to Valerie Brown (*Oregon Historical Quarterly*, Summer 2007). These thousands didn't show but the city did generate and collect a music scene that featured all the influences of the period – blues, psychedelia, and folk. Touring bands that had special impact in the late 1960s included The Grateful Dead, and Dan Hicks. It wouldn't have been too unusual for these influences to be politely discrete in local bands such as The PH Phactor Jug Band, Melodious Funk, The Nazzare Blues Band, Portland Zoo, The Sodgimoli Jug Band and others. If so, that surely changed when a small invasion of musicians a couple years older than the hippies began to show up from points east.

*

David Lightbourne had performed with friends and classmates in Iowa while he attended Grinnell; these included Tom Newman, Clark Dimond,

Ellis Simberloff, and Peter Cohon (later Coyote). An April 21, 1962 Grinnell Folk Club concert saw a double-album private release and features David performing two songs before an auditorium full of enthusiastic and knowledgeable music fans. This generation of student had followed rock and roll in junior high, and then found in 1958 that the record industry had tamed it and as David would say, "Dick Clark took it over." The music obsessives in high school then discovered a truer folk music underneath the bogus pop-folk, or folkum as *The Little Sandy Review* might call The Kingston Trio, Brothers Four, Harry Belafonte, etc. David at 19 sounds influenced by Dave Van Ronk, and The New Lost City Ramblers; he was discovering the blues but hadn't worked much of that into his sound yet, though he is already playing finger-pick style. And it's clear by the audience reaction as David is introduced as "a performer of social import" that he is cutting a figure on campus where he also wrote a column in the paper. Clark Dimond, also on the album, writes,

> "We shared our knowledge and our repertoire at Uno's coffeehouse, which was run by Zal Lefkowicz, later to become actor and producer Zalman King. Mescaline was available by mail from Texas. I remember the police doing an ashtray sweep looking for evidence of marijuana. David was playing onstage at the time they came in. Next to his foot was an open quart bottle of mescaline, and David just kept on playing and the cops left."
> (CD, July 16, 2010)

David grew up in several places as a young child due to his father's death in WWII when he was one. I figured Dave probably had a memory of a brief idyll with his mother and her family before she remarried when he was about four. His sister Priscilla writes:

> "My maternal grandparents, Isaac and Emma, were from southern Indiana and Kentucky. My mother used to tell many stories of how much music there was in the house. They were tenant farmers, so incredibly poor, but each evening they would either sit on the porch or in the living room and sing, one harmonizing, one on lead. This was the house that David grew up in, at least until he was four, and then visited often after that. In someone else I might say they were too young to soak up the atmosphere, but I wouldn't say that about David." (PL, July 20, 2010)

The new family moved near Elmhurst outside Chicago and David was preternaturally media-wise when it came to radio drama, comics, movies, and early television. His stepfather had played trumpet for the Dorseys and Paul Whiteman and left the road to sell instruments to kids and schools. The Lightbourne family's daily radio program featured the kids; David said they had radio equipment under their kitchen table and a special phone line to send the show live to the station; he was eight and playing accordion. The show ran in 1950-51. David saw Elvis Presley in 1957 at the International Amphitheater, the first Presley performance up North. David switched to guitar; he saw Mike Seeger in 1958, Rev. Gary Davis, Mike Bloomfield, and Elizabeth Cotton in 1961, Ramblin' Jack in 1962, and in 1963 he worked for Bob Koester at Jazz Record Mart and roamed southside blues clubs with him to see J.B. Hutto, Junior Wells and others; he got to know Bloomfield and saw Skip James, Son House and Howlin' Wolf, and was a charter subscriber to Minneapolis' *The Little Sandy Review*. He was to record a folk album for Koester's Delmark label but the British invaded, Dylan plugged in, and the folkies surrendered.

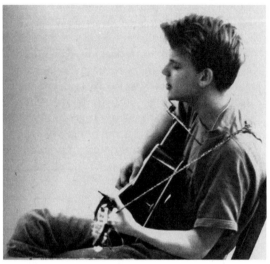

DL, GRINNELL COLLEGE, CIRCA 1961.

Here's something David wrote for himself, setting the early scene for his high school cohort in 1958 with Elvis in the Army and rock and roll on the ropes:

> "We had spent four full years up to '61 largely listening to music, frequently driving distances to see it live, when no one our age did that. By 10th grade... I had started my lifelong ransacking of American roots music record catalogs and made no apologies for any lack of savvy. I knew that older hipsters knew more about political folk music, and bluegrass, and blues. But I prided myself in also keeping AM Top 40 in my cross-hairs as well, and older music freaks despised that stuff on principle to their loss. I'm trying to remember 10th grade now: Leadbelly, Big Bill Broonzy, Woody Guthrie, Cisco Houston, Pete Seeger, Brownie & Sonny,

Bob Gibson, Odetta, Blind Lemon Jefferson, Josh White...."
(DL circa 2000s)

David enjoyed Grinnell and talked about his music-minded classmates and friends often. He took the third year off and spent a year in Cedar Falls/Waterloo where he made some friends he'd need in 1967 when he had enough of his first job in the straight world at R.R. Donnelly in Chicago. He was on a white-collar career ladder and somewhere between his older uptight co-workers sniggering about co-eds or the blacks, he balked, returned to his Waterloo friends and drifted into their drug-smuggling enterprise, dubbed The Company. He writes,

> "I was only twenty-four in 1967, but already like a lot of other people in America, somewhat desperate to cling to the visions of unfulfilled action that had been promised earlier in my life. Action, drama and incident... Accident and movement... In some weird way possible, yet in the civilization of depressed content – the sublimation of sexuality sideways – the opportunity to be aggressive, still something to snatch and grab.... The deal was to pay the expenses of the trip, a quickie, from a small town in the hinterlands of the remote Midwest, quickly to Chicago and thence to Mexico City. We were going to bring back as much as $500 would bring in the best available Acapulco Gold, which used to be available on the farm for prices around $6.00 a kilo.... The last time friends of mine had done it, their interpreter had taken along a pistol. This was sheer madness in the hallucinatory glitter of our truly psychedelic childhoods." (DL, circa 1990s)

In this peripatetic pre-Portland period, Lightbourne was probably trying to figure out how his interest in writing and music could be applied without winding up a hollow careerist who might as well be pulling down a salary at Donnelly for all the good it would do the culture. If he wrote he'd want to write as Miller or Genet wrote; if he played music he'd want it to be as true as Koerner Ray & Glover, or Mike Seeger. Dave spent a long week on the Strip in Los Angeles catching Albert King, Steppenwolf, Canned Heat, and others before settling into Cambridge, Mass. for a year. He doesn't appear to have performed while in Boston though he followed the vital music there – The Remains, Jim Kweskin & the Jug Band, Taj Mahal.... In Fall 1969 he moved to Eugene, Oregon. David lived with his Iowa friend Warren and their girlfriends while Warren ran what Tom Newman calls "a hippie hangout" called Alice's Restaurant. Tom writes, "Wherever Warren lived was always the center of activity for everyone he knew." In a fictionalized version of these days Dave describes a certain character as "being Pisces, active, restless, impatient with the stasis in things, with perpetual momentum for stirring up, shaking down, bilking the town in the only really effective way possible, the corruption of its youth however such may be accomplished." Did I mention Dave said these instant "youth-culture food parlors" Warren set up wherever he went in Iowa and Oregon were inevitably crawling with runaway girls?

*

In Eugene they also found Al Malam, another former Iowan, who David thought had the best singing voice on a white boy. Still does, though he's gone by the name Al Rivers for decades now. In early 1971 David and Warren moved to Portland. They and Tom Wood, also from Iowa and who'd been in Cambridge as well, now set up to run their Mexican loads up to the rather dry environs of rain city. In a cassette tape dated November 1972 that David made in a Cuernavaca hotel room, he, Colleen, Tom and Warren mostly swat cockroaches and laugh about David's attempts at emergency Spanish when they were evicted the day before at gunpoint from another hotel.

Portland liberalized its restrictive licensing of bars for live music presentation in 1973 and Portland stages quickly filled up with acoustic country-blues specialists as Manhattan, Bucks County, Vermont, and other formerly happening scenes emptied out of talent such as Steve Weber, Robin Remaily, Dave Reisch, Jeffrey Frederick, Jill Gross, Peter Langston, Fritz Richmond, Gary Sisco, and others. They were liking what they were hearing and seeing in Portland. Bars like The Inferno, The Euphoria, The Earth Tavern, The White Eagle, The Leaky Roof, Key Largo, The Grog House, The Dandelion, and Sweet Revenge were soon showcasing The Holy Modal Rounders, The Clamtones, Michael Hurley, The Metropolitan Jug Band, The Fly By Night Jass Band, Puddle City Bluegrass Band, Al Rivers and others. Lightbourne was quoted in the *Oregon Journal*, "Portland is sort of a refuge for '60s folk musicians" (2.4.1980), and he looked forward to luring Dave Van Ronk next. These guys were just hitting their stride too. They'd been perhaps a bit too green in their first attempts to sound blue or old-timey. Now they were ten-plus years into their music-making. They had all manner of criminal sidelines (drug-use of course, but also smuggling, shoplifting, drug-store raiding, arson, and maybe even a crime or two against nature), they had hip young women to inspire them now whose own estate-sale obsessions guaranteed the apartments and houses where they lived or passed-out in were furnished with the finest in

DL, BUCKHORN BAR, LARAMIE, CIRCA 2000; PHOTO: JOE CARDUCCI.

Handwritten note:

GRINNELL SCARLET AND BLACK - AUTUMN 1965!
A MIXED BAG TO BE SURE; EMBARRASSINGLY PRETENTIOUS AND INTELLECTUALLY MISTAKEN AT KEY JUNCTURES; BUT PRETTY DAMN GOOD FOR 1965 NOTWITHSTANDING. DICK WATERMAN, SON HOUSE'S MANAGER, WAS IMPRESSED AND GRATEFUL FOR THE ADVANCE PUBLICITY; SHUCKS!

David Lightbourne

trains and rivers

I've been asked to say something by way of introduction about Son House, the Negro blues singer, prior to his performance here tomorrow night, and don't know exactly where to begin.

For one thing, Son House is one of an older generation of Negro country blues artists who were born in the Mississippi "Delta" region, recorded a few "race records" in the 20's and 30's, and then disappeared back into the bleak obscurity of the northern Mississippi countryside. And unlike many of the rediscovered country performers currently singing to the college folk "revival," Son House is "pure Delta," which means he helped invent and develop some of the most haunting, driven, bitter and psychologically-intense music in Western culture. From Charlie Patton, Son House and Willie Brown through Robert Johnson to Muddy Waters, and John Lee Hooker, the Delta Style is the "mainstream" in country blues, the central point of influence for every other kind of "blues" music from hillbilly to sophisticated jazz to rock-and-roll. It is also, according to Newsweek, "our finest native-born music."

The original Negro blues were conceived — somewhere, at some time — as an extension of group music into a form in which the individual singer could improvise freely around some introspective, personal theme. The metaphor "the blues" has come to be associated with many things, but it originally meant the total rejection and alienation from society felt by the rural Southern Negro, experienced in the harsh, practical terms of his daily existence. An intense environment was bound to produce intense individuals, and it was the illiterate artists in this outcast society, the singers and untrained country guitar-players, who captured this intensity in its most brilliant and hallucinatory form.

The creative blues artist had to have the poet's outlook — "the ability to state the truths of his time and place lyrically." The music of Son House is thus the music of poverty, exhausting labor, the fears of the Mississippi Negro under the lynch-law government of the 20's and 30's, as well as the loves and yearnings of an intellect sensitive to a Dostoyevskian predicament. On another level it is the music of a tragic vision trying to cope with the particulars of its destiny.

There are, of course, many factors which make this kind of cultural event inaccessible to a white audience. Country blues performers were often shy, introverted poet-guitar players, and regardless of individual personalities the country blues are most often intimate soliloquies, painful admissions in a private dialogue between the artist's emotional and artistic sensibilities. The best blues performances are always improvised and spontaneous, the singer choosing his theme and actually putting the song together on the spot, relying on his own inventive abilities and falling back if necessary on the thousands of stanzas and phrases which are "commonplaces" in blues lyrics. Then too, harsh voice, thick accent, and a primitive and unpolished musical style add to the problems of a formal presentation.

All too often there is a tendency to dismiss this Negro music as an inevitable, but nevertheless unpleasant reminder of what this country has done to its colored citizens. This kind of attitude is doubly gratuitous in that it ignores the artistic excellence of these Negro singers at the same time that it crosses them off in history as the unfortunate victims of a regrettable cultural lag. The truth of the matter is that the American South created the circumstances for a remarkable variety of man, of man driven to the physical and psychological borders of human endurance, and that from this remarkable, historical voyage this manner of man brought back a new version of human experience, and was forced to invent — out of illiteracy and ignorance — a new kind of human art, that was capable of telling about the terror of that trip.

GRINNELL COLLEGE, *SCARLET AND BLACK* 1965 COLUMN.

old-growth wood craftsmanship and twenties accoutrements. They really were off-the-rails and out-of-hand in formerly tidy, rain-scrubbed backwater Portland.

The Holy Modal Rounders came through Portland in 1971 and except for Peter Stampfel, they decided to stay. They were instantly a big attraction in their new town and though the lineup always did go through its changes the band was stabilized when Jeffrey Frederick's Clamtones moved to town from Vermont in 1975. Lightbourne dashed off this bit about local color on a large pharmaceutical post-it pad:

> "In those days, not quite the mid-70's, high times came with seemingly no effort, a serendipity of sex, drugs, and rock and roll spurred by hip capitalism and an explosion in entertainment options. When the magnum rock quintet (version of the) Holy Modal Rounders hit Portland in 1973, we all rolled over onto our opposite hip, blinked groggily, and whispered, 'No shit?' excitedly. PDX already had a rich local rock band culture going back before 'Louie Louie' to the 50's. Folk rock had seen a great new generation emerge, while Melodious Funk, (and the) PH Phactor Jug Band, had opened for the Dead in the early years in a nod to their own jug-nik origins. The Rounders conquered (like a Roman company)." (DL, circa 2000s)

The Seventies serendipity happened differently around the country. The common ingredients led usually to an egalitarian suburbanized arena rock FM youth culture which didn't last too long, but which pushed its boomer elders into a politicized adulthood of singer-songwriters or bluegrass. It was different in Portland: smarter, more sophisticated, almost as if the promise of that most vital thread of the folk & roots movement had somehow survived there alone to incubate into its own rock and roll culmination – one knowing but natural, deduced from music recorded in the twenties, re-discovered in the fifties, and here delivered in the seventies. The music took off locally on its own power. Nick Hill calls the Rounders of this period "the hottest touring dance band in the Northwest". The regularly packed the Rainbow and the Central in Seattle as well. But the drugs came with the musicians. Tom Wood left Portland when the high times spooked him, but he did not leave drug-smuggling. Warren stopped going to Mexico; David made one more trip, but then Wood, alone, was killed outside Acapulco in fall 1977. The business of maintaining the high had got big and violent.

Music

*

I was part of a punk recalibration which in its early years was often puritanical in its determination not to be drunk or stoned or wired like the rockers, the hippies, or the disco crowd. And as the punks, unbeknownst to them at first, were going to have to reinvent their own radio and record industries it was just as well to be sober. And further, given that punk would be music with "whiter," more forced rhythm, pot's vaunted musicological aid was initially dispensable.

What is striking to me about this Portland scene was how dance-oriented their bluesy psychedelic rock and roll was, even when acoustic. In the sixties I was too young to do anything but listen to the radio, and later too disaffected to go to high school dances in the early seventies, and by then hard rock and punk rock weren't for dancing, thanks largely to the influence of the British Invasion. The laid-back singer-songwriter bunk made sure that one of punk's initial demands would be that you at least stand up in the presence of live music. But David always talked about dancing, its presence or its absence, and how in his ideal music, a band performance was responsive in the live moment to the best dancers on the floor. This certainty of David's and Jeffrey Frederick's especially, brought women into the Portland audience, whereas they were drifting away from commercial rock audiences elsewhere for disco.

DL, PORTLAND, CIRCA 1980.

Colorado writer Elliott Johnston interviewed Lightbourne in 2008 and asked him about his role in the mid-seventies Holy Modal Rounders:

> "All I did was occasionally get onstage and sing the Stampfel parts when Weber would do a song and it desperately called for a higher voice. Then they'd just tell me to play lead electric guitar. The real relationship was, everybody in Portland could rent a Victorian mansion for $125 a month... The one I rented, I lived with Marcus and Weber. So in other words there were like seven

people dividing $125 a month rent... But what Weber finally told me to do was, 'Why don't you start your own band?' And I think he was tired of me getting onstage with him. 'Why don't you start your own fucking band?' So I did." (DL, Oct. 12, 2008)

I imagine The Metropolitan Jug Band would have come together anyway, despite the impression David leaves. In fact, unlike his friends, he managed to get out of a scrape with time-served in early 1978 so I'm guessing that forming The Stumptown Slickers, which evolved into the MJB, as well as his *KBOO* radio program which also began that year were part of his attempt to move himself past the harder, heavier drugging that had begun four years earlier. He was back in jail in fall 1979 while I was staying at his apt to save money for a November trip to London to meet the Rough Trade folks (we were moving Systematic down to Berkeley to help them set up in America). Christine, another Company turista was also in the place. David wrote from jail, "In this situation depression is too dangerous to cultivate, and discipline works quite well. Little things mean a lot: I'm doing exercises, taking showers, brushing after every meal – it's literally amazing!" It took the slammer to get Dave to brush his teeth. He also writes that his bandmates were a blessing and thanks me for doing his Fifties show for him. I remember *KBOO*'s blues host Tom Wendt being down there in case Dave hadn't made any arrangements. Tom was another music-first Portland fixture; Dave told me Tom sold his blood so he could buy blues records. Those were the days...

But as regards the Metropolitan Jug Band, you don't get a Fritz Richmond joining your band unless it's his best option. Fritz was a star in the early 1960s Boston folk scene with Jim Kweskin & The Jug Band and a noted recording engineer as well as a friend of John Sebastian – he named The Lovin' Spoonful. In the 1990s and thereafter Fritz played in Sebastian's The J Band, and also in ex-Kweskin band-mate Geoff Muldaur's Jug Band (as well as a last Portland outfit called Barbecue Orchestra). Fritz was the foremost jug and washtub bass player of the revival years. He'd been on the Vanguard and Reprise labels, and Fritz had engineered albums for Elektra's Paul Rothchild and others in Los Angeles (The Doors, Jackson Browne, Bonnie Raitt, Lonnie Mack, The Everly Brothers...). Tom Fitting describes the beginnings of the MJB as he and Kevin Robinson playing guitars together and Kevin bringing in Hugh Frederick on harp and Dan Lissy joining quickly, singing and blowing jug. "Hugh or Lissy introduced David Lightbourne to the trio in late 1978, and the foursome started playing as The Stumptown Slickers. It was clear that David was a powerful presence in the musical direction...."

Dan Lissy told the *Blues Notes* paper in 2004 that The Stumptown Slickers included Billy Hults as well and lasted a year with a regular gig at The Long Goodbye and opening slots for John Mayall and John Lee Hooker. Lissy left and David sang and they played as a trio for a bit in early 1979 as The New Stop & Listen Boys. Hugh brought in David Dearborn on washboard and they became The Metropolitan Jug Band by spring, playing Fridays at the Leaky Roof Tavern. Tom Fitting writes:

> "From my tapes, it looks like Fritz Richmond approached the band on 7/13/79 and sat in then for the first time, and I recall he was there every time we played thereafter... [W]hen Fritz asked if he could sit in... Hugh was coy but let Fritz come on stage, although he told me later that he recognized Fritz... and was fully aware of Fritz's pedigree." (TF, July 15, 2010)

The MJB represented David's musical vision, but that's not to say he lead the band otherwise. The Kweskin band often tilted away from blues and jug band styles toward vaudeville-style jazz and kitsch. There was zero kitsch in David's bands. He knew the best songs, the best players, the best playing so he never shrank from hating or just ignoring lesser stuff. And he knew that rock and roll was acoustic music first, as it was as late as Elvis on Sun. And he further knew that if rock and roll was radical it was also of a tradition. It was not progressive, but rather regressive. Lightbourne wrote recently: "We regress to do battle, we regress to make love, we regress to dream."

But this did not get the band recorded. Tom writes, "Fritz was very clear about recording. He insisted on professional recording using the record label's support, nothing less, and we did not have a label. We had several different discussions about it, and he would not budge." Dave never regretted that to my knowledge – there's loads of tapes and he could always pull out his guitar and go to work on anything he wanted to hear – but once I thought about it after he joined me in Chicago in 1995 it annoyed me. I wasn't having a good enough time at SST once we were solvent to have thought of recording the MJB for SST. I should've done it regardless. Fritz didn't realize that the record business was ending even then as the easy money and access he'd known evaporated. And maybe, with what he enjoyed about Portland life, he was lulled out of awareness that he was no longer in the record industry loop. What I think he feared happening was the band recording itself with local resources and having some substandard product marketed on his reputation. Big mistake.

Life Against Dementia

*

One of the great things about the early rock and roll era was that musicians were all coming from an organic folk culture that, though it took advantage of the electronic media, was not yet altered by that media. Musicians could sit in with players they did not know and find their way to sync up. So lineups were more fluid. Still it could take an hour to sync up; David often mentioned seeing Howlin' Wolf in Chicago and being surprised at the shambling versions they were putting out until about forty minute in. David often talked about the rhythmic sense of his generation of players versus some player who might be deep into the same blues canon but being younger couldn't quite settle into the same wavelength; he even marveled that he and Steve Weber didn't really have it together. When I saw the Metropolitan Jug Band at the Leaky Roof in 1979 Billy Hults was subbing for Dearborn. Billy played with everyone sooner or later in the Portland scene. His bands (The Fly By Night Jass Band, and Billy Foodstamp & the Welfare Ranch Rodeo) had more fluid lineups than most but he got good results. There is a live clip of Fly By Night doing The Memphis Jug Band's "She Done Sold It Out" which is usually findable at *youtube*; it's the single best video representation of the Portland scene that I'm aware of. The clip features:

MJB BUSINESS CARD; ART: ROBERT ARMSTRONG.

> John Ward - vocals, harp
> Billy Hults - washboard
> Kenneth Turtle Vandemar - guitar, kazoo
> Stu Dodge - fiddle
> John Dominegoni - bass
> Robin Remaily - fiddle
> Richard Tyler - piano
> Peter Langston – mandolin

Nick Hill guesses it's an outtake from sessions that yielded a six song EP around 1974, and he thinks he recognizes Mike Lastra and David Lightbourne on the floor towards the end; I can't tell. Peter Langston who had been in Portland Zoo, writes, "I believe that was filmed at Rex Recording where we had just finished mixing some recordings of our bluegrass band, Puddle City. As we were leaving we ran into our Fly By Nite Jass Band friends rehearsing and they invited me to join in." (PL, July 14, 2010)

Remaily and Tyler were then in The Holy Modal Rounders, though when the now Portland-based Rounders-Clamtones toured to the east coast to record the "Have Moicy!" album with Peter Stampfel and Michael Hurley, Weber dropped off the tour long enough to miss the recording session. Lightbourne thought "Have Moicy!", credited to Michael Hurley/The Unholy Modal Rounders/Jeffrey Frederick & The Clamtones, was the masterpiece of their scene, though it was recorded on the east coast and Stampfel rather than Weber held down the Rounders franchise. It was recorded in two days in July 1975, mixed in three. Hurley told *PopWatch*, "You probably just don't have the software to know how good I feel about the 'Have Moicy!' release. So many people have told me that they love it, it changed their life, it turned them on to old-time asskickin' hillbilly, it lead them to a superior love life, it brought them much wealth and still remains a favorite after 20 years or 10. Everytime I listen to it, it sounds more together; it sounds like a bunch of loonies too."

Thereafter, some of Hurley's mob, David Reisch and Gary Sisco, threw in with the Portland crew and Michael himself was pulled inevitably to Oregon. One could find different combinations of all these players in any of a number of bands. Lightbourne and Richmond also played 1984 gigs as The Justin Other Jug Band with Mark Goldfarb on guitar and vocals, and Randy Griffin on harp. And Earth Tavern fixture and music-writer Dan Lissy who'd been in The Stumptown Slickers continued to play with David and others.

Another one-page essay I found in David's effects, tells of yet one more wayward folk musician on the scene in 1973 playing his own depressive low-key ballads:

> "At the time we all lived, four or five of us, in a little one-bedroom house down by the freeway at the very edge of the black and hippie enclave in Portland called Dogpatch. Colleen, Weber's girlfriend at the time, came calling at ten o'clock one morning, way too early, and I woke up in my loft in the utility room cursing the daylight. Somebody in the front room had taken down the little 1868 Martin parlor guitar, D-8 or something, with a great-looking dark spruce top, and the music sounded like jazzed folk, or folk swing or folk soul.

> By the time I got up and down and out this geeky little guy with a Jimmy Durante hat and Ray Charles sunglasses had played a real sweet set and Colleen introduced me to Tansy Ragwort. (We got to the west coast in the late sixties, and one of the first topics they got your attention with in the regional media had to do with cattle dying all over eastern Oregon from eating Tansy Ragwort. At the time it sounded like this was the deep down hard-core uniquely Oregonesque local exotic lore.)
>
> The real Tansy Ragwort wrote really pretty love songs with simple folkish tunes using jazz-substitution chords on acoustic guitar with classic 1930s changes. He'd been opening for the Holy Modal Rounders that week in Seattle at several venues and grabbed the ride south as a great chance to check Portland, Modal Rounder World Headquarters." (DL)

Tansy's actual name was Steven Bernstein, as he was known later for his poetry; he died by his own hand in 1991.

*

There've been revolutions in American music all along of course, but in Portland this backwater mix by postwar pop culture radicals seemed to start with fifties rock and roll and then retreat into the past. Often acoustic or half-acoustic, it was metaphysically, if not always musically, a blues-style revolution. It was not dreamy and righteous as in the former folk-style, or self-absorbed and mercenary as in the singer-songwriter mode then current. As Jane writes above about her time with David in Cambridge, "From the different sixties' themes – political, music, black, drugs – we were black and drugs."

David printed out a post to the "Have Moicy group" by Nick, maybe the only member who insists on the importance of the west coast Rounders against the general indifference. In his post Nick writes about a Portland classmate, also a musician, just then deceased:

> "I am reminded of a day I spent at Weber's house in Portland when he was living with Colleen on SW 1st St. I was all of 15 at the time, and Craig would have been about 18. I had just stopped by to visit and was surprised to see Craig Mayther there, tripping out of his mind. Obviously he had taken heroic doses of acid, and maybe something more ferocious. He was large, and out of control, foaming at the mouth. Doctor Steven Weber was

in. Attending to this LSD overdose with all the bedside manner of a saint. Administering B-12, and generous doses of gentle old guitar ballads to cool the huge man's disturbed sense of being." (NH, June 6, 2005)

David may have performed similar ministrations but I remember most his story of his first heroin customer who received rather more cursory treatment when David found him turning blue on the floor of his bathroom. He managed to save the guy's life and send him on his way, but that was how he learned that you never let a customer use your bathroom on the way out.

I found this short note, which by the looks of it was written by David in the last five years or so:

> "I'm inclined to a totally apologetic attitude about the Great Portland Oregon Heroin Plague, roughly 1974-1994. Fucked up the very best and brightest, the talented and everyone else. Weber played his central flashpoint position to get the ball rolling. Ricardo, Dolores, Fat Freddy, Shade Tree, at one point Rube & Pam the Gorgeous. The listed would fill a damn data-base, and Oregon bureaucrats probably have a good one, hard to access. Start at the easy end with the clockwork thud of obituaries, Here an O.D., there an O.D., everywhere a-, not to mention a few suicides.
>
> One of my road buddies from Iowa, running to dodge the draft as well as to escape an FBI dragnet for a failed Florida Panama Red load, set up shop with a mixture tested at 80% opiates coming down from Vancouver. He cleared a hundred grand a month for a spell. We played our part, and probably a dozen younger kids did too much. Not a good way to begin, self-indulgent, spoiled and bored. Things were way better when Steve just hit me from his cotton for driving him to cop. I could take it or leave it.
>
> I personally don't care for the shit. I quickly learned how a whole other kind of normal fellow, the ambulatory depressed, could and would soon commit any and every imaginable desperate act to assure the sustenance of life itself. I'm sure it beats all the anti-depressants by a mile, with the only downside lifelong constipation. Not at all like these pills that make you go postal. But I only liked it because I needed it. Getting it often proved an unbelievable adventure, and man did it feel wonderful suddenly

getting well. I way prefer pot.

    The Greeks said everything in moderation and about the best time I ever had took place the afternoon Jeffrey and I went over to Danielle's to do some good white. We had two guitars. That's really all I remember. As soon as we realized how amazingly well we clicked we never looked back. The one day in my life I could never begrudge a tip of the top hat to King Dope, shit, smack, dog, do, H, beige, boy, etc." (DL, circa 2000s)

    I got to Portland from Hollywood in fall 1977 and got to know Dave because we both worked at the Cinema 21. I was the janitor and would clean the theater after the last show cleared out around midnight. Sometimes he'd hang around the theater but usually I'd do the job alone with a small radio on which filled the big empty theater space nicely. (One night I was mesmerized by a piece of contemporary classical music and got a pencil to write down what the announcer said; it was the 1978 debut recording Górecki's Symphony No. 3 and I never found a copy until a lesser British version came out twenty years later and went platinum.) I might get done about 3am and I'd check to see if Dave's apartment light was on. It usually was and we'd talk in his place, or go to the QP diner a few blocks away. I didn't know anything about drugs I didn't hear from him. In his place he'd be dabbing the tracks on his arms with some skin restorative while we talked. He was off heroin then and had never liked cocaine, LSD, or alcohol. I met Weber once at Dave's apartment but had no idea who he was. I left Portland when we moved Systematic Record Distribution to Berkeley at the end of 1979 and soon enough it was clear by his letters that he was back on it, plus he was starting to mention some of the Portland punks I'd known who were now crossing paths with the older scene.

*

I found a cassette in David's collection that records a quiet late-night fifty minutes or so of Steve Weber in 1977 moving through one tune after another, singing and playing guitar for Dan Lissy, Pamela Boswell Marcus, and Christine Van Kamen. It begins with David reading discographical information about Frank Stokes and adding to that what he knows about how the metal masters were found near Grafton, Wisconsin nailed to chicken coops as roofing shingles. Then David is either unusually quiet or has left. Lissy is still recording and to prompt a version of "Cocaine Blues" out of Steve, he asks him what he knows about cocaine. Steve answers, "Well you take some cocaine you feel like a new man, and next thing you know the new man wants some too." Steve plays it and another dozen songs, four of which he reprised the next year in New York with Peter Stampfel as part of the "Going Nowhere Fast" album. Weber sounds far less comfortable in the New York recordings and so the tunes are as a consequence not as delicate and beautiful, or in the case of "Junker's Blues", not as perverse as the Portland home recordings. And yet the album's liner-notes by John Swenson are at pains to dismiss rumored Portland recordings of Peter and Steve and cheer on the abuse his co-producer lays on Steve, "working at a breakneck pace by haranguing him constantly during breaks until Weber retreated behind the microphone for solace." New York for ya.

The women of the Portland scene shopped resale, wearing what twenties dresses could bear up under the crush in these bars and the wear-and-tear of the strange new sexual customs still then unfolding. The protest flyer nearby concerns Jeffrey Frederick's apparently routine exclusive use of the women's johns at bars. The flyer's protest features already routine feminist attitudes with descriptions of behavior somewhat more in the true spirit of the times. Here's David again, writing decades later about this flyer and that night. (A Warning: David wrote this for himself with perhaps no editor or reader in mind...)

> "The flyer makes the big dustup unnecessarily complicated and confusing. It vanished overnight so this might be the only surviving copy. No one took it seriously just like no one took the cat fight seriously from the get go. Needless to say, anywhere Fat Freddy had a gig, he only pissed in the women's shitter. Supposedly men's cans turned his stomach. In truth, many women swear it's the opposite – Hey, gals, come on in!
>
> Either Jeffrey walked in on Hannah or she walked in on him. Probably told him to get the fuck out of there. But then she made the fatal, suicidal mistake of flinging his hat into a toilet bowl.
>
> The poor dumb cunt had no possible way of knowing that a bindle of heroin lay tucked inside the hat's sweatband. She thought in all honesty she was just being a righteous bitch. No damn harm, No damn foul. Fuck the hat you fat fucking fuck! Dear sweet Jesus.
>
> A cross-cultural misunderstanding of tectonic proportions: Put a twenty dollar match-head of Persian beige inside a hundred dollar hat. The hat would maybe be the real deal in price for vanity stage drag. But Jeffrey would happily pawn a pair of Stetsons, even trade 'em, for one good hit.
>
> How in holy hell could poor Hannah possibly comprehend this alien universe she had stumbled into – where the men all shit in

the women's, which sees no room, no rest." (DL, circa 2000s)

I should explain here several of David's unique circumlocutionary habits. He often paired the euphemism "freakin'" with the very word it was meant to take the edge off of, namely the F-word; hence, a likely sentence: "If he wants to go out of business I'd be glad to burn the freakin' fuckin' place to the ground for him." Another strange tic of his involved how someone, anyone, might edit themselves in conversation by ending a sentence with "blah, blah, blah..."; but Dave was moving much to quickly to make do with just three "blahs" so he'd use freakin' fuckin' five of 'em! Dave was a great editor and proof reader, but I'd say his verbal editing needed editing.

David's girlfriends were often buyers and sellers of vintage threads re-released on post-Carnaby street, post-earth-mother fashion via former timber-baron estate-sales and auctions so these mogul's dissolute scions could buy heroin from David. He was in the used records stores and his girlfriend was in the resale clothing shops. It was a division of postwar post-labor, an archeology of one postwar golden age so as to prolong the last bit of a second postwar golden age. One thing that bears mentioning is that the earliest of our postwar bohemia spun from homosexual men born between the wars. Bohemia after the Beats was generally hetero but at first shaped by the pre-birth-control Pill years when women, pairing up, children and/or marriage were the threat to their plans to avoid the straight work-a-day world. So those born during WWII were often misogynists going into the sixties sexual revolution, and they could be lets say a handful during it. Their girlfriends were of necessity quite their match.

*

In Boston and Chicago and elsewhere acoustic/delta/Piedmont/blues/etc. was already being presented as if behind glass in a museum for the progressive delectation of that element of the sixties generation which wished to retire into a lifestyle. But in Portland Oregon, these musician-criminals couldn't help but make that music live again as twenties-style rock and roll in something like the manner of the great jug bands of Memphis. I mostly missed it as I wasn't looking for that. Lightbourne's fifties' rock and roll knowledge seemed more relevant to me and the punk rock I was beginning to deal in. Thank God I did go and see his band a couple times, once at the Leaky Roof and once at a practice at either Hugh Frederick's or David Dearborn's house.

The hip tavern culture of Portland peaked in the eighties, probably with the election of bar-owner Bud Clark as mayor in 1984. He claimed his bar crowded "butt-to-belly", the Goose Hollow Inn, served 200 kegs of beer a month. The movie *Drugstore Cowboy* (1989) may be the nadir; it is based on events committed by friends of these musicians only subtracting all of their style and wit and taste. Lightbourne's friends were co-stars in the actual nonfiction newspaper coverage; I found a set of clippings in his things of the arrests and the sentencings, and also a newspaper photo of a pharmacist with a framed photo of Matt Damon on the wall behind him. Dave would tell some insane Portland-era story and I'd again remind him that we needed to re-write that truth-never-told and make Danielle in that small house in the shade of the sheer back wall of Fred Meyer's the star of the show. Her front room was a Marx Brothers' state-room scene waiting to happen with all the human traffic, the antique bric-a-brac and David's complete run of *Rolling Stones* lining the walls floor-to-ceiling. The pitch would've been: Maisie in the crack-den, call it Superheroine.

In one of David's many semi-filled journals-diaries-notebooks there is this, immediately following a short note dated Feb. 16, 1983 on basketball dynasties:

> "It was all quite predictably freaky. I burst into Warren's without knocking last Sunday, the 7th, and got three sawed-off shotguns pointed at me. Narcs as thugs; at first I thought 'bikers' before things slowed enough to notice the down vests and hiking shoes. They almost blew my ass out of the universe nose-first, perhaps to a parallel realm where mu-mesons reverse/implode in time. After holding me face down on the floor and kicking me a lot I talked my head off and they found a hundred dollar paper in a wallet next to where I'd been on the floor, pocketed the heroin, wallet and all, and said why don't you split. So I did...." (DL, circa 1983)

David was then the star of the top tavern attraction in town, playing four nights a week.

It couldn't last. They each on their own schedule stopped their drinking or drugging, or they died. Some spent time in jail, Dave among them. He almost never drank anything other than Coca Cola but he gave up heroin a second time in the mid-eighties, though he continued to recommend it for depression; he considered all of Big Pharma's search for the perfect anti-depressant utterly redundant and hypocritical. Until I read Sisco's blog I didn't appreciate what an a-hole I was drinking a beer in front of Michael Hurley, who does a manful job pretending to love his cup of tea while his Boone & Jocko cartoons tell you what's really on his mind.

David had a number of friends who disappeared late in life into relationships with women that seemed combination rehab-matrimonies. He referred to these lost souls in the past tense, and described them as having married dominatrices. Dave's girlfriends over the years were all good-looking, hip and smart but his own troubled childhood meant that he was pitched mightily against fatherhood and so these women left him to pair off with more user-friendly men, though many stayed in touch with him and counted on him for occasional blasts of information from out beyond their new normal.

*

Dave left Portland gradually, spending the late eighties in Phoenix with his mother and stepfather, actually taking law classes to assure her that he'd be able to provide for himself. He then went on the road as the audio-video tech for his brother Michael who was conducting sales seminars in the Rentrak video rental system. During these tours Dave hit every used record store in the country and re-connected with everyone he ever knew and respected as he went, and he would tell you all kinds of stuff, like what he found when he went looking for the Augusta house where Blind Willie McTell was born.

David's brother Michael told me two very interesting things while here to move his brother's effects, both about Michael and Priscilla's father Kirk Lightbourne – David's step-father (his father, Kermit Loe, was killed in WWII when David was two). Kirk, who'd played trumpet in big bands until he got his front teeth knocked out in a drunken brawl while on tour. (Paul Whiteman Violence Must Stop!) Just before David went off to college in Iowa he had a big argument with Kirk who perhaps resented paying for it. Michael who was thirteen didn't understand the argument except that it was scaring him because David was getting the better of his father until, as Michael tells it, Kirk picked David up and set him in the trash saying, "You are garbage." David never went back home after that. In retirement in Phoenix, Kirk was an in-demand piano-tuner and he got to know Alice Cooper, Glen Campbell and other notable musicians in the area. Michael believes that his father began to soften on David as he recognized that what I'll call the rockstar traits of Alice and Glen were the same things he'd been seeing in David since he barged in on young David's idyll. But as a former big-band musician he had no respect for folk music per se, whether it was stepson David's or his own son Michael's, who on the face of it was quite successful himself in the pop end of early sixties folk music. As Michael puts it, his father though quite rowdy in his big band days, played ballrooms in tuxedos and "never saw the musical merit of this genre of music."

*

In January 2007 Dave was at Jane's in New York and The Holy Modal Rounders and Michael Hurley were in Portland doing gigs around the release of a documentary film called *Bound to Lose*. The film's makers knew it was important to present in Portland, though the film does not cover the band's Portland years. Dave wrote an email on the details of his impending return to Wyoming, and filled me in on what he heard about how things went back in his own stomping grounds:

> "They took some good photos at the PDX bash, one in particular of Hurley & Reisch. Hurley looks like he's on a roll. Reisch had the sound-guy do digital 32 tracks off the board but noted that, often, one side of the stage had no idea what the other side was playing. His admonition: 'Tapes don't lie'. Four fiddles, three washboards, two saxophones.... equals Tennessee Klezmer. Still being billed as Weber's one last chance to resurrect, apotheosize, or take petulance to the mountaintop. Nobody even remembers that he was virtually run out of town as corpses fell on every side. Nor do any of these morons remember Martin & Lewis, Laurel & Hardy.... or even Dan & Connie. Stampfel, meanwhile, has made a bigtime outback comeback." (DL, Jan. 10, 2007)

David could be impatient with writers or filmmakers when they didn't seem to know what they were talking about. He smiled when he told me the filmmakers had said they hoped to portray "the love between Peter and Steve." Dave didn't exactly mean to imply they hated each other, but he meant that the self-esteem generation might never figure out that once the focus had been on music first, and then drugs, girls, and life in America, and only after that maybe camaraderie, perhaps touched with something resembling love. The literature on bands like The Minutemen or Dinosaur Jr hinge on the ability of Music itself to bring together the nerds with the jocks – nerds do not make good drummers and only genius-grade music can lure some happening high school dude to associate with his weirdest classmates – it may be touching, but it isn't love. How much more likely necessary was it in 1963 that music brought the two pathfinders of The Holy Modal Rounders together? (Peter began hearing horror-stories about Steve from Antonia as early as 1962; Steve was in Bucks County down the street from Hurley.)

To be fair Dave himself should have written these books and films on the blues, or Dylan, or The Rounders, or Mike Seeger, Mike Bloomfield, Frank Lloyd Wright, Marshall McLuhan, Elvis Presley.... It's hardly their authors' fault he didn't. What is their fault is that they somehow didn't locate him during their inadequate research phase. Dave was nothing if not the world's premiere expert talking head. When Weber heard of David's death I'm told he said, "There's a lot of people who talk a lot, but David always had something to say." Only a rank amateur filmmaker by the name of Elwood Snock ever knew enough to point a camera at videocamera at David. We look forward to seeing some of that footage at the White Eagle on August 7.

*

There aren't too many gaps in my book *Rock and the Pop Narcotic* of a size sufficient to embarrass me but my missing that Oregon scene is surely the principle one. And I was so close to it! Dave might have recorded for Delmark in the mid-sixties when he worked at Bob Koester's Jazz Record Mart; he might have recorded for Adelphi in 1970; nothing panned out until we got The Stop & Listen Boys album together in 2000 for a label I put together with Bill Stevenson of The Descendents and Black Flag – bands that were among the reasons I left Portland and Berkeley for Los Angeles. Fortunately there is a ton of additional recordings of David and his bands from both the Wyoming era and the Portland era, and perhaps we'll find material from the sixties as well in this crate of ancient reel-to-reel tapes he'd been toting around for years. We'll know soon.

*

I had a vague idea that aside from what Coca-Cola did to his teeth, that drinking it all day long might presage some kind of nightmare diabetic finger-failure that you hear about in the pages of blues history. But Dave got stronger on the guitar in his sixties. Laramie of all places offered him both weekly solo venues (at Provisional Café, Cowboy Coffee, The Fireside, Muddy Waters Coffeehouse, The Buckhorn Bar) and places to play with his band The Stop & Listen Boys (The Old Centennial Café-Beartree

Tavern, The Trading Post, *KUWR*, *KRFC*, and many one-offs). We talked through each Upland Breakdown since 2000, trying to bring out the best players he and I had known around a loose idea of acoustic blues. He was thrilled and even a touch nervous when he could bring out to our centrally-located middle-of-nowhere another of his old music compatriots: Michael Hurley, Gary Sisco, Al Rivers, Jane Cohen-Pellouchoud.... Every few years I'd ask him if he thought there'd be any chance of bringing out Peter Stampfel & Steve Weber, or at least Weber. He was sure it couldn't be done and I figured he knew. But that would've been something. Something for Wyoming to fear.

    David's theory on health issues was to avoid doctors and hospitals because they'd insure that you'd have a lengthy twilight of failing abilities and mobility. He didn't want that and didn't let on when he was in pain, mostly because a childhood bout with rheumatic fever meant that he had often had pain; he apparently learned to just ignore it. I found his stray reference to insomnia due to "phantom chest pains" in a diary entry on a run to Mexico, and that was 1972. So I suspect he didn't have any expectation that death was approaching. He was on the phone until about 11pm Mountain time to his old Portland pal Kevin Robinson the night of Thursday April 29th talking about a song lyric he was working on, and the coroner had his death come between 10pm and midnight. I found him at 9:30 the next morning sitting on the floor wrapped in his blanket, as if during the heart attack he tried to get up off the sofa he slept on. But this time it was more than pain.

(originally posted at The New Vulgate, *No. 56)*

Rock Against Concrete

Though I listen to the radio and play some old favorites, I don't follow music now. But I have a deeper sense of what it was that happened across the 20th century as American folk musics started getting transmitted to other folks through media. This piece is something I posted at The New Vulgate in March, 2011. It doesn't really resolve itself, but then what does other than "Supernaut" by Black Sabbath.

When fifties greasers stuck with their rockabilly thru the sixties, and sixties mods stuck with their music into the seventies it wasn't as reactionary and destructive as it was when the hippie-boomers of the late sixties/early seventies dropped out and took over. This was because the music business was suddenly an album-based economy and as such, much bigger business and more pretentious. The 78 rpm and 45 rpm singles economy worked efficiently in terms of culture and economics for decades; more chances were taken on more talent more quickly at less cost. Things started to slow down when albums were no longer low budget collections of a couple hits and a bunch of filler and covers designed to favor publishing companies, but instead became ersatz novels, major statements from the artist-gurus themselves alone. Recording an album at a single shot and releasing it first, followed by a number of singles released on a schedule from the album was beyond the capabilities of most bands. This left the door open to a kind of conceptual *musique concrète* hi-fi demonstration record like "Dark Side of the Moon", and even lead a traditionally skilled band of singer-songwriters like the Eagles into a poisonous pretension that really offered far less song-for-song than their average Nashville contemporaries at a fraction of the costs.

David Bowie is best seen as a late British Invasion success in America who just squeezed by on style in the last years of arena rock-AOR. The albums themselves are virtually unlistenable, both the "rock" albums which do rotate in and out of some classic rock playlists, and the "art" albums which do not. Each was the embalming of a style once full of life – the Stooges wise-guy lumpen rock, and the German psychedelic romanticism of Neu! In his review of a new Bowie bio called Starman Nick Crowe writes that author Paul Trynka notes Bowie's early musical failures in the mid-sixties but calls them "crucial," true-believer that he is. Somehow the earliest Brit rockers managed to get into a conversation with American forms, and the later generation used Bowie to avoid that. Even all those punk bands triggered by the Heartbreakers, the Ramones or the Runaways never consulted them again. Trynka, breathlessly I'm sure recounts Bowie's down time with real Art. Crowe writes:

> "Struggling in anonymity made him absorb the concepts being explored on the fringes of the art world. He also acquired a habit of interacting with cultural figures – often on a whim – which he never lost. In 1967 Bowie met avant-garde mime artist Lindsay Kemp and took him on as mentor, touring and performing with his decadent troupe. With Kemp he discovered a theatre of identity, which would prove indispensable to his later approach; it is this relationship between Bowie's experience and his music that drives Trynka's narrative." (*Starman*)

No doubt.

Meanwhile, the new album era near-vanquished the singles world tied to hit radio as it was. It lost the center of its adult audience, leaving it with young teens and pop music got sweet and unheavy and oblivious to the world outside. Further meanwhile, at that very moment the Ramones were recapitulating the classic singles idea, only fully contemporary, but couldn't get airplay on AM or FM. It's easy to forget that for their first two or three albums punk didn't mean anything in the way of a sartorial challenge beyond a de-greased urban juvenile delinquent look updated with long hair! The stripped-down songs and presentation, though, ran full up against reigning liberal pretension which was still on a roll. The Ramones were such fertile songwriters that they tried all kinds of things with production and movie tie-ins over those months and none of it worked. Lee Abrams, Jan Wenner and the other young hip powers-that-were took the Ramones personally in a way that the old singles-era world simply could not have. Just in simple provincial New York City terms they were rejected. As Legs McNeil told *Juice* magazine, "I mean, c'mon. The Ramones never played Madison Square Garden. The Ramones were never invited to play on 'Saturday Night Live'. To me, that's a slap in the face." It may prove that they belonged on both bands of radio in 1977 that they are today on radio and over the P.A. systems at MLB, NHL, NBA, and NFL games, but it's like a little Hendrix on the classic rock FM or AM oldies stations, it doesn't really boost the musical IQ of the audience. It's too late for that.

What got programmed in the late seventies had an increasingly post-sixties British feel: Just the George Martin aspect of the Beatles records but none of the music's rock and roll ambition; plus middle-period Pink Floyd and David Bowie strategies. Soon what the Brits call "post-punk" displayed Bowie-damage rather than Ramones influence and Pink Floyd wash with David Gilmour's expressiveness eliminated. Johnny Rotten had famously appeared at his Sex Pistols jukebox audition wearing a personalized Pink Floyd T-shirt with the painted-on words "I hate" added above the band's name. The only Sex Pistols influence that survived in the U.K. was their manager's: that rock and roll was dead, and sell-out conveniently the new measure of your contempt for music and capitalism.

This was realized audibly as new sounds emphasized texture rather than playing. For the listener it's simpler, to the point of boredom, to respond to texture, say those simple two or three note patterns with heavy sustain etc, on a U2 record – turning the guitar into a processed wash that cannot be musically nimble – than it is to respond to musical expressiveness.

My brother recently picked up a copy of Jimi Hendrix's "War Heroes" album and let me burn it. I had played his LP copy a lot when we were in high school in the early seventies and Mark had a band named after the album's best track, "Midnight." Listening to the tune now reminds me of a lot of what we came to expect in that great period of rock and roll. "Midnight" is the instrumental Experience trio recording for themselves as they often did on tour (the record was posthumously released in 1973). Hendrix is really at a peak in this 1969 instrumental track where he seems able to command the subtlest inflections musically on the guitar itself but also technologically by playing his amplification and foot pedals at that same unimaginably high level – the second round of the solo towards the end contains my favorite bar he ever played.

I remember in the early seventies wanting to hear sound detach itself from the limits of its instrumentation, and this is that to the max. (It must be said that U2 is a uniquely shameless proposition, their film doc explaining the blues to America [Hey Paddy, steal some blues, *please!*], suing Negativland but then stealing their schtick like the human Xerox machine they are and calling it ZooTV, and The Edge[!] in that doc trio-ed with Jimmy Page and Jack White?! Has to be a comedy-doc, right? Bono couldn't just go home and save Ireland, could he, ya think?)

Power and pretense to defend, the new powers chose to risk boredom rather than excitement and the best post-Ramones bands expired at even smaller sales levels, though they often found that the single format could be used on a completely underground level, almost as if selling off a demo run in collector shops. Those raw singles were where the excitement was risked as a matter of course. Boredom was risked in the technological experiments increasingly conducted by engineers and designers in the real record business. Synthetic percussion, even in a hard rock sound, invites the listener's lower brain to zone-out rather than engage. And that's what folks were encouraged to prefer within ten years of Jimi's death.

*

But let's pull back before I start repeating myself. It is not well understood that American popular culture was highly refined back when our schools still did their job. Our pop culture was a high culture and the great pretenders here and abroad came to hate that. The American forms were vulnerable to our own elite culture which was European derived and oriented, but less than classical in its achievement. That American elite, was angry that the American crud all around them here had saved their heroes there. And in England and on the continent including the U.S.S.R., elites got even angrier as Americans celebrated that victory in music and movies through the fifties, and they began to champion and make perverse work, art against art. American popular culture's success overseas eventually brought the arts low – not quite as low as the popular arts are overseas where the balances between high and low are reversed, but certainly lower by design. The *Economist* just reported:

> "The success of a film outside America is not purely a marketing matter. As foreign box-office sales have become more important, the people who manage international distribution have become more influential, weighing in on 'green-light' decisions about which films are made. The studios are careful to seed films with actors, locations and, occasionally, languages that are well-known in target countries. Sony cites the foreign success of 'The Green Hornet' (Taiwanese hero, Austrian-German villain) and 'Resident Evil: Afterlife' (Japanese location) as evidence of that strategy. Big noisy spectacle travels best. Jason Statham, the close-cropped star of many a mindlessly violent film, is a particular Russian favourite. Films based on well-known literature (including cartoon books) and myths may also fare well. Films that trade on contemporary American cultural references are about as popular abroad as an oil slick on a NASCAR track. (Note to our non-American readers: NASCAR is an American sport involving fast cars.)" (*Economist*)

Do you remember how good *The Last American Hero* was? Not important. But just about true.

The countercultures over there going back before the Surrealists had once used the American popular arts against their own high culture hierarchy but the Wars ended that pattern. That Brit love of fifties rock and roll, rhythm and blues, and country and western that was so productive from 1962 to 1974 was finally rejected by the glitter, goth and punk revolts against, actually, their own gray socialism. Had nothing to do with us really.

(*originally posted at* The New Vulgate, *No. 87*)

Arguing With the Fish – The Minutemen
This was written for the book, Spiels of a Minuteman, *put together by Mike Watt and a publisher in Montreal doing bilingual nice-looking small books. So it's my debut in the Francosphere.*

Rest in peace? The Minutemen?! They ate anxiety for breakfast and by lunch were farting peace of mind. Such rumble pie as would have split other bands/friends for life. There was so little peace around them that I suspect any rest they got was something more aggressive, like, say, oblivion. And it would take something more aggressive still to finally sunder them.

When I think of the Minutemen I think of a band that laid everything out on the table. Whether they were alone in their practice pad, or on a local stage before an audience of friends, or on tour before an audience of strangers, if something crossed one of their minds – especially something like George dropping a beat, D breaking a string, or Mike misfiring – said thought was said and underlined, heaved onto the table like stinkin' week-old flounder. Strangers might wonder at all the pointing, yelling and laughing going on amongst the three of them as they played. It seemed there was some other show going on inside of the one they could hear – the one the Minutemen called "the schtik."

Now this "schtik" happened to be issued from what certainly was one of the most intense bands that have ever musically combusted. With just guitar, bass, and drums – and further with D's trebly narrow sound, Mike's resoundingly physical counterpoint, and George's determination to play on 16ths and 32nds no matter the tempo – they chose to play a music that could be easily heard in its constituent parts (once you found your way into the physically demanding presentation) and so mistakes would be out on the table as well. Other bands' players might hide in the soft-focus wash of chording guitars and shadowing bass-lines, not the Minutemen.

Once strangers acclimated to "the schtik" they became friends who reveled in their unique anti-glamour. The Minutemen were funnier in performance the better you knew them. Only then might you know that Boon, Watt, and Hurley were critiquing each other's playing, or were ranking on each other's stage moves – Watt warning a leaping Boon against going

OPPOSITE: D. BOON, WHISKY, JUNE 1982; PHOTO: GLEN E. FRIEDMAN.

through another stage, Boon reminding a stumbling Watt of the time his knee went out and ruined the gig. I recall Mike trying to convince D. that when he did his Townshend jumps he wasn't actually elevating his body, only kicking back his feet for a split second. D. thought this was absurd, but in truth he really didn't want to think about what he looked like. In performance he was looking for some kind of exhausted high. D didn't dwell on how he looked and this made for one of the louder fashion statements of the punk era.

D. used to talk about how anyone could do it, but that just wasn't true. Most people are afraid of other people, of themselves, and what those other people might think of them. And this goes double (at least) for performers. Cool is considered so important that people often become cold pursuing it. Well the Minutemen ran hot. They brought their practice-pad manners on stage out of a compulsive need to be true – they so hated what fear and its exploitation by show business had done to rock music.

When they toured, usually just the three of them in a van, they'd be arguing about civil war history all through the South as the place names rolled by. The civil war was always their number one war with a bullet, but they'd tussle over the Big One, or even the War of 1812 if it happened to come up – it did. Like most members of the southbay bands that ended up on SST they had gone to arena gigs all through high school and at odd times they'd start taking about the time they saw Gentle Giant open for ZZ Top at the Long Beach Sports Arena, or Uriah Heep headline over Mahavishnu at the L.A. Forum or some other such crazy bill. They didn't talk about The Ex or Gang of Four; they did talk about Wire and the Pop Group but not as much as they talked about the Who and Creedence Clearwater Revival.

They were realists, constantly undercutting the threat of pretension with slang and scatological counterpoint. To recoup after the "Project: Mersh" 'stoop' Mike told me their next album might be called "No Mysteries." (It wasn't.) But when I mentioned this to the Meat Puppets they visibly recoiled. They were desert mystics; the Minutemen were harbor empiricists. They were sentimental in their realism too – they loved those stinking fish because they were from San Pedro. They had a blue collar turf-consciousness and code of brotherhood that on the east coast causes problems musically. But in California these three so enjoyed taking their Pedro stench north to Hollywood and east to America that the evangelism of their open-hearted faith meant you were included too. Because of the intensity of their relationship inside the band, they enjoyed mixing it up with friends about art and politics or anything else. But it took just a whiff of true schtik to discomfit them. In other words they were quite often yelling at their friends, whilst speaking reservedly to the suits – ripped and pinned though those suits might be.

They accommodated each other at the top of their lungs. They kept a running tally of each other's infractions but they graded on a curve. They paranoiacly tried to deduce who each other's song lyrics were written about and wrote misperceived responses to challenges never made and laughed as the fish piled high on the table and Pedro stench overpowered even *Rolling Stone* and *MTV* at the other end of the country. Their unpretentious approachability makes them the most unlikely of the legendary lost bands of the punk era. There's the revolution, D.

Minutemen were Reactionaries
This was written as liner notes for the 2010 release of the one recording extant of the Minutemen's first band, The Reactionaries.

For most of the music world – or rather the much smaller rock world – of the early 1980s, the Minutemen seemed to arrive fully formed, as if from some other planet. Questions must have immediately crossed minds: Where are these guys from? What drugs are they on? Are they carbon-based life forms? Those reactions were understandable, as it was the 45-song, double 33 rpm "Double Nickels On The Dime" (SST 028) that introduced the band to most folks outside of Los Angeles.

If I remember right, the initial sales jumped from the five thousand range for "Buzz Or Howl Under The Influence Of Heat" (SST 016), to fifteen thousand for "Double Nickels". (Of course all those releases sold far more after the day.) D. Boon, Mike Watt and George Hurley were always deflecting the effusiveness of fans in clubs, or in interviews – it was part of their charm. But think about it, the Minutemen were telling kids that they could pick up instruments and do the same! Nobody who saw them live believed that for a second.

I was at Systematic Record Distribution and got their first record, "Paranoid Time" (SST 002), from the label and ordered it for distribution to shops around the country. It was hard enough for me to discern how great they were from that and their early follow-up records and compilation tracks. To my ear, I don't think I really heard what they were capable of until they were playing the Anti-Club regularly in 1983-84. There was just so much music packed into their short, fast tunes. And at each gig a few older, simpler tunes were replaced by new, even more masterful tunes.

At their first San Francisco gig at the Mabuhay, Dirk Dirksen (who ran and MC'ed the club), strolled out on stage to introduce them and the first thing he saw was a four-foot long set-list taped to D.'s mic-stand and Dirk said, "What is this, the history of music?!" It was! When we recorded the long tail of the song "More Spiel" for "Project: Mersh" (SST 034) I joked to D. that he had just laid down a six-minute history of the guitar solo. At SST, hearing guitarists Greg Ginn, Joe Baiza and Curt Kirkwood all the time, it was easy to underestimate how great a guitar player D. was. That radical reformation the Reactionaries performed on themselves to become the Minutemen encouraged that, because it elevated Mike and George to co-lead players.

But their world-historical, musical summation had a history as well. And that was their late-seventies band, the Reactionaries. Mike and D. had known each other since junior high. They met Martin Tamburovich and George Hurley at San Pedro high, although they wouldn't claim they knew George because in Watt's words, "he was a happening cat," whereas D., Mike, and Martin were on the not-so-happening end of the high school social spectrum. As George tells it: "For a long time Mike would ask me to play music with him. He wanted to jam out, but I really wasn't into it 'cause I was a Surfer then and he was sort of a geek. I don't know, we were kids. Finally, I agreed to it." This kind of transgression of school social hierarchy is common when music brings young kids together in their first band. It's an under-appreciated aspect of the power of music.

Thankfully The Reactionaries recorded a practice in their attempt to get gigs so we have these 10 songs to contemplate. What you can hear are the rudiments of the Minutemen's sound, only unlike most bands, they only got rid of stuff as they improved. D. is already a good guitar player with his trebly sound in place. Mike and George play more standard-rock bass and drums parts, and Martin sounds like he belongs on the mic, though the quality of the lyrics varies widely.

Chuck Dukowski saw them and reports, "Martin was a cool singer and I liked his style." They were just out of high school and though they already had their obsessive interests, the lyrics (by Mike, Martin, and friends outside the band) show an awkward adaptation to the punk style as they understood it. Like a lot of lyrics by seventies punk bands, television is of particular concern – punks who were determined to create a music scene thought watching TV was a fate co-equal to Death.

In February of 1979, Chuck and Greg Ginn were flyering a Clash / Bo Diddley / Dils show at the Santa Monica Civic when they met D. and Mike. The flyer was for what would be the second Black Flag gig and it was going to be in San Pedro. D. and Mike were amazed to learn of a gig in Pedro and Chuck hadn't known there was a punk band there, so he put The Reactionaries on the bill. It was their first gig; they played with Black Flag, The Descendents (their debut too), The Alley Cats, The Plugz and an impromptu mini-set by The Last. A world-historical night, however many paid at the door.

The Reactionaries played only two more gigs, opening for The Suburban Lawns at their practice pad in Long Beach. They made a pass at getting a gig at the Other Masque up in Hollywood, but the band was falling apart. Mike's description of D.'s loss of interest in The Reactionaries is interesting. Apparently D. didn't offer his songs to The Reactionaries and then found them another guitarist (Todd Apperson) so he could quit. They broke up around mid-1979. George found a band in Hollywood called Hey Taxi! and is on their 45. Though soon enough, D. and Mike regroup and eventually pull George back into their new, improved mess after their new drummer (Frank Tonche) walked offstage and quit during their second gig.

At the Minutemen's first gig (May 1980), Greg asked them to do a record for SST.

Armando and Saint Vitus
Armando Acosta (1952-2010)
I heard something about Armando leaving the band, then Doug Sheppard sent me a link to Armando's angry blog entry. Dave explained that Armando was ill and his playing affected; they've become an important draw in Europe over the years. Then Armando died. I posted this in early December, 2010.

There was no longer long-shot on SST than Saint Vitus. And as long as it was, it was slow too, but slow like the tortoise. As the band became a fixture on major summer festivals in Europe these last fifteen or so years they surely trod the bones of many a long forgotten hare. I generally preferred slower, heavier music ever since I found it somewhat difficult to settle for anything else after first hearing Black Sabbath at a neighbor's house in 1970. When I came down to L.A. and SST from Berkeley in 1981 I considered Flipper my favorite band. In that sense I was ready for Saint Vitus when I first saw them.

But in practical terms at SST in spring 1982 I wasn't so sure about doing their record. Black Flag was going to halt their deal with Unicorn so we moved out of the Unicorn offices near the Tropicana in West Hollywood and down to a one-room office on Phelan Ave. in North Redondo Beach. Black Flag rented time at a practice studio called Pax in Carson where Overkill practiced. Though we'd managed to release the Minutemen's "The Punch Line," and Saccharine Trust's "Pagan Icons" albums soon after I came down, those records were already in place and I didn't do much on those. But we also had the early Black Flag singles to keep in print, and the ill-fated "Everything Went Black" vault comp, plus we'd already recorded the first Meat Puppets album, the basic tracks for the Overkill album, and we still had the Stains album and an earlier Overkill 45 to get released. And we had no real cash flow separate from Black Flag's live revenues; we wouldn't for another two years. Yet here was Greg and Chuck telling me I had to see this new band they'd heard over at Pax.

I think this was April 1982 and Black Flag was working Emil into the band and preparing for the Summer tour. I went over with them and met and watched Saint Vitus play their set. The first thing you noticed was Armando's drum kit! The damn rack toms petered out to a size smaller than bongos, and he had layers of cymbals, and double-kick drums of course, but also a couple floor toms as large as most humans' bass drums! You couldn't even see him behind the kit and Armando was big! The whole band looked at first glance like they might have missed that it was now the 1980s. Then you'd catch the visual and audio Germs references and find out that they saw bands at the Fleetwood as well as the Long Beach Sports Arena, and they were the only SST band conversant with UK punk bands like Discharge.

Dez was of course immediately, totally into them, and possibly it took Henry, Mugger, Spot and I a nano-second longer. My concern was how would we budget for another album release with no cashflow, so when Greg asked what I thought about doing their album, I responded, "How about a single?" Obviously I hadn't yet clocked the tunes' running times, nor figured on how wide a groove those low-end rumbling progressions were going to require; they couldn't do a 7" 45. Spot found that one of the

SAINT VITUS (MARK, DAVE, SCOTT, ARMANDO), REDONDO BEACH, 1982; PHOTO: NAOMI PETERSEN.

Media Art guys had opened up Total Access studio in Redondo and he had just run the Descendents through it so he booked an overnight – ten hours for $200 if I remember. The recording began with load in at 10pm August 16, 1982 and went til about 9am the next morning. Dez and I went in with Spot. He used the studio's main room with its carefully calibrated angles and acousticly perfect design merely to run the amp and mic cords and power cables out to a larger raw space that Total Access rented but hadn't incorporated into its business yet. It must've been about 25 x 100 feet with a fifteen foot ceiling. Cement floor, steel roof. Spot remembers,

> "When we got into the studio – the big live, cement room at Total Access – I couldn't help think: 'Now it's time to show BF how it's really done!' The Vitus guys left me alone and didn't try to over-theorize anything. Aside from a few ambient miking tricks, it was a real straightforward setup. Armando's drum set looked tricky at first but was actually a piece of cake even with 4 tracks dedicated to the toms. No sonic surprises or nightmares. Only one overhead mic, and I refused to pull the front heads off the bass drums. One of my favorite recording sessions ever!" (Spot)

Spot is referring to the fact that Greg and Chuck seemed already, even early in the "Damaged" tours to be thinking about their own slowage-to-come as it might apply to Spot's end of things on the touring at hand and the studio work to come.

> "Greg was seriously obsessed with the idea of the album sounding dark and sludgy – i.e., anti-punk. In that regard, 'My War' was a dismal failure since none of the tracks or performances lent themselves to such treatment. Hell, Saint Vitus had been honing their sound for years! They had it down in their sleep!"
> (Spot, Dec. 4, 2010)

As I understand it Dave Chandler, Mark Adams and Armando Acosta got together as Tyrant in 1979 with Dave singing until Scott Reagers joined and they changed the name to Saint Vitus after one of their songs. They appeared they might be Satanists but their crosses were right-side up; they were actually Christians leavened by some high school drugging, thereafter they mostly just drank beer in my experience. Their first fans were from the lowest circle of Narbonne High in Harbor City. I heard Dave's room-mate Louie say that a guitar tone whirring across the top of one of their songs reminded him of doing cannabinol and Dave and Mark started nodding and laughing.

According to the obituary placed by the Acosta family Armando grew up in West L.A., went to Venice High, enlisted in the Air Force and was an Airman First Class. If I recall he then had a short career as a cop before doing freelance security for Don Dokken and others some might wish to lay hands on. He kept in touch with Dokken and he even produced one of their later albums ("C.O.D." in 1993). Armando moved to San Pedro in the late seventies and joined Tyrant; the others lived in Lomita.

As soon as we came out of the studio with the first album's basic tracks, all done live that night, Spot made some cassettes so Black Flag on tour was listening to it. I was at SST, and Bill Stevenson was getting into it too. The Descendents were into fast playing so it really made a double-take impression with them. Bill came around SST a lot as he was getting their first album, "Milo Goes to College," out and for him it was the song "Zombie Hunger" running through his head. He'd be air-drumming as he came into SST sounding out *"bom... bom... bom-bom-bom... chicka-blam, chicka-blam."* Those long slow songs really were open to what Armando could do with all those drums. Of course he didn't use all of them to create the principal slow-mo syncopation set-ups that fascinated Bill. But there'd be a use for each of them down the line of albums. The longest, slowest song they did that first session, "The Walking Dead," isn't on the LP but was put out on 12" EP in the UK, its twelve minute crawl-haul occasionally peals the arrangement back to just the drums and one gets an amazing audio portrait of Armando trudging along alone in that big space, the drums slapping back in a room-acoustic counter-syncopation.

It took us almost a full year before we were able to spend another two hundred bucks to mix the album. We got it released some time in early 1984. It wasn't the first album that I'd been in the studio for but it's the first one I had some input on, plus I worked out artwork with David Chandler and Naomi Petersen. She was just becoming our go-to girl for photographs and she really clicked with them. I thought she might be disappointed to begin work on them since no-one knew who they were and they weren't punk-looking to say the least. But they were goth in their way, and she liked them and loved having a reason to do some graveyard shoots.

I'm probably over-emphasizing how many slow songs they did. The double-kicks got plenty of work-out, most notably in "White Stallions" off the second album, "Hallow's Victim," which also features "War Is Our Destiny," another barn-burner. (There's a nice performance lip-sync music video of this song that we made that got so little response it hasn't found its way onto youtube.) This second album was recorded right off of their first real tour, opening for Black Flag from the east coast and across Canada in winter. I talked to them about rotating a few of the new songs into each gig on the tour so that they'd really have them down when they got back. We went straight into Total Access, the main room this time, and it was the sharpest they ever played in the studio. Even a strenuous practice regimen, never their style, is no match for recording right off a tour, only most bands don't play new songs live before they are out on record and so the recorded history of rock and roll suffers. Not that album.

Scott Reagers left the band when the touring was too much for his girlfriend. I thought the band'd never find a decent replacement. You should've seen who replaced Merrill in Overkill; there just weren't a lot of choices. But they'd talked to this guy in D.C. on their tour, also named Scott but better known as Wino, and he'd given them a cassette of his band, The Obsessed. Wino came out and we began to prep "Born Too Late." I remember being surprised when Dave promised that this was going to be their metal album. I thought, "Oh I see, 'Hallow's Victim,' was a punk album in the world of Vitus." Wino fit in great, of course, and for a lot of people "Born Too Late" is the quintessential Saint Vitus album. It is slower and perhaps a tad heavier at its best, and Wino's voice is lower and more naturalistic in approach. Spot had moved to Austin so we had Mike Lardie engineer at Total Access – he slipped some noise-gates past me then which now I hear quite clearly.

The next album, "Mournful Cries," is another favorite of mine. I stayed at Dave's while I was out in March 1988 and found out how much he likes watching *"Green Acres"* reruns. He lived in the front house of a duplex owned by Mark's parents who lived in the back. We ate back there and the Adamses were like working class Ginns, really nice folks and the place crammed with flea market tchochkes.

The band practiced in a shed behind a crack-house in Torrance and they worried they might get their amps impounded or stolen before the studio date came. Whereas for the first album the band could only conceive of playing the tune in its live arrangement, by now they practiced rhythm arrangements for the studio so we could lay down a consistent sound-bed and more carefully set a sound for the solo and overdub it. We were getting real pro by our lights, but you could tell the Music Grinder Studio folks up on Melrose had never had any other band come in and pound out an album's tracking and mixing in four straight twelve hour days. On "Mournful Cries" Wino plays second guitar on some tunes which worked out great; he's got the best rhythm sense of any guitarist I've heard, something elastic akin to John Bonham's drum-feel.

Listening to these great Saint Vitus slabs of sound in these studios was better than any live P.A. or LP or CD playback could possibly be. For the song, "Shooting Gallery," we were going to have a fade-out so I was to signal them when to stop playing the final descending pattern, only I forgot as I was just listening to them play it – totally zoned out until they filled the two-inch reel of tape with it! They came out of their room laughing at me. One Armando-supremo touch is in the last song on that album, "Looking Glass." Somehow I hadn't picked out what he was doing in practice but suddenly under the solo he just went supernova on the cymbals hitting down deliberately with both sticks through two overlapping cymbals on both levels creating an elongated, particularly destructive-sounding bash as Wino (I think) bends and shreiks his melodic climax. Dave had a surprise of his own, springing those little scratchings on his strings after the riff strikes. Amazing first take!

They were getting somewhere too. I remember *Flipside*'s review of the first album where Al just couldn't understand the point of the record, but there was a nice feature with photos on the band in a late 80s issue. They won some respect for doing their thing from the beginning and the world was beginning to go their way. There was a funny cartoon ad for somebody in *Forced Exposure* that pictured a walking cliché of a long-haired flannel-wearing Seattle rockhound depicted slack-jawed and carrying a Saint Vitus album in one hand and a Soundgarden album in the other.

Some time after "Mournful Cries" was released Dave called me in Chicago and told me he couldn't get Greg on the phone and they had this offer to go to Germany to do an album and tour. He wasn't sure it was a good idea so we talked it through and since he figured Greg was less interested in them now they went for it. After they signed to do the album "V" for Hellhound in Berlin in late 1989, then Greg called....

It's another great record and they've done more, most notably "Die Healing" with Scott Reagers back after Wino left to reform The Obsessed. A particularly... I want to say witty, performance on that album is "In the Asylum," certainly it's hard to compare what Scott and Armando are doing here with anything anyone else has ever done – it's comic-doom that bears relation to some of the Ramones' great mental tunes only with completely different sound dynamics.

With all the activity in Europe Armando often played on rented drums. There's a lip-synch music video for the song "Fear" from 1992 with Christian Lindersson on vocals; you can actually see Armando over the top of his small rented kit!

I think of all the early SST bands Saint Vitus probably got along the best. It's Dave's vision you'd have to say but he pretty much grew up with Mark and Scott, and then Armando was such an easy going guy, it explained how they could make this long tortoise run. They didn't practice daily like Black Flag did so they didn't get on each others nerves. Wino has a vision as well and so his relationship with Dave has had its ups and downs but I was glad to see them back together to play these European dates recently. They even did a rare Los Angeles gig a couple years ago where they got something like respect from Hollywood and all. They never really "made it," they just concentrated on the writing and playing of album after album of inspired music.

Given all that it was a surprise to hear from Dave that he'd replaced Armando after some 2009 shows in Europe. In what is probably a January 2009 San Francisco performance (rather than 2010 as labeled) of "Look Behind You" which Dave introduces as the band's first song, Armando is wailing pretty solid though he could slur on some of the faster rolls as he does here. Apparently Armando's health had been deteriorating and it was affecting his playing. In a backstage video on *youtube* he looks a little thin and he shows some large swelling on his lower throat. According to the band's statement his last show with Saint Vitus was April 29, 2009 in Stuttgart. Armando got angry – something hard to picture – but he felt well enough to complain about his treatment online. He obviously loved being in Saint Vitus, whatever little it got any of them in the greater scheme of the music Industry. They did love it and these back-end gigs were certainly great proud fun for them all. That summer they were apparently slotted just before Mötley Crüe at Roadburn Festival in Holland. They've announced they'll record another album soon with Wino on vocals. It'll be another great album, but I expect it'll sound strange to my ears with no Armando churning down in the music's engine-room. He passed early Thanksgiving day, November 25, 2010 at Providence Little Company of Mary Medical Center in San Pedro.

Now that I can't see him play drums again it occurs to me that I haven't seen them play live since a gig at Raji's in Hollywood with D.C.3, and Across the River in late 1985. Time flies whether you're having fun or not. When I was working on my Naomi/SST book I got back in touch with a number of people. Also caught up on my L.A. punk lit which included Brendan Mullen's books. I'd known him slightly from the old days but hadn't been in LA or in its music scene in his Masque heyday, but I was aware of his documenting those days with his writing. We got together at his place and he showed me his archive of stills and flyers; he also showed me his coachhouse studio with his records and drum kit and DJ'ing turntables. He was very interested in finding out about the various nooks and crannies he'd overlooked in his books about the massive sprawling Los Angeles music scene of that era and I got the idea he might do an addendum to *We Got the Neutron Bomb*. I wouldn't have guessed Brendan wasn't long for this world either, he was still so enthusiastic about music and life. I made him some cassettes of LAFMS bands, Secret Hate, Across the River and other stuff, but it was the first Saint Vitus album that blew his mind; he'd never heard it:

> "Freaked out... sounds so great on these bitchin' new speakers I just got for my dj'ing .... another fucking great track to obsess over ... when I freak out over a song or a track ... it's like adrenaline... inspires my ass to keep on keepin' on. SV (the song) so rocks like that... Also crazy for that sound you guys got especially the drums and bass... that warm, booming bassy breathing sound which pans out superswell on the new speaks which have MONSTER depth. Wait till you hear it, maybe you'll flip, too... How do you get that drum sound.. haha? Wouldn't I just love to know the secret recipe.. haha." (BM email, June 1, 2006)

It was a pleasure to turn him onto it all those years later.

Saint Vitus for some were the most important band on SST Records; it's amazing how many different languages a google search for Armando's death brings up. For others they're just a name of something they're sure they'd hate. To my mind it's the quality of the more overlooked bands of the South Bay area of Los Angeles back then like Saint Vitus, Saccharine Trust, Overkill, Slovenly, Secret Hate... that really tell the tale.

It occurred to me when Ray Farrell wrote me about how he remembered responding to the early SST releases I sent up to him in attempting to get him down to SST. He was still up in Berkeley very involved in that music world and he referred to the SST bands as "neighborhood bands," which made me think that that might be the secret, maybe only in the south bay did rock music continue to be a folk music like rock and roll had been for the sixties garage bands and the rockabilly bands of the fifties. Ray closed, "I used to wonder if St.Vitus was taken seriously enough amongst a stable of groundbreaking music associated with punk. They were the real thing. I'm serious about their legacy... I hope Dave keeps it going." I'm sure Armando does too.

(originally posted at The New Vulgate, No. 75)

The Obsessed, Mk II
The original version of this appears on the 2006 reissue of The Obsessed's 1991 album, "Lunar Womb," as liner notes. It was good to have positive reason to touch base with the guys again, after having reconnected with them the year before about Naomi Petersen's death; her photographs feature in the Meteor City reissue as well.

I first heard The Obsessed in 1985 at SST. Dave Chandler brought over a cassette, a.k.a., THE CASSETTE. Saint Vitus had just come off a Black Flag tour and was losing vocalist Scott Reaghers to his fiance. To my mind this was very bad news. I assumed it would not be like Black Flag finding a new singer; Saint Vitus would have to draw from a metal scene that was total bullshit – especially the peacocks who thought they could sing – and with less audience to offer. Dave wanted my opinion on whether this other Scott they had just met on the east coast might fit into their sound. I can't say I was immediately blown away by the tape but I could tell that Scott Weinrich was no cheese-meister. Amazingly, it seemed there was someone on the east coast working on the same wavelength as Saint Vitus! Soon Wino was in L.A., in Saint Vitus and on SST. While working on the "Mournful Cries" recording in 1987 I got a dub of The Obsessed tape and thereafter got addicted to its slow, heavy, psychedelic grooves.

Saint Vitus soon left SST for the German label Hellhound. In late 1989, after they recorded "V" and "Live," Wino mixed the better Obsessed recordings that had constituted THE CASSETTE for release by Hellhound. (The rest of those early tunes have popped up throughout the rest of their catalog.) The Germans asked Wino to put The Obsessed back together to support the release and once the new line-up was together, Wino worked up new tunes as well, and so Saint Vitus had to replace another great vocalist! They was mad.

The Obsessed, mk II, came together in Los Angeles. Scott Reeder (Great Scott, another one!) remembers meeting Weinrich at a Saint Vitus / D.R.I. / Across the River gig in Palm Desert (May 16, 1986). I'd first seen Reeder in Across the River opening for Saint Vitus at the Anti-Club (July 2, 1986); I walked in on their set and was amazed how powerful and soulful they were; I immediately turned on my tape recorder. Reeder played barefoot – always a good sign in a bassist. I had just left SST but I called Chuck Dukowski and told him to get AtR into the studio; they didn't though they did record them live at the County Line festival later that summer.

Scotts Weinrich and Reeder first played together at a generator party in August 1986. Wino recalls,

> "I jammed with Scott (Reeder) at this gorgeous Malibu cliff-side party, he on drums. That's where our friendship started. No-one from the desert crowd knew I played guitar (at first Wino only sang in Vitus), or knew of the Obsessed, except Henry (Rollins) was in the process of turning folks on to it. So Scotty got behind the kit and I picked up someone's, maybe Mario's hollow body Gibson – magical!" (Scott Weinrich, 2006)

Mario was of course Mario Lally of Across the River (and later, Yawningman, Sort of Quartet, Fatso Jetson); he was playing bass during this jam.

Drummer Greg Rogers was then jamming with bassist Danny Hood and guitarist Dave Van Heusen. Greg and Danny had a band called Acid Clown that Chris Gates (Big Boys, Junkyard) had turned Wino onto. When it broke up Wino began working with Greg and Danny. When Danny was killed in a motorcycle accident, Scott Reeder, who had moved to L.A. when Across the River broke up, joined.

Greg writes of the early period of The Obsessed, mk 2:

> "We toured Europe in the spring of '91 and recorded 'Lunar Womb' immediately after that in Berlin. The sessions went great. We were in good shape from touring and tracked all of the basics live. If I'm not mistaken, we tracked and mixed the whole thing in 7 days. Tracking 'Lunar Womb' was a trip because we hadn't learned the song yet. Wino would show us a section, we would record it, then he'd show us the next section, and we'd punch it in next, and so on. There were times when we didn't know if we were actually recording, listening to playback while we were playing, pre-rolling for a punch-in or what... It all went pretty smooth and we had a great time doing it. It's still by far my favorite recording experience." (Greg Rogers)

Greg says some of Danny Hood's early contribution survives in the opening tunes of both "Lunar Womb" and "The Church Within" albums.

Standout moments of the "Lunar Womb" album begin right away. "Brother Blue Steel" announces itself with a brutal fanfare that drops quickly into a lowriding riff from which Wino tosses off a lazy slow-handed lead figure before the vocal begins... You know you bought the right album within twenty seconds max. "Hiding Mask" was my favorite track from THE CASSETTE and I missed it when it wasn't on the first Obsessed album. It might be Weinrich-the-songwriter's best work; it's the song Rubin should've had Johnny Cash do.

Uptempo is not my favorite thing The Obsessed do, but "Spew" and "No Blame" are the two great faster tunes they did. "Spew" is an instrumental and the best place to hear the band's seventies prog influences. As Greg mentioned they recorded just off a tour and no amount of practice is a substitute for that. And I would guess that "No Blame" is Wino's explanation of leaving Saint Vitus for a chance to do his full thing – one of his best vocal performances therefore, as its his life in music he is singing about. "Kachina" and "Back to Zero" are great chugging riffs that open up into psychedelic passages and "BTZ" is another great lyric (it and "Bardo" are sung by Reeder). "Endless Circles" cuts matters down to a sub-riff figure that opens up only to slam right down; another great tune first heard on THE CASSETTE. The title track is slower, heavier prog especially in its bizarre song-length intro which Greg is describing above. That leaves the fast "Bardo," the riffed melody/psychedelia of "No Mas," the mixmaster "Jaded" which bulls thru heavy chug, prog wind-ups, and rolling psych passages, and then the noise-drone afterbirth, "Embryo" – not too shabby as lesser tracks go.

After this album was released in Germany the band gigged in California and Arizona, recorded a little, and did one quick tour to get to a New York showcase for the Columbia label folks who signed the band. Scott Reeder left to join his desert buds in Kyuss for their last couple records and Guy Pinhas replaced him on bass for the last Obsessed album, "The Church Within." Of the "Lunar Womb" line-up Wino writes,

> "Greg was a big inspiration to me with his integrity and sobriety, and Scott's genius shone on Embryo, his riff – he wrote at least half on Lunar Womb – when he completely down tuned a strat, hooked up an original Golden Throat mouth-wah, filled his mouth with water, laid on his back and made the coolest noises ever recorded!!!!!" (Scott Weinrich)

But the story doesn't end, even with "The Church Within," another great album.... It goes on to involve Shine, Spirit Caravan, The Hidden Hand, and also Goatsnake, Probot, Place of Skulls, and even Wino-Vitus reunion gigs! Such a blizzard of obscure names but these bands and players are giants, invisible though they may be to most. As Greg Kot wrote in one of the few aboveground comprehensive reviews of the Weinrich body of work, "There is a secret history of rock, one that lurks undocumented between the official chapters, one that isn't preserved in the Rock and Roll Hall of Fame or discussed in exhaustive 10-part television documentaries." (*Chicago Tribune*, July 15, 2001) The Obsessed, as well as everything else Scott Weinrich has touched, is part of a major chapter of that untold history. And as metal, punk, and rock itself lose touch with the blues, psychedelia, and their own histories, the Obsessed (and the rest) sound more important than ever – kind of like the last rock and roll standing.

The Algorithm of Radio's Death Spiral
If cartoons are not a bit over the heads of kids, they fail with those kids. Music radio is cynical but the programming isn't over the head of a munchkin. This went up at The New Vulgate *on Oct. 21, 2009.*

"The Song Decoders" in the *New York Times Magazine* is about the internet radio-service Pandora's Music Genome Project, an attempt to log and cross-ref "hundreds of data points" that are alleged to determine what it is a listener hears in a song and will presumably search out in other songs.

Well, okay, here's what Pandora tells you about three songs that Chris Collins of the *NV* checked out for me when I told him I was working on this:

"Black Sabbath *'Hole in the Sky'*
Features of this song:
- hard rock roots
- mild rhythmic syncopation
- repetitive melodic phrasing
- a twelve-eight time signature
- mixed minor & major key tonality
- groove based composition
- a vocal-centric aesthetic
- electric rhythm guitars
- a dynamic male vocalist
- triple note feel
- similar songs are: Smashing Pumpkins *'Today,'* Motörhead *'We Are the Road Crew,'* Ministry *'Supernaut,'* Led Zeppelin *'Houses of the Holy.'*

Amon Düül II *'The Return of Ruebezahl'*
Features of this song:
- electric rock instrumentation
- extensive vamping
- minor key tonality
- electric rhythm guitars
- an instrumental arrangement

- similar songs: Kennelmus *'Goodbye Pamela Ann,'* Nektar *'The Nine Lifeless Daughters of the Sun,'* the Avengers VI *'Heartbeat,'* the David *'Mister, You're a Better Man Than I,'* Wigwam *'Pig Storm.'*

Black Flag *'In My Head'*
Features of this song:
- punk roots
- electric rock instrumentation
- a twelve-eight time signature
- minor key tonality
- a vocal-centric aesthetic
- electric guitar riffs
- a dynamic male vocalist
- triple note feel
- similar songs: Jesus Lizard *'Uncommonly Good,'* the Birthday Party *'Say a Spell,'* Shellac *'Canada,'* Heatmiser *'Dead Air,'* the Butthole Surfers *'Sea Ferring.'"*

Pandora notes after each song breakdown, "[t]hese are just a few of the hundreds of attributes cataloged for this song by the Music Genome Project." I don't doubt that but as Ray Farrell tells me the tunes suggested by non-genome software at All Music Guide or iTunes are not so different. (Ray went from Rather Ripped Records to *KPFA* to Down Home to SST to Geffen to eMusic to RoyaltyShare to finetunes so he about knows it all – rode the boom and the crash in rhythm.) Just posted at *Arthur* is an interview with Josh Homme and John Paul Jones where Jay suggests that no matter how fringe the artists one enters into Pandora, the algorithm gradually moves you "to the center. It doesn't run around the edge," which Homme then christens a "Vanilla-ator."

Satellite radio attempted to please the music consumer by programming many channels by micro-genre – a thousand narrowcasts. But what they play is ordered from over the heads of the on-air talent, even when that be music people who know far better what to play. Pandora's answer is a more mechanistic attempt to fix what was broken back when radio got rid of all it's music people. But Pandora does not want music people back either, because they might commence to listen, respond, and program with little regard for business considerations. (Managers and labels often threaten to withhold their big stars unless their newbie-foists are programmed.) Things could open up in uncontrollable ways, recombining as they might.

Music people as such were driven out of radio by 1973 or so, and since then earlier versions of these Numbers people created this death spiral which promises radio station owners better targeting of existing listenership and then proceeds to deliver smaller and smaller audiences as people tune out radio itself.

Station-owners' answer has been to switch formats, but these too have the same problem: Country or R&B or Rock or Pop formats can only profit marginally from the ebb and flow of each other's deterioration. Why? Because a programmer must build an audience through contrast and drama, and he needs to know music much better than the listeners, the sponsors, the sales people ever will. He has to be assembling and educating an audience for music that does not at first exist.

If the DJ himself has a clue and a personality you get something like you once had after ASCAP (American Society of Composers, Authors, and Publishers) and the musicians union mercifully pulled all their professional pop music off the air in a bid to halt the playing of records over the air. They'd colluded to prevent this for a decade and clearly felt they could stone it for another. Radio then founded BMI (Broadcast Music, Inc.) to collect performance fees for the country and blues they'd been filling the air with for a year before a settlement was reached. To the astonishment of the musicians union head James C. Petrillo and ASCAP, BMI's signings out of ghetto and holler stayed in the air, laying a path for Sun, Chess, and the rest.

In any case there was nothing but the Race and Hillbilly charts in Billboard for early rock and roll: Bill Haley on both, Elvis Presley on both.... The Pop Chart wasn't really conquered until Elvis' end run around pop radio formats via a run of appearances on network television programs: "*Stage Show*" - CBS, "*Milton Berle*" - NBC, "*Steve Allen*" - NBC, "*Ed Sullivan*" - CBS. Thereafter Elvis, Chuck Berry, Gene Vincent on all three charts, and if there'd been a Gospel chart....

But it was a golden age due more to the music than media. American balladry had blued up under the influence of black Americans, and then it rhythmed up after the Civil War as Rags, Stomps, and varied Dance crazes washed over the music culture via early twentieth century jazz which was then further disseminated through the new media of records, radio, and then film and television. Rock and roll had built up a head of steam.

But radio and records gradually were taken from the hands of music people and low-life hustlers, and delivered into the hands of suits and swells, lawyers and accountants. And as done elsewhere they standardized products and routinized their selling. Music folk had to leave the business-side. Soon enough they were getting thrown out of the music-side too.

Something I like to do is periodically keep my eye *off* the ball. Well maybe keep it in peripheral vision, but look around a bit – see who is moving where while attention is elsewhere. It can be enjoyable after a rec-biz career like mine to relish each internal crash of its collapse, but what's more important is that as the old major labels threw themselves against the web, they did manage to rescue copyright for the big music publishers (Warner-Chappell, EMI, SonyATV, Universal...) to now wire up that web. Publishers do their promotion behind the scenes for satellite radio, advertising, television and movie soundtracks, etc. The promotional *working* of songs isn't as visible as billboards and record shop display ads anymore, although *NBC*'s signing Bon Jovi as "performer in residence" to be "seen and heard across the multiple brands and platforms of NBC Universal" was so ridiculous they figured they'd have to make it visible.

Ray thinks Pandora's new social networking feature that shows the playlists of others who have requested the same song is going to open up the system to knowledge beyond what their software scientists can isolate and identify. It also allows one to listen to what they've downloaded so may prompt more lawsuits.

But all these mechanisms to replace the old radio model that worked, turn music-hunting into something analogous to code-writing when what a listener needs, especially a young one, is have their code written by the ambient programming of a musically rich culture that comes at him or her from all directions in all styles, live and recorded. There still are music people in this country, Ray and Jay for two, but media has damaged content. There's no doubting that at this point. And as the music industry people go about their survival drills they don't see another way even as they claim to be looking for nothing else.

(*originally posted at* The New Vulgate, *No. 16*)

Frank Navetta and The Descendents
I wrote this for a book that Jordan Schwartz and Dave Markey were putting together. Not sure what came of that, but once Frank died I reworked it and posted it at The New Vulgate *on March 17, 2010.*

In 1980 I wasn't aware of the first 45 by The Descendents, "Ride the Wild/It's a Hectic World" (Orca 001). It was recorded by Spot at Media Art in Hermosa Beach in September 1979 with help from Dave and Joe Nolte of The Last. The 45 was released in early 1980, though undistributed anywhere but stores in Hermosa Beach, Redondo Beach, and at Zed in Long Beach. The first Descendents I heard was the track, "Global Probing" on the second New Alliance compilation, Chunks. SST had turned Mike Watt onto Systematic Record Distribution, where I was, which was easy enough since he and D. Boon were working for Greg's SST Electronics company, assembling his tuners. Later in 1981 The Descendents "Fat" e.p. came out on New Alliance and I ordered it immediately for distribution around the country. It was one more idiosyncratic masterpiece of what was coming to be known as L.A. hardcore.

But on that first single the band was a trio: Frank Navetta on guitar, Tony Lombardo on bass, and Bill Stevenson on drums. I saw Frank and Tony again in 2006 at Bill's studio in Fort Collins, Colorado. Frank told me that The Descendents started with he and Dave Nolte woodshedding some tunes on acoustic guitars in the Noltes' garage in 1977. Dave was the youngest of the Nolte brothers and not yet in The Last. Bill knew the Noltes and loved their band. He lived in Hermosa Beach just around the corner from the Ginns but was barely aware of Black Flag, then called Panic. Nolte introduced Bill to Frank and he joined The Descendents in late 1978. Frank was 16; Bill was 15; Tony's age was and remains classified.

Frank and Bill had fishing in common and Bill's friend Pat McCuistion was, like Dave, a close associate of the band and co-wrote or inspired songs including "Weinerschnitzel" and "All." Bill told me that he'd go out fishing with Pat and on bad days when they hated everybody they'd troll small islands and rockpiles off the coast and shoot seals. Bill writes in the "Hallraker" album liner notes, "Pat insisted that we quit writing 'stupid girl songs', and start writing about things that really matter – like food and fishing."

They practiced by LAX and then down in Long Beach. Tony was in Long Beach and his band shared a nearby space with Rhino 39, and The Cheifs' guitarist. Tony heard the racket Frank and Bill were making and went over and sure enough they needed a bassist. "Ride the Wild," written by Frank shows the influence of The Last. It has a relaxed sixties pop guitar and vocal approach (all three sang together, plus maybe Dave). "It's a Hectic World," written by Tony points to their own sound with its speed and foursquare urgency.

Frank's dad prevented them from playing gigs until finally he managed to escape and play a party in Long Beach. Bill's mom prevented them from playing what would've been their first gig, somewhere in O.C. Their second gig was the San Pedro Teen Post with The Plugz, The Alley Cats, Black Flag, and The Reactionaries on February 17, 1979. Good gig. It was Black Flag's second gig too, and The Reactionaries first – they soon morphed into The Minutemen. Dave still sang for these first gigs but the Descendents continued as a trio looking for a lead singer. They played one show with a girl named Gwynne singing on Nov. 9, 1979. It's hard to believe they even knew a girl back then. One can't exaggerate the extent to which the Descendents were uncool at school and put upon at home. Frank, Bill, and Pat found solace on the ocean; they didn't fish like I thought of fishing on lakes in Wisconsin... they pulled heavy, commercially desirable fish out of the Pacific Ocean and sold them for cash, the kind that if their classmates possessed was simply given to them by rich, styler parents.

The band added Milo Aukerman on vocals in late 1980. Milo was an unhip brainy kid. I remember Bill telling me that an old friend of theirs had drawn the cartoon of Milo for the first album (when I was drawing the second cover after his original style), but I see on the Descendents website that this was hardly true. Roger Deuerlein was actually a high school nemesis who'd fixed on Milo to torment via cartoons and posters. Some friend. (And some balls for Bill and Milo then to make Roger reprise his caricature and thereby force it cool by his own hand on the cover of their classic album! – btw, Frank's brother Mike drew the three-piece Descendents on the cover of "Ride the Wild.") The new four-piece Descendents recorded the Fat e.p. the following March with Spot at Music Lab in Silverlake. Spot writes, "It was definitely the 'bonus cup' era so the vibe in the room was pretty manic."

I left Systematic and Berkeley for SST in September of 1981 when its offices were near the Tropicana in West Hollywood. That's where I first met Bill Stevenson – he did an emergency tour with Black Flag in December when Robo wasn't let back into the country after UK dates. I didn't really get to know him and his bandmates until we moved SST down to Redondo Beach in spring of 1982. In June 1982 Spot recorded the album, "Milo Goes to College," at Total Access in Redondo. While Black Flag was out touring for the "Damaged" album (Emil drumming now), I went to every Descendents gig with them and got to know them well. The Descendents were just getting to where they had a gig every weekend somewhere in the greater Los Angeles area. All the gigs seemed to be at small bars with foot-tall stages, and as they weren't a hardcore attraction yet they were easy to listen to from the best sounding spot on the floor – just drums and vocals thru the little house PAs. They drew twenty to thirty people back then. When Bill told me The Descendents pre-history and gave me a copy of the first 45, I hooked him up with Joe Pope who took over at Systematic when I left (Joe was in the band Angst, too). That first single then got out around the country.

FN, COURTESY MARIE NAVETTA.

Bill stopped by SST in Redondo Beach often. He worked at Jerry's Tackle on Aviation Blvd – Jerry was Keith Morris's dad. Rob Holzman, first drummer for Saccharine Trust and later Slovenly, went to Mira Costa High School and remembers Bill and Frank in the hallway before class just in from pre-dawn fishing off Catalina Island, their smelly clothes covered in fish slime. Bill was pointing out classmates as they walked past, noting, "I hate you... I hate you... I hate you..."

"Milo Goes to College" seemed like it was going to be a farewell album. But Milo could maintain his involvement while he went to college; he was probably the best punk-era singer there was. Who was any better? H.R.? Johnny Rotten? Henry Rollins? Gary Floyd? Maybe, maybe not. The Descendents were never better than in the years 1982-83. They played in East L.A. at the new Vex with The Nig-Heist and Suicidal Tendencies (July 8, 1983). Even though we expected it to be a dangerous neighborhood, for some reason we all got there early and had to sit around out front just waiting to be knifed. I sat in the Descendents van with them. If it had been Black Flag's van someone might be getting a blowjob in the back while the rest mind-fucked about music or bio-anthropology. If it had been the Meat Puppets' van there'd be a pipe passing back and forth while they tripped out over the latest misunderstanding between them and the punk community. In the Descendents' van they mostly just drank coffee and vibrated with bitter resentment at their place beneath the lowest rung of the social world. They were rungless! Mugger was still 17 and standing out front of Vex's with his arm around Gina, who seemed like his first real non-driveby girlfriend. This was a bit much for Frank, Bill, Tony, and Milo to have to watch. It was a real Descendents moment I was privileged to witness, though it was undoubtedly tempered by the fact that they knew I worked with Mugger at SST. I also went up with them when they first played San Francisco at the Mabuhay (Jan. 1, 1982) with The Effigies. Good gig. It was the farthest they had been to play and I remember that their impression of San Francisco was that it was like one giant urinal.

Thanksgiving, 1982. Frank invited me over to his family's house for turkey dinner. We never turned down a meal at SST and Black Flag, Mugger and Spot were out on tour. I think Frank wanted to show me off to his dad, but how can I put this... his dad sucked. He was a great provider, a type-A achiever and the family – Mom, Dad, 3 sons, 3 daughters – lived in a nice house in Manhattan Beach, but Mr. Navetta was severely disappointed in son Frank. I don't remember how many of the other kids were there but I remember one of Frank's sisters desperately trying to keep things light and positive in that house every time father insulted son, the founder of one of the most important bands in rock and roll history. Frank's sister Marie wrote me recently, "If anybody was trying to make peace it was either Barbie or myself. To tell you the truth, it used to break my heart to see the way Frank was treated by my dad. All of us suffered, my dad really did suck!" I got an eyeful and an earful, but I did get to eat, and I got to see where Frank pulled his great, no-bs songs – classic Descendents bursts like "My Dad Sucks," and "I'm Not a Loser," songs that still reach kids in a direct, honest, funny way as that first album of theirs is the best-selling record of that scene and era – it is a young kid's right of passage. Frank also drew excellent artwork for their flyers and the "Fat" cover. Bill once marveled to me at Frank's guilelessness – he'd left the "Fat" e.p. artwork lying around the house and his dad picked it up and saw that the band had a song called "My Dad Sucks" triggering yet another round of abuse.

I'm glad I got to see the Descendents often while Frank was in his band. In that era of they played only a handful of gigs outside of L.A. The rest of the country never saw Frank play. It's hard to explain today that there was a desperation to play back then that accounts for the power

"WIFE" BY FRANK NAVETTA.

"PICASSO" BY FRANK NAVETTA.

those songs and recordings and bands have. Times changed fast and one thing I meant to mention last week in my piece on Repulse Kava is that by the end of the eighties a band could be that good but not try very hard to keep it together because they just didn't need it in the same way the bands I knew at SST did. The Descendents kept going as Frank wanted them to but I don't believe they ever really could replace him, and that desperate energy of his. That he did start his band and follow through on it despite being just about the last human being that the existing music audiences wanted to see up on stage, may have made it so much easier for kids later that maybe they simply can't be as good.

I saw them once more – Frank, Tony, Bill – in 2006 at the Blasting Room in Fort Collins, recording basic tracks for an album of new songs by the early line-up. I had arranged for Dave Lightbourne to record the day after the Upland Breakdown and was amazed to see the Descendents going at it in Studio B. I took a couple photos thru the glass but didn't want to interrupt them. I came back down the next day to ask Frank and Tony a few questions about the beginnings of the band. Glad I did that. Frank died back in Oregon in 2008. According to the obit in the Florence, Oregon paper, he left behind two daughters and a son.

FLYER ART: FRANK NAVETTA; COURTESY BRENDAN MULLEN COLLECTION.

That summer when I was alone at SST Bill would often burst in after Descendents practice and vent his frustration with his bandmates. My favorite was the time he came in making wretching noises, "Ugh... Achh...! UGH!!! Milo thinks he can sing!" But when Frank told his bandmates that he would leave the band I didn't hear anything about it. First Ray Cooper was added as a second guitar and they played for most of 1983 as a five-piece (see clip above; Mi Casita, Torrance, Cal. January 14, 1983). Frank must have seen that things would be fine with the band and only then did he leave in November 1983. He left L.A. too for the south coast of Oregon where he fished and painted and got married. Pat, who Bill refers to as the fifth member of the band, was lost at sea in a 1987 storm. Bill wrote, "He had 15,000 pounds of fish onboard, so I guess you could say he died in heated pursuit of All."

I left L.A. in mid-1986, spent about ten years in Chicago which by then The Descendents were reaching regularly on tour. Then I moved to Laramie where I got back in more regular touch with Bill Stevenson because he had moved his All-Descendents-Blasting Room-O&O operations just down the street to Fort Collins. Tony was no longer in The Descendents either; Stephen Egerton and Karl Alvarez were now in the band and Chad Price made them the band All when Milo was too busy pursuing his academic career on the east coast. The Descendents were friends, and at first they were each other's only friends. Bill was good to Frank and kept him paid up on all royalties due from his old songs that were now selling so well ("Milo Goes to College" sold about five thousand copies in its first five years of release, and over a hundred thousand copies in its second five years.) Frank was living in Bill's garage in Fort Collins one summer and having occasional trouble with still undiagnosed schizophrenia and bi-polar disorder according to Frank and Marie. I saw him then and he seemed himself, same hoarse high-pitched voice, a little fatter, a little hairier; he told me he was doing a lot of fishing back in Oregon.

In 2002 I drove out to L.A. to peddle screenplays and stopped by the Ginns. I read the papers over huevos rancheros at Calimex and later walked around the last few streets of old-style beachside houses. Walking back up Pier Ave. I thought I saw Frank, but it couldn't be – I had just seen him in Colorado. But it was him. He looked like a mountain man with long hair and now a beard too; he said he'd just walked up from San Diego. He looked it. I was afraid to ask if he was going to his parents' house. I thought Raymond might like to see Frank but didn't feel I could invite him to the Ginns because I didn't really know what shape he was in. When I got back to Wyoming and next saw Bill and told him I'd run into Frank on Pier, he was surprised but then not so surprised and told me that he'd had to ask Frank to leave after he had some kind of fit that disrupted work at the recording studio.

Here's Frank's last song contribution to The Descendents, mk 1; it clocks in at 37 seconds on the "I Don't Want to Grow Up" album which was released in 1985:

"Rockstar"

Rockstar
Poser
Asshole
Loser
Satisfaction
Recognition
Leave me alone
Rockstar
See if you can do two things at once
Go away and leave me alone

Rockstar
Asshole
Loser
Satisfaction
Recognition
Leave me alone
Let's exploit rock and roll
To its fullest potential.

Frank Navetta; ©Alltudemic Music (BMI)

He wrote that song, recorded it, and then bailed. Over the years he looked more and more like Jack London's Sea-wolf. But Frank was much too nice a guy. He was just a sea-dog.

Marie Navetta wrote me, "Frank forgave everybody before he passed away, his parents and everyone who hurt him; he was just full of love. He talked to us about his relationship with God, he was ready and really he couldn't wait to see the Lord."

It was Frank who named the band The Descendents in 1977. What do you think he meant by that?

(original version posted at The New Vulgate, No. 37)

Radio Programmer Tip: 3 Tunes, 2 Segues, 1 Story

When Hit List *magazine started up in the bay area I liked the people involved and thought I should try to write something about the bands up there I was into before I left to go back to L.A. They didn't run it but I posted it at* The New Vulgate *on Aug. 5, 2009 and it received more comments from some of the principals than any other posting.*

Negative Trend – "Black & Red"
Flipper – "Shine"
Toiling Midgets – "Preludes"

Negative Trend were of the first generation of San Francisco punk bands. These were all inspired by the then final album by The Stooges, "Raw Power," mainly because it was the best record you could buy for 50 cents in 1975, and was also the best musical style you could attempt to pull off, having just copped your first ten dollar guitar on that very 50 cent inspiration. The market for underground rock had shrunk overnight to the point that The Stooges' label Elektra dropped them after "Fun House." (*Dropped after "Fun House"!!!*) David Bowie's management company moved them to England where soon enough MainMan had second thoughts. Eventually, Columbia released "Raw Power" in the U.S. and then quickly remaindered the album. These cut-out copies were snatched up and anyone looking for "Raw Power" after 1976 had to pay import prices. The market for underground sounds had in fact shrunk to the young musicians just beginning to form their own bands knowing nothing of any collapse but maybe radio's, and certain that they and the noise they'd make would wake the dead.

These were not college boys. Unlike today, the mid-seventies music scene was one of drop-outs inhabiting city neighborhoods bereft of hope and pretension as the late hippie/radical scene either bottomed out in drug use or retired to college town arcadias. The drugs these players were taking they were taking without pretension. Mind expansion? Yeah right. Initial drug pretenses were folk scene clean and had been laid low by the motorhead impulses of Grand Funk youth. Revolution? Yeah right. The draft had ended, then the protests ended, then Nixon resigned, then Ford became president, then the hip young congressional class of '74 cut off aid to South Vietnam, then it fell, then a bloodbath in Vietnam, then Carter, then a bigger bloodbath in Cambodia, then a war between Vietnam and Cambodia, then a war between China and Vietnam, then the Mullahs took Iran, then the Soviets invaded Afghanistan....

No, this music generation's excitement was about a lean mean music that looked to The Stooges, The Velvet Underground, and then suddenly The Ramones as models. They disparaged the just collapsed hippie pretense while making stylistic gestures in the directions of pre-hippie fifties/sixties rockabilly/garage approaches.

Negative Trend was formed out of the ashes of one ground-zero nexus of early San Francisco punk, Grand Mal, which in 1977 split into Trend plus The Offs. I never saw Negative Trend though I did know their first singer, Rozz, as he bounced between SF and Portland, where I was doing punk radio on *KBOO* and turning an import record store called Renaissance into what we thought of as the first modern independent record distributor, Systematic Record Distribution. Negative Trend released one four song seven inch which was quickly out of print with nary a copy leaving the west coast. They played the bay area, toured the Northwest once, went to LA to play and record with a new singer, Rik L. Rik (formerly vocalist for LA band, F-Word). He replaced Mikal Waters as singer. F-Word had been on the Posh-Boy label, which probably owned Rik from his head to his anus. They recorded for Posh and then Robbie goes and has the Simpletones re-record the music and releases it under the Rik L. Rik name. They just didn't know about that kind of shit in SF. Robbie must have thought this was pop music and was going to sell. It actually did in Los Angeles where media wasn't in full hippie lockdown.

Flipper was formed by Trend's rhythm section, Will Shatter and Steve DePace, guitarist Ted Falconi, formerly of a band called SST and Ricky Williams who had floated away from The Sleepers for a moment (Rozz filled in for him). While in Portland I met a kid from SF named Bruce Calderwood who showed up with his girlfriend, Diane, who was one of the early Portland punks and moved back and forth between the cities. Bruce put the locals on edge slightly as he was a big city punk and Portland was definitely a backwater. He talked about this band he had back in SF called Flipper. He lolled around Portland for a month or more so I didn't figure the band was much of a full time career move for him. He had replaced Ricky who then floated back to The Sleepers. I don't think he ran into Rozz while in town.

Systematic moved to Berkeley at the end of 1979 and I caught up with Bruce quickly as he worked at the folk label, Kicking Mule, just up the street. I saw Flipper gigs at Dew Drop Inn in Berkeley, and the Sound of Music in SF before they began to get onto bigger hall gigs. I bought a small Aiwa cassette recorder to tape their gigs because they were pretty abstract in those days and very flexible in their treatment of their tunes; it was tough to recall just what had been so great about them. Subterranean Records and Target Video recorded Flipper and three other new SF bands "Live at Target" in February 1980 and Subterranean put out the album which included three tunes by Flipper.

Systematic had a label but my partner was not easily interested in this or that band so I kicked a few hundred dollars to Steve Tupper and we called the first Flipper 45 a Subterranean-Thermidor co-release. At the recording session at Hyde Street in late October 1980 they did five tunes, "Ha Ha," "Love Canal" (both released as the 45), plus "I Saw You Shine," "No Tears Wasted," and "Boom Boom." It was great to see the live tunes finally go to tape. I'd only been in a recording studio once before in Portland (Neo-Boys), though I had recorded my brother's band in early seventies at junior high dances on a four-track if that counts. I just watched and listened. I remember being sure that they would go back and clean up that hellacious amp-noise of Ted's before the tracking began. Boy was I dumb.

The sessions were great and it was an honor to be there. "Boom Boom" was never released (another version of it was recorded but unreleased by a post-Flipper band of Will's called Any Three Initials). All five tunes were recorded one day, and mixed on another day. Steve Tupper told me that "Shine," and "Tears" were later re-recorded for the first album, "Generic Flipper," but I think for "Shine" maybe just the vocal was redone. At the mix session I remember Bruce laughing with Will and Steve (the ex-Trends) as he told them of calling Craig Gray immediately after Flipper had recorded to inform him that he had been ripped off. Bruce meant that "Shine" was "Black & Red" reworked, so to speak. Craig was ex-Grand Mal, and the Negative Trend guitarist, who was just then turning the final Trend line-up into the Toiling Midgets with ex-members of The Sleepers. [Craig's comment was he didn't remember any call, so perhaps it was Paul Hood that Bruce called.]

I first saw The Toiling Midgets on a Saturday when I walked up to Telegraph Avenue to check the record stores and do some writing at a coffee shop. I heard a band playing from the campus at the end of the street. It was a three-piece grinding out instrumentals in a mid-tempo Stooges-style. They had set up on Sproul Plaza and though a lot of students were milling around the campus walkways and the Telegraph Avenue sidewalks were jammed, just about no-one was checking them out. And the Midgets weren't checking the kids out either. They played with heads down and Craig and bassist Jonathan Henrickson even turned in toward the drummer, Tim Mooney. They were playing outdoors on a sunny day in the middle of UC Berkeley for themselves, as if practicing. That's as good a picture of the new rock underground's relationship to youth culture as represented by college students at an elite and allegedly hip California university. It took me a few tunes to guess that they had to be The Toiling Midgets, a new band I had heard about. Tim Yohannon came by and he confirmed that. In essence they were the final line-up of Negative Trend after Will and Steve had left for Flipper and been replaced; then Rik had returned to LA and they became The Toiling Midgets.

I talked to Craig a bit after they played, and saw them play elsewhere as they added members but I never got to work closely with them. However, Thermidor did release their second album, "Dead Beats," though that was worked out more by Jon Boshard, an MFA from UCB who started Thermidor with me. The first Midgets album, "Sea of Unrest," was to have been the first release by the US branch of Rough Trade, which had opened in Berkeley in 1980 in collaboration with Systematic. The Brit honchos vetoed it on the grounds that it was too damn good to bear the Rough Trade brand. It was then merely manufactured and distributed by RT under the label name, Instant. "Sea of Unrest" features Ricky Williams on vocals, but by the second album they were essentially an instrumental band (Ricky sings one new one and a cover of his own Sleepers tune "She's Fun" on the "Dead Beats" album). Ricky was in the Sleepers, Flipper, and The Toiling Midgets and few today know his name. He died years ago from the toll taken by chemicals on top of his own faulty body chemistry. His death was noted in *Rolling Stone*; his life hadn't been. The Toiling Midgets are still occasionally together and have recorded great stuff with Mark Eitzel (of American Music Club) on vocals.

But returning to the theme of this piece: the "Dead Beats" album closes with an instrumental called "Preludes." It may be called "Preludes" because "Black & Red" was likely the first tune Craig Gray wrote back in his Grand Mal/Negative Trend days, and "Preludes" though at first quiet and sketchy builds into that same damn riff, here opened up to a simpler, more abstractly resounding crescendo. It is Craig returning the song to his own band. It is unknown to me whether he called up Bruce to inform him the song had been repossessed.

Will died of an overdose and his death was noted in *Rolling Stone*; his life hadn't been. Flipper did an album for Rick Rubin (who had been in a NYC Flipper-rip band, Hose, whose 45 was Def Jam's first release). The "Generic" album got reissued with major label distribution through the deal; Steve Tupper considered he got hosed on the deal. The Toiling Midgets "Son" album was released by Gerard Cosloy's Matador label. The

Negative Trend EP was reissued by Subterranean as a 12" EP. A great 1978 9-song demo with Rozz on vocals was released as Rozz & Negative Trend by the old White Noize label, but I was told it really was a Rozz band rather than an alternate Negative Trend line-up. Meanwhile, The Sleepers discography was compiled for CD by Tim/Kerr Records. Not much conceded by the marketplace for music of such quality, but then, foolish youngsters that they were, they began their rock and roll ventures from the very point at which The Stooges' wheels fell off. "Deserve's got nothing to do with it."

Oh yeah, and in 1997 Sony/Columbia's Legacy CD re-issues of classics out of their vaults suddenly decided they were gonna re-mix "Raw Power" before putting it out. Iggy had declined to mess with it when Henry Rollins offered to set it up after his sound engineer found the album's multi-track sub-master tapes in Europe. But faced with Sony's decision he jumped into the project and it finally got the re-mix it deserved (Bass!), along with colorful but diplomatic Ig-speak liner notes on the convoluted story of the production of the record in 1972-3. The underground exhumed.

(originally posted at The New Vulgate, No. 5.)

Renaissance, Systematic, and Rough Trade

I saw the BBC doc about Rough Trade and when The New Vulgate's London *contributor Steve Beeho wrote up the accompanying book for us I thought I'd write a companion piece. It went up on Aug. 18, 2010 with Steve's piece plus articles by Ray Farrell, Joe Pope, and Johnny Myers.*

(Note: A new, smaller, Independent Distribution system for rock music was a necessity in the mid-seventies. In fact the reigning powers that were/are made us reinvent the rock label, the club circuit, and radio outlets, too. As a generation our bands weren't good enough to air, though The Ramones can now be heard all over MLB PA systems. And after we and others did the work we now have to hear it called by the diminutive "indie," used as a flavor of major label college rock. If that's what it means then everything below is a lie.)

Renaissance was an import-only record shop begun by three guys who'd worked at Music Millenium in Portland, Oregon, and thought they could do it better. They couldn't, partly because Millenium was everything to everyone, and according to Archie Patterson just this month, they still are driven to carry everything against all sense decades later. Archie was hired out of Fresno on the basis of his *Eurock* fanzine to run Millenium's import division which included a mail order service. The Renaissance guys had already left Millenium and their idea included continental releases such as now classic German psychedelic bands (Popol Vuh, Tangerine Dream, Harmonia, etc.), but by 1977 its bread and butter had devolved to their chagrin to supplying Brit or German or Japanese pressings of iconic audiophile recordings of stuff like Pink Floyd's "Dark Side of the Moon," or Michael Oldfield's "Ommadawn." Should there be any groove noise or even a single -pop- they'd bring the damn disc back the next day for a refund.

But the Renaissance guys liked reggae as well and stocked Brit and Jamaican pressings of great classic stuff. Those 12" 45s cut and pressed in Jamaica were so damn hot that you quickly learned to junk any audiophile tendencies you might have caught, because those records *popped* like a mofo. As it happened one of the three guys travelled to London sometime in 1976 or '77 and wandered into Rough Trade Records in their earliest days when nothing but reggae played over the shop turntable. At that early point most of the earliest punk had been on major labels and the independent label and self-released flood of singles in 1978 had not yet dragged the shop into service as the London nexis of the new.

By the time I wandered into Renaissance in late 1977 the shop was run primarily by Peter Handel. Peter was what NW folks recognize as a Reedie – a graduate of the semi-experimental Reed College. He was a stoner and really into the Stones and reggae, and also Patti Smith. He's the one who began ordering the import 45s that Jem Records was offering (Sex Pistols, Clash, Jam, X-Ray Spex, Buzzcocks, etc.). I liked Peter and began to run the shop for three hours in the afternoon and close it up for him; I'd get one album or three 45s for pay. I have pretty cools records from that time. Peter was interested in checking out this reggae shop in London his ex-partner had told him about so he went over in early 1978. Everything was changing fast in London and he was inspired by what Geoff Travis, Richard Scott, and the others had going on; it was hip and righteous and though increasingly involved in the kind of punk rock Peter didn't particularly care for, he could tell it was culture going somewhere.

If I remember he mostly bought reggae for himself that time but he thought we should start up a mail order service along the lines that RT had going so we ran ads in *Rolling Stone* and *Creem* and *Slash* magazines and began to collect a customer list. I had stumbled onto the Dangerhouse catalogue at Longhair Music where Jennifer LoBianco worked. I'd already seen her play with Formica & the Bitches at what may have been the first punk gig in Portland. Jennifer told me she got them direct so I bought them direct too. She later worked for us at Renaissance and her new band, The Neo-Boys, practiced in the shop.

I don't think Peter thought that the various small American labels would ever add up to anything; the country is so large that it took years for anything to develop – years that often meant the bands that initiated events here or there were long gone by the time any results were seen. But in London Peter could see it work in a concentrated, one-city national form and he began to think about distribution as well. By early 1978 I was doing the first punk radio show on *KBOO*, playing the latest Brit punk and American releases and locally, The Wipers joined The Neo-Boys as world class musicmakers. Also Portland saw west coast bands like The Screamers, The Zeros, The Dils, The Weirdos, Crime, Pink Section, and others.

We distributed the Dead Kennedys 45 so they asked us for a gig and we set up two shows at the Long Goodbye (The Fix opened). Jello was enthusiastic about our vague idea to move to the Bay Area to set up shop next to a planned Rough Trade US. RT had been selling to individual American record shops and having trouble getting paid and filling orders.

They sold to Drome, Wax Trax, Yesterday & Today, Time Travellers, and most of the important shops around the country. Most were collector shops that nevertheless had respect for these new small label releases that could be hard to track down. The first 45s had come out of Ohio, New York, and others places by bands with sounds all over the map like Television, Patti Smith, Pere Ubu, Residents, Chrome, Devo, The Last, Half-Japanese, Negative Trend, The Zippers, The Dils, The Urinals, etc. Peter worked with Geoff and Richard on the phone and I was writing for American samples and buying those for distribution/mail order and the shop. Over the counter sales in Portland didn't amount to much but the mail order and distribution was beginning to happen.

Peter convinced Rough Trade to just refer American shops to us and we'd work our better price to a low mark-up and do domestic promotion for their own in-house label releases. So we took their promo list and combined it with what the DKs worked from and whatever anybody else had and sent out the radio and press copies beginning in 1979. Peter returned to RT in London to talk about the move to the bay area and laying the groundwork for splitting our American record shop accounts with them once we all got set up. This meant we did about a year long run to increase our accounts by combing the out-of-state yellow pages at the Multnomah Library and blindly mailing our wholesale catalogues to just about any shop that looked hip or more often, just a used or collector shop. We made plans to start a label while in Portland but it was complicated to deal with the local bands and they didn't seem to understand what we were building. Peter and I both sported beards which no punk would countenance until Peter Saville shots of Joy Division with facial hair cropped up years later. I wasn't about to shave to the gods of punk.

In London a second time Peter sat in with Geoff and Mayo Thompson for the cutting of lacquers for Cabaret Voltaire's "Mix-Up" album and he told me was so bowled over by the sound he was sure it would be a massive hit – I think they were all high. He also found out that Rough Trade would be doing Pere Ubu records so we booked them for Portland just to get a look at them. Hardly anyone came and it cost the business about $1500, but Peter didn't flinch; they were great (The Ziplocs opened). I flew to London so I knew what they were doing and they knew who did the catalogues. I stayed with Richard and liked him fine and still owe him five bob which I needed to get to Heathrow. I'd also gone to Paris to visit SCOPA (P.P.U., Illitch...) and to Sweden to visit SAM Distribution (saw Ebba Grön too). While in London I managed to meet most of the RT crew including Allan who was about to meet us in Cali, plus Steve Solamar of Object Music, the Better Badges guy, and not too many others though I did get to see Geoff see off the Fall as they went to NYC for the first time. I missed the days of the doorless Rough Trade john that had so impressed Peter. But I saw a couple good shows, one at Oxford where D.A.F., still then a four piece, really impressed me. I talked to the one American at RT, the late Scott Piering, who did promotions and he concurred that the building RT catalog might use a bit more rock as it seemed suddenly rarer in 1979. Mostly I spent days walking around London while I had the chance - big town.

We packed up a rental truck and moved to Pinole, California the day after Christmas, 1979. Peter, his girlfriend, and I. We got a space on Heinz Ave in Berkeley, just down from the Berkeley Barb offices. We got going as fast as we could set up with the new name, Systematic, and we immediately reissued the first Dead Kennedys and Pink Section 45s on our new label, Optional Music. I got an apartment in walking-distance of the office, up near the Ashby BART station, and Rough Trade's first "agents" in town were Vale, of *Search and Destroy* magazine, and a guy named Craig, a manic man about town who was about a perfect opposite of Vale. They'd been getting sixes of each Rough Trade release so we knew that RT counted on them to be hitting the bay area media, mostly the excellent college radio stations

(*KUSF*, *KALX*, *KFJC*), Greil Marcus, and probably a commercial station, plus that hunk of deadwood at the *SF Chronicle* Joel Selvin. I think Herb Caen may have gotten records too in the run-up. Soon Allan Sturdy flew in and he, Vale, Craig, Peter and I began to gather at Peter's, or the Systematic office, or at Allan's house in Orinda. Allan was a great guy, a tall, thin, red-haired stoner with a Jamaican accent and great little quirks like for example being unable to pronounce "San Francisco."

Peter aced me out of half ownership of a company with negative value and since I knew it was a mistake to move to SF rather than LA, I stayed out of Peter's relationship with RT mostly, though I saw Richard, and Sue Johnson and Pete Walmsley on their various stateside stretches. Walmsley's name was on King Crimson's "Larks Tongues" and "Red" album covers so he was like reg'lar Limey royalty to me. Richard studied baseball when he could, and Sue broke up Peter's relationship with Lynne. Peter caught the collective-meeting disease from Rough Trade which wasn't exactly relevant in a two-man office. One day he said we should have regular meetings, and I said, "Well I'm right here, what do you want?"

SF saw a few more good gigs because RT was there but the mother label became more purely English in some way that prevented it truly participating in the American music underground then being built up one kid at a time by Black Flag, SST, Systematic, Dutch East, *Flipside*, *Forced Exposure*, Alternative Tentacles, *Touch & Go*, and others. Souled American was the great exception to this rule at RT later in the 80s when interest finally swung to American bands in Europe. I mostly built up Systematic's reputation as the place for American independent releases, in particular the heavier

L.A. and D.C. stuff, which was fortuitous as Peter had let our bill with Rough Trade grow to a size which got us put on hold. As the Optional Music label wound down, I started Thermidor hoping to do the Monitor album and other stuff I couldn't get Peter interested in. Thermidor was

myself and Jon Boshard and a sometime-third, Johnny Myers, who'd put us together in between trying to manage Flipper. Jon and Johnny each had radio shows at *KALX* too. Thereafter I explored the limitations of the bay area which were thankfully many and I left for LA and SST before the end of 1981.

At SST I was finally at the center of what was happening in this very large country, which even then under the latter years of the major labels' dominating platinum ethos, had no apparent center. I was also as close to the artistic process of bands as any non-musician can be. When Joe Pope took over Systematic I made an effort to convince him to move it to LA so SST could have a simpatico distributor within reach – the better for tour promotion and advertising coordination, etc. Might've worked but that Colorado boy loves San Francisco.

Vale describes the beginning at his *ReSearch* blog,

> "I had been the first American hired to help launch Rough Trade USA (Rough Trade, a U.K. store and record label, had been stocking my punk tabloid *Search & Destroy* since its very beginning in June, 1977). I had rented a storefront in North Beach on Grant at Green Streets, a block from where I lived, and had set up the retail and wholesale operation, with help from Allan Sturdy (a white Rastifarian; and 'Peter and Sue,' seemingly always hunched over canary-yellow bookkeeping sheets, presided over by the tall, rail-thin founder, Geoff Travis)." *(Vale)*

Aquarius Records was the long-time hip shop in SF, and then Tower Records was damn good in SF and Berkeley too. The buyers at Tower Berkeley were very loyal to Syst; Georgette went on to work for RT US and then RT London if I remember correctly, and her successor Joe Pope (of the band Angst) eventually left to work for us. Peter ultimately gave Systematic to Pope for the assumption of what sadly turned out to be the insurmountable debt run up to RT UK.

In bay area retail terms, RT was trading on its underground cachet but that only went so far, though its exclusive with Factory Records with its simpler lux-gothish come-on could go quite far with impressionable Americans.

I was too busy on the phone or filling boxes for UPS to hang much at RT so allow me to cede the floor to Johnny Myers, friend of yore and rumored third leg of the Thermidor triumvirate. Johnny was the best on-mic college radio DJ ever and his *KALX* interviews with Black Flag and Flipper are legendary and were instrumental in the University Administration deciding finally that only registered students could have programs. [You'll have to look up Johnny's spiel; lengthy edits are still up at NV and the whole thing is up at his *Mog* page.]

(*originally posted at* The New Vulgate, *No. 59*)

Drink the Repulse Kava

I forget what brought this piece on, but it might have been that after revisiting what I witnessed in L.A., S.F., and Portland, I wanted to revisit the other city whose scene I had experience with. Also, Repulse Kava spun apart just before the art rock scene in the city gained notice and they seem unjustly forgotten. Posted at NV March 11, 2010.

Bill De Leonardis met John Seden in a hallway at the School of the Art Institute of Chicago in July 1986. John was wearing a Sonic Youth T-shirt and they discovered they were both into punk, hardcore, and free-jazz. Bill says, "Although my move to Chicago was to attend art school, my decision to go to SAIC was predicated on the music coming out of Chicago and the region." The "distinct arty edge" of bands like Naked Raygun, Big Black, Articles of Faith, and the Tar Babies was unlike the bands he knew on the east coast. "Although I had been in some straight up hardcore groups, I wanted to be in a group that was like The Minutemen meet the Bad Brains and filtered through King Crimson." The original RK duo was pretty abstract but they built a somewhat more conventional lineup from fellow SAIC students:

> Bill De Leonardis – bass
> John Seden – vocals, noise
> John K – guitar
> Chris Levack – metal, noise
> Kerry Brown – drums

They lasted a few months and several performances this way before the other three quit to focus on school. De Leonardis and Seden, rather, quit school to focus on the band full-time and find similarly committed bandmates.

Ads in *The Reader* and *New City* listed as influences The Minutemen, King Crimson, Void, The Stranglers, Led Zeppelin, and Bad Brains. Craig White responded. He'd just quit the hardcore band No Empathy. Craig was a black kid from the southside who, when I asked him what he grew up listening to, mentioned being into his older brother's Guru Guru albums! I worried about Craig cause he seemed to live on jelly donuts.

They played a bit with drummer Brian St. Claire but he was soon replaced by Andy Young. Soon in 1987 the new line-up was playing hardcore shows and opening for White Zombie, Flaming Lips, and Friends of Betty. Peter Margasak saw them and interviewed them for his fanzine, *Butt Rag*. Peter asked them to do a single and they recorded three songs – "Coercion", "Sabotage Time", and "Value of His Own Simplicity."

Bill picks up the story: "Upon release, the e.p. was chosen as *CMJ*'s record of the week. From that point, people started to buzz about us, including Gerard Cosloy. I think the e.p. had been out about a month when Andy told us unexpectedly that he was leaving the group. We would later find out that he had joined the cult Jesus People USA. As we had a show coming up and wanted to continue to forward momentum, we asked my friend Virus X, who had previously been the drummer of Articles Of Faith. Virus obliged to help us until we found another drummer but did not want to commit to us as he was predominately involved with the Revolutionary Communist Party. After an ad was placed, we brought on board Craig Hall. Craig played a few shows but his style was ultimately incompatible with our sound. He left amicably and joined the group God's Acre, who Repulse Kava played with many times."

Another set of ads brought them drummer Bob Rising. Although Bob was more rock oriented then the rest of the band Bill says, "I think he was intrigued by a band that loved hardcore and art rock and had multiple part to their songs... his considerable skill brought the group back into focus." They did a second record for Butt Rag but made it just two songs ("The Daddy's Crowbar" and "Judging") as they were beginning to husband tunes they hoped would make an album that some bigger label such as SST, Touch and Go, or Homestead might be interested in.

Bill again: "'The Daddy's Crowbar / Judging' 45 came out in '88 and was reviewed by Byron Coley in *Spin* and received a good amount of press. We played some shows on the east coast. We believed that it was a matter of time before we were signed... Of course, nothing happened. I really don't remember what happened but John quit – I think it was just personality conflicts and disappointment. Craig, Bob and I wanted to continue so we reinvented ourselves as an instrumental trio."

I first saw Repulse Kava on Feb. 17, 1989 at the Cubby Bear. I'd moved back to Chicago in late summer 1986 and bought a four flat near North and Ashland and spent most of 1987 rehabbing it. Then I began to go out and see some bands again and I resumed work on my book, *Rock and the Pop Narcotic*. RK were opening for Eleventh Dream Day and Doug McCombs introduced me to Bill before they went on and he was excited to talk about SST, The Minutemen, and what I was doing in Chicago. We talked standing outside the entrance to the club overlooking Wrigley Field.

Life Against Dementia

I remember he told me how he'd had his hardcore mind blown in 1984 at a Black Flag gig by their support band Saccharine Trust when singer Jack Brewer knocked himself unconscious with a liquor bottle and the band kept playing around him until he came to and resumed singing. Repulse Kava's set was great. Craig, Bill and Bob were the best, hardest art-rock trio since Robert Fripp kicked Jamie Muir out of King Crimson. Craig's fingers reminded me of Hendrix's; they were so long and nimble it made what he was doing look really easy but your ears could tell how sure his effect on the frets was. And Bob's drumming was great as well. He didn't just rock the groove, he also had all these trip-ups and syncopations to set the song up within a rhythm arrangement. Bill too is a natural whether he's on a fuzzed out bass or a guitar. I remember that John Seden was there too and went up and reprised his vocals and turntable noise on the singles that they felt people might be familiar with.

CRAIG WHITE, BILL DE LEONARDIS OF REPULSE KAVA, CIRCA 1989.

While on the west coast from 1976 until 1986 I kept an ear out for what was going on in Chicago and had largely been disappointed. Even the important bands (Mentally Ill, Special Affect, Ono, Naked Raygun, Effigies...) didn't seem to work it. The whole town seemed to accept that only the clubs on North Clark were important. It sure wasn't like Los Angeles. Chicago bands would turn down gigs in the suburbs, Black Flag would play anywhere. But by the late eighties it seemed that the Wicker Park area was opening up as a second club area, more hospitable to new bands doing different things. I first noticed that Chicago had more good music going on than had been apparent while listening to WNUR in 1987 as I worked on my building. I found the two-hour Saturday show of local music that the station's music director Octavia did was better than the rest of their programming, and it was a great station. What may have really turned Chicago into a rock scene again was how cheap it was to live there in those years. It collected a generation of hip kids leaving Minneapolis, Ohio, Texas, and elsewhere who were attracted to how easily you could live and get by in the city. When I bought my building the rents for the two bedroom apartments were $200/mo. Once I fixed them up a bit I gounged $325 for them!

Tim Adams of the Ajax mail order catalog-cum-fanzine had launched a label and Repulse Kava recorded their album, "Flow Gently Sweet Alpha," for him. I worked on it with them and watching Craig, Bill and Bob work out their arrangements in the basement of Bill's apt building near Damen and Division was like watching skilled woodworkers putting together very sturdy, artistic and functional three-leg stools. Bill now considers that the album was a bit too rock even with the musique concrète interludes that were added from other sessions. The mixes sounded sharp and heavy, but we were the first band through a brand new studio and the test pressings came back disappointingly flat. If I was thinking quicker we'd have just sent the cassette mixes to John Golden to cut. Instead we did a quick re-e.q. and let it go. Still, the Repulse Kava album is a major Chicago landmark from that period. I don't think they played another gig even though it got released in Europe as well.

Joe Baiza's post-Saccharine Trust band, Universal Congress of, came out to Chicago three times in the late eighties and they stayed with me and must've told Jack Brewer they'd had a good time because he came out when I suggested he could do some recording and a gig with Bill De Leonardis and another new line-up, now called just Kava. Bill says, "I was very happy with what we did with the shortened Kava. I only wish that we had released more of the stuff we had done with Jack." Those sessions were also a lot of fun. John was back with Bill and a new drummer Peter Kessell. They did a kind of improv free-rock with Peter skittering around skillfully on his drums more like a bop drummer than Bob's stark rock effect. I remember Jack was really thrilled with their abilities and how easily

BILL DE LEONARDIS, JACK BREWER; CHICAGO, AUGUST 1992.

they could put together interesting pieces for him to speechify over. After years spent waiting for Joe Baiza's exacting demands to produce SaccTrust arrangements, Jack loved the racing productivity of Kava. He was also amazed that he could have a beer with his hot dog at Duk's; I explained to him that it was partly a German thing, and partly that it was owned by a cop. I put out a 7" e.p. of the Brewer-Kava stuff but we never did get the album out. The idea was to edit in some of the recordings made at an improvised Lounge Ax gig too (Aug. 13, 1992), to insure the album was truly insane. I think I remember them playing live on-air at WNUR too. But suddenly, there was no band, and then not even a record business.

    Bill was working at Facets and we started a videotape company called Provisional with Dave Lightbourne and released a number of films and videos and produced a couple small features. Bob and Craig have parts in *"Rock & Roll Punk"* and the two of them played in the band Seam for awhile. Bill moved down to Knoxville, plays music, and occasionally has to listen to me tell him that Repulse Kava shoulda hung around another couple years.

(originally posted at *The New Vulgate*, No. 36)

Cheese – How Much Will Money Buy?
This came up when I was driving back from Illinois and began to pick up Cheyenne's hard rock station. They were playing my favorite Filter tune and it got me thinking about the top of the garbage heap. This was posted at The New Vulgate *Aug. 17, 2011.*

The old SST parlance was based on surf-lingo when it wasn't coined by Spot, Mugger, Medea, Pettibon, Black Flag, the Descendents, or the Minutemen themselves. This randy Cali patter never had more impact than on the early Black Flag tours north or east out of Los Angeles to serious socio-agitprop punk precincts. In town it was simple raw beach and harbor jive, though the SST/Church bohemes loved wordplay, hippie jargon, and subversive crudities. "Cheese" in the lexicon referred to a kind of false rock. We used it mostly in relation to metal, as in cheese-metal, in particular the lighter show-metal style that came in with Van Halen. Greg was struck by their monotonous single beat, used in every song. I didn't hate every Van Halen song but did describe Eddie's guitar solos as "frictionless whiffery." It was also clear by 1982 that what had been interesting punk-related rock and roll (a.k.a., new wave) was quickly devolving into similarly processed, industry-friendly shuck and jive. You could once stand to listen to Elvis Costello or the B-52s, but no more. But the thing about what came to be called hair metal is that it could never fully ditch the guitar or the general rock and roll band template, no matter how much abuse the form might take from Industry-hands like managers, A&R men, producers, engineers, session musicians....

In 1981 *KROQ* was still playing a lot of tunes off of Los Angeles punk records. When the "Damaged" album came out they were playing "Rise Above," "TV Party," "Six Pack," "Thirsty and Miserable," "Police Story," and "Gimmie Gimmie Gimmie." The station also played deeply into albums by X, the Adolescents, the Circle Jerks and others. But come 1982 *KROQ* tightened up around the rock-is-dead Brit-pop that followed Malcolm McLaren rather than the Sex Pistols themselves. These synth-based New Romantic groups at most used guitars to create washes and textures that could done to by engineers in a way that expressive playing could never be treated. Such sounds sit still and bear more echo, eq'ing, and chorus; indeed many of these effects were often piled onto single note themes a la Flock of Seagulls "I Ran." By mid-1982 we no longer listened to *KROQ* at SST. If rock stations were on it was usually *KMET* or *KLOS*, so we had a working knowledge of the beginnings of hair metal.

In October 1981 while the Meat Puppets first album was being worked on at Unicorn's studio, Daphna brought in an advance pressing of the unreleased Mötley Crüe debut. Chuck and Greg and Laurie O'Connell (of Monitor, then managing The Meat Puppets and working at Unicorn) remembered Nikki Sixx's earlier band, London, which had been a late Hollywood glam failure so they were interested even though the new band was barely known. We listened to it a several times over the studio monitors and talked about whether or not it was a piece of shit and/or whether Unicorn should release it. Who knows what Daphna was really doing but Mötley Crüe's management was looking for a major label deal and couldn't find one. The impending "Damaged" release had made Unicorn a logical plan B, especially since her other signings were commercially intended AOR or CHR pop (Joe Chemay, J.D. Drews, Frankie Blue) and Daphna was burning through her cash forcing them to chart.

I only liked the last tune, "Piece of Your Action," which had a lower-pitched, less hysterical groove that the band managed to more-or-less pull off. The album came out in November on a self-released label through Greenworld (the Torrance distributor was just beginning to reorient itself toward releasing records as Enigma). The release made a splash around town and Elektra picked it up a few months later. The other big kick that ignited the Sunset Strip metal scene was Ozzy Osbourne's solo career. His band (originally called Blizzard of Oz) featured L.A. players and when the first record got big airplay and the tour happened, the aimless session-musician post-arena-rock scene on the west-side went Metal.

Arena rock (1969-1974+) dried up after the AOR formatting of underground FM meant that playing together as a band was no longer the currency. This was suddenly true whether you were Humble Pie or Gentle Giant. Kiss was probably the first band that really couldn't play and made it anyway on studio precision and live spectacle. Lesser bands of that era such as Grand Funk Railroad, and Black Oak Arkansas still had good players in them (B.O.A.'s drummer Tommy Aldridge became Ozzy's drummer) but they tended to be underdeveloped as song-writers as well as undisciplined players in line with the indulgent, looser musical culture of the album era, and the fact that the arena had became a kind of free-fire-up zone for pot-smoking in a way that bars never could, plus kids could attend. In other words, a less critical audience.

Lee Abrams' spreading AOR programming service replaced hundreds of individual locally-based programmers and drove expressive, played music from the airwaves with his constricted "Superstars" format and fostered studio-based cheese-rock. There were still kids knocking themselves out trying to master chops off their Yes or Zappa albums, but the music culture began to be shaped more by what got played on the radio, and the major labels followed suit by narrowing what they signed, and then leaning heavily on recording studio technicians to process the songs for AOR programming. A band like Pink Floyd comes close to telling the story technically as they went from recording inspired psychedelic pop on four-track machines to producing turgid bone simple *musique concrète* to audiophile specifications on 24 track machines. They managed to get included in the AOR format on concept album pretense, rather than "progressive" playing. Lee Abrams seemed to think his mix needed some Art and "Dark Side of the Moon" was it. (Abrams actually appears on Alan Parsons Project albums – Parsons engineered "Dark Side"). Most of the AOR playlist constituted rock bands from the arena world that could saw off their edges: Alice Cooper could, Mountain could not.

Punk came along at this point and was a perfectly organic, logical development as surprising as many of the bands were. It was a classical, roots retrenchment coming at the end of the baroque prog era. But even the less radical, overtly retro-styled punk era bands like Blondie, DMZ, The Last, The Pop, etc., couldn't sneak past the Programmer – maybe they should have hired him as "manager" which he did on the side. The first Cheap Trick album was a beautifully rendered hard rock pop album produced by Jack Douglas who'd done the early Aerosmith albums, and they were stone-walled as well – they came back with a Tom Werman-produced marshmallow that still barely got any play, just the song, "I Want You to Want Me," a much bigger hit now than then (such backwards phenoms are common and another gift of the radio blockade testing word-of-mouth's viability).

The south bay SST bands had mostly grown up at arena gigs in LA and Long Beach and so when I came down from Systematic to run the office I found an interest in hard rock on the part of Greg, Chuck, Mugger, Dez and Bill that I hadn't found in the San Francisco punk world. We went up to SF once and before the gig went up to *KALX* above UC-Berkeley campus to do Johnny Myers show and it turned into a cheese-rock bacchanal as we thought of the worst bands and threw their LPs on and pulled them off (the station had them all, even Saga!). Spot did his Jello Biafra impersonation and announced that The Dead Kennedys were going metal prompting hate calls from faithful *Maximum Rock'n'Roll* readers. Mike Watt, D. Boon, Jack Brewer and Joe Baiza knew the stuff but had somewhat expunged it from their sensibilities, whereas The Meat Puppets and of course The Stains, Overkill, and Saint Vitus were all arena-grounded as well. Simon Reynolds tagged SST "progressive punk" in his book, *Rip It Up And Start Again*, a Brit-orientated understanding of how such playing could still be going on within punk which was supposed to have killed off rock and roll.

The Brit-punk analog to Pink Floyd was Joy Division. They lost their singer to suicide rather than acid, and they changed the name of the band to New Order, but they similarly emptied out what in their case had been a rather stately, Stooges-derived rock. In New Order they stopped what playing they'd been capable of, leaving sequencers and samplers and syn-drums to be hung onto a bass melody. Even the singing was emptied out by Bernard Sumner who had been the guitar player and now as often played synthesizers. New Order also switched to a funk-style rhythm, though funk had rarely sounded whiter. This was certainly cheese on white bread, though hardly appetizing to anyone looking for rock and roll.

The Industry did without rock and roll, but after Mötley Crüe's and Ozzy's successes what came to be called hair-metal was accepted by radio and the new *MTV* (Lee Abrams a consultant here too!), and so more such bands were signed by the majors. The best of this stuff may not even be cheese: Guns n' Roses, the Sea Hags, Dirty Looks, and a few others. Def Leppard's success was another influence. They'd brought producer Mutt Lange into the song-writing process by "Pyromania" so that their *musique concrète* had a more efficient pop and rock delivery than Pink Floyd, but sounding just as embalmed if not cryogenically frozen. Sweat? Stink? Funk? No thang kyew! Lange took songwriting credits, but songs are rearranged, rewritten, and otherwise done-to by producers, A&R, and various other staffers at the majors, and something similar happened even on independents. This kind of interference can improve a band's lax arrangements but they improve them the same damn way every time. As non-artists, technicians have at best an literal memory of pop and rock hits with an outside-in understanding of the writing and arranging of songs. So their contributions are insultingly Pavlovian rather than uniquely Freudian, and based on proven past precedent and thereby only serve to close the circle on the art.

But in the cheese section, there are the finer cheeses, and these all the way down to the utter pop-intended Velveeta are good enough to interest the American audience, even as that audience is further and further subdivided into small closed-circles of interest for the benefit of marketers. Before local stations forfeited programming decisions to Burkhardt-Abrams a Gillian Welch might have had an impact in Top 40 radio. Instead she's circling *NPR*'s closed-circle, not even Nashville's. Abrams aside, the late seventies audience for music were being asked to accept the Ramones, Television, X, etc., in their preferred mix of Pat Benatar, Gary Wright, Gerry Rafferty, Van Halen, etc.

AC/DC was a last major music breakthrough for the old arena circuit at the end of the seventies; they opened for Kiss so how could they miss. They possessed much of the old Brit-blues rock bravado that many of the better cheese bands displayed less fulsomely with less grounding. Of that cheese the following are notable:

Billy Squier – "In the Dark"
By 1980 there'd been many botched attempts to new wave-up hairy hard rock but this is one that worked. Hell, now you hear Kraftwerkisms in Nashville hits, but I like how the song's 1981 video cuts to the wavester with his goofy haircut in those parts. This was probably an early MTV clip, something for everyone, even a little something for Lee I reckon. Squier was in a failure called Piper and seemed to move his concept toward the Raspberries, only his rock-tease fanfare has real impact – the wavester isn't on camera in those moments. In retrospect I can remember signs that Greg Ginn was losing interest in what it took to be in a band. He thought one might do non-cheese solo music, and got interested in what Ronnie Montrose was doing with machines. Once I walked into Total Access when Greg, Henry, Kira, and Bill were dug in working with Dave Tarling on songs that became the last two Black Flag albums. Along the floor were about a dozen rolls of two-inch recording tape. Half of them were marked "Loose Nut," and the rest were titled, "The Squier Sessions." Apparently for a second or two Greg intended "In My Head" to be his first solo album and he even did some vocal tracking. Hard to picture that, but there's your Billy Squier influence on Black Flag.

Dokken – "The Hunter"
Dokken recorded at Total Access and I generally liked their style of songwriting and playing. The tunes were slower and lower-pitched, and George Lynch was one of the better guitarists in that cheese-whiz style, though in his later Lynch Mob band, a nice slice of cheese like "Dream Until Tomorrow" suffers with no Don Dokken on the mic. I think they hate each other.

W.A.S.P. – "I Wanna Be Somebody"
There was interest in W.A.S.P. around SST because Blackie Lawless had been a rock fixture in Hermosa-Redondo record stores and clubs – the Fleetwood if not the Church itself – and Dave Tarling of Media Art/Total Access who engineered the first Panic-Black Flag sessions had shepherded W.A.S.P. through demos, showcase, and signing. We saw their showcase at the Troubadour and it was the first gig I had my tape recorder taken away from me, thus no animal blood smeared my Aiwa; this was the real record business, and sure enough Tarling was supplanted as manager and

producer upon the band's signing to Capitol.

Sword – "Stoned Again"
This I first heard on *Z-Rock* in Chicago; it was hard rock ABC satellite programming from Texas programmed by (*wait for it...*) Lee Abrams who was attempting to squeeze money from the metal underground since Metallica had refused to go away even without AOR play or music video play. Sword were Canadian and don't know what happened to them, but in a moment of clarity they sure got this riff identified.

Kix – "Cold Blood"
This band never made an impact on me until after reading Chuck Eddy rave about them I re-checked the *MTV* slog-pile tapes I used to make. That man knows his cheeses! They play good within the parameters set by music-loathing radio industry players, and they released many albums of rockin' mouse-bait.

Winger – "Seventeen"
There is a live *MTV* clip that got my attention back then. They are obviously great players – the drummer, Rod Morgenstein, had been in the instro-prog Dixie Dregs – and here they are beating up on their own defenseless pop song, even though the average *MTV* viewer might have preferred a lip-synced version. The dancers are directly in front of the band which plays from a short stage on this New Year's TV party set and the band is responding to the best dancer, and it is carnal beyond its leering lyric.

*

Because heavy metal, or now merely Metal, as a culture is so unconcerned with getting respect, hair metal or pop metal was able to thrive while a metal underground was rebuilt from the ground up by Motörhead, Pentagram, Saint Vitus and others. It was Metallica that broke through for this underground and though bands graduated to major labels the style didn't threaten the hair metal style on radio or *MTV*. Rather it did (along with Brit post-punk pop) stop the surfacing of the punk underground which had two years on KROQ in LA, but never surfaced elsewhere around the country at all. Metallica gave up on LA to move to San Francisco, which says a lot about what was called speed-metal's isolation from commercial metal. The move didn't hurt Metallica, whereas kicking out their only songwriter, Dave Mustaine, did leave them stringing together fret patterns and drum arrangements in lieu of songwriting and getting by on generic athleticism, attitude, and branding. While Mustaine in Megadeth wrote many great and distinctive tunes with the interlocking melodic logic of Bach sustained somehow through a chaotic alcohol-fueled run of line-up changes, Metallica had to struggle to keep their lead-guitarist's cheese impulses in check while learning song-craft from producer Bob Rock. Not going to happen, but at least they took less time to fail.

By the late 1980s the parallel record industry that a number of us created for our era's rock and roll began delivering significant sales numbers despite the radio blockade still in effect. American major labels had by then been bought by Japanese companies, Sony and Panasonic, and the German company, Bertelsmann, and to the record industry's eternal shame this is what it took for them to begin signing rock bands again, out of the nominal punk underground then being repainted "indie" no matter what size label it was on. This led mostly to new flavors of cheese, as if you needed to be told. (Hello Soul Asylum! R.E.M., come on down! Goo Goo Dolls, *chupame la verga!*) One wouldn't call the retro-styled Smithereens cheese, and the limit placed on their radio play is probably proof of that. Rage Against the Machine may not be pure cheese, but they did have cheese-flavored guitar. Tom Morello can't even play a straight up cheese-whiz solo so he squeezes out foot pedal sound effects, uniquely lame and perhaps the cheesiest as the kids eat it up.

Nirvana was the hinge of history for punk rock or whatever new wave/indie diminutive they were using back then when their second album went platinum, produced not by Jack Endino, but by Butch Vig of the budget Wisconsin cheese variety-pack: Spooner, Fire Town, and Garbage. Nirvana went on to Steve Albini for the last album, but Kurt Cobain's suicide obscured a true assessment of his talent. He was a fine singer and writer-arranger but he was not much of a guitar player and not getting any better. Once a platinum-selling, yea, an arena-rock god, Kurt might have continued writing many albums of tour-spiel just as many of the first wave of arena rockers had. Kurt no longer lived in the real world of his audience though it was his self-imposed punk burden that he had to pretend he did. His anti-metal etiquette seemed to imply that his indie movement was sturdier musically than it proved. And I guess Courtney Love prevented him from experiencing and writing his own "Hey Lawdy Mamas," and "Mississippi Queens." Bummer, because Dave Grohl sure ain't writing them.

Before you knew it there was Classic Rock in two flavors. Punk form shorn of edges moved on through the better bands like Green Day and Fall-Out Boy, but you might guess, the rest were *fromage*:

Puddle of Mudd – "Drift and Die"
These guys were on Limp Bizkit's Flawless label thru Geffen so one won-

ders where all the gold and platinum went. I think the current band isn't the same except for dude – the Industry had no use for those other guys. Dude plus hirelings recorded a fairly successful record with Bill Stevenson at the Blasting Room, but radio and *Fuse* video play no longer sells plastic. After I heard and liked their new single "Psycho" I asked Bill about it and he said, "You remember how we used to make fun of how much money they wasted at major labels? We had no idea!" There'd been so much re-tracking and re-mixing and mastering between Fort Collins, L.A., and back in Colo, that Bill and crew couldn't even be sure they'd done any particular final mix. This earlier tune, though, was the third single off their breakthrough album and though it has a nice, solid breakdown they use a keyboard wash in place of a guitar solo. It's not really the lyric but the video that seems to comment on how a garage band from Missouri is spun to cheese.

Filter – "Where Do We Go From Here"
Totally a B-grade band, but you know in movies B's are usually more interesting than the A's at least since sound came in. Not quite so true in music, but this one is quite nice. They probably had a chord progression and lyric, and the producer set their chromatic effect into an arrangement that amplifies the ideas, such as they are, into a fine pressed cheese curd.

Ashes Divide – "The Stone"
This is like one of those 1970s solo projects by some dude in a band you've heard of but don't know the individual players' names. Free bassist Andy Fraser wasn't exactly Paul McCartney but he got a solo album out of "All Right Now" and this dude has some networking connection to Tool at a remove of several option agreements. Some guys only look insane while they can efficiently parlay the weakest link into a one-off that goes places, or at least to WalMart. I pointed this tune out to Lightbourne when it came on the radio in the car once and he said, "I have no idea where this comes from." I told him Pink Floyd and goth. Dave didn't use the term "cheese" but he believed such music was the product of people who were scrubbed of any and all folk culture traces.

Good Charlotte – "I Don't Wanna Be In Love"
At this far end of punk there are no longer traces of The Stooges or The Ramones or even Black Flag. Musicians influenced by those bands tend to play a kind of abstract folk-oriented psychedelia – generally they don't step into the rock band heavyweight ring. The old kind of punk expression was denatured by Nirvana, *et. al.*, yielding the processed cheese we now all know but rarely love. (Curiously, Cobain was obsessed with the metallers

who'd show up at his band's arena gigs but Nirvana's biggest fallout has been to provide a new template for Christian rock.) This tune of GC's, though, uses late hair metal strategies in the way of bringing distorted keyboards up underneath the guitars for more easily simulated rock-like texture. Still, I always turn the volume up in the car when this one comes on, so you know, maybe I um, kind of love it. I just wish it was the worst rock-like substance on pop radio instead of the best.

*

Today in Hollywood, session-musicians all look like scum-of-the-earth with tatts, piercings, interesting facial hair..., but they live like businessmen, hit their marks and don't actually smell like bikers. They are well-scrubbed, so to speak. I imagine players no longer arrive in Los Angeles with a band, but leave their high school or college bands behind and arrive solo. As those were likely highly derivative if not actually cover bands of one metalesque or punkesque closed-circle or another, they arrive in West Hollywood, start making the scene and look to combine and recombine in as many projects as it might take, claiming to like everything and as its all the same, why not? Nobody knows who might make it and need a bassist or second guitarist. They may hope it isn't Evanecsence but hey a gig's a gig. They duly attend classes at Hollywood's Guitar Institute of Technology (I asked Spot once whether some player was any good and I thought he was joking when he answered, "He's one of those Guitar Institute of Technology guys.")

The technological revolution now sends any acoustic phenomena through processing via multiple digital filters for the benefit of engineers. This limits quality playing so that poor playing can pass for adequate. It's no longer easy to identify a weak-ass rhythmic base. The full use of digitally programmed percussion allowed them all to sound as good as any cheese band, because basically we're all listening to the work of the same dozen or so engineers whatever the band's name and whether they've sold their souls to Satan or pledged them to the Lord. And this has led even to actual non-cheese Christian rock, for God's sake, my favorite being Flyleaf. Of course strictly speaking, Saint Vitus are a Christian band, but I worked on most of those and Lee Abrams never heard them.

(*original version posted at* The New Vulgate, *No. 111*)

Peanuts... Jellybeans... MET-Rx Protein Bars...
I had no particular idea where this would go but I had the idea for it during the last Presidential campaign and just prior to the launch of the New Vulgate. Craig Ibarra, an old SST hand, offered to run it in his fanzine, The Rise and Fall of The Harbor Area.

The American political system proceeds according to a base-two system. Every two years the entire House of Representatives is up, plus one third of the Senate, and every other two-year period the Presidency. These overlapping bodies ratchet right or left and rarely line up to give either party a lock on Washington. It often seems the wisdom of the American crowd rarely tests out either party's ideas without the hurdle of the other party tempering in counterpoint. But when the branches do align, politics manifests itself culturally in an unusually strong way. There is a superficial level of influence like increased sales of peanuts on Carter's election, or jellybeans at Reagan's, and then there is a level that normally proves *too* deep. Young voters and high schoolers excited about Barack Obama's election can hardly be expected to acclaim any program of universal public service. This has been on the Democratic Party's back burner since the Reagan era, but now that they have the power to pass it there may not even be a proposal. The idea tempts them because they see how Peace Corps and AmeriCorps volunteers vote. It seems a nice way to mint Democratic voters; it can't be a simple military draft though because that might mint Republicans.

No, any real cultural response will manifest itself more in counter-formation to the new political zeitgeist.

The last time one party owned Washington was the middle four years of George W. Bush's two terms. The time before that, the first two years of Bill Clinton's administration. These periods didn't do as much culturally as at first it seemed they might, although the *political* backfire in each case was loud and clear. Famously overheard during the Thunderbirds flyover at the Clinton inauguration were boos followed by actor Ron Silver's protest to those booing that they were "our" planes now. Democrats in the Clinton administration and those in the majorities of Sen. George Mitchell's Senate and Speaker Tom Foley's House then duly struggled with their impulses and history over whether to use their planes to continue enforcing the Kurdish No-Fly zone in northern Iraq, or in Bosnia, in Kosovo, in Afghanistan, in Rwanda.... Before they knew it Newt Gingrich was Speaker and Sen. Bob Dole majority leader.

Bush's first term was clouded by the disputed vote in Florida and then unnaturally jolted into unity by the 9/11 attacks; that unity gained his party the Senate but then the Republicans lost both houses at the six-year mark, leading to a fake trench warfare – fake because the war in Iraq was not stopped by the Democrats who still seemed spooked by the price their party paid over the Vietnam bug-out. The party leaders judged that an immediate defunding and pull-out was the one thing that might turn the election the Republicans' way. And for his part in this theater, Bush went along with the legislature with nary a veto until this last year of his second term. (9/11 did seem to permanently re-align Ron Silver, however.)

These two recent periods of single party alignment didn't have staying power because the country's demographics weren't aligned as well. And for that to happen anytime after WWII, the baby boom had to be fully involved. And the last time that happened Jimmy Carter was the political beneficiary. The voting age had been lowered to 18 for the 1972 presidential election (Nixon won that youth vote!), but until 1976 only the leading edge of the baby-boom was able to vote and its voting power didn't fully register. Carter was a new face, governor of Georgia, and his religious faith brought in fellow evangelicals even while key early fund-raising support was provided by Georgia-based Capricorn Records and the Allman Brothers. He surprised the favored Democrats in Iowa and the primaries; they were seen to be too invested in the battles with Nixon (Frank Church), the failure in Vietnam (Hubert Humphrey), or hippie idealism (Jerry Brown). Carter promised a turn of the page on Ford, Nixon, Johnson, the Vietnam War, the hippies, the radicals, Watergate, the riots, the bombings, the assassinations, and he beat Gerald Ford. His presidency didn't quite work out even so, and then Sen. Kennedy actually challenged a sitting president of his own party, softening him up for Ronald Reagan.

Reagan beat Carter, just after Margaret Thatcher replaced hapless Labour P.M.s James Callaghan and Harold Wilson in the UK. She truly altered the course of Britain, privatizing nationalized industries, pulling the state back until London became the world finance capitol it remains. Reagan never had Republican control of the House and Speaker Tip O'Neil fought him on domestic issues but supported the military build-up and the re-engaging of the cold war. But Reagan's election, as a signal that the sixties ethos had hit the wall, was quite potent.

The punk era is too often misinterpreted as a response to this rightward move. What is correct is that Thatcher and Reagan relieved the anxiety of the cultural milieu and tempted punk from its original profound existential revolt to mere political protest, which hardcore, as a simpler and younger phenomenon, made quite reductively.

Punk as a sensibility goes back through the Stooges to the goofier edges of garage and rockabilly, but for our purposes it began in 1975 when bands like Television, Pere Ubu, the Dictators, the Residents, Chrome and others began to record. The early punk era bands were all over the map musically but they did share a certain stripped down approach to sound, as well as a radical drop-out indifference that Richard Hell termed "blank." That ethos was subtle, absurd and unnerving to the mid-seventies rock and roll world of hippie triumphant. It was as if a younger generation had suddenly rejected hippie and made stylistic alliance with sixties garage and fifties rockabilly. With the Weather Underground cooling out after their days of rage, the S.L.A. incinerated by the L.A.P.D., and Manson in prison, the new mellow consensus of the day suddenly didn't include the next turn of the rock and roll screw.

Punk bands in the early phase of this challenge were regularly chastised by a new class of rock and roll burgher. Music never heard, nevertheless proffered song titles, record covers and band names enough to set off the rock critic, the record store clerk, the erstwhile mellow dude.... But *Blank* went largely unplumbed by the rock writers and experts of the day and then was quickly blown away by imported tabloid representations of the Sex Pistols that began after the Bill Grundy live TV interview in late 1976. *The Filth and the Fury*, a documentary about that band makes much of the hot London summer of '76 and the piles of uncollected garbage on the streets and the frivolous musical novelties being dumped on British kids. The U.K. political landscape is different from that of the U.S., but there too punk had a dysfunctional left-wing political backdrop that lent its blank features a Weimar cast despite – or right down to – the occasional swastika. As Legs McNeil, co-founder of *Punk* magazine in 1975, recently recalled in *New York* magazine, "The left had become as oppressive as the Republicans."

There was a classic mid-seventies documentary about New York too; it was called *Death Wish* and it painted the city as given up to criminals – a rural/suburban rightwing fever-dream. And even post-blank, in the first 45 by Dead Kennedys, "California Über Alles" (1979), Jello Biafra, famous scourge of Reagan through the eighties, instead rips on Governor Jerry Brown. (Brown who famously dated Linda Ronstadt who got yelled at by Elvis Costello when she covered one of his songs on her fake new wave album.)

History is fun, but what about now? Might the Barack Obama administration, with its alignment with both houses of Congress make a Carter-like counter-cultural difference? And I don't mean an increase in fundraising concerts for the environment. I mean an audible difference, a drop-out difference. Edward Abbey famously contrasted Culture and Civilization in his 1968 drop-out journal, Desert Solitaire: "Civilization is the wild river; culture, 592,000 tons of cement." Overstated, perhaps, but it is true that culture often leaves nature out so as to put as much padding as possible between Man and Death, and thereby attract a larger audience looking for comfort and reassurance. This strategy works for a while, then pays dwindling dividends until a cultural revolution brings nature back via a new realism. Punk was that once in reaction to the buffered hippie rock-turned-pop of the Eagles, Peter Frampton, Fleetwood Mac, Carole King, Boston, Chicago....

If this Civilization/Culture wheel does not turn, it will be because those media that once channeled music and moved it to people have been dissolved, leaving music to spill thinly like water over any and all programming from ads to videogames to check-out monitors, to the Superbowl.... Music was once far more than a life-style accessory. And if it isn't bad enough now with eight year olds pleading for iPods and twelve year olds cell-phones, experts predict a techno-singularity wherein these gadgets begin to drive their own evolution and really test Man's (or Kid's) ability to connect with anything but cultural batting and the mirror. I recall losing interest in television and radio and sports as I got involved with music in the mid-seventies. Maybe the sheer connectedness of kids today prevents the development of a drop-out culture. Surely the ubiquity of the signs of past subcultures on today's nominal adults gives one pause – their tattoos and rings, Harleys and leather can be read as the toting of the scalps of the vanquished.

On the other hand, dropping out for these irradiated, immediate kids might actually come to be a simple matter. These days living without a cell-phone is practically pulling an Edward Abbey.

There might be a lot of useful anxiety in the culture as President Obama inevitably fails to live up to naive expectations, and then struggles with his own party as the usual Republican nemeses are suddenly impotent bystanders a la 1976. And this time, once again, the baby boom looks to be doing its part. As it ages it becomes ever more insufferable.

It used to be that the network news programs were the principle ad venues for the Geritol demographic. Now try to watch a baseball game on TV. It's a non-stop deluge of Flomax, Cialis, and Scooter Store ads. I expect a class action suit any minute on behalf of electrocuted Scooter users caused by Flomax failure or Cialis success – those four-hour erections they warn about. The old Geritol demo knew how to age with grace whereas narcissistic boomers must be portrayed by actors and models at least two decades younger and decked out in designer casual-wear, riding bikes and wearing helmets – God forbid they might injure a single brain-cell! I'll hazard a guess that the first sign of a healthy new youth culture will be a cruel dismissal of aged boomers. Perhaps the flavor of McCain jokes during the recent campaign is a harbinger.

Punk was a revolt of late boomers who'd been inspired by the early boomers' adoption of southern rock and roll, but punk was suppressed easily by the music businesses built by those older boomers. Now the boomers have stretched their dominance over the span of what in earlier decades would've been three discreet generations of prudent, productive adults. Current young people understand their music doesn't stand with the music of the early punks, hippies, and rednecks. Since the end of the 80s they have shown too much respect for their cultural elders as part of their congenital non-committal, no-risk slacker slide through what might have been their prime, but sadly has been fairly sub-prime instead. Those younger, well we'll see.

(*originally published in* The Rise and the Fall of the Harbor Area, *and posted at* The New Vulgate, *No. 9*)

Baroque Is Dead

This was a half-step towards the title piece perhaps. I submitted it to the Village Voice *and Chuck Eddy responded I'd have to peg it to some release. And that was before* New Times *bought it. Didn't bother doing that, but you'd think I could have come up with a better title.*

Where are we in music right now? If we answer that question we might make a reasoned guess as to where we're headed. Industrial strength rock/pop/youth culture is five decades old and though certain things have changed, the cultural patterns remain. Stepping back from the panic of the latest Pop Moment as brought to you by Viacom, Clear Channel, Conde Naste, AOL-TimeWarner, Sony, Fox, Disney, and Vivendi, and breathlessly interpreted by everything from the *New York Times* to O.C. *Weekly*, from Wenner Media to Transworld Stance, one notices the heretofore unregarded rococo frippery of even its most macho rockband manifestations.

And another question: What's this "we" shit?

In the seventies, the energy of the British Invasion and the rise of the album format hit the baroque wall with Gentle Giant, Genesis, and Yes – all fine bands but stylistically speaking, punctuation rather than new openings. Even outside of the general pop/rock realm of that day, the formal momentum ebbed with the dry conceptualism of Henry Cow, Faust, and Neu, signaling what, retreat? Advance? Time for the Ramones? American Baroque was not so clearly discerned and tended to involve less determined departures from the more organic and deeper American musical stew. Parliament, The Tubes, and Kiss certainly looked the part of baroque, but their music remained quite rooted in earlier music traditions, as opposed to Moments.

Seventies baroque was resisted by elements of surviving American founts such as the blues (Led Zeppelin, ZZ Top, Bad Company), country & western (Graham Parsons, Crazy Horse, Eagles), and garage (Lou Reed, Slade, Thin Lizzy), though music aside, most of these as well came to adopt quite rococo looks. ZZ Top's included a stage-full of texas ranch critters and Nudie suits for everyone; the others' excesses were related to psychedelia, English music hall, thirties/forties revanchism, and homovanguardism. The tables turned starting in 1975.

Punk in the beginning was a lumpy mix of garage, glam, sixties classicism, fifties classicism, and art-music. Mid-seventies American bands that are considered punk avatars such as Pere Ubu, Suicide, the Residents, Chrome, Electric Eels, the Dogs... were as much continuities from earlier artists such as the Velvet Underground, the Stooges, and Kraftwerk, as they were the signal gauntlet-tossings of something new. Once the punk mode was sure of its lexicon, adaptations were indeed made in every possible direction: C&W, disco, blues, old-timey, R&B, minimalism, cabaret, bel canto, opera, et. al. It became a generation (or two)'s summary take on the general musical environment they'd inherited. It took longer to reach the top of the charts than had the sixties or fifties summary attempts – in fact as they had charted throughout their lifespans they were less contrived, more immediate fusions than summary attempts. The Wailers, for instance, one of the first non-southern and therefore not country, blues or gospel-rooted rock and roll bands, had a hit with an instrumental called "Tall Cool One" (peaked at #36 on June 1, 1959) four years before they changed the world with their lumpen, trashed-out version of "Louie Louie" (peaked at #2 on Nov. 30, 1963).

It took 15 years from the Ramones non-moment for Nirvana and others to hit big with sounds informed by seventies/eighties punk rock. As many as three typical band lifespans set end-to-end had expired before the Punk Moment of 1975 registered in the pop charts (ignoring the new wave hits "Whip It," "Heart of Glass," etc.). This makes it a tradition, albeit one perverted by its years underfoot. (Again I speak of America here; the less rooted English pop culture with few exceptions fit fifteen peripatetic mayfly lifespans into that same decade and a half.)

It was easier to see baroque in the mid-seventies, especially if you were at ballroom and arena shows with bills mixing the naturalistic (West Bruce & Laing, Lynyrd Skynyrd, Stray Dog) with the decadent (Queen, Angel, Tubes). Today, baroque is less borrowed wholesale from Europe and Broadway than it is abscessing from within formerly spartan styles as punk, metal, blues-rock, rap, and folk. The Cali surf-bum's utilitarian generation of long cut-offs against the sun as one sits on a board waiting for a wave, his flannels-as-jackets for the beach cool or desert nights, were seized upon and mutated into high-end specialized bogus-wear for rain-dwellers, gangbangers, and fashion-heads. The appreciation of the stitching and thread-count of materials assembled in Taiwan-not-China, Los Angeles-not-Mexico is where some of this generation chooses to press its harshest aesthetic judgments.

What is generating this? Well, the time is long passed when cutting your hair and going punk was like walking the plank of the good ship H.S. Status. Much of the early Los Angeles punk violence was generated when the put-upon early punks who'd paid dearly at high school for their choice of music and look, suddenly, at a Germs or Black Flag gig, found themselves the new norm and the isolated and outnumbered jocks and hippies suddenly vulnerable. But today's high school punks, even the ones with tattooed cocks and steel balls under their skin have status and girlfriends and cars and credit cards. They are the new jocks, and just as likely as well to be pot-heads, meth-heads, class presidents, or teacher's pets. You know, they are formerly a subculture, but one now so successful as to no longer be rationally generalized about, like the longhairs were circa 1976 – when they might be Jesus Freaks or Manson family, or Bill Gates. However, we can generalize about the music of both subcultures from the period of their total social conquest, and that is that it sucks.

With the mass-middle dropped back in *en masse*, it pays no price but to merchants. And barreling out of the nineties with money to burn, things got baroque *faaast*. We have punk, hip hop, Dead, folk, redneck, techno and metal versions of a pre-fab demi-monde for social tourists. There's no dropping out today; it's back to working for the weekend, or interning your way up the bowels of the Man. Kids have been raised on television programming rendered by marketing hacks determined to pander more and more fiercely at them. In my youth we waited and waited through the saloon singers, the foreign circus acts, kidstuff puppet shows, and show tunes to see the Rolling Stones or the Doors play; we were spared the full-bore focus of the television industry. Today's kids suffer media-burn – media now vertically integrated and what was once broadcasting is now narrowcasting, soon to be laser-focused solocasting (tivo, custom sponsored programming, my netscape, bloggers, etc.). The kids aren't alright; they can't tell an authentic musical attempt, from a reverse-engineered prototype-for-the-next-fad floated into subcultural niches by cut-out guerrilla marketing firms staffed by pop-junkie judas goats cashing the checks of multinationals.

The band/artist vehicles for these product lines have no locale, they are from colleges rather than dropout scenes and their drive to be famous is unsublimated in any musical craft, art, or band format imperative. The managers, A&R men, label heads, producers and engineers prefer blank slates in any case and out of colleges these come pre-filtered. The more distant the Street and Garage are from the pop zeitgeist, the more power redounds to these apparats, and power settles in with them all the more securely when they begin to retool new media around the very process of hit-making, a la *VH-1*'s "Bands on the Run," and the various music websites' contests where the winners get voted into recording sessions or contracts.

There are willful dropout scenes but they have largely also dropped out of music as anything but a social trump card warding off the uncool. The varied metal, punk and experimental branches are for the most part musical dead-ends driven by suicidal teen-age frustration – you won't listen to me so I'll make sure you cannot even approach my music. The death metal scene seems determined foremost to drive off any females as well as provide a rationale for their being gone. This is symbolic suicide in terms of male mythos, but a real death to music. This metal's ties to blues and garage rock are severed; it is a "music" that starts at Slayer and one more turn and they'll be irrelevant too. The sophistos seem finally to be stalling in their ten year determination to differentiate themselves from the success of Nirvana with the great unwashed; whether they will try to sellout or buy in will be determined by whether they go for kitsch or something new. I'm not optimistic here; unfortunately there are young hipsters in hot lofts everywhere who want pastel soundtracks for their cleverdick lives. But seventies punk was better for the interest of the pretentious in picking up instruments. But if they won't play rock music, they'll just rerun the Talking Heads or Police, lifting third world ideas to fake-ground the pop whoring, as if the blues and rock itself were just plain exhausted.

Radio has been a deadly influence on musicians since 1973. The early eighties was the last time any generation of musicians arrived rooted in those rich programming mixes of Top 40 AM and freeform FM. Since 1983 then, music has gotten thinner and thinner sounding. It's been left to music-obsessed kids to buy or borrow CDs enough to augment the anemic radio and TV music programming. This doesn't work because to grow musically they need to hear music that is beyond their present ken – music that is by definition not what they are looking for but which will over time makes its richness apparent, if only through their own better product. Only radio rotation accomplishes this because like the monkey and cocaine, left to his own devices a human will seek his favorite buzz over and over and spiral into narrower and narrower stylistic tropes. When I was in eighth or ninth grade and impatiently waiting for *WLS* or *WCFL* to play Blue Cheer, Amboy Dukes, or Frijid Pink again, I got interested in Henson Cargill, Peggy Lee, and Sam and Dave as well, and was the better for it.

Distribution and media are about to become one. What is likely to result from this on the street is more room for a music underground. On-line pioneers will be lucky to survive the entrance of the major labels to the game. The global overlords of these congloms are not likely to countenance giving middlemen any oxygen. Their subscription models will empower the music publishers like nothing since blues, country, and rock and roll first threatened ASCAP's sheet music/orchestra empire. ASCAP and BMI allied with the majors will find television and film even more critical to launch hit songs when the album format is finished and all anyone is purchasing is essentially radio. With songs standing alone – no b-side, no album – the band and even the self-directed singer like Madonna will be replaced by studio projects serving the song. The publisher's demo will become the whole game; the pop music world will be as Nashville. And this will open up space for another rock underground to get a running start.

Today, metal and alt bands have trimmed influences to just their contemporaries in a circle jerk dance of death. While youth culture's boardjocks have virtually broken the bonds of gravity and pushed the inner ear and lower brain to feats once sensibly considered impossible, Music and Film, whether made by lumpen or sophisto have retreated, and proudly.

I'd advise a young musician-to-be to listen to oldies radio, preferably fifties and sixties rock and roll, R&B, and C&W, to augment his or her own CD or vinyl research, and to not, under any circumstances, go to college or watch *MTV*. When I was at SST (1981-86) Greg Ginn, when not on tour with Black Flag went out virtually every night of the week to whatever seemed the most promising gig. This was a guy who never drank alcohol, in a city where it takes at least an hour to drive anywhere. Today, what bands would seem so promising to a young music fanatic that they would induce him to drive crosstown and put up with the discomfort of the typical rock club while stone sober? Why? When you can chill in your crib watching *MTV* "documentaries" about wrestlers, cheerleaders, teen sex-lives, and houseful after houseful of consumers being consumed?

The rave culture, like the hip hop scene, is more purely a social scene. Here the male energy of the DJs and performers is servicing a dance imperative which means they're essentially, aesthetically pussy-whipped. A non-dance aesthetic push in hip hop lasted for about two years and two groups – Public Enemy and N.W.A. Now it's all Barry White, with attitude of course – oh my yes, just listen to that language! The ravers are looking to reach a euphoric trance and machine beats and Euro-washes of harmony and melody are the tools for that. Though even then, it takes some serious pill-munching to sell the deal. The rave intelligentsia keep trying to pump up its progressive ambitions but the audience keeps asserting its need to dance – the history of rock and roll in sterile, farcical, microcosm. When the next crop of high school girls decides these are boring scenes they will become so and dry up and blow away.

Currently young women are in rock audiences most often when there are gender considerations (The Donnas, Sleater-Kinney), or racial identity considerations involved (Seam, Blonde Redhead). I'm not talking mainstream sit-down audiences where attendance is juiced by commercial radio and styled-out venues where you pay your way away from the rock and roll rabble, I mean rock bands still playing rock venues with cruddy sound and messed-up toilets. The presence of women in these clubs for rock bands is a barometer of the economic health of rock music. But the rock/pop/youth culture need be on a down-scale jag for that to occur. And what comes after Baroque? That's right. You may be educable after all.

If the right young dudes can get real on the tools, they may catch the turn of the great culture wheel. The early punk bands missed it through no fault of their own. What's left of big rock has lost its ability to galvanize any but its own shrinking fan-base. This is all Billy Corgan seemed to talk about in his interviews on the final Smashing Pumpkins tour. His band and that small bundle of breakthrough bands had blown it, if you're thinking big enough. The last Stone Temple Pilots album, the new Tool album, the next Queens of the Stone Age or Pearl Jam album won't do it no matter how great they may be. Before the late seventies punk chart hits in England there had been a wave of retro chart-action from Dr. Feelgood to straight-on reissues of the early Beatles singles. Before the Nirvana chart breakthrough in the US, the ascendant classic rock radio format laid important groundwork with the young audience that knew nothing of the best blues-based rock of the late sixties/early seventies. That was the better choice for a high school kid in 1988 than what contemporary radio and MTV were foisting.

Perhaps today, the mania of MP3 file collecting has broadened what is listened to by high school kids. What is available on reissue and youtube and cable and wireless music services is greater than ever. The young need a less musty evaluation of the past to direct them past mere nostalgia to what they can use. What's current musically that might be relevant to a start-over movement among the young might be the new blues, some of alt-country, and a handful of stoner bands. Certainly we are very close to the point at which, in an echo of what happened in 1973 and 1959, the sharpest kids decide that what music is being programmed and sold is completely ignorable. Such a break with the present pop moment is what would be necessary to create a new music.

The Indie-worlders decided they liked sitting at the kids' table. They wouldn't risk the disappointment we lived with at SST. The Meat Puppets on the eve of recording their first album were obsessing on Led Zeppelin's "In Through the Out Door" album, in particular the stumbling, resounding big rock of "In the Evening." Later bands were happiest engaging in kitschy thriftstore one-upmanship over stuff that was picked over by Boyd

Rice and Monitor a full fifteen years earlier. Status in their cool hermetic universe was enough for these impacted passive-aggressive megalomaniacal bourgies. Nirvana felt judged by this scene and wasted much energy on atonement for success. Most of this stuff devolved to solo or duo projects without rock intent. Though ultra-cool rockband tropes such as Jon Spencer Blues Explosion, Nation of Ulysses, the Make-Up, At the Drive-in now regularly appear as contrived attempts to revive a dimly remembered more lively approach. But they are merely the gutted and stuffed carcasses of a musical animal that once roamed the earth as the Stooges, Ramones, Mötorhead, Avengers, Wipers, Black Flag, Minor Threat, *et. al.* They make as good a baroque endtimes signal as Staind/Slipknot/Mudvayne, or Kid Rock/Limp Bizkit/Insane Clown Posse, or all that R&B-on-ice in outerspace on *MTV*.

Tattoos, studs, makeup, ripped abs, roid-rage, rap-metal, wrestling, goth, Hefner, baggies, long shorts are finished. When you dominate the pop world you are just around the corner from being absolute nothing for ten years. Hip hop will learn this as Country did, as Alt-rock did, as hair-metal did.... Get in line behind Flock of Seagulls and Cinderella for retro-trend of 2011. Thanks to Ralph Nader, the fallen legal profession, and a now ideological female influence, young kids are strapped into car-seats from birth, forced into kneepads, elbowpads, and helmets just to ride a goddamn bicycle, and doped with anti-depressants if they get excited about anything. Puberty today is largely about tossing all this shit and doing an inverted double 360 on any wheeled or board conveyance. That's all fine and dandy but if these high school brats coming up don't start giving us some music that's new and alive we'll have to fire up the draft and get 'em ready for what's coming with China. That could be what it'll take to forge the kind of dudes who hear and play music like their lives depend on it.

Music Killers in the Pop Mausoleum
I got a call from Keven McAlester editor of New Times LA *who wanted to publish a piece on this theme and he remembered that it figured in* R&TPN *so he called. He cut out the Bowie abuse but here 'tis.*

Foo Fighters' drummer William Goldsmith quit when after recording the new album in good faith he found that Dave Grohl went back in and tracked over his drumming. Bad move in terms of the band ethic, though the real crime here may be drum-meister Grohl fiddling around with a guitar. No doubt Grohl played the drums slightly better and no doubt the engineer nodded gravely when Dave expressed his doubts about Goldsmith's tracks. But what Dave might not know is that the engineer, with perfect pitch Industry cynicism, was further dreaming (while nodding) of ditching the drums altogether so he could strut *his* stuff.

Social Distortion has two drummers, one for studio and one for live. Of course the records make no mention of this in deference to the band ethic. The question then becomes, who if anyone is the drummer on what they refer to as their "live" album? Mike Ness' solo album, then, is essentially the same difference and market research toward the jettisoning of the Social Distortion band baggage. Maybe Mike can fly solo and lease the name to four members of his fan club; it'd be ashamed to let all those S.D. bin cards go to waste.

The Cranberries for some reason have a band name but anything coming out of England's thin music culture and unforgiving music Industry is bound to be fraudulent in band terms. These particular charlatans tour with a guy who plays the piano from under the stage while what's-her-face bangs away on a hollow prop. When Metallica begins recording an album, the drummer works solo for a month because it takes that long for his engineer to go through every single percussive incident and move it into its perfect proper place as determined by the computer soft-ware. To do this drums must be recorded with perfect separation so that microphones pick up only the individual drum or cymbal they are set on, and not the neighboring drums or cymbals. This is accomplished by atomizing the instrument and the performance with noise gates which choke off everything but the strike itself. Then an ambient delay must be added to disguise the dead isolation of the percussive incident and simulate a room space. Or more easily the drums can be set for mere use as triggers that send an ideal canned percussive incident to tape. This way every hit is the same hit and can be more easily moved around by the mix computer. Or the drums can simply be dispensed with and programmed from the desk. These are the ways to squeeze out any possibility of musical incidents. Nobody's gonna confuse this stuff with jazz, but the lingering band ethic nevertheless demands such brave technicians pose as just another garage band.

It's not that these folks cannot play, so what's the problem here?

The Monkees fought for the right to play on their own records after being cast individually to portray a fictional band. They did sing, but only mimed playing the instruments on TV and on stage (the real players were behind the curtain!). They won a shot at it as they were all musicians and the project was such a success, and the greater pop culture in the late sixties was rock-determined and band-focused and capable of shaming the music's producer Don Kirshner into it. The Monkees were a fictionalization of Paul Revere and the Raiders by producers Bob Rafelson and Jack Nicholson. It took the success of the Beatles and all that followed, however, to convince *NBC* to greenlight the series. The Raiders began in Idaho in the late 1950s and were one of the great garage band pathfinders, led by a Jerry Lee Lewis acolyte. Yet Revere had to ditch his piano for a Vox organ once they got management and got to LA from the Northwest. Paul Revere tells William Ruhlmann in his liner notes to their box set, "I wanted us to be black and bad." Their recordings from 1960-64 are led by Revere's boogie piano and Mark Lindsay's sax blowing. They got a guitar/organ/harmony make-over and when they got so big they could tour forever, they did. Paul Revere wanted to rock and roll live before audiences, so he let his producers begin to use session players to record the stuff back in Hollywood while the real band was out touring. They'd fly in to do the vocals and learn how to play their new tunes later.

Did this matter? What is the band ethic, and what is band music?

Today virtually all rock music is recorded to radio programmer specs, despite the fact that almost none of this music will ultimately be programmed. It's all nonetheless offered up to this digital processing willingly, even desperately by the bands themselves, aided and abetted by managers, A&R men, mixers, producers, and engineers. The "music" thus processed is as thrilling as wallpaper. And with such carefully, expensively designed wallpaper, any reasonably interesting painting, never mind the rare masterpiece, must be kept off these walls. Thus the few remaining bands capable of good or even great playing willingly deface their music in the studio. Engineering standards devised to survive the ridiculous panoply of radio broadcasting compression settings destroy music that will never get broadcast.

Whole audiences listen to nothing but ice cold digital sound manipulation instead of music. The dumber the audience gets the more perfection they require: perfect regularity, perfect pitch – a perfectly sterile sonic environment; Patti Page couldn't dream of being so whitebread.

The efficient use of today's standard digital outboard gear requires that the original signal be generated in either a dead studio or sent direct into the mixing board. Further, subtle shaping of chords or notes by bending strings and the tactile profile of any genuinely musical player threatens the effectiveness of these digital fogs and chorales. These effects work much better and more subtly when chords and notes are executed foursquare (un-blued, as it were) and preferably by keyboards. Then these discrete blocks of consistent texture can be tweaked with equalization, delay settings and white noise exciters to render sensual presence. And these sonic blocks work better with synthetic percussion. A drummer and his bandmates reincarnating a song get inspired and never play it the same way twice. This is called Music. But here in the studio it is needlessly unpredictable and makes later overdubs impossible to synchronize. So get the click track up. On second thought, just lay down the click track. Send the band home. We're left with lushness, not edge; aspic not jam.

Earlier outboard effects were physically generated in small concrete chambers, or underground lockers, or by metal plate reverbs. These less artificial echo effects decayed naturally. The high end died faster than the low mids. The American Recording studio in Hollywood had a meat locker buried underground. Listen to Steppenwolf or Three Dog Night recordings and you hear a warm, wet, even luminous reverb that placed the music in a psycho-acoustic space we recognize from our lives in the real world.

Digital technology can in theory do anything it's programmed to do, but who's doing the programming and what are they after? Who wrote the Compact Disc program? An audiophile? To what specs, classical or pop? Certainly not rock music specs. The widening of the audio spectrum from the LP to the CD has principally achieved the expansion of the market for recorded music to dogs and whales.

When digital delay settings decay in an unnaturally replicated full frequency fade, music is essentially frosted. That's fine for pop music generated on digital keyboards jacked directly into the mixing board, but rock, blues, and country are hot forms. The icy, breathy digital come-on you hear in Def Leppard or late Van Halen recordings is a candied, narcotized substitute for the steaming meat and potatoes that rock music once offered. The only heat R&B, once *the* hot form, can generate today is freezer burn. (Note that in hip hop videos the sound is intimate and nearly reverb-less and at psycho-acoustic disconnect with the image of the inevitable wide, high-ceilinged stage whereupon two dozen dancers shake four dozen buttcheeks.) In today's faux-R&B, the tin pan alley pattern of the singles market has interfaced with the modern record Industry technocracy completely – aided and abetted by an increasingly cosmopolitan, increasingly ignorant audience. Indeed, this is an R&B increasingly sci-fi in its hysterical self-loathing flight from the American earth of roadhouse, kitchen, church, juke, whore-house, etc. (Again, see the videos.)

Nearly ten years ago the muzik technocracy had to contend with a sudden pop surfacing of an ostensibly more authentic punk approach to rock. But from the first this commercial breakthrough was prostrate before radio. Producer Butch Vig's account of the recording of Nirvana's follow up to "Bleach" in the May '98 issue of *Mojo* makes much of his laboring to convince Cobain to layer the guitars. Then mix engineer Andy Wallace came in to program drum samples and additional outboard effects for guitar and voice. What should have been a solid, earthshaking musical document thus was turned to candy for radio's use – high pop rotation for a month, then never mind. After recording the follow-up "In Utero" in a rock honorable stripped-down style with Steve Albini, Cobain critiqued "Nevermind" to journalist Jon Savage: "It's too slick. I don't listen to records like that at home. I can't listen to that record.... I think it's a really good record, I have to admit that, but that's in a Cheap Trick sort of way. But for my personal listening pleasure, you know, it's just too slick." (*Guitar World*, Oct. 1996) (Note: the first and best Cheap Trick album was produced by Jack Douglas and presents them unapologetically as a hard rock band, unlike the later records which are what he is referring to.)

Wonder of wonders, though, this time the radio programmers actually broadcast tunes from "Nevermind"! On the public airwaves!!! Turns out Kurt had blue eyes and so *MTV* had to program the "Teen Spirit" video.

Long term rock-style listening satisfaction had been subverted by the disassembling of performance and the processing of the parts – Taxidermy. "Layering guitars." Is that like feathering hair? Vig's group, Garbage, is state-of-the-art Taxidermy. Consider the received nature of such a project. Certainly they're into Big Star, the Velvets, the Stooges, all the cool wild stuff that is now safely enshrined and thus mandatory to like. Good move, cheeseheads – checkmate, even. The rhetoric of band ethic has been solved for this era. Studio nerds have colonized rock and the greater pop culture is once again merely pop-determined. This era's Boston got hip to this era's rap. Built to last, not for speed. Alas, there will be no suicides in Garbage.

After the success of "Nevermind," engineers known for designing the sound of the more pliable metal bands were suddenly scrambling for punk or alt-rock sessions just in case commercial metal tanked (major label signings only please). One old school punk band faced with an arrogant metal engineer who answered no questions and used his own outboard mystery boxes to make them clank like surfers in knights' armor, fired his ass, only to see him turn on a dime, now crawling, pleading, and begging to stay involved on any terms. He needed the credit - the new street cred.

Now of course everything has settled down; in fact, it's collapsed. The losers went on drug binges, or got honest work recording advertising jingles. The same half-dozen winners mix everything the radio programmers accept. But they accept less and less. Lately radio is fond of editing song choruses of a handful of current hits and dosing listeners with the even smaller, more proscribed format of the station ID - a pop suppository. And it allows them to play one less tune per hour (Thank you, Jesus!). The Industry nervously demands re-editing of song arrangements in the writing, recording, and mixing phases, or even as late as the mastering. Increasingly it's no longer Verse/Verse/Chorus/ Verse/Chorus because radio can't afford to make the audience it's made wait that long for a payoff. (Solos disappeared decades ago.) The Chorus comes quicker now and sometimes there just isn't a verse at all (Chumbawumba? Crass!). It took from 1974 to 1991 to re-educate the pop listener so he could appreciate something other than Toto or Journey. Radio and *MTV* programmers lobotomized that pop listener in less than half the time. They strip-mined this audience, winning their puny ratings share battles while the great war (audience size) was lost (to country, hip-hop, banda, internet, games, board-sports, wrestling, comics, porn...).

Radio programmers have the music Industry by the balls; it's their doing. But their game is disappearing up its own ass. One hit blunders abound and follow-up albums litter the cut-out bins. This is inefficient as it means every hit is a fluke that must be broken from scratch and no follow-up can build and re-coup from its success. *KROQ* programmers complain that there is no audience loyalty and that what they need are more Pearl Jams only without all those annoying rock band issues (Foo Fighters to the rescue!). *KROQ* calls for rock bands to send them their tapes - more perfect pitch Industry cynicism. (Any tapes sent were surely recorded over with the latest techno and goth wallpaper by UCLA interns.) Getting fired will not be punishment enough for their like.

Until the next rock retrenchment, we are stuck with the pneumatic singer-songwriter. Beat box Bonos posing as Dylans. Listen to all those smoky baritones. Oh the things they've seen and felt in their lives on campus, on line, and at the mall. Plus, they're so enigmatic! All these monkeys with computers jockeying to be the conscience of their generation - sign me quick before I'm thirty and have to go back to grad school. Lenny Kravitz has a new rap to replace the old one about real playing and real tube-amp recording just like the sixties, man! The new rap explaining his discovery of the hitherto unsuspected nonsell-out viability of synthetic percussion should really be: Hey man, a dude's gotta eat (shit). Like Ness going solo, Lenny has been forced to accept pop methodology to obtain the airplay necessary to maintain major label distribution. But look at Kravitz: he's the mediated image of the sixties reverse-engineered by someone who no doubt listens to some good old music, but he listens as a fan – he is not a musician, I don't care how fast he can play scales. What good is being a black Jewish hippie if you got no rhythm, can't write a tune, and don't have a psychedelic bone in your body?

Women make better pneumatic singer-songwriters because at this late date beyond feminism, they have more to say and they come almost entirely free of band ethic baggage. They get their backs up less as the engineers and managers go to work on their tunes. We'll soon see whether the pneumatics burn out the way the organic singer-songwriters of the early seventies did. What if they don't?! Don't look for a Neil Young to rise from their midst.

The late period alt-rock bands, largely conceived by college kids under the influence of platinum punk, fit right in to Industry needs; they could hardly imagine a move that might hurt their careers. When Iggy threw himself into a mixed crowd of motown greasers and long-haired gearheads in the early seventies and moved no Stooges product did he land on anyone? Yes, and real trees fall everyday in the forest though no-one hears jack. But Cobain's dive into the drums had a European festival audience with camera present and fed back into the *MTV* platinum loop. Did Kurt then land on anyone? No, I told you he jumped into the drums! And the video was lip-synced so nobody in the platinum audience heard him hit the drum-kit and its microphones. We only saw it.

Kurt's gesture was authentic enough and the camera was just Dave Markey's super8, but the social success overwhelmed musical considerations both among the hipsters Kurt wanted in his audience and the climbers and metal-heads he did not. Thus Iggy's silent gesture can be said to have moved music and launched all manner of incredible bands (Ramones, Avengers, Black Flag, Minor Threat), while Kurt's eye-splittingly loud gesture yielded Industry-friendly porridge (Weezer, Everclear, Bush).

Rock began when the instrumental bands in the north and west took up the southern rockabilly and R&B approach and began working it out with the emphasis on playing (they didn't generally possess the vocal grace of southerners). This band-focus was dramatized most successfully later by the Beatles, though they also introduced other arch, derisive tendencies which the gathering pretension of college-boy counter-culture encouraged. These tendencies found their true voice in David Bowie, who kicked around London in folk and blues guises for years before he caught the cultural and Industry zeitgeist. Interestingly, he used Iggy as his stalking horse/stuntman and then picked out the safer, less risky options for his own career. (His innovative recent securities offering on Wall Street guaranteed by future royalty earnings sold very well.) Bowie reversed this band-focus, assembling them for recording or touring as needed. Such assemblies are generally incapable of developing a true band voice and the sound gets generic or arch. But the recording Industry, the broadcasting Industry, and the talent management Industry don't have musical considerations in mind: One face will do and it won't be the guitarist's, the bassist's or the drummer's.

Rock is no longer rock and roll – the interface that a half-dozen root forms had with the electric future. Now it is free standing and has less organic ties to those root forms all of which themselves struggle. And it is no longer an interface with the future. It is merely a vital musical setting prefaced on the small band format. As the self-consciously futurist solo artists race toward downloading their personae unto immortal web-lives, rock music can seem just another Luddite pursuit, bracketed with the blues, bluegrass, and other forms tamed by time. The future may actually come some day, but for now the techno soloists seem to have to backslide into rock formats to tour in support of their releases – Industry imperatives, again. Like the hip hoppers before them they have a hard time coming up with anything much more innovative in presentation than a 1979 Sammy Hagar concert (Hey Cleveland, show us your tits!).

After platinum punk, metal Grammies, alternative gold, and rock museums, stoner rock alone has the loser sensibility immune to the siren song of radio play. Sleep, Fu Manchu, Goatsnake, High on Fire, Core, and Nebula may not rank with Queens of the Stone Age, and Spirit Caravan but they have recorded some great tunes. Queens and Caravan come respectively from the last great recent bands: Kyuss, and the Obsessed – i.e., they are not young. Queens debuted on the Man's Ruin label, gave their masterpiece to Loose Groove, and are now getting a push into radio by Interscope with their fine but fairly processed new release, "R". Spirit Caravan is bouncing between independent labels and therefore still releases powerful, essentially live-in-studio music.

The young band today must consciously challenge the musical ignorance bad radio has bequeathed them. Unfortunately, rock music is largely about the cultivation of instinct, and therefore pre-conscious and vulnerable to its surroundings. In the old days, pre-1973, you could bone up on music by listening to the radio; now that just dumbs you down.

And no longer is music fed by a stream of middle class drop-outs and risk takers; now the middle class liberal arts grads descend *en masse* like locusts on each and every sub-cultural acre, leaving most music sounding pre-masticated, pre-digested, and fully received.

A pop act today might merely pick stoner manque as schtick (Hello Monster Magnet!). But even received, stoner rock remains a foolish career move, and therefore, alongside a few other cranky music-focused subcults like the Chicago improv scene, is a last best hope for musical reconstruction. This can happen while the Industry is busy trying to settle the internet frontier – the natives are way restless. Copyright will be protected, but the Industry will fail because mass culture itself is failing and the new medium is uncentered. When Elvis died, Lester Bangs wrote that as we'd never again agree on anything like we agreed on Elvis he wasn't going to say goodbye to Him, he was going to say goodbye to you. And the stoners go, "All right now!"

Meat Puppets II
All Tomorrow's Parties had the Meat Puppets playing their second album in 2008 and I was asked write about that album for the program.

Curt Kirkwood – Vocals, Guitar
Cris Kirkwood – Bass
Derrick Bostrom – Drums

Produced by Spot and the Meat Puppets

If I remember the story, while in high school Curt played lead guitar for some older guys in a working cover band, while jamming on the side with brother Cris on bass. The oldest Kirkwood stuff I have on tape is from 1978 and features them rounding out a Phoenix College classical quartet; they play it straight even on their electric instruments which mix novelly with flute and violin. Their friend Derrick followed punk rock and convinced them to form a band. The Meat Puppets soon got to open for Monitor, an art band from Los Angeles making one of its rare forays out. I first heard about them from Laurie O'Connell of Monitor; I've repro'ed her 1980 letter to me about them in my book about Naomi Petersen; Laurie didn't follow punk rock but really liked them. Chuck Dukowski tells me that it was the Sun City Girls who opened for Black Flag on their first trip to Phoenix and that they didn't see the Meat Puppets until they shared a bill in Riverside, California.

The Meat Puppets were playing L.A. and S.F. regularly by 1981, and once I left Systematic Record Distribution in Berkeley for SST in L.A., I often went out with Black Flag on short runs to Arizona or up the coast, with the MPs often on the bill. Laurie put the Meat Puppets on L.A. shows with Monitor, Non, Nervous Gender, and Human Hands. Chuck worked the Meat Puppets into the SST scene via gigs with the Minutemen, Saccharine Trust, the Descendents, and Red Cross. All of the early SST bands were first and foremost *live* bands – the Meat Puppets most of all. Their treatment of their own songs and the covers they'd seemingly pull out of the air was always musically different and exploratory.

coming in September: the new Meat Puppets album on S.S.T. Records

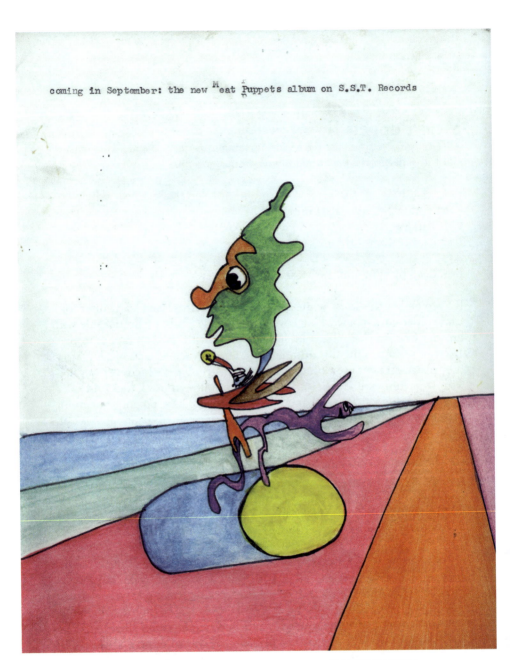

MEAT PUPPETS PRESS RELEASE, 1982; ART: CURT KIRKWOOD.

Once in Berkeley some punk purists' complaints were rewarded with a set-long noise jam; other gigs might resemble a tightly focused picking parlor, or stomping biker rock or hazy psychedelia. Then they'd go into the studio and come out with yet another surprise. Recording the early Meat Puppets was trying to catch lightning in a bottle. This was successfully done by my lights only five times: "In a Car" off the first 45, "H-Elenore" from the "Keats Rides a Harley" compilation, and "Walking Boss," "Melons Rising," and "Saturday Morning" off the first album. Those tunes are *live-in-studio!*

Derrick explained to me as they prepared to record their second album that from the beginning of the band Curt and Cris could play anything, and now that he also could play anything they were no longer a punk band. "II" is the best balance of their early, wilder approach and their later professional approach. Spot tells me that the basic tracks were done in under eight hours, but the overdubs were bumped by scheduling problems (we had to work around Dokken and Great White at Total Access Studio in Redondo Beach). Cris walked back to SST early one day and we had a good conversation about art and drugs in the unusually quiet office as night fell. I remember Curt, Cris and Derrick as the kind of low-key, deep people you'd be talking with and no-one would think to turn on a light so you'd end up talking in the dark with only the flashes of their lighters when they fired up their pipe. So anyway, Dokken's "Tooth and Nail" turned out great as we all now realize, but then, rather than wait around, the band went back to Phoenix. Spot flew out and they finished the album at a small studio called Chaton. Total time: about 35 hours he reckons.

We didn't have a record player at SST so I heard the album mostly from the final eq master cassette Spot brought back from K-Disc mastering. Even then, we didn't play cassettes that much either. Spot would check his tapes on a small cassette box as sessions progressed from tracking, mixing, to the mastered version. Mostly we had the radio on at SST: country, black, rock, college, big bands & ballads, Hispanic.... SST was a live music record label; we documented the best live bands before they destroyed themselves. Greg Ginn, Chuck, and Spot were doing this from the beginning of the label when Black Flag first recorded in January, 1978. Even when they had no money they'd run bands like The Minutemen, Saccharine Trust, The Stains and Overkill through the Media Art Studio in Hermosa Beach just in case the bands didn't last – hardly the m.o. of any other record label I can think of.

We didn't consider the Meat Puppets college rock or hardcore any more than we thought Saint Vitus were. The bands that lasted more than one record had to figure out for themselves how much to cede to the inhospitable, often deathly studio process; most ultimately just surrendered to it. To Spot's credit he was never the undertaker.

Unlike their first and third albums, "Meat Puppets" and "Up on the Sun," "II" perfectly integrates all the wild psychedelia, close picking, light/heavy, fast/slow, tuneful/atonal experimenting they'd been doing for years. Once it was released they went on their first U.S. tour, and then went out again with Black Flag. In this period the guys in Black Flag, the Minutemen, Hüsker Dü, Saccharine Trust, and Saint Vitus all raved about the Meat Puppets' gigs they were seeing. And we – each other – were the only people whose taste we trusted, so that's a judgment that'll do until Kingdom come.

Just before they went into Total Access (a 3 day lockout this time) to record "Up on the Sun", they played at the Music Machine and sounded more like Steppenwolf. I'm still waiting for that album! The first three Meat Puppets albums put me in mind of the three middle-period King Crimson albums of ten years earlier: "Lark's Tongues" is rough and spacey like "Meat Puppets," "Starless and Bible Black" is the most vivid representation of the band's live, experimental search to find its voice just as "II" is for the MPs, and "Red" of course, like "Up on the Sun," is fully realized and therefore the band would likely only falter from thereon. It must be an iron law of rock.

But I hear good things about the reconstituted Meat Puppets from folks who remember their lightning-in-a-bottle days. Be nice if they could at least bend that iron law.

(original version published in ATP's "Don't Look Back" 2008 program; this version was posted at The New Vulgate, No. 18)

Folk and the Pop Narcotic
This revisits aspects of my Lightbourne, and Nelson pieces but in this I get to make fun of Sean Wilentz and Dylanology, posted at NV on Sept. 8, 2010.

Christopher Shea at *Chronicle.com* on Sean Wilentz's book, *Bob Dylan in America*, deals mostly with Wilentz the historian. Shea's section on Wilentz's view that scholars easily let their contempt for politics color their work, as in the stressing Lincoln the orator, thereby removing him from politics, is great. But unfortunately it does eventually get to his Dylan book and here again we see the class problem of rock and roll (and politics) reigns.

I haven't read any book on Dylan and have barely listened to anything other than his hit 45s which I liked when I heard them back on AM radio. But I did listen when the late David Lightbourne would talk out his otherwise unwritten Dylan book, and that puts me well ahead of anyone else, no matter how many cockamamie Dylan books they've read. And that's because Dave saw the revelation that was rock and roll circa 1956. (See his essay, "Elvis Up North," at *The New Vulgate*). At age 14 Lightbourne didn't understand the sources of its power but he spent the rest of his life tracing its tributaries and got as close as anyone. He followed folk and blues from *WFMT*'s *"Midnight Special"* and Studs Terkel programs, to the blues and folk clubs in Chicago, to *The Little Sandy Review* (see that essay at the *NV* too), but primarily he collected music backwards from the last contemporary southern practitioners back to the music released in the twenties and thirties which he explained in an interview included on the recent Lightbourne "Tribute" CD, actually documented Southern music styles going back to the 1880s depending on the age of the artist recorded circa 1930; he called that first burst of recording for the gramophone "a time machine."

David knew that Bob Zimmerman was another Northern rock and roll fan who as a budding musician first had to figure out whether you might not *have* to be Southern, if not all the way black, to play this music. Bob also had to figure out whether you had to be Christian too since the church figured so prominently in any Southern white or black musicians' development. It's no surprise that middle class white kids didn't want to know about the gospel interests of Elvis, Jerry Lee or Johnny Cash, but one wonders if gospel music kept dropping out of the literature of rock and roll, rhythm and blues, blues, jazz, and country and western, because the left, not to mention the Jewish left, were opposed to it and uncomfortable around churches. And yet Southern church music remains the great trunk of the American tree of music. Amazingly enough, just in the last ten years, the gospel hand-clap has replaced the snare drum in American pop music!

In the late 1950s Northern rock and roll tended to be instrumental because singing was often the real barrier. Most Northerners went to church or synagogue but the services were nothing like down South. What singing people did up North was more likely popular song. The mix of black and white in the South is right there in the accent and it's in the singing of any cracker as well. And that's true for blacks as well – there is white in their music and voices – though one might have to be fully *Afro-African* to hear it that.

David also remembered that Dylan could really sing at first. Bob just had to figure out *what* to sing, and since he didn't grow up in a rock and roll church he'd have to fake it. Dylan was busy thinking his way to this fakery using his prodigious intellect, borrowing/stealing from Koerner Ray & Glover, Paul Nelson, Woody Guthrie, and Jack Elliott. Elliott was the obvious model, but Guthrie meant more in New York so he'd stretch his truth in that direction – he didn't want to wind up on Prestige or Folkways, after all.

Shea writes, "Wilentz adopts a fly-on-the-wall perspective as he listens in on tapes of the recording sessions for the double album 'Blonde on Blonde,' in which Dylan's create-on-the-run approach collides with the stoic professionalism of Nashville studio pros." This is Shea, not Wilentz writing, though it is his book Shea is summarizing. Neither apparently understands that Dylan is recapitulating rock and roll's impact on Nashville ten years earlier. Dylan's "create-on-the-run approach"?! Those Memphis rock and roll thugs destabilized Nashville's company town game as they inspired Northern teenagers. But Nashville is a writer's music town and as we are seeing today writers/publishers are the last men standing in the music game. Dylan understood Nashville was the way out and back, once again, but he sure wanted to bring along some of the fire that lit in Memphis.

Separating Dylan from rock and roll (and America!), here done by the scholar who can discern and object when that's being done to Lincoln.... Craziness! Crazy, class-blind, automatic writing.

The folkie lens is still preventing American rock and roll from being discovered, for all the books and monographs. The middle class sophistos didn't want to know those Memphis cretins, but they were suckers for the British Invasion. They thought they learned about black music from Britain! What was Dylan to do? He was banking on this ignorance because it implied he was self-authored, certainly he wishes he was, and yet that's his nightmare as well. Dylan wanted his songs to resonate through American culture as if they were authorless for all anyone could tell. Ingmar Bergman (*the* auteur!) also indulged in this fantasy; Bergman suggested he wished to be as the artisans who built the landmark cathedrals of old Sweden, old Europe, and are unknown.

Dylan's celebrated run-on/turned-on period embarrasses him. He wasn't affected so much by The Beatles in 1963 as by The Holy Modal Rounders. Those two guys (Peter Stampfel and Steve Weber) knew everything he knew and more but they didn't have to fake or pretend anything because they weren't plotting out a career. Their understanding that their music was rock and roll even at just fiddle and guitar was thug-like.

Wilentz prefers to fantasize that Dylan was studying 19th Century newspapers on microfilm at the NY Public Library when in fact he was banging one muse after another like Bergman. The fan is a killer and the more pretentious he is the more deadly. Wilentz will write no book about the Rounders. He is the Dylanologist he requests not to be described as. Dylanology is the aggressive misunderstanding of a musician so as to not risk the accidental learning of anything cold or unforgiving about oneself or by extension one's generation. You can quote me on that.

(*originally posted at The New Vulgate, No. 62*)

The Upland Observer, Aug. 30, 2004
"The Observer never sleeps soundly"
We did a decade's worth of annual folk-blues music events here in Centennial until Lightbourne died. I started writing them up for my email list.

Breakdown Lowdown
Dream Gig of the Year, or Haberdasher's Nightmare?

It was sunny all day Saturday but still cool so with pickers like Hurley, Spot, Hurwitz, Lightbourne, and Safran we thought it best to run the show inside the tavern this time. That meant no wandering toddlers or canines in the picture, but the mountain rummies were pleased to not have to negotiate the leaving of the bar nor the braving of the sunlight to hear the blues.

After Michael Safran's instrumental, baroque/new age improv stylings, after David Lightbourne's twenties/thirties delta pickings less his Stop & Listen Boys but accompanied by his custom-made jazzhorn, after Spot's now seamlessly complete fusion of Celt-surf-garage-blues-jazz-beat-dada-gaga, the Rocky mountains finally got a looksee at the heretofore merely hearsaid Michael Hurley.

I personally have never seen the party-determined rabble of Centennial's Beartree Tavern so focused on every note of music played. He started on his banjo, moved on to guitar and finished on the fiddle, and with his calm workmanlike spell-casting Hurley pulled us all into his timeworn time-warp. The set peaked when major land-owners hereabouts of sensible Scandinavian derivation were observed tapping their toes when Hurley pulled 1951's top-ten Patti Page hit, "Detour–There's a Muddy Road Ahead," out of his cap.

But all that wasn't enough so we pulled Michael Hurwitz out of the woods. Michael Hurwitz is Wyoming's take on American traditional music. This bear of a man left Centennial years ago when its Pop.100 hubbub got on his nerves; the 'biler gearheads down in map-speck Albany had him pulling out his shotgun one too many times so he moved up to Alta on the back side of the Tetons. He is a native whose been playing since the late sixties and in his various band configurations has been pulling twenties blues, western swing, and classic Nashville through his cowboy paradigm.

After his rare solo set Hurwitz lead the entire troop through ramshackle jams on "Will the Circle Be Unbroken," "Waiting for a Train," "Let the Mermaids Flirt with Me," "Liza Jane," "Six Days on the Road," "Low and Lonely," and several more already even now lost to memory if not posterity. Spot was on banjo, Hurley on fiddle, the others on guitars with Hurwitz calling out the solos. The beautiful advantage to moving inside was their ability to play on into the night. Only Michael Safran went bareheaded, but the hats riding the crests of the rest of this encore jam safe-to-say made this event a true haberdasher's nightmare. Goodnight Harry Truman, wherever you are.

Stray Colorado, Texas, Nebraska, and South Dakota plates were sighted along the shoulders of Hwy 130; *KUWR* DJ Miss Tillie came by, Murf and Linda from the other Centennial music hotspot (Trading Post) were in the house. Murf came in on crutches but was later seen flying across the dance-floor with Linda – cured by the power of Hurwitz's guitar. Spot slow-danced with Jan, the President of the Laramie Film Society made the scene with his First Lady or maybe leading lady in booth #2, UW profs and co-eds made appearances, the Mayor was spotted drunk, ex-Detroiter Marc told tales of witnessing cool stuff like the first Psychedelic Stooges gig and the MC5 "Kick Out the Jams" weekend during breaks in the action, and even a Muddy Waters Coffeehouse barista was spotted, creating quite a stir. There was a brief moment of silence observed for Singing John (R.I.P.) when the Mayor tripped over the power strip; but John can still be heard importuning the Stop & Listen Boys on the live CD of the first Upland Breakdown and then singing his request himself when Dave shut him down. Tried but failed to record this one too.

No bears were sighted except on the napkin drawings over the urinals (my favorite has papa bear returning home covered in lipstick and mama bear saying, You've been out hibernatin' around on me again!). Lightbourne and Safran are back to Laramie, Hurwitz to Alta, Spot to Austin, Hurley to Astoria, and I've got deckwood to clear.

Thanks go to the players, Jill and crew at the Beartree, Lightbourne in his pr cap, Don Woods at *KUWR*, Ted Hill and Kristianne Gale at *KRFC*, Kevin at Kinko's, Aaron at the *Laramie Boomerang*, and Holly at the *Casper Star-Tribune*.

Upland Breakdown 2005 falls on Saturday, August 27. Next year, then...

The Upland Observer, Aug. 30, 2005
"The Observer never sleeps soundly"
One year later another Upland Breakdown, more fretting about the weather, etc.

Breakdown Lowdown
Pizza Dough Shortage Prompts Run on Green Chili

Your correspondent took an extra day to recover from severe social overdose (SSO) as the population of Centennial, Wyoming trebled or so for the Sixth Annual Upland Breakdown. What's more, the population of my house rose some 500%. I may have to move soon.
    The Breakdown had everything this year: perfect weather, hot girls, cool dudes, and one great musician after another. The coolest dude was surely noted rock critic, self-styled archivist, and amateur chemo-therapist Byron Coley, in attendance with his unaccountably well-mannered son, Hud. Did my best to introduce Mr. Coley to every low-life in the valley for a visit he will surely puzzle over at least 'til he hits Idaho. Byron wore dark sunglasses but if you got close enough you could stare right through his dilating pupils to the very back of his skull. There was a tie for hottest girl: little Maya of Blue Diamond, Nevada shut down most competition with her pink leather Barbie boots but it was her satin gloves sealed the deal. However, a certain rookie math prof was equally distracting; Teach will surely find herself flunking or slapping near every boy in her class, and probably half the girls too. I know what goes on, I saw Tom Wolfe on the TV...
    David Lightbourne joined by Shaun Kelley on standup bass got the music jumping early. The two of them are two-thirds of the Stop & Listen Boys of old, way back in the twentieth century. Dave pulled out one Mississippi or Memphis tune after another interspersed with originals from LaRamie. Birgit Burke followed with accompanist John Lyon on a set of Appalachian folk, gospel, olde English ballads, and an original or two; instruments played by the duo included hammer dulcimer, mandolin, fiddle, guitar, and banjo. Michael Hurwitz & the Aimless Drifters and their smooth cowboy blues once more pulled every last rancher, miner, and rummy off nearby ranges, claims, and barstools; the resulting dance-steps resembled nothing so much as a

Mexican rodeo under attack by killer bees. Spot pushes his Toyota up our hill almost every year and he kept the demanding dancers going with Jimmy Reed's "Aint That Lovin Ya Baby," and his own "If You Dont Like Me Now," and "Ministry of Funny Dances"; also emanating from Spot's banjo, fender and acoustic guitars were Celtic, Bop, and rock and roll-influenced spaatmusik. (Michael Hurley cancelled at the last minute when his dates in Montana vaporized on account of the aforementioned state acting stupid; they're practically Canadian up there, you know.)

After the show the sun duly set, the fire was lit and an impromptu session took place, led by the well-lubed John Kidwell on banjo. Following him down one hearty musical dead-end adventure after another was Lightbourne and the newly shaved-up ex-hippie-Mike on guitars, and Shaun Kelley on something that looked broke off from a didgeridoo. Everybody eventually drifted across the highway to the Trading Post for Hurwitz & Co.'s late set.

During the afternoon a heavily made-up couple in fancy attire that set the dogs to barking come off their range-rovering real estate tour and were heard guessing that the hubbub was some kind of private party. They're even coming up from Aspen...

One of Centennial's seasoned rummies was observed acourting two lovely ladies when his brain, awash in all the known psychedelic properties of wood and/or grain alcohol, decided to tell them and I quote: "I never been with two M&Ms before. "When pressed he explained after thoughtfully wiping away chin-dribble, "M&Ms are ladies between menopause and medicare. " I'm guessing he ain't ever going to be with no two M&Ms either...

In other news, The Library pub's India Pale Ale is out at the Beartree Tavern, and Easy Street Wheat Beer is in. Score one for the Fort Collins, Colorado brewing industry against the Laramie small-timers. Also, the mayor reports some graduating frat boys tore the door off of the only squad car in the Centennial Police Force, and boy is that stuffed smokey bear behind the wheel ticked off about it. What are they teaching kids these days over at the U?

Thanks go to the musicians Dave and Shaun, Birgit and John, Mike Tommy and Josh (for the PA too), and Spot and his many personalities, also to Jill and her crew at the Beartree Tavern, Aaron at the *LaRamie Boomerang*, Carrie at the *Casper Star-Tribune*, Don Woods and Tom Wilhelm at *KUWR*, Ted at *KRFC*, Jan for her email help, and Mike at Snowy Range Graphics. Next Upland Breakdown is Saturday, August 26, 2006.

Upland Breakdown, Aug. 26, 2006 (1427 a.h.)
This too went out by the telegraph a few days after the event.

Breakdown Lowdown

Sure was a lot of music flying around southeast Wyoming this past weekend. And a lot of out-of-state plates lining the highway around Centennial's Beartree Tavern last Saturday. The first drama, not counting John Martz's food poisoning in Greeley, was whether the gray skies would let us set up outdoors. It didn't rain (much) but was a bit chilly for optimum playing. So it was indoors again and the stray kids and dogs had to make do with the patio bonfire and warm-up workouts while the Breakdown moved into the bar.

The delay meant the reunion of half of Trouble in the Yard (Kelly Trujillo & John Martz) was cut to keep to the ruthless precision of our schedule – apologies. And so direct from Vermont began Gary Sisco, Clamtones alumna and drummer to the stars, but here playing guitar and singing songs from his new release, "The End of the Trail," which features a Michael Hurley painting on the cover and playing by Hurley, Frederick, Reisch, Remaily and more. His set was easy, comfort blues in line with that of his pals and a great start for the day.

Spot was up next and he tore through some old favorites and dug up an old spot-topical ballad, "Sextant," concerning a certain earlier over-there bit of nasty business now newly relevant, though he didn't tempt the fate of God's clear-channel wrath (*silence...*) by bringing up his sharing a certain state with a certain prominent pol.

Michael Hurwitz & the Aimless Drifters were up next and before we could ponder whether he himself is one of the Aimless Drifters or merely has them under particularly onerous personal services contracts, he/they laid out a great set of their prairie blues. They haven't sounded this good since the Great Albany Wyoming Pig Roast of 1999. The set prompted a run on his/their new CD, "Coyote Blue," the sales champ for '06 ('27) at the merch desk.

Somehow the gods of ranchin' and fossil-diggin' conspired to make John Martz available for his first Breakdown in four years, and first Stop & Listen Boys reunion since the Knitting Factory two years ago. So Dave

Lightbourne, Martz and Shaun Kelley, augmented by Jane Pellouchoud on washboard and John Kidwell on trombone, raised the roof, and at this elevation that's some trick. This had to be the ghost of twenties rock and roll that David is always talking about (Hurley calls Lightbourne the Informaton).

Michael Hurley followed but it wasn't the Sensitivos backing him as falsely advertised, but folk-star Josephine Foster sneaking up the Rockies to accompany Michael on lap-slide and vocals. There were no complaints. Hurley stuck to his electric guitar and picked his way through a set of lovesick blues. I felt like tellin' him, Hey look who's settin' right next to you and cheer up for Goshsakes!

The Places closed the Breakdown but they turned out to be Amy Annelle unaccompanied this time. Amy played a thoughtful mix of striking originals and familiar classics both of which served her great voice well. While tuning up she explained she usually played taped noise-loops between songs but wasn't sure we all wanted to get weird – see what I mean? Thoughtful!

That wasn't the end of the music by a longshot either. Hurwitz rounded up his Drifters for a late set with Spot and Kidwell reportedly involved. Spot woke up rough but I was off down to Colorado to the Blasting Room to record the Stop & Listen Boys w/ Jane, Kidwell, Billy Broderick, and special guest author/commercial archeologist, Arthur Krim. Arthur was the star of the session with his autoharp-led treatment of "Louisville Burglar" – I had to patiently explain to Arthur that, no we could not rush release it on wax cylinder and even if we could we wouldn't need a B-side. (Also of note: Bill, Frank, and Tony were laying down cool new Descendents tracks in Studio B; Hey Milo, duty calls.)

Back up in Wyoming Spot sat in again for a Hurwitz Sunday matinee at the Beartree for those needin' an eye opener... after Mass, I mean. And then there he was again picking with Martz, Kidwell, and Broderick at Lightbourne's Sunday night Scam at the Buckhorn Bar in downtown Laramie. They brought it down a bit and Spot sang "Sunny Afternoon." THAT closed the Breakdown weekend for me, but they kept playing. KOCA was playing spooky Hmong vocal music while I drove back to Centennial in the dark.

Overheard at the Breakdown:

1) A Middle-aged man leading his women into the Beartree was stopped and told there was live music, he turned on a dime and said, "Mildred, we're outta here." No word on who the other woman was.

2) Gary Sisco relaxing at the bar after his set: "It's great to see that there's a scene somewhere in this country!"

3) And at one point I was alarmed to see Michael Hurley talking to some old timer. I warned Michael, "Don't listen to him; he's my dad." Michael said dad was telling him that he could tell by the song lyrics what was on all the musicians' minds. I assured Michael that my dad did in fact know what was on his own mind, me being one of nine kids and all.

Thanks to Jill and crew at the Beartree, all the musicians, esp Michaels Hurwitz (for P.A.) and Hurley (for bringing Amy, Josephine, and Gary), Lindsay Olson for paparazza services, *Arthur* magazine, Laramie Beverage (the New Belgium Sunshine sold out before I thought it safe to take a sip!), Don Woods at *KUWR*, Ted and Kristianne at *KRFC*, Aaron at the *Laramie Boomerang*, and Kathleen at the *Casper Star-Tribune*.

Hope to have Souled American out for next year's Upland Breakdown. Stay tuned.

Breakdown Lowdown on the Eights

Colorado was a bridge too far for the Breakdown. They're just too busy with all that's more interesting down there at a mere mile high. This went out as an email.

Two years ago we asked Souled American to play the Upland Breakdown. They couldn't and then last year's bill came together so fast that we couldn't ask them again when they were ready to do it. So this year we finally got it together and further set up a second day of Breakdown in Colorado. As the powers-that-be-Colo do not want to rebuild their side of the highway of death-287 they are writing a lot of tickets to keep college kids and truckers from dying on those steep curves and sleep-inducing flats. Unfortunately this affects average, innocent lawbreakers such as myself too. The early flyering trips cost me plenty; I was even nabbed from the air by Sky King hisself.

The music began on *KRFC* in Ft. Collins when Michael Hurley appeared on Friday's "Live@Lunch" where between songs, hostess Beth Malmskog dug deep into Hurley's heretofor unsuspected special diet of moss, lichens and rotting wood pulp. She also got a few wired words from Spot in his post-24-hour-drive mode (strangely I can notice no difference). Pre-festivities continued at Coal Creek Coffee where Spot, fresh from another hour of driving (287 again) and four hours of sleep-like stasis, played hot caffeine-fueled further elaborations on tunes from his new album, "In the Bag," which also features bodhranner Albert Alfonso.

SE Wyoming had rain most days in August but it was particularly dark and wet up to last Thursday, then it passed and Saturday at the Beartree in Centennial was a perfect day, people came out, tourists wandered in and Birgit Burke and J Shogren made their way thru excellent acoustic, sit-down Berryesque rock and roll. That's the problem with the Breakdown – the bill is full of headliners! Ralph White, formerly of Austin favorites, The Bad Livers, then rummaged through his instrument collection, playing and drawling his roots phantasmagoria on fiddle, banjo, squeezebox and perhaps mellotron (I stepped inside for an emergency Odells Cutthroat Porter) from his solo albums, "Trash Fish," and "Navasota River Devil Squirrel."

Gangs of three foot gunmen suddenly were running through the crowd. (Wyoming's reprobate toyshops deal cap-guns to anyone whether they have ID or not! Luckily for the music there appears to be a waiting period for rolls of caps.) I was warned by one cold-eyed hombrito never to admit I'd seen him, and when the posse came looking I asked its gun-waving leader what the varmint had done and was told he'd murdered his father is all. This was a lie cause I'd just seen his father gobbling jalapeno green chili pizza. Or could be that's what killed him and it's all a misunderstanding.

Over the din of imagined gunfire the Stop & Listen Boys rocketed through a set of twenties rock and roll featuring guitar, bass, trombone, washboard and jazzhorn; they started with "Staggerlee" in the contagious spirit of bloody mayhem. This year Michael Hurley picked his way through his set on just his electric hollowbody, Betsy, or maybe that's the name of his car, speaking of the price of gasoline caused him to fly and leave his banjo and fiddle at home. Michael played great new songs from his just-released album "Ancestral Swamp" (*Gnomonsong*). As the sun set Souled American began their sit-down electric rural psychedelia. It got dark except for the line of Christmas lights behind them and the bonfire in front of them. Can't imagine a better setting for their music; the families and tourists had gone but the rest were lined up on the benches around the fire riveted to a rare chance to see them and hear tunes from their next album. After the show Birgit, Spot, John Kidwell and others jammed around the glowing embers.

Sunday's Breakdown was on the patio at the Swing Station in LaPorte, Colorado, just NW of Fort Collins. Their stage is framed by two impressively large willow trees – another beautiful setting. Music began with a short opening set by Mike Safran, returning from the 5th Breakdown. A rainsquall shortened it further, but looking west over the Rockies we saw we could wait it out. Then Spot, and the Stop & Listen Boys played their sets. Fully warmed up as he was, Spot found even more space/time for previously unsuspected note-particles by splitting the atom right there on the neck of his guitar. The Stop & Listen Boys played this set without John Kidwell's trombone, so they had a more rural feel. (When not on stage Lightbourne seemed to be conducting an ex-girlfriend convention – no firearms involved.) The Places, which here featured Amy Annelle on guitar and vocals and Ralph White accompanying on fiddle, played a more old-timey style than Amy's solo performance last year. Amy reports she had a psychedelic experience facing into the now clear sky sunblaze; so did we. Michael again stood and played alone, but seemed to rock in place a little more emphatically this time. And watching Souled American bring the sun down two evenings in a row was some privilege. Hearing

Chris and Joe work their way thru the new song, "Libertyville," is to be awestruck.

The music ended, the musicians moved along their tours, and the banditti were cleared out by their parents. Rock and roll. Law and order. Something's got to give. See you next year.

Thanks go to all the musicians, Jill and crew at the Beartree, Brad and crew at the Swing Station, Melissa at Coal Creek Coffee, Justin Cooper, Beth Malmskog, Elliott Johnston, Tom Wilhelm, Ted Hill, Jane Schuman and crew, Jan Leonhardt, Frank Kelley, *Arthur* magazine, and Odells Brewing Co.

The Last Upland Breakdown Lowdown, 2010
This one got posted at The New Vulgate *in addition to going out by email. It wasn't ever going to be a true music festival but it was fun while it lasted.*

We had great weather on Saturday which always means good attendance as Centennial, Wyoming is a tri-state daytripper destination for anyone wanting to get out of the front-range traffic or great plains heat and up into the mountains. Tourists outside the area tend to think Yellowstone at the other end of the state so we don't often see them, which is fine by us as the grizzlies over there need feeding. But those in the know streamed into the Beartree's side-yard all afternoon and evening to fill in around the music diehards who've long known the Upland Breakdown is the mark of quality.

Upland Records was begun as an imprint of O&O Records which the Blasting Room Studio in nearby Fort Collins started in 1998 when they began to scheme to get some of the spec recordings they believed in released. Wretch Like Me and Chad Price's side-band Drag the River were the first sessions for release – Wretch on O&O, Drag the River on Upland. Chad's job #1 is vocalist for All – Bill Stevenson's Descendents line-up when Milo isn't available. The rest of Upland's roster took shape easily enough with David Lightbourne having put his Stop & Listen Boys together in Laramie, and Spot, our old SST compadre now producing his own music and touring from his adopted home in Austin. We also released records by Grandpa's Ghost, a rural Illinois concret & western band.

We started the Upland Breakdown in 2000 at the old Murph-the-Surf's, then called the Old Centennial Café, and now called the Beartree Tavern. It was the perfect venue as it was possible to move the music inside should the weather turn, which it will on occasion, though I hasten to add that the snow never amounts to much in August. I think the music tended to be better when played indoors on those occasions (Breakdowns 4, 5 & 7) due to something deep inside the musician's psychology – fresh air and sunshine just don't agree with 'em. And audiences can be somewhat distracted as well, even though the Breakdown was never a three-ring circus in the modern style of outdoor music festivals.

As you might imagine Upland Records, while still selling catalog, stopped releasing new titles back in the latter days of the Phono era and since then the Upland Breakdown has been wholly unburdened with commercial aspiration; rather, we focused on that holy grail of music-fest success, complete plumbing failure. Unfortunately Jill has augmented the drainage capacity just a flush or three ahead of our annual testing of it. Still, thought we had a chance Saturday to go out on a real low note.

Lightbourne and I began talking about Upland Breakdown 11 soon after 10 was over. I spent five months with my parents in Illinois but made a preliminary lineup announcement on March 16 just after I returned to Wyoming. Nothing but the photograph remained of that announcement – the only shot of Wyoming Hwy 130 facing east I've used on any of the flyers which always featured a scene one might see on one's way to the Beartree (unless one is some hardcase arrived from over the mountains Saratoga-side). Even Jake & Joe, regulars at Lightbourne's Buckhorn Sunday Nights, morphed into a five-piece called Oatmeal Stumble by the time the real, corrected announcement went out in late July. I got it out before I was obliged by The Hand of Fate to drive to Portland, Oregon for the Tribute-Memorial concert for David Lightbourne.

Wyoming was well represented at that event at the White Eagle Tavern by many of the players who played with David over the years at the Breakdown, the Buckhorn and elsewhere. And this year for the 11th and final Upland Breakdown it was all Wyoming musicians once again.

Here's who played over the years as best I can remember – there are slight discrepancies between who played and who was announced and/or appeared on the flyers – not that we were untogether or anything! But in the all too short passed times, I'd've just called up Dave and asked him...

1, 2000 - The Stop & Listen Boys, Spot, Drag the River, Grandpa's Ghost, Michael Hurwitz.
2, 2001 - Grandpa's Ghost, Stop & Listen Boys, John Martz, Maggie Simpson.
3, 2002 - Drag the River, Stop & Listen Boys, Leghorn, Mumbletypeg.
4, 2003 - Spot, Stop & Listen Boys, Michael Hurwitz, Maggie Simpson, Birgit Burke & John Lyon.
5, 2004 - Michael Hurley, David Lightbourne, Spot, Michael Hurwitz, Michael Safran.
6, 2005 - Michael Hurwitz, David Lightbourne, Spot, Birgit Burke & J Shogren.
7, 2006 - Stop & Listen Boys, Michael Hurley, Josephine Foster, Gary Sisco, The Places, Spot, Michael Hurwitz.
8, 2007 - Souled American, Stop & Listen Boys, Michael Hurley, Amy Annelle, Ralph White, Spot.

9, 2008 - Stop & Listen Boys, Michael Hurley, Precious Blood, Al Rivers, The Alltunators.
10, 2009 - Stop & Listen Boys, Al Rivers, Michael Hurwitz, Black Crow White Crow, Spot.
11, 2010 - J Shogren Shanghai'd, Ben Slater, Oatmeal Stumble, Mike Safran, Jeff Duloz.

(*originally posted at* The New Vulgate, *No. 60)*

From the Northwest Desk of Joe Carducci...
This was written in Seattle after spending a few days in Portland to attend an August 2010 Memorial concert for David Lightbourne and was posted at The New Vulgate *soon after.*

It was seasonably muggy in Portland but as I haven't lived there since we moved Systematic to Berkeley in 1979, I forgot how summer works here. I'm now calibrated to a short high-desert summer. But the Tribute concert for David Lightbourne was a labor intensive affair so I didn't get to walk around in the northwest-side-and-downtown environs I once trod with David. He had a show on *KBOO* ("David Lightbourne's Rock 'n Roll House Party" - titled after Art Linkletter's early, enduring TV program) and I got mine thru his ministrations. We also worked together at the Cinema 21.

David's brother, Michael, lives well south of there and I had to put time in on David's primo collection of twenties/thirties blues-oldtimey albums, merely damn fine collection of fifties/sixties folk-blues albums, and pretty decent collection of everything else until about 1970 or so. After that it's all Koerner Ray & Glover, or Hurley or Clamtones or Rounders continuations. I got about half of Dave's albums categorized and alphabetized last week. Have to do the rest another time. While I did that there were rehearsals going on in Michael's front room as David's friends from Cambridge and Wyoming worked out their tunes for Saturday. In the lead-up to the Saturday event itself I revisited *KBOO*'s punk program and we also did a live interview and music program for David. (Those shows are archived at *KBOO*.)

I also wedged in meetings with two old friends, Archie Patterson and Randy Jahnson. Archie founded the *Eurock* fanzine in 1973 and he dropped his 700-page doorstop of an anthology on me which happy to say includes my Sadistic Mika Band album roundup from 1978. We caught up on our separate moves up and down the west coast over the years and I answered the inevitable question, Whyoming? Archie had the insane record collection because he was once upon a time the only person in America interested in German psychedelia, et. al. But it's gone, he sold it, put down your crowbars you'll find nothing but a happy couple in the house now.

Randy directed those music videos of the Minutemen and Black Flag that people are always amazed even exist when they see them. He also wrote the screenplay for *The Doors* (1991) and other films. He moved up here recently from Pasadena where he once told me he was out-of-the-Hollywood loop even down there. So I guess the internet is dissolving the Hollywood game too. We met for a beer at another McMenamins monster salvage job. They aren't bad for a ubiquitous hippie-era corporation but it is sad to see a classic Portland elementary school (Kennedy) turned into a playground for today's Portland arteoisie. The walls are covered in Portland artists' works except for the odd enlargements of old school portraits of various classes and faculty groupings – they seem a different race of people and their images may function as a kind of scalp-taking by the new race. Everything now in Portland is somebody's idea of green-and-improved and a man can't even pump his own gas in Oregon. Randy is nevertheless doing a rewrite of my "Yeung Girl" script and it looks like it may get made.

The official artist for David Lightbourne's Stop & Listen Boys, Maya Carducci, showed up with her family and so I spent time with them. Steve Weber's ex-, Essie Weber, was seen prying Maya's drawing off the wall of the White Eagle Saloon (McMenamins again), but the event was winding down and I hear she has a great Holy Modal Rounder poster archive so it's in good company. You can see that drawing at *NV 56*. Anyway Dave's friend from Iowa-days in the early sixties, Tom Newman kicked things off with a spoken piece on David's coming of age at Grinnell-and-thereafter, after which the music started and never stopped. It went past the 2am closing time (I want the State of Oregon to know – David-the-criminal to the end!).

It was an exceptional evening of music with many notable figures from around the country's music scenes from Oregon to Vermont. Lots of talking about David, lots of his old friends reconnecting after decades, lots of young folks blessing their lucky stars they crossed paths with Sleepy Dave Lightbourne, and everyone in the White Eagle was riveted by Michael Lightbourne's set which began with "The Midnight Special," theme song from the *WFMT* program of the same name which he and his brother secretly listened to every week and began them on their blues and folk paths. Each tune prompted a telling story told and Michael's ballad, "Ode to Davy," with its classic folk-song storyline kept everyone straining to hear every detail in the epic that was David.

(*originally posted at The New Vulgate, No. 58*)

The Nig-Heist
When Drag City Records decided the world needed the Nig-Heist album re-issued, naturally they called me. Mugger's bomb dropped in 1984 on Thermidor. Ego Trip was the smartest of the hip-hop mags that proliferated in the nineties. Paul Sommerstein, then at Matador Records, faxed me questions and I answered after conferring with the former Artist occasionally still known as Mugger. Paul got more excited as it became clear to him that, sure enough, the Nig-Heist might reasonably be bracketed with both Black Flag and black culture.

5.9.98

Paul.

Yeah, I expected to hear from *Ego Trip*. Thanks for the *NYPress* article; it's a pretty good piece. I don't know what Matador has released lately but I know I'd like to get copies of The Toiling Midgets LP you did a few years ago, and the "Half-Cocked" VHS that I think you released. Thanks.

1 Context?
JC – The Nig-Heist wasn't intended to make any larger censorship point. It was a natural outgrowth of Mugger's personality and the musical interests of the Black Flag road crew (Mugger, Spot, Davo and others). As Black Flag was one of the first independent touring bands and many of their first gigs were informal DIY garage-jobs done for whoever asked they got to be known and respected quickly.

They were fearlessly casual Southern Californians who yet spent an ungodly amount of time and energy forging an extremely exacting music and then doing the grunt work of releasing and promoting their own records. They cut quite a profile around the country in much more depressive and reactionary situations. They were far more accessible than the Ramones had ever been and Mugger and Spot as the roadie and soundman were even more off-handedly intimidating in their easy scamming grace because, after all, what kind of dudes of color (Spot is black and Mugger is some kind of SoCal mutt) would be hanging with the Flag ("White Minority" and all). And if you didn't know they were crew, you'd take them for stars.

In a *Maximum Rock 'n Roll* interview the Texas band M.D.C. complained that Black Flag's records were so intense and then they'd roll into town and it was, "Alright! Where are the broads?!" That was Mugger being Mugger and also Mugger fucking with American Crass-wannabes.

When Mugger was a kid he had a band with two black kids who were sons of doctors. Their parents wouldn't let Mugger come over so they practiced in Mugger's garage. Spot is a musical wunderkind and back from Black Flag tours they'd have time to horse around on the band's equipment at the Church or Media Art studio where Spot could always scam late nights because he lived there. Mike Watt put out a call for contributions for his record label's compilations and the Nig-Heist debuted with an anti-hippie jam called "The Nig-Heist" for the "Chunks" EP. This tune was written by Mugger's friend Henley who was Darby Crash's boyfriend – let's say one of them, Darby was very progressive.

Later in '81 I left Systematic for SST. We all slept on the floor for the next two years. The first thing Mugger told me was to watch out for Spot because he might try to slide it in during the night. These two roadcrew superstars and some bass-playing chick named Teri came out of the Unicorn practice room with a cassette recorded on a mono Panasonic portable. Song was "Walking Down the Street" and sounded perfect for the record label I'd left behind, Thermidor, where we'd wanted to release a series of un-single-like 45s. Mugger didn't have a tune for the B-side so we decided to etch a plea to get laid onto the back. John Golden shrugged and smilingly commenced etching on another lacquer. This 45 should now be worth $200 but it's only worth $25.

Later, Spot no longer went on the tours, and Mugger became soundman and Davo was roadie. Black Flag tired of getting on stage late because every damn punk band in town had to get on the gig, so they began delivering the whole show: Nig-Heist opening, an SST band in the middle slot and Black Flag. This regularly touring Nig-Heist was made up of Mugger, Davo, and bits of Flag and other crew and they debuted just as the audience outside LA began to grow. These kids were from high school and were used to running in groups. (Early punk was made up of loner misfits – Nice to meet you.) These new kids made up rules and fashion etiquette. They'd misread Black Flag and extrapolated or reacted themselves into tight little purist codes. Then they get to the Black Flag gig and see what, Toxic Reasons? Youth Brigade? Sorry, welcome to the Nig-Heist, junior. This early hard-core audience scene was a rigid boys club and not at all like the loose over-the-top Los Angeles culture the early SST crew was coming from, Mugger being one of the first of 'em.

1b Joke band?
JC – They weren't a joke band and Mugger was annoyed when the shuffling of players in Black Flag shuffled the Nig-Heist as well and set the music back to relearning the set. Still, we needed Mugger to leave the endless tour and work the SST office with me as the label got busy, so the Heist was gonna go down. The album, alternately known as "Understanding Basic Economics" or "Snort My Load," was done during extended down time as Black Flag fought a court battle over the "Damaged" album.

2 Common reactions?
JC – I only saw west coast gigs. The most common response was "Fuck you hippie, you suck." Musically and sexually the Nig-Heist was ridiculing this new hardcore scene's idea that you could do without the seventies or music history generally. If the heckler had a girlfriend Mugger would start in on her, or if he didn't Mugger would naturally assume that he and his bros were homos and proceed from there. I remember a San Francisco gig after *Maximum Rock 'n Roll* had given up on Black Flag as hopelessly politically regressive and we talked about this because of something friends had heard to that effect on *Maximum*'s *KPFK* radio show, and so Mugger took it upon himself to interrupt his normal string of interruptions between Nig-Heist tunes to demand that *Maximum*'s one female, Ruth Schwartz, come up onstage and be butt-fucked. This was the first Black Flag gig that the *Maximum* collective hadn't showed so they only got to hear about it. And no doubt they did; it was shockingly uncalled for, and therefore extremely funny. Mugger felt bad afterwards because he didn't even know who she was. I told him not to worry, you can't abuse anybody who lives in San Francisco enough.

There were some arrests for nudity on stage on the final Nig-Heist tour, some of which involved game (and possibly gamy) female volunteers from the audience. I repro Mugger's mug shot from Denver in my book.

3 Name?
JC – "Nig-Heist" was Mugger's comeback term when his friend Eugene (the bald black kid in *Decline of Western Civilization*) cracked on his white boy stealing to get by in Hollywood. It became his synonym for rip-off. Useage: If Mugger couldn't find his pen he might say, "Spot, did you nig-heist my pen?" (Mugger used pens to draw cocks on boxes of records waiting for UPS.) One idea for the album cover was to have Spot and Mugger with television sets under their arms being chased out of Watts. That was rejected by Thermidor bigwigs for not being insensitive enough. It was Spot's idea to have Knucklehead getting a blow job, and my contribution

to have the blower be Chatty Cathy with Knucklehead pulling her string. Thank you very much. It was Mugger's idea to title the album 'Understanding Basic Economics – James Flanigan.' What a sicko.

Declassified Records, Dear Audio Buff
Henry sent new blank TDK SA-90s to Charlie, and he'd return his blues on the most beat-up used cassettes available behind bars. We decided to give him his own imprint rather than put him on SST, and named it after a Lightbourne concept. I used a pseudonym to write old style record label blarney. It was not released.

Dear Audio Buff,
You hold in your hands a rare and exciting recording. It is a recording the likes of which too often goes unheard. Whether entirely obscure or whether notorious in some way, many worthy recordings languish in private collections available only to scholars. Despite the current wide range of worthy and necessary independent record labels for the dissemination of the recorded word and music there remains a desperate need for an unbiased outlet for certain types of de facto classified information.

It is for this reason I and my associates have initiated this company, Declassified Records. We intend to search out and obtain the rights to materials that existing record labels may have ignored, feared, or simply been unaware of, thus barring your access to said material. This potential narrowing of the information spectrum is of proper concern to us all.

The recording we hereby declassify may provoke or unnerve or outrage or even horrify the listener. We can only hope that it does for it is in the reconciling of new information that shocks our systems, with our own ideas and perceptions of our common and personal realities, that our assumptions are tested and new insights risked. We trust our intentions will be understood in this project. Your comments and suggestions would be appreciated.

Alexander DiHerrerra, Mexico City, D.F.

The New Wave

Posterity Alert. I forgot about this one. It ran in the Clinton St. Quarterly, *a Portland paper in Spring 1979. We were building mail order and distribution at Renaissance (pre-Systematic) and I did a punk radio show at KBOO. It's pretty bad but I was writing to a kind of post-rock hippie art crowd, and it says something about that period.*

As the music Industry divested itself of all the problem artists (Wildman Fischer, Captain Beefhart, New York Dolls, Iggy Pop, MC5, Dictators, Nico, etc.) it had collected in the late sixties/early seventies and got down to serious megabuck business with marketable brand name product (Led Zeppelin, Rod Stewart, Boston, Who, Dylan), more and more people began looking elsewhere for imagination and individuality in their music.

A group of bands from West Germany became surprisingly popular because of this. Though these included Tangerine Dream, Kraftwerk, Can, and Amon Düül - bands that allowed the prospect of popularity in the United States to lead them into sell-out via artistic concessions, slick production and embarrassingly bad attempts at English lyrics - they also included Faust, Cluster, Neu, TSS, Uli Trepte, and maybe Klaus Schultze - bands that insisted on their artistic vision and either continued to produce distinctive music or died trying.

Beyond West Germany, excellent bands began recording in France (Etron Fou le Loublan, Heldon, Lard Free), Finland (Wigwam), Poland (SBB, Test), East Germany (Puhdys) and other places. Most of the records being imported at the time by American distributors were uninteresting remodeled versions of British or American forms but the bands named above were/are actively attempting to articulate something, rather than simply pursuing a well paying job (stardom).

Unfortunately these bands were not recognized as an important alternative to the musical status quo by enough people to have affected that status quo. It was left to others to reactivate the Anglo-American music scene - to make the music culturally, politically, and personally valid again.

Of the active bands in the Anglo world of the seventies that can be considered to have artistic depth (Eno, King Crimson, Henry Cow), only David Bowie can also be considered to have been popular enough to have had wide influence on the prevailing musical atmosphere. But by the mid-seventies Bowie, like the establishment bands, had cut touring in the UK to one date in London a year.

In Britain music is much less the casual interest it is in the US and soon British kids began wondering why they should accept a situation where they must consider themselves lucky to get to London for that one Bowie show, never minding that the show itself takes place in a huge stadium where they would have to take it on trust that that orange haired speck really was Bowie. This situation was soon intolerable and all it took was some real touring by an unknown New York band called The Ramones to remind the kids how it's done.

The music establishment, if they paid any attention at all to them, thought the Ramones were a bad joke. Now, four albums later, some edict has been handed down at *Rolling Stone* magazine and the Ramones have been cleared. Its okay to like them. They still won't admit, however, that the Ramones were, rather, a good joke and that they, *Rolling Stone* and the other reputable rock media were the target of that joke.

Think of it, all the old stale forms of western popular music have had their revenge on rock and roll that replaced them in the fifites and sixties. Barry Manilow is Frank Sinatra in disguise. It really gets convoluted when all this muck insists on calling itself rock music. Because when a band comes along that just so happens to be rock and roll incarnate the "rock" media do not recognize it.

Duplicity breeds cynicism and the British bands that formed in the wake of the Ramones were that, at least in so far as their attitudes to the music world they inherited. At the same time, though, they were honestly optimistic and hopeful about the culture they were making because now thousands of kids were out creating for themselves instead of lining up to buy the new Ted Nugent album. Overnight, bands began putting out their own records and the more overtly political made it a point to turn down any offer from the Industry.

There are now perhaps a thousand bands in both the UK and US alternative scenes. (There are at least ten in the Portland area.) This many bands of course do not all play what is commonly called punk. "Punk" as a term is only useful now as a general name for the new alternative music whether it be electronic (Human League, the Normal), avant rock (Pere Ubu, Chrome, Metal Urbain), or rock and roll because punk has created the milieu wherein these bands were appreciated.

The punk explosion has also put in touch the various alternate musics that had been developing in secluded corners of the music world in addition to reawakening people to the important music of the past. So someone in touch with the cultural opposition today is likely to listen to and draw upon reggae and dub music out of Jamaica and London's ghettos, reissued albums of sixties' punk and psychedelia (Red Crayola, the Remains, 13th Floor Elevators), reactivated and new rockabilly bands (Ray Campi, Carl Perkins, Matchbox), the continental bands (Etron Fou, Magma), in addition to the wide variety of sound and attitude within the new punk music (from Pere Ubu to the Dils to John Cooper-Clarke to DNA to the Screamers to Wire and on and on).

This active subculture provides the perfect audience for an album like the Plastic People of the Universe's, recently released in France. This band has not been together for years due to the Czech government's curious habit of throwing the band members into prison. One member has recently had his sentence doubled to eighteen months. And since Dubcek, the band and others of the cultural opposition have, of course, had gigs cancelled and broken up by police etc, etc. This album was released by a policial group in France once tapes had been smuggled out of Czechoslovakia. Aside from some hippie excess (Czechoslovakia's last major rock infusion from the West came in the late sixties) their attitude is strictly of today:

> "Instruction" (translation)
> ...Throw away your brains,
> Throw away your hearts,
> Throw away everything
> That makes men out of you.
> Be changed into swine.
> Be changed into swine...

The sarcasm reminds one of you-know-who.

The extent of this new culture is easy to ignore in this country due to have constricted the normal channels of art dispersion (radio, magazines, television, the record industry) have become. So unless one was never out of touch with the largely ignored links between the sixties' alternative culture and the current one, or happened to move in circles that included the nearest local outlet for it (assuming there was one), one could quite easily be oblivious to it as an option. That someone might also continue to believe that punk has more to do with spit and vomit than freedom of action, which is too bad. No doubt the local scene could use that someone's participation.

Whether all this activity is just energy expended will of course depend on what the eighties bring. If they are as lifeless as the seventies; it could be. But considering that the current tax cuts mean that neither will the underclass have its condition bought off any longer by the state, nor the upper middle class creative types have their CETA money to play around with, then add the prospect that the draft will be reinstituted due to population drop and the need for "better" material for our next adventure, and one can see that the same old contradictions are lying just below the surface. The civilized nations of the world are still intent on feeding upon their young.

And when it comes to music that inspires people to challenge what is, its not Dylan or the Stones or Jefferson Airplane any more. And it sure has hell ain't Boston or Heart. Open ears and an open mind will tell you, its Metal Urbain or the Dils or Crisis or Alternative TV or Siouxie and the Banshees or the Clash or Public Image Ltd or X-Ray Spex or Stiff Little Fingers...

Sadistic Mika Band

Posterity Alert. This was published in Eurock #12, November 1978. I'd moved up to Portland the year before and met Eurock's Archie Patterson on day one, David Lightbourne a couple days later, the guys at Renaissance Records a week later and saw Formica and the Bitches play that winter.

"Sadistic Mika Band"
"Black Ship"
"Hot Menu"
"Live in London"

In the early '70s while the US and UK music industries were honing their production techniques so as to allow vacuous no-talents to pose as earnest musicians, Japanese kids were still coming to terms with basic rock and roll. Those bands with a serious air like Men Tan Pin and Creation put out albums in the British blues vein. The first Sadistic Mika Band album however, was and remains unique in its bold mixture of blood and guts rock, electronics and lyricism, in addition to the striking production by main man Katoh and the flashy tackiness of the cover art. "Dance is Over," "Arienu Republic," "Shadow Show" and "Picnic Boogie" are the rockers. "Dance" is fast-paced and Katoh's vocals are so hot they're shredded. "Arienu" has an infectious chorus and powerful theme. "Shadow Show" exhibits Tanaka's lead guitar. "Picnic Boogie" closes the album with rambunctious good humor. It has blues riffing, shoo-be-doo-wops, wah-wah guitars and a soaring chorus. The other cuts range from light and airy songs to playful and quirky with spicy electronic and percussive hooks.

At this point SMB fell into Chris Thomas' hands and his production moves the sound from a flexible rock and roll to studio progressive. BLACK SHIP bats only three for nine. "Time Machine" is straight ahead rock with strong Mika vocals, but a weak rhythm section bottom; "Yoroshiku Dozo" is only an intro to Side Two, but its jaunty sax is a highlight; "Sayonara," the album closer, is a beautiful acoustic lament with Katoh's light electric guitar and organ bringing it to a close. The rest of the material is mainly pedestrian progressive funk. There are moments of interest, but they are buried deep.

HOT MENU released in '75 is a bit better. "Time to Noodle" is a fast instrumental romp; "Aquablue" picks up its smooth lyricism into a nice bouncy chorus; "Mada Mada Samba" has nice Latin sounding acoustic and laconic humor; "Hi Jack (I'm Just Dying)" has a pretty e-piano intro and ends with a synth theme that gains in intensity as it repeats. It, along with "Okinawa (Strange-Fish)," "Style Is Changing," and "Tokyo Sunrise" are the only SMB songs with extensive English vocals. "Tokyo Sunrise" begins with the drug-tired Mika talking to herself as she fumbles to mix a drink over a lonely western sounding guitar and ends with snoring, a blowing wind and acoustic guitar. "Okinawa" has interludes of exotic percussion; "Style Is Changing" has a soaring guitar line; "Funky Mahjong" is funk with an imaginative vocal arrangement and "Mummy Doesn't Go To Parties Since Daddy Died" is passable.

SADISTIC MIKA BAND LIVE IN LONDON is a bad recording all around with persistent hiss, a mix that leaves the bottom out and lifeless performances. Passing interest is generated only in sections of "Time To Noodle," "Silver Child," and "Black Ship." It shows that SMB were not hot musicians. It was Chris Thomas' heavy hand that constructed a progressive Muzak around them. They should have stayed a rock and roll band, they had the chops for that.

Tangerine Dream – "Sorcerer" (MCA)

Posterity Alert. See the film, but the trailer is the masterpiece. Star Wars *opened at the Chinese then was bumped for* Sorcerer *which was expected to be huge. It emptied Graumann's of even tourists while* Star Wars *sold out the Hollywood Theater from 9am on. One week later* Star Wars *was back at the Chinese; it ran for months and the world ended; I moved to Portland. This is also from* Eurock, *September 1977.*

According to director Friedkin in the album's liner notes, Tangerine Dream sent him ninety minutes of music for the film's score. Of that ninety about forty-five are contained on the album and of that, only about ten are actually used in the film. The only sustained use of the music is over the end credits. The two cuts used there are "Betrayal (Sorcerer Theme)" and "Grind" which are also available on a single.

"Betrayal" is the only piece that sounds unforced. There is inspiration behind it and the music is direct and confident. It has a charging rhythm that plays against a murky, ominous undertone.

It is the lack of tone that makes the rest of the music fail, at least as far as soundtrack music for such a doom-laden film as SORCERER. "Grind," "Rain Forest," "Impressions of Sorcerer," and "Search" are all far from being lousy pieces of music, but they are moodless and incomplete musical ideas. Moodlessness can be blamed on the musicians, but the faded endings and under three minute average running time indicate that MCA did its own editing.

EUROCK, VOL. II NO. I, SEPT. 1977.

As far as sound dynamics SORCERER has interesting moments. Froese's guitar work is light, clean and rounded in "Search" and "The Call," but too wild and rocky in "Impressions of Sorcerer." "Impressions..." also has some unexpected synthesized Latin percussion that works well. The melancholy synthi-flute heard on other Dream albums also appears here on "The Journey" and "The Mountain Road" and an effective synthicricket sound runs through "Rain Forest." "Main Title," and "Abyss" contain the wildest ranges of sound on the record, including the deep foreboding buzz over which light bubble-like sounds skitter in "Main Title," and the subdued drone that evolves into a panic-paced battle of mellotron and synthesizer before falling apart in "Abyss."

There are many valid sound images in SORCERER, but a combination of editing and T. Dream's recent veer towards the rock market sabotaged the creative process whereby those images would have been integrated into music with artistic vision. As it is, SORCERER is further evidence that they are stuck in a holding pattern.

Books.

~

End Times for the Hero: The Batman & Frank Miller

(I'm no expert on comics, we weren't allowed them as kids, but something I said about Peru's Fujimori in my New Vulgate *piece on Lori Berenson sent the L.A. Review of Books my way so I gave it a shot. I expanded it for the* New Vulgate, *plus a little extra here.)*

When we easy-living post-mod children of the post-war boom reach back for handfuls of cultural humus to ground our own reveries, it's usually twenties-thirties modern whether we realize it or not. Our conscious backstop is WWII, which mobilized the men, transformed the homefront, and lived on through the cold war where we wore the white hat globally. This began to break apart in the sixties but not fully and not soon enough to save them with the black hat. However, baby boom myth liked to portray the 1950s humus as sterile, and this more recent golden age wasn't made direct use of until the punk era had run through its immediate sources and found itself fascinated with Johnny Cash, Link Wray, et. al. The attachment to the Roaring Twenties and the Depression tends to be reflexive. Harry Smith began it for us in the early 1950s with his excavation and representation of songs and art from back before the war ("The Anthology of Folk Music," Vols. 1-4). The influences continued thru folk music and the blues revival. And early hippie-era graphics often trolled the twenties for inspiration; R. Crumb is famously only interested in twenties music. And just a year ago music photographer Jenny Lens was insisting on the silent vamps influence on the seventies punk female look, especially in L.A.

But in this ongoing borrowing, the sunnier appetite of fans is in a footrace with the sour drive of university adjuncts as they interrogate the hero or at least knock the white hat off him. The collegiate plaintiffeoisie has some ongoing need to pose as their own supercritic-hero dragging into the dock some stand-in for their parents. American WWII victory culture was that intimidating, and the burdens of the cold war that intolerable to the generations that followed, who must have suspected that any achievements of their own must necessarily pale in comparison, or even have questionable authorship given the headstart in a clear field the thirties-forties provided us.

The Superman franchise has been easier to relaunch and so it has greater continuity through comics, movies, television, merch. Bob Kane's answer to Superman bears a heavier load, and as a creature of the night can even be sucked into that still spreading after-the-fact revisionist *faux* category, Noir, from which there is now no escape. Batman and Johnny Cash both got caught on the goth conveyer-belt to noir at the end of the nineties. If all those gospel recordings and all his praying couldn't save the man in black what chance did the Batman have?

Superman had a six-year gestation before anyone saw him, whereas Batman was ordered up one weekend to reproduce Superman's sales figures. If Jerry Siegel and Joe Shuster pulled from science fiction and the Jewish legend of the Golem, Kane pulled rather from films: two Roland West films adapted from the 1922 Broadway hit, *The Bat*, as well as from Douglas Fairbanks' *The Mark of Zorro* (1920). West's 1926 version featured sets

THE BAT (1926).

by William Cameron Menzies and was shot by Arthur Edeson with Gregg Toland apprenticing; West remade his own film as a talkie titled, *The Bat Whispers* (1930). Both films are visually innovative comic mysteries – what used to be called "old dark house" pictures. In these films (and the play) a master thief wears the mask and cape. He baits the police with mocking notes and the earlier film even features a bat signal. Fairbanks played Don Diego as a louche fop so as to better disguise the masked, stout-hearted, acrobatic Zorro. Superman's Clark Kent alter ego tracks closer to Zorro, both feature comic relief as women despair over the uselessness of the alter ego, wishing he might be more like the hero. The mask Bruce Wayne wears to become Batman had an interesting pull on young boys and their heroic fantasies. The mask promises that one's deeds will speak for themselves and reveal one's true identity, rather than the grubby little kid one actually is. The Lone Ranger used this aspect as well.

Batman debuted in *Detective Comics* in 1939, one year after *Superman*. *Dick Tracy* had debuted in *Tribune* papers in 1931. It was Chester Gould's daily comic strip that set the crime-fighting scene and discovered readership appetite for an implacable force for justice against criminal impunity. This appetite was struck in twenties Chicago. The big town was an instant city of new money and immigrant poverty – the biggest crap game ever, where America bet that masses of Catholics could be made over into Americans, and that blacks might had a future here as well. Prohibition had failed to dent Catholic drinking habits, and they re-charged cracker racism of the south with grave peasant fear. Marcus Garvey was promoting repatriation to Liberia in the twenties. It wasn't clear this bet would be won. But Bismarck was right, "God has a special providence for fools, drunks and the United States of America," though he too (Bismarck, that is) had his doubts about Catholics. America's enemies at home and abroad would thus do well to surrender, drop rifle or pen and emigrate or immigrate as the case may be. The immigrants that did come and the blacks who came north understood finely in a first-person risk-reward sense that beneath all the roiling cruelty of the city a better deal might be had.

Mayor Anton Cermak was one of those immigrants; elected in 1931 he made a political machine out of the ethnic stew spilling through the neighborhoods. Convention still has it that Giuseppe Zangara was aiming for Franklin Roosevelt went he shot and killed Cermak, but FDR wasn't even the President yet and wasn't standing near Cermak. In Chicago, given the pace of events ahead of Prohibition's end and the approaching World's Fair, no-one doubted Capone, on his way to jail, and Nitti, who'd survived assassination by the Mayor's extra-legal thugs, had sent the Sicilian sharpshooter to hit "Pushcart Tony." Chicago was the capitol of the country until FDR's New Deal and the War resized the Federal government only to see the national imagination shift west to Los Angeles come the forties and fifties.

The superhero phenomenon arose from young sons shamed by their immigrant fathers who couldn't speak English and worked unheroic though often quite dangerous jobs. They kept their heads down while bootleggers and white slavers fought for streets in a wide open town. They understood only the old country ways and saw this crossfire as a kind of WWI redux – a Chicago World War – fought by ethnic mafias rather than states – the Italians, Poles, Czechs, Slovaks, Serbs, Croats, Irish, Jews, and blacks all had their rooting interests in the crime-family battles. So did the Pols and the Police, and sometimes even the miniscule WASP elite. Newsprint was the cultural currency. And little boys burned for a response to this impunity and from the early thirties they found it in *Dick Tracy*, radio's "*Lone Ranger*" and "*Green Hornet*," and *Superman*, and *Batman*. Picture those kids helping their European-born or former sharecropper fathers read *Dick Tracy* at the end of the day.

Chester Gould introduced high-tech gadgets and super-villains but Tracy himself was not quite a superhero; the other superheroes would be more fully owned by the kids.

*

Frank Miller, a lover of Gotham, has his Dark Knight Batman-reset nod to this Chicago source with a reference to Commissioner Gordon's "sketchy" early days as a Chicago cop. (Now there's some story loam: Dick Tracy's departmental rival.) And Batman's Gotham continues to feature the human scale surface street bridges one sees rising and lowering over the Chicago River rather than the few massive arterial bridges that barely connect Manhattan to the other boroughs. But Miller picked the right superhero to adapt. The original can be improved. Kane eventually built up a distinctive gallery of arch-criminals, but graphically, only the title-page portraits of "the Batman" really hit with the power of an arcane icon, and DC Comics didn't dare commit graphically to a night-world of black-and-white and so Batman jumps around in an incongruously brightly colored night. None of Hollywood's black-and-white chapter-serials based on the comics were any good, but the four *Dick Tracy* features made in the mid-40s look great and point to the kind of production Batman in particular would've benefited from (these were directed by William Berke, Gordon Douglas, and John Rawlins). Another missed bet was the quick addition of sidekick Robin which insulted all but the youngest reader. If Batman can't be a brooding loner in the night, who can be? Robin appears one year into *Batman*'s run in *Detective Comics* when he is still battling run-of-the-mill criminals and syndicates. Another issue later is the first free-standing *Batman* No. 1 comic and it introduces The Joker.

Frank Miller in his introduction to the collection *Absolute Dark Knight* makes veiled reference to Frederick Wertham's 1954 anti-comic book polemic, *Seduction of the Innocent*, where the good doctor accused *Batman* comics of being "psychologically homosexual." In the mid-sixties, *The Realist* revisited Wertham for laughs but also for real in John Cochran's "Batman and Robin were lovers." Of course in the sixties we may be juvenile but we aren't authentically modern anymore, though the comics are still being issued and in fact the pop zeitgeist-grabbing "*Batman*" television show is just around the corner. *Mad Magazine*, *The Realist* and underground comics are publishing funny, derisive, lewd versions of famous daily strip and comic book characters and it seems the backroom cynicism of politics, newsroom, and showbiz has invaded our living rooms. I often think of Jack Brewer's poem for the Saccharine Trust piece, "Emotions and Anatomy", which ends:

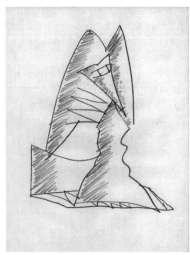
JOE CARDUCCI.

"Because the world is perverse
We must live through our imaginations.
When our imaginations become perverse
All that is left is... is... is..."
(V.A. – The Blasting Concept, Vol. II)

Miller responds to the over- and underground subterfuge by enlisting a female Robin (the original Robin, Dick Grayson, has gone bad) which contemporizes this aging Batman's world, adding sexual tension to Bruce Wayne's lifelong commitment to honor his parents, murdered back in the roaring twenties of impunity. Miller is grounded in the original real thing of comics, so while influenced by the underground comics of the sixties and seventies he doesn't surrender to them. He writes that human nature is "immutable," and with this simple declaration he throws off much of the worst political pretense of the last century. The sixties version of that pretense was dumbed-down New Left cant and proffered by poli-sci washouts or pseudo-artists who moved in the wake of the old left, the civil rights movement, rock and roll or Crumb. The hippies sought the natural man until one named Charlie showed up. Face it, the only New

Man possible in the world of comic book crime-fighters is the next hideous black-hearted mutant announcing himself with some insane outrage – like Manson, id in full effect.

Miller loves the melodrama of the comics form and speaks in an interview of hoping to cause his reader to slow down for appreciation of the art against the impulse to race along the storyline. A story chopped into a procession of frames colliding and sparking off each other makes the comic a better illustration of Eisenstein's theory of montage than film, because the motion picture, or living picture as it was called in its early history, finds its initial power in the framing of motion. But when a comic book run is collected and reprinted in bound editions, much less an extravagant, large, boxed, hard cover glossy re-framing of form like this edition, it's cheap glory is corrupted by promising too much. The graphic-novelization of comics is a wrong turn as sure as Cinerama was for cinema. I never saw the original issue of Miller's work and I'm sure those who have, value the high-tone reproductions of the original artwork now available but in terms of storytelling it shifts the weight away from story and the normal porn of form to the distracting fetish of printing specs.

*

In Miller's Batman stories it's the corruption of truth that the electronic news-media yields and wields that concerns him. In Kane's original, newspapermen are merely bumbling fools blaming Batman for crimes he is hot on the trail solving. Now the omnipresent faces on screens seem a willful chorus of some sealed-off collective id – reporters barely see the streets and by the end its *"News in the Nude,"* cutting to spokesmen, fuming heads and a holographic president.

In *The Dark Knight Returns* (1986) Miller placed a middle-aged Batman in a seventies New York that inspired films like *Death Wish* (1974), *The Warriors* (1979), *Defiance* (1980), and *Escape from New York* (1981). In *The Dark Knight Strikes Again* (2001-2) Batman is fully aged and now the internet deepens the corruption of truth as the superhero's own fans band together to counter television's calumny and succeed mostly in presenting one more obstacle to necessary action by the hero. Miller catches a New York at the end of Mayor Rudy Giuliani's tenure. The one-party polity had turned to a Republican who was seen as a last hope crime-fighter, and amazingly he delivered and head-manned newly ascendant Gotham to the point that even the suits claim they miss the old Times Square. As reward Giuliani was exiting the stage a lame-duck laughingstock, dragging himself towards divorce and chemotherapy. And then super-villains attacked from their secret lair on September 11th.

Miller writes of his Dark Knight stories,

> "Much of what I was after was to use the crime-ridden world around me to portray a world that needed an obsessive, Herculean, half-maniac genius to bring order. But that was only half the job. I saved my nastiest venom... for the vapid, pandering talking heads who so poorly chronicled the gigantic conflicts of the time. What would these little people do if giants walked the Earth? How would they regard a powerful, demanding, unrepentant hero? Or a villain whose soul is as black as death? Fifteen years passed. I found out. I was halfway thru *The Dark Knight Strikes Again* when the Twin Towers collapsed and thousands of my neighbors were slaughtered." (*Absolute Dark Knight*)

The Dark Knight Strikes Again couldn't thereafter be the "affectionate romp" he intended, but it was too late to change its title to, say, The Dark Knight Strikes Out. While the art's color shifts after 9/11 into an unhinged computer-chromaticized scheme – not quite air-brush minimal, not quite psychedelic – the story skids out into an end-times for the hero as Batman – Bruce Wayne under mask and cape – begins to break down due to age and the pressure of a seemingly hopeless battle. The overwhelming weakness of the city around him means even the legion of attending superheroes can make no difference as each that throws in with Batman and Robin are quickly preoccupied with simple survival. They mostly do.

The superhero of the world of comics is a profane version of the story of Christ, and not far removed from those mortals who intervened in the histories of their similarly collapsing nations – Fujimori, Pinochet, Franco – and were called fascists for their trouble. A simple question, *Compared to what?*, comes to mind.

But the world of comics must be a single city – the city as planet. It's a mistake to acknowledge Chicago or Washington as Miller does. Cataclysm in Gotham reminded its citizens that they needed Giuliani, but he never should've run for President; President of what? For him there is nothing but his city. There are limitations to the pop metaphysics of comics and they are not forgiving. The world they describe implodes at the slightest attempt to redeem their father-son twenties inheritance in sixties social science terms. In eighties London, Alan Moore and David Lloyd tried to rationalize terror in *V for Vendetta* by turning Guy Fawkes (a militant Catholic to the right of Franco) into a Nechaev of style and taste who delivers freedom via propaganda-by-the-deed, the destruction of the structures of bourgeois democracy, something of an *idée fixe* of both national socialism and international socialism until the cataclysm of the forties. Moore and Lloyd surrender to sixties-seventies subterfuge; they make Miller look like a genius for accepting that comics can bear no redeeming beyond what a son can describe to his father in this strange new world.

American Culture From and Against the Rest
The web and DVD availability makes classic American culture like "The Fugitive" available to anyone who knows to look for it. Somewhere I hope there's kids discovering it and talking about it. I doubt it. Posted at NV on March 16, 2011.

Americans are among the last people to understand the depth of their own culture. Most American audiences took it for granted that they'd hear Bing Crosby or Louis Armstrong or Hank Williams or Elvis Presley when they turned on the radio, and they'd expect to see Mary Pickford or William S. Hart or Robert Taylor or Jean Arthur when they went to the movies. Popular lit they'd pick up from the drugstore rack might be Cornell Woolrich or Dashiell Hammett or Luke Short.... But American Studies specialists from Humanities depts generally overlooked these artists in their moments, preferring developments in Europe or what they called literary fiction, some of which is good, most of which lies unread. They have preferred American artists which directly reference European work, whether German expressionism, British theatrical convention, French new wave, or even Italian westerns. Without such Euroid markers – normally laid on thick – the elite audiences are simply at a loss. They live in America as vicarious ex-pats so cannot admit to being at a loss and take this out on the American artist generally by ignoring him.

There have been exceptions such as Vachel Lindsay, Manny Farber, Paul Nelson, Robert Palmer, and precious few others. In one of the nuttier books I've read recently, *The Red Rooster Scare: Making Cinema American, 1900 - 1910*, Francophile professor of English at Drake U., Richard Abel proves that the Western was invented to drive the French film giant Pathé from American screens. It's a handsome book full of interesting factoids and illustrations but it forges its Euroid causality and just last night I watched an Edmund Cobb western, *The Courage of Collins* (1927), which is a Pathé production, though by then the company was run by cowpoke Joseph Kennedy.

America does not have a high culture, though it participates in Europe's. Europe, Asia, and Africa have rich but often dying folk arts, but they have false, trivial pop cultures. Their cultures interface with modernity via the necessary local media and marketing environments that are debilitating of those already weak arts. American arts are acclimated to the media environment since the country was still becoming itself as the arts and media environments grew up, and with no high art the best minds were often found grinding out all manner of pulp or pop. African pop is better than European or Asian pop as you might expect, though it suffers relative to black American pop for its not having centuries of deep accommodation to European balladry and hymnals as well as coming late to a modern media environment. Latin America has its own better pop environment but its cultures often left blacks to their own African devices and so the rude world-historical interjacency whereby Anglo-Scots-Irish balladry and West African ritual musics finished each other off yielding blues, jazz, country, and rock and roll did not occur and yield Hispanic versions. The most interesting music found in Latin America tends to be more purely African or Iberian inheritances.

There's been too much going on in American popular culture for the audiences to do anything but enjoy, and the intellectuals to do anything but ignore.

For these and other reasons it's great to find out that one of the less retarded academics, Stanley Fish, has written a book about the ABC television program, "*The Fugitive*" (1963 - 1967), and that it originates in Fish's liking the show. Jenny Diski reviews *The Fugitive in Flight: Faith, Liberalism and Law in a Classic TV Show* in the *London Review of Books* and knowing nothing about Diski I'd assume the book might be better than the average *LRB* reviewer might understand; she does fault him for fan-like *faux pas*. But it's also true that if she's British she'd not likely suffer the kind of Anglophilia that would preclude interest in watching great TV-size actors driving primo Ford Galaxies and Falcons around on the gravel roads of a lost small town America. Such Anglophiles reside in America. My guess, anyway. She writes:

> "Kimble, unencumbered by houses, wives and lawns, can become his almost zen-like essential self, a vacuum that is the essence of his personhood and which must be protected from all interference and attachment. He becomes a wandering monk, or given the homilies he's inclined to dish out, true though they might be, more like a peripatetic life coach. His humanity can't say no when asked for help, even if it puts him in danger of discovery. But although his medical expertise means he can fix the odd broken leg when necessary, his help consists, for the most part, of showing and explaining to the strangers who ask for his help that the solution to their troubles is within themselves, in their capacity as individual, rational humans – at which point their eyes shine, and, having proved they don't really need him, he runs

once again for his life.... This is the fugitive's freedom, and also his condition of isolation: the dark side of liberalism, Fish calls it." (*London Review of Books*)

I'm inclined to forgive a large amount of double-domeage when it comes to *"The Fugitive"* because it was obviously some kind of telepathic mid-sixties harbinger of the late sixties. The final episode, a two-parter in August 1967, set and held the record for audience-size for years, and when it was over America promptly went berserk.

Ed Robertson's fan book, *The Fugitive Recaptured*, which I have read is full of interesting information about the series. Roy Huggins created it after producing *"Cheyenne," "Maverick,"* and *"77 Sunset Strip."* He tells Robertson, "Although I was tired of producing westerns, I loved the freedom of the western hero. I wanted to transfer that total freedom of the western protagonist... onto a character in a contemporary setting." His problem was how to keep the lead from looking "like a bum." Richard Kimble being a fugitive MD falsely accused of murdering his wife was the answer. Huggins was thinking *I Am a Fugitive from a Chain Gang* or *The Wrong Man* which Robertson considers a noir theme and locates it in late fifties-early sixties television programs like *"M Squad," "Naked City,"* and *"The Untouchables."* Quinn Martin produced the series with a version of *"Dragnet"*-style realism, only we're riding with the wanted man who is innocent and therefore low-key and paranoid, even as he searches for the one-armed man who did the crime.

BARRY MORSE, DAVID JANSSEN; *"THE FUGITIVE."*

The show also was an adaptation of the old fifties anthology programs, with just David Janssen common to every episode (his co-star Barry Morse playing Lieutenant Gerard showed up every few episodes still chasing him).

The setting, the cast of characters, his job and his name all changed every week. Apparently Huggins had some trouble selling the idea.

We lived a block from school in the sixties so we walked home for lunch and reruns of *"The Fugitive"* ran at noon. (Because it had such a famous closed ending it hasn't been the desirable rerun property you might think.) While my younger brothers and sisters were watching *"Bozo"* every noon I got to watch the first three Acts of *"The Fugitive"* but never got to see Act IV, never mind the Epilog! I only knew Kimble got away because he was in Salinas one day and the next day he'd made it to Decatur. While I saw it as some kind of fantasy of autonomy, living as I was in a house full of kids, parents, grandmother, and various parakeets and hamsters, I found out that Dave Lightbourne had been watching it at Grinnell with all his proto-American Studies hipster friends. One day in Chicago in the mid-nineties he quoted from memory one of the narrator's Epilog dispensations: "A city with 10 million lights casts a hundred million shadows, each one only a passing refuge for a man on the run – a man like the Fugitive." That one ran in an episode written by George Eckstein, "See Hollywood and Die", which aired November 5, 1963. Undoubtedly that generation of college lit student saw *"The Fugitive"* as related to Jack Kerouac's *On the Road*, and Twain's *Adventures of Huck Finn*, and as well exhibiting a grave tone warranted by the times unlike the rest of network television programming.

Sometime in the seventies American culture began to wind down as all the high/low, black/white, old world/new world contention resolved themselves in a now fully middle class, aestheticized, politicized, internationalized world of product. Since then, rather than capitalizing on cultural down-time by grounding students in this rich past of new world Classics, the schools just throw more dirt on American music, film, and literature. And then still they look overseas for answers, when we know that even when interesting foreign responses to modernity are really missing a dimension, and as such are basically responses to American culture itself. World music doesn't rock; at best it lilts.

You don't expect culture reporters to understand this when culture critics don't. Still it's disappointing to read in the *Wall Street Journal* how the latest thing in television programming is borrowing and translating Israeli and British shows. Amy Chozik and Joshua Mitnick write in "Coming to America":

> "[A]s the world gets smaller, and original ideas harder to come by, Hollywood producers and agents are looking elsewhere, and they say they've found signs of a Promised Land. Israel, though

faraway, isolated and war-weary, is culturally more aligned to American TV tastes than almost any other country. The nation's small, but highly educated, technologically advanced work force largely speaks English and has grown up on U.S. shows and movies, even if their own shows are in Hebrew. 'It feels very much like a 51st state,' says Ben Silverman, former co-chairman of *NBC Universal*....." (*Wall Street Journal*)

Actually we've been watching recycled British forms since the early seventies, and the current mode of contest and reality programming is Japanese in origin. Ideas are never hard to come by, but idea men can easily be driven away. Hollywood's businessmen are now college educated and the cult of Twain, Jack London, Hemingway, is long gone from the place. There's a bit of Warhol to it though. Ya think?

(*originally posted at The New Vulgate, No. 89*)

Misrepresentational Art
I liked the New Republic's *art critic Jed Purl's vituperative cover story so I bought his book, which is a more sober history of the New York art world. I meant to send it on to my uncle who lived in New York in the fifties and painted for himself (this book's cover features his favorite), but he died before I could send it. This was posted at the NV.*

Finance in its decadent phase became the tail that wagged the dog to the detriment of American industry and large patches of America itself as real estate. But extreme-finance which leveraged assets to the very edge of walking-the-plank also loosed up what industry survives and helped accelerate the creation and development of new industries like those associated with computers. It's no small achievement that seventies' garage tinkerers were able to find capital enough to assume wireless ubiquity today. The powers that were (IBM, ITT, Ma Bell...) didn't see it coming. The Chinese attempt to order up some innovation top down will likely fall short, just as the Japanese attempt did. An American advantage remains.

As in business, Art was reconfigured by such decadent leveraging too. Here the loose capital was invested in mass higher education. With no strings attached students piled into film schools, comics studies, rock courses and the like, forgoing as kids will a complete meal and cutting directly to dessert. The skids for the current juvenilia were greased by the sour political cadres who long ago impuned Western Art right down to the oil in the paint and the pronouns in the texts. Nothing of any real politick remains of all that, but its remaining advocates don't seem to recognize what came of that as their sterile mule-child. I suspect there is some sort of American advantage remaining in Art as well, but it's much harder to discern.

Camille Paglia is the best known contemporary critic of these conditions in the world of Art and her insistence on the necessity of tradition, especially the route the pagan imagination took through the Holy Roman period is heroic I'm sure. *The New Republic* maintains a good art critic named Jed Perl, which seems heroic as well in this age of publishing. He got the cover of the mag back in 2007 for his vivid critique, "How the Art

World Lost Its Mind." Inside the issue the title was rendered: "Laissez-Faire Aesthetics: What money is doing to art, or how the art world lost its mind." In the story he riffs on exhibitions of art by Lisa Yuskavage, John Currin (got the cover-booby prize), Fernando Botero, and Bob Dylan, plus Miami Beach's Art Basel. Certainly money is a problem, where it is and where it refuses to go. What is rewarded and what punished. Perl's beat includes the galleries and museums of New York and a few other cities and the art they anoint. That trashing of gravity-defying garbage was impressive so I bought Perl's book of 2005, *New Art City: Manhattan at Mid-Century*. I'm no expert but the book is readable and well-illustrated (if all b&w), a fine narrative of how the energy of modern art moved from Paris where it barely survived WWII, to New York City. Exiles were important as he tells it, especially Marcel Duchamp.

HENRY CARLSEN.

Roger Shattuck's earlier portrait of emerging Modernism in France from 1885 to WWI, *The Banquet Years*, focuses on Alfred Jarry, Henri Rousseau, Erik Satie, and Guillaume Apollinaire. Shattuck makes much of what he terms a "theatrical aspect of life," a "light opera atmosphere" that characterized *la Belle Époque* but also begged questions: "Was it a revolution? A liberation? A victory? A last fling? A first debauch?" Shattuck has it the first World War opened the artistic mainstream to brewing avant-garde currents. But then Modernism split right and left and was doubly compromised, except for what escaped to America.

Perl refers to art critic Clement Greenberg's setting of New York against Paris at its post-war start:

> "In 1948, just as a new generation of artists was streaming into New York, Greenberg argued that the life of the avant-garde in New York was a sort of hyperbolic version of the avant-garde life of Paris. He said that New York artists were living a life 'as old as the Latin Quarter; but I do not think it was ever lived out with so little panache, so few compensations, and so much reality. The alienation of Bohemia was only an anticipation in nineteenth-century Paris; it is in New York that it has been completely fulfilled." (*New Art City*)

Perl has it that the city's call on artists' time changed the formerly rural idyll of American painting until an on-the-street theatricality was "an aspect of everyday life." He quotes painter Larry Rivers' assessment that "Pollock was the first artist in America to be 'on stage'." That strikes me as generational blindness to all that occurred in terms of art, media, and celebrity in America before what I've called the WWII backstop, but for the world of New York artists it may be true and is probably significant. Perl has Duchamp's "almost fossilized cynicism" inspiring, if that's the word, the "cheerfully self-absorbed nihilists" Jasper Johns and Robert Rauschen-

NINA CARLSEN.

berg "who were quickly followed by a generation of whatever-the-market-will-bear nihilists, the generation of Andy Warhol and Roy Lichtenstein."

Perl notes that the city's art critics, Clement Greenberg, Harold Rosenberg, Hilton Kramer, and others came to be more important, even overpowering, as the art began to fail at the end of abstract expressionism and into Pop. He writes of Greenberg and Rosenberg:

> "Both critics were so insistent on giving the excitement of the art of the present some kind of overarching, systematic relationship with the experience of the past that they threatened to rob the work of art of its independence...." (New Art City)

He quotes Kramer's observation that "'the relation of the critic to his material has been significantly reversed' by the coming of Pop." He notes Pop's suspect nostalgia and ultimately its mercenary endgame. He characterizes its career knowingness as "history sickness," and syncing up with what Dwight Macdonald called "mid cult" leads high culture to become "in many people's minds, a dimension of popular culture." That and the fact that the middle class's work-allergic children were clambering into MFA programs that were now conceptual and critical rather than grounded in tradition or technique leaves us here now.

  New Art City makes clear where Jed Perl's *New Republic* pieces come from. The wonder is he continues. In "Laissez-Faire Aesthetics" he noted the bankrupt characters profiled in *New York* magazine as "Warhol's Children" and the re-bidding up of until now unappreciated and therefore un-fully exploited late Warhol, before writing, "Warhol is the evil prophet of the profit motive. His portraits of Chairman Mao can look positively visionary at a time when container ships full of neo-Pop Art are emerging from China."

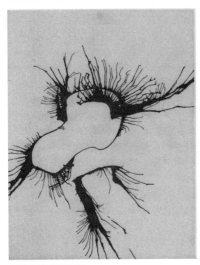

JOE CARDUCCI.

  Perl's current piece on Robert Duncan's *The H.D. Book*, written by the poet known as H.D. in the years 1959 to 1964, is a meditation that only begins with the book. Perl responds to it in part because it is a time piece, "Duncan's modernism is at once lofty, optimistic, activist, and open-minded." Duncan's "great enemy" is T.S. Eliot "for being so quick to isolate tradition from the present." All of this is of a piece I guess, and it fits with my sense of the long 20th century evolving of America's small-p popular arts of music and film. Music, Literature, Art, all of it seems one long collapse – a collapse predicted by the Vatican no less when Western Art was separated from religious observance. All good work increasingly being done by those slumming from their true potential, yet elevating lower forms of first folk, then popular, and finally mass-media arts. In this great collapse there have been centuries full of amazing, wondrous whorls, eddies and side-flumes. But still there is only an inevitable general sinking and settling to stasis. Los Angeles, in other words.

(originally posted at The New Vulgate, No. 80)

The New York Times Criterion

The New Criterion pays special attention to The New York Times *and it doesn't take much to get me going on them either. This ran at* The New Vulgate *on Nov. 24, 2011.*

The *New Criterion* for November features an excerpt from William McGowan's book, *Gray Lady Down: What the Decline and Fall of 'The New York Times' Means for America*. The excerpt is titled, "Pop goes the *Times*", and focuses clumsily on the *NYT*'s "treatment of film, television, theater, music, and other arts." I'm sympathetic to his general thrust but the piece is an illustration of how slow on the uptake the Right has been on popular culture if not the arts themselves. This has left an entirely corrupted and inadequate Left to have its way with the arts. The issue is all but impossible to get into focus today because so many erstwhile critics, consumers, fans, scholars... have begun producing art since there seems to be money fun and fame attached to the arts as they went Pop under the demographic power of the baby boom. Then Pop culture invaded the Humanities and weakened aesthetics – the Critic vanquished Art and proceeded to produce mere Culture in place of Art. Such Culture is far more politically settled and easier to market in the near term.

The *New Criterion* is designed to fight a rearguard defense of Art against all this, so it's easy to sympathize. But their defense of Art is as Art was before Elvis and Warhol, but that line leaves so much outside their ken as to invite dismissal. I always wondered why the publication wasn't titled The Old Criterion, or just The Criterion. Seems like calling it *New Criterion* was throwing in the towel on some level. And there's so much righteous objecting and critiquing for them to do!

I liked the old *WSJ* as it was edited by Robert Bartley, and the CNBC television hour that the editorial board did with Stuart Varney was a lot better than the half-hour they do now on *Fox News Channel*. Bartley didn't look like he cared at all about the mechanics of performing on television which is quite rare and unlike his replacement Paul Gigot who had done *PBS*'s "News Hour" for several years. The hippest writer on the board and the shows was/is Dorothy Rabinowitz who projects a classic Manhattan hauteur though she's currently wasted reviewing television. I once caught a *NYT* television program on the local *NY1* cable channel but its primarily a vehicle to tout that week's Sunday *Times* features.

There wasn't much on music or film in the *Journal* until Bartley died and Gigot took over, though movie coverage got the head-start. Now with Murdoch's ownership the paper is about as hip as it's gonna get. But it doesn't have near the ambition the Times has when it comes to arts coverage. McGowan makes easy points about the politically interested and invested compromises the *Times* makes whenever it disapproves of some development or is suddenly embarrassed to have missed the early stages of some phenom. Coverage of books which it finds uncomfortable is elided when its felt the attention a *Times* review would get the book is oxygen it would otherwise not get. This is different than the ignoring of Rush Limbaugh, his arrival in Manhattan, his turning civics into compelling radio, his best-selling books, his effective connecting up the *WSJ* editorial board with just-folks out across the country; the *Times*' determination to be up to speed on all matters of American culture failed them here and they backed into coverage of Limbaugh with a profile of him that acknowledged the book had gone to #1 on their own chart yet not been reviewed. Such media-figure political books are now a deluge, and certainly the *Times*' obsession with Sarah Palin since the McCain ticket lost is somewhat shaped by their earlier failure to note activity out between the University towns of America.

The *Times* did cover Limbaugh-fan Camille Paglia's first book fairly quickly given she was unknown, but *Sexual Personae* was published by Yale and easy to identify as likely significant. And her text was hip enough in simplified Manhattan terms (references to The Rolling Stones, movie stars, etc.). Hers was also an Arts corrective – not in full sync with the *New Criterion*'s but an interesting update of it. (My own books haven't been reviewed in the *Times*, even the revised edition released by Henry Rollins' company in 1995 was elided, though of course here we're talking about a Pop Music regime-past whose understanding of what was important was perversely only relaxed by Nirvana's pop success and any back-checking would be painful for the paper of record. My third edition was pitched to the *NYT Book Review* section editor, but by 2005 you know...)

Though Books and Music are important to the *NYT*, they only attempt comprehensive reviews with regard to Films and Theater. Obviously, they couldn't hope to review every music release, or live performance, or every book published, but it does probably mean something that movies rate so important – even those that do not come with advertising budgets, even those played from DVDs in pizza parlors. One of the marks against former *Times* editor Howell Raines when he was on his way to being fired was his front page placement or even the assigning of an article on Britney Spears in the early days of what I counted as her third life, this one her red-shift blast-off as new media supernaut. She wasn't drying up and blowing away and the micro-paparazzi with all that bandwidth and syndication to feed were metastasizing into something new. Raines was ahead of that curve, and perhaps right as well to put it up front rather than in Arts.

McGowan writes:

> "Part of the late 1970s Sectional Revolution, in which the *Times* became a multisection publication bulging with soft news and life-style journalism, was a greater use of market research and polling of target constituencies, especially in the area of cultural coverage. The research explained that the *Times* needed to 'reach out to a new generation, people whose attention spans were shorter,' Warren Hoge, the assistant managing editor, told *NPR*. It needed to replace its older readers with a new generation, one that was educated but 'aliterate,' meaning they did not read much.... Over time this transformation crowded out coverage of high culture in favor of an oddball, wink-and-nod popular culture. 'The entire social and moral compass of the paper,' as the former *Times* art critic Hilton Kramer later said, was altered to conform to a liberal ethos infused with 'the emancipatory ideologies of the 1960s'.... The change was met by disaffection and derision within the paper's newsroom. Grace Glueck, who ran the culture desk for a while as replacement editor, was one of the disaffected and famously once asked, 'Who do I have to f[...] to get out of this job?'" (*New Criterion*)

Hilton Kramer has been co-editor and publisher of the *New Criterion* since he left the *New York Times* in the early 1980s, so presumably the limitations of William McGowan's book are the generic Manhattan limitations.

Back before Raines went a Britney too far, Sridhar Pappu in the *New York Observer* recounted the murderers' row of the *Times*' recent glory years:

> "For years, particularly from 1967 to 1990 under Mr. Gelb's direction, the culture section of *The Times* served as the repository of New York's most distinguished cultural critics: Harold C. Schonberg and Donal Henahan on music; Hilton Kramer and John Russell on art; Walter Kerr, Stanley Kauffmann and Mr. Rich on the theater; Clive Barnes on dance; Renata Adler, Vincent Canby and Janet Maslin on the movies; Ada Louise Huxtable and Paul Goldberger on architecture; and Jack Gould, John O'Connor,

> Walter Goodman and John Corry on television. And in dance, literature and cabaret, *The Times* ruled the waves. Even readers who hated those critics read them." (*NY Observer*, Jan. 19, 2003)

Some of those critics are even good, just as some of today's are good. If they are any less lethal it becomes academic so-to-speak when the varied arts are failing as they are.

The paper is now fully a national paper. It sells only perhaps a couple hundred thousand copies in New York City, and those in Manhattan. In the city itself, the *New York Post*, the *New York Daily News*, and *Newsday*, each outsell the *Times*. The marketing department is especially visible in the Arts and Travel section; each dip into Chicago theater or L.A. taco trucks or Austin filmmaking or Portland coffee trends is an attempt to juice distribution in those now important markets for the *Times*. Certainly this has begun to temper the old Manhattan-bound politik – it was harder for the cosmopolitan literature-based Old Left frame-of-reference *Times* to molt unto a Pop-based New Left *Times* hip to developments on the West Coast than it will be for this new rootless pop provincialism to sell itself to the coming faithless cell-phone "readership." The television ads for the *Times* tell you who they think these young 'aliterates' are, and that maybe they want the paper just on weekends.

The political element of the *Times* that concerns McGowan and Kramer now seems weakened everywhere under the effect of the web and the general dispersion to formlessness of what media remains; only *NPR* seems strengthened as an influence-magnifier for the *Times*. When there was talk of the paper going non-profit I thought I heard a harmonic.

(*originally posted at* The New Vulgate, *No. 73*)

Paul Nelson - First You Dream Then You Die
I'm not in the reviewing game at The New Vulgate *but David Lightbourne had introduced me to Paul and told me about Kevin Avery's two Nelson books. I was glad to get copies of both books; I wanted to know more about Paul's life and I needed to read the other title for my upcoming film book. This was posted October 2011.*

> "Dave Gahr and I were standing five feet from the stage in the photographers' pit. It was just incredibly exciting. You could hear the boos sort of, but I've actually heard the tapes played back years and years later - that's very tame stuff. It wasn't this volcanic thing that we all remembered. It was quite tame. But it changed me. I mean it completely changed my- to me it was something that I wanted to know more about. 'Like a Rolling Stone' is just a key song for me. And I just didn't want to work with people who wanted to put that down."

- Paul Nelson, Jan. 24, 2000

There's a sudden bonanza of Paul Nelson material in the form of two books put together by Kevin Avery in the years since Paul's death in 2006. Nelson was best known as one of *Rolling Stone* magazine's top music writers and editors in the late seventies, but he was also the A&R man at Mercury who signed the New York Dolls, and he was the editor of *Sing Out!* who quit when electricity came to Newport '65. He also happened to be the inventor of rock criticism and the music fanzine in the form of *The Little Sandy Review* which he and his friend Jon Pankake plotted out at the end of the fifties in Minneapolis.

Avery's book, *Everything Is an Afterthought: The Life and Writings of Paul Nelson*, is an admirably unorthodox construction that starts with a bracing 180-page biography of Paul followed by a 265-page collection of Nelson's music writing, primarily that from the seventies focusing on the artists he was particularly drawn to. The second book, *Conversations with Clint: Paul Nelson's Lost Interviews with Clint Eastwood 1979 - 1983*, are transcriptions edited by Avery of interviews that were to yield a cover story for *Rolling Stone*. The failure of Nelson to deliver that story begs the question that is the riddle of the man – What is a critic? This is a very old issue. The Bible is the Creator's story; Satan is the critic who doubts and attacks the Creator's Revelation. We can be glad that Satan is more the Deconstruction mode of lit-crit rather than rock criticism as we've known it. Paul was looking to be a constructive critic of music and artists he enjoyed, but it was also important to him to "knock" offensive things, especially in record reviews. His early work in the *Little Sandy Review* (1960-64) was less ambitious than the long-form features, but it was a better period for music than the period Avery's compiled, primarily from 1974-1983, though there was much to knock in the folk music era, particularly what the commies were proffering as music of the people, or what the record biz was manufacturing as folk which Paul and Jon referred to as "folkum." The *LSR* covered more rock and roll in the two issues Barry Hansen published after buying it for a dollar in 1964. He'd been their blues writer and is better known since as Dr. Demento. (A 1966-67 issue was published by Gordon Wickham who had also paid a dollar for the privilege.)

In terms of our world today it was Paul's and Jon's decision to write some record reviews, type them up in folded booklet format, print three hundred copies, staple and send out to record labels, and take to shops that was an act of World Historical importance.

Nelson's later literalist m.o. of deep listening and repeated interviewing of artists who maybe could sustain such investigation is dated in a way that his *Little Sandy Review* patter, or his signing of the transliterate New York Dolls are not. In a January 2000 interview with the late David Lightbourne (see *The New Vulgate*, No. 4 for his history of *LSR*) Paul characteristically downplays any particular vision or genius, and whenever Dave mentions a favorite *Little Sandy* curt dismissal of some insult to American music Paul begs off his assumed authorship to emphasize the contributions of Pankake. They did not credit themselves individually because, he laughed, "We started meeting these people!" Their modest breakthrough publication got noticed quickly by record labels and they mixed with musicians at the University of Chicago Folk Festivals and the Newports. Paul also underlined the fly-by-night aspects of their run of issues from 1960 to 1964: "We didn't want to say 'June issue' because it might not come out til October.... We were probably both more interested in movies. This just seemed like a ridiculously easy field to get into." It was also a scheme to earn free records. (By the time Paul moved to New York in 1963 he and the others were taking individual credits. Three issues were then overseen by Paul from NYC before he was hired to edit *Sing Out!* Magazine.)

The *LSR* introduced the wise-ass fan voice that we have more than enough of now, but back in 1960 had probably not been heard or read since the twenties at *Photoplay* or in certain newspapers. The voice features good-humored, often exaggerated enthusiasm for what it likes and witty trashings of what offends it; and over both actions is a subtle tone that both acknowledges the absurdity of treating American folk and pop culture as worthy of treatment formerly reserved for high art and serious literature, and also justifies and demands such treatment. Hollywood had incorporated this attitude organically in its meld of the other arts during the silent era, and then at the end of the twenties Ben Hecht and others brought it to dialogue and acting from newspapers. But it didn't last long. The Depression and especially the WWII mobilization became a formidable backstop back beyond which our era's postwar popular culture was largely ignorant. Harry Smith's "Anthology of American Folk Music" was an early fifties backwards breakthrough to the forgotten commercial country and blues of only twenty years before. And the recycling of twenties silent comedy and early thirties westerns for fifties children's television programming was another massive breach past this WWII wall. In terms of criticism in popular art, only Manny Farber's film criticism begun in the early forties ranks higher than Paul's work in the LSR as pathfinder, though music operating closer to the ground makes Paul's influence the greater.

Paul Nelson was born in a small town in Minnesota in 1936 and though he was twenty when Elvis Presley and rock and roll made their entrance, he was not a rock and roller. Lightbourne was six years younger and was (DL's Elvis recollection-review of his first tour-date up North is also at The New Vulgate). These birthdates before the war's end mean more than dates do once we're safely into the baby boom and the rock and roll era. Dave was just another Chicago-area kid playing accordion except that he was extremely interested in radio and television and got wind of the early Elvis appearances on "The Dorsey Brothers Stage Show," "The Milton Berle Show," "The Steve Allen Show," and "Ed Sullivan" because his stepfather had been a professional musician. Dave switched to guitar and then as rock and roll was tamed by the deaths and sell-outs and the ersatz teen idols in the late fifties he became a folkie. Paul had been first a movie fan; there was no television signal in his town and he told Lightbourne that he did not listen to clear channel stations from the south. In terms of music Nelson had always been a folkie. By his own reckoning he went rock and roll when Dylan went electric in 1965. And when everyone around him at *Sing Out!* rejected Dylan's electric set at Newport that year, he quit the mag.

Paul knew the young Bob Zimmerman from his Minneapolis days. Lightbourne understood Bob Dylan as a fifties rock and roller whose folk period was part of his musical education, and further that it was his protest-singer phase that was a Hibbing songwriter's tactical sell-out, not the "going electric." These were loaded and misunderstood events for the younger, boomer generation - the second generation through the rock and roll grinder, and one more pretentious and culturally distant from rock and roll for its college education. Lightbourne used his folkie period research to identify an earlier rock and roll in twenties delta blues and Memphis jug band recordings; he knew rock and roll as an acoustic folk music.

One of my favorite stories about this acoustic-electric disconnect occurred in a location even more remote to rock and roll than the Northern Midwest or Northeast. It is recounted in Robert Palmer's book, *Deep Blues*. Muddy Waters was invited to London in 1958 on Bill Broonzy's recommendation, so he brought his amp and Otis Spann with him from his current line-up, but the London blues scene then was thinking trad-jazz and skiffle which were their cockeyed ideas of Dixieland and Jug-band music. They got an early look-listen at contemporary Chicago blues. They were polite in their disappointment; they'd expected Muddy to sound like he did on the Lomax recordings from the Delta. Four years later, 1962, you can imagine the now electric blues scene in London is picking up steam and Muddy is invited over again. This time aiming to please he comes alone with just his acoustic guitar. Again, the Brits are very polite about their disappointment.

Regarding influences on Dylan, certainly the debut albums by the Holy Modal Rounders (psychedelic old-timey recorded in 1963, released in 1964 on Prestige), Koerner Ray & Glover (acoustic blues from Mpls, produced by Nelson in 1963 for Elektra), Michael Hurley (the bent balladeer's "First Songs" recorded for Folkways in 1964), and the Paul Butterfield Blues Band (white-led Chicago blues band together in 1963, first album 1965 on Elektra) were what inspired and/or forced him to move beyond his initial models. (Members of the Butterfield band plus Barry Goldberg, another young white Chicago blues player, accompanied Dylan at Newport 1965.) Young white players who were not from Memphis were beginning to go off the rails of model popular entertainment. Alot was in the air: Kerouac's On the Road, ABC's "*The Fugitive*," Paul's *The Little Sandy Review*. Jac

Holzman credited the *LSR*'s attitude and reviews with changing his idea of what to release on Elektra Records.

Forty years later Dylan all but confirmed the influence of these artists on his own development by *not* playing their songs on his three year radio program, "Theme Time Radio," which was otherwise quite a good and generous deed done by him. (It had to be him playing this stuff for radio programmer/music-killer Lee Abrams to be involved.) But of the artists Bob did play only Lou Reed was active in New York City in ways pre-Velvets that might have shamed him back to rock and roll.

What's most impressive about Avery's biographic half of the book is that he's produced both an intimate personal biography and a comprehensive professional bio as well. He's talked to virtually everyone that Nelson inspired or mentored in rock criticism starting at the *LSR* but especially in the latter half of the sixties and into the *Rolling Stone* years. These knuckleheads are a who's who of American rock criticism, God help us. Most were of the baby boom but seemed to have had their rock and roll baptisms in the Thames. Whatever memories they didn't have of humid, mossy southern rock and roll meant the best music was often wasted on them; they had rootless preferences for novelty, style, lyrics and accents. In their birthdate-determined uni-mind it seemed Dylan went electric because of the Beatles - maybe this was Jan Wenner's contribution to musicological assumption-jumping. The album was the preferred format in the folk scene and albums began to define the more pretentious collegiate experience of rock music by 1965. There was great rock and roll made in this period, here naturally, and now in Britain as well, but a kind of class-based misunderstanding of the object of music writers' alleged expertise was developing and it going to be a problem. The working class, non-Southern rock and roll of 1958 through 1963 by such as Eddie Cochran, Richie Valens, Johnny and the Hurricanes, Dick Dale and the Del-tones, The Wailers, Paul Revere and the Raiders, The Belairs, The Beach Boys, etc., was discounted or ignored, and no matter the R&B in their sounds or sets the British Invasion given credit for introducing white Americans to black music. It was write there in black and white in the *Rolling Stone* magazine. The 1970 *Rolling Stone* review of Richard Meltzer's book, *The Aesthetics of Rock*, which had been written in the mid-sixties, complained,

> "It seems that Meltzer is unable to grasp the qualitative transformation that differentiates fifties jag-off rock from late sixties accomplishment." (*Rolling Stone*)

Imagine that! Though I commend Mr. Mangelsdorff's construction, "fifties jag-off rock," and commend the music he's decrying.

Nelson himself was increasingly serious in his criticism. He understood that he could over-focus on lyrics of his favorite songs and artists but he generally remembered to step back and assess the playing and sound of the recordings. But he'd obsess over Jackson Browne lyrics as if Jackson was the lead in a detective novel. Then Paul became the continental op; he would fly out to L.A. or to some stop on a tour and get to know him on a friendship-level to write his *Rolling Stone* features. All very lit-focused, even framing the biographical information that was sometimes hard to pry from his subject through the tropes of pulp. Paul did steer clear of the more common problem his trainees indulged in the socio-political grading of lyrics and general righteousness. He'd launched the first fanzine to fight that kind of reductionism in the old pinko folk movement. But as lyric-focused as Paul could be he also heard the music in the mess the New York Dolls were making and knew it was important. He worked hard to sign them to Mercury, right after signing Mike Seeger! In *R&TPN* I had ripped *Rolling Stone* in general for Nelson's review of the first Ramones album. I thought the use of a cinematic framework to understand the band was an admission of cluelessness. Now I see that Paul used film analogies in every music review and that whatever the problems at *Rolling Stone*, Paul could hear it. And perhaps no other writer at the mag had the stature to get that positive and prominent a review past Wenner. (The review isn't in Avery's collection.)

Nelson arrived at Mercury Records from editing *Circus* magazine:

> "I was freelancing a lot, mostly for *Rolling Stone*. But my main job was editing *Circus* and writing about two-thirds of every issue: most of the articles, all of the record reviews, and even some of the letters section, wherein such literary notables as Nick Adams, Jake Barnes, Frederic Henry, Dick Diver, and Lew Archer often wrote to tell Gerry Rothberg, the publisher of *Circus* and my all-time favorite music-business employer, what was what."
> (*Everything Is an Afterthought*)

He explains he took the Mercury job when he got writer's block from all that writing. When I came upon Paul's mention of writer's block I thought at first he might be referring to his attempts at fiction on the side, but it seems he actually froze up writing *Circus* jive. Paul tried his hand at mysteries and then screenplays while writing about music for his livelihood. From my experience, I don't recommend getting into the nonfiction grind of criticism or journalism until after one has mastered fiction as that mastering is not a part-time job. I mostly avoided essay writing because I could feel it a threat to my ability in fiction, even after I was out of the record business, and even after my rock book attracted offers. I did do four years of compression-criticism in Systematic mail order catalogs where I had space for five words-or-less to describe records, and another four years of PR jive at SST and other labels. Now in my fifties I can dash these things off quickly, but I'm no reporter and not the perfectionist young Nelson was. But it is sobering to consider the shadow cast over everything he did write by his failure with fiction. Is criticism a true writerly profession that one can devote one's life to? It would seem not judging by rock critics.

For me Paul's strongest music writing in this collection is his 1975 post-Mercury after-the-facts narrative of his involvement with the New York Dolls for the *Village Voice*. He summarizes:

> "The dreams of so many good people died with the New York Dolls.... I think those kids from sweet Ioway were wrong, or rather perhaps that they never really had a chance to encounter the group on any significant level: on the radio or as part of a major tour. Instead, the band's philosophy of instant stardom and limited, headliner-only bookings proved to be the stuff of dreams. Even a cult favorite must eventually face the nation as a whole, but the Dolls never played by the rules of the game. Neither did the Velvet Underground, and their contributions will last. At times, when I am feeling particularly perverse, I can't blame either of them." (*Ibid.*)

There's a lot in that paragraph intimating the desertification of rock and roll to come, or rather to the banishment of rock bands from labels, press, radio, stages, and retail for nearly fifteen years. As someone involved in the forced building of a parallel music business of our own labels, press, radio, stages and retail, it's interesting to see the inside of the Dolls' Industry adventure through Nelson's eyes. The failure of the band was, like that of The Stooges, an early warning shot from a handful of formerly hip culture apparats who were beginning to exert control over rock music through the business of media. In that period, and later, only Lester Bangs, Richard Meltzer, and Metal Mike Saunders would prove they could be trusted with the music as critics. New writers would pick up on their approach, though they would write mostly for fanzines styled unknowingly on the *LSR* model or short-lived start-ups hoping to be a post-boom generation's *Rolling Stone*.

Nelson's forty-page essay on his five years (1970-75) at Mercury, "Out of the Past," is another highlight of *Everything Is an Afterthought*. Previously unpublished and apparently written in the mid-1990s, it is a classic portrait of the kind of record label dysfunction that was indulged in a period when the fecund American musical cornucopia could overwhelm any cabal of mountebanks in its path. Mercury, still then a Chicago hq'ed large independent, was capable of selling a lot of records but Paul describes the operation as "Two rock & rollers in New York against twenty bookkeepers in Chicago." His notes from just before a big A&R meeting at headquarters include this description of a preliminary get-together:

> "[A] bunch of us got into a discussion with (label prez Irwin) Steinberg about the record business in general and Mercury in specific, and it became very apparent that Mercury would never be more than a second-rate label, at best. Steinberg's new theory seems to be that R&B, country music, and classical music are both safe and long-lasting, and that rock & roll is just too crazy to bank on." (*Ibid.*)

Nelson mentions his own "snobbish" indifference to Mercury artists Sir Lord Baltimore and Uriah Heep in the piece and elsewhere Jay Cocks (then *Time*'s critic) said Paul startled him once by telling him he didn't "get" black music. Cocks also says, "Paul was one who deserves the word critic; the rest of us were reviewers." I imagine that critic Paul had a higher standard to meet before he felt he had "gotten" black music than the more reflexive reviewers who likely couldn't imagine they weren't getting a whole lot of stuff.

Avery seems to have interviewed all of those reviewers and Paul was a mentor or editor to most of them. In Avery's hands his life becomes a Rorschach test for how they feel about their own compromises as the paying gig of rock critic followed rock music itself out the door courtesy Lee Abrams, Jan Wenner, and others who preferred to bank on media than its formerly crazy content. To a qualmsless entertainment pr specialist like Anthony DeCurtis it seems a simple matter what Paul should have done. It's interesting to hear from virtually every one of those guys. While they clambered into the nearest paying gig (management, production, fake books, movies, tv, pr...), Paul preferred to focus on his screenplay and indulge his deferred interest in movies by working at Evergreen Video in Greenwich Village. His co-workers there are full of great stories about Paul's tastes and his impatience with customers with none. In a footnote to a *Rolling Stone* piece on Rod Stewart presented in the book as a more complete version assembled from the published version, various drafts and a book edit, Avery inserts a personal aside from Paul that sounds like it's from the raw taped interviews:

> "I've debated time after time whether, Jesus Christ, get a regular job and settle down, or should I keep going this crazy way, being broke all the time and have a good time? I finally decided I should keep going this way, being broke all the time and having a good time." (Ibid.)

He's telling this to Rod Stewart! Michael Azerrad asked Paul to write up something on the bluegrass he was listening to for *emusic.com*, but he passed on the chance. Charles Young tells Kevin, "Paul wanted to keep bluegrass pure for himself. He wanted to be able to listen to it without any of the fuckery of rock journalism messing up this music that he loved." Surprising tributes to Paul come in recollections from many of his seventies rockstar quasi-friends. Some knew him well from that period when even stars were expected to be real for their public.

I met Paul a couple times in the early aughts as Lightbourne was interviewing him. We had gotten Lightbourne into a studio to at last record the music he'd been working on since the fifties and booked a Monday at the Lakeside Lounge so Paul could check it out on his night off. It was Dave's Laramie trio with Shaun Kelley and John Martz, The Stop & Listen Boys, with Trip Henderson sitting in on harmonica. Halfway through the set Paul leaned over and said, "What a repertoire!" (It was all delta blues, Memphis jug, or original.) Dave had known and played with Mike Bloomfield, Steve Weber, Fritz Richmond, Michael Hurley, Maria Muldaur, and others through the years, but I know that being able to play his set for the co-founder of the *Little Sandy Review* was one of his highlights as a performer.

Back at Jane Stokes' pad (she's also an *NV* contributor) I had mostly talked films with Paul. He talked about his western screenplay like it was something just about done and he seemed to think he could get Clint Eastwood to read it when it was ready. It was depressing to learn from Avery's book that there really was nothing so discrete as a screenplay, but more a huge stack of unconnected scenes or settings. Screenplays are really the only thing I've been interested in writing since back in high school when I'd pass time thinking up sight-gags like it was still the twenties. I would never have gotten involved with music had Hollywood circa 1976 made more sense to my young self. I treated the music business as temporary and as a place to learn how art works in the world of business. Because of Abrams, Wenner, et. al., and how the damage they did backed up the entire major label system, it was mighty small business. I felt the rock music lifers of my era had been sold a bill of goods by their musical inspirations and then, unsigned and unprogrammed, left to take rock and roll back to the porch, like a folk form before radio and records, unwritten out of rock and roll history. For me, I was never going to stay long in my record business, but before I turned back to screenwriting I was determined to in turn write those apparats and failed critics out of the rock and roll present and future.

I didn't finally master the screenplay until sometime after they stopped using them. The post-studio system movie industry runs on a fear that generates a Brownian motion of insecurity that must work itself off on everything submitted to it; they don't need anything masterful for it must be disassembled to its atoms anyway. Masterful can only depress the intelligent among them. I gave Paul a copy of my western script hoping he'd give me a copy of his. He didn't and I hope mine didn't depress him.

When friends want to chop me down to size (can't be done) they often insist I am just another rock critic, no better than all those guys I reamed in *R&TPN*. Robert Christgau referred recently to "the cant" of sixties writers, that criticism was "parasitic" and to be avoided. Paul was one of those deeper critics who so loved certain work by certain artists that he obsessed about jumping the fence and becoming the Creator - Satan's compulsion. Lionel Trilling (who referred to criticism as "secondary, an afterthought") was a high culture version of this. He was probably the best post-war American literature critic, and he wrote fiction enough to realize his limitations and stopped, but he had options in the world of scholarly publishing that Paul did not. Paul had an ass-wipe like Wenner, or friends not much more solvent than he.

My vague sense of Paul's actual living situation, which I got from Lightbourne, was that he was trading off a more comfortable life by his determination to stay in Manhattan. I've moved all over west of Chicago, and not many travelled this country more thoroughly than David, so we'd just shake our heads over what some folks will put up with. In their conversation on Lightbourne's tapes Dave explores their common small town Midwestern origins and mentions how much he liked living in Laramie. He'd been dug deep into the Portland music-drug scene when I convinced him to leave it for his own good and my benefit. I could offer him free rent until he found his footing, an album deal of sorts, and Jane helped him with some emergency dentistry - emergency because she didn't want to be seen in public with him anymore. (Like Paul, Dave drank Coca-Cola as others drink coffee or alcohol and had the teeth of a hillbilly to prove it.) Paul received similar help but Manhattan doesn't allow for free rent.

Speaking of alcohol, *Everything Is an Afterthought* provides the original uncut version of an amazing piece on Warren Zevon. I never cared about Zevon because he's a piano playing singer-songwriter and the bands on the albums aren't playing well together. But the Nelson m.o. meshed with Zevon's messed-up alcoholism as he crashed through one hair-raising false-ending after another. It's more a portrait of Zevon's self-excavation by an intimate than it is rock criticism. But there was no place for such work. Charles Young suggests "they" might have rationalized running it at length by treating it like a Hunter Thompson special. But Jan tells Avery:

> "He was really writing for his own purpose. And I suppose at the end of him writing that perfect piece that he wanted to write about Warren that got it all and explained all where Warren stood in the West Coast literature of the dispossessed or whatever the fuck - that in his mind that was so perfectly clear it should be published as is. It takes that kind of ego and that kind of thought, which Paul had, to think of something that vain." (*Ibid.*)

Jan preferred the sane probity of Hunter's digressions. Paul is quoted elsewhere telling Bruce Hornsby (!): "Actually, I quit *Rolling Stone* because it was just getting too much to deal with Jann, who was like a coke maniac, an alcoholic.... He was really out of control." (Jan changed the spelling and pronunciation of his first name after touring Gstaad in the early seventies.)

When Wenner came out of the closet in 1995 I thought, "Man I wish I'd known that!" How can anyone make any sense out of the doings at *Rolling Stone* or Wenner Media or the Rock and Roll Hall of Fame without knowing that? The books about the magazine by Robert Sam Anson and Robert Draper are clear that he needed his wife's money to keep the magazine afloat (could she still be company vice president?!), just as he needed record industry help at other moments. And what, he's in the closet all through that?! Daydreaming of, which is it, John or Paul? He leaves San Francisco in 1978?! He opens the door for *Spin* magazine by dropping the musical ball and even lets *Spin* make coverage of Aids research its one major non-music subject?! If it wasn't for the Experience Music Project he'd even have a choke-hold on the History of Rock and Roll. Craziness....

By the time The Ramones set a template for the Reformation, Jan was like a debauched Pope of the dark ages using the mag to work Hollywood and Washington, tooling for heinous I presume. RS left SF just as its punk scene coalesced; it moved to NYC right after its punk bands had broken up or left for the perpetual touring necessary for lack of media oxygen. Had the mag stayed in Frisco it would have been impossible to ignore the Mabuhay with its distinctive cabaret presentation of bands by Dirk Dirksen, or the radicals presenting bands at the Club for the Deaf, or eventually Bill Graham Presents himself, or bands like The Sleepers, The Avengers, Dead Kennedys.... There might've been an organic relationship as the old rock halls of the sixties scene were resurrected as venues for the punks. And the rise of Silicon Valley might have given Wenner a more radical entrée into the corridors of power than glad-handing sell-out. Plus Castro Street was right around the corner. But Jan was done with music as Paul soon found out.

The other Paul Nelson book by Kevin Avery, *Conversations with Clint*, is made up of the interviews Paul did with Eastwood for what would have been a 1980 *Rolling Stone* cover story hung on the release of *Escape from Alcatraz* (1979). The interviews continued as Paul worked his m.o. at a level he'd never reached before. But he kept postponing the piece so that it couldn't hang on *Bronco Billy*, or *Any Which Way You Can*, *Firefox*, *Honkytonk Man*, or *Sudden Impact* (1983). Eastwood's productivity must have intimidated Paul. Clint was laying groundwork to be a winner in a system where the stakes are higher and the odds longer than any in the music world, and not less so for his having to find his footing as the movie studios began to implode from the time he signed as one of the last contract players at Universal in 1954. Nelson was simpatico with Eastwood or he wouldn't have gotten so much out of Clint; these are great interviews and tell us much about how Eastwood thought about Hollywood, film in general and the ones he was making.

Eastwood does route the interviews and he eventually gets impatient with Paul and it becomes clear that he was counting on the *Rolling Stone* cover story to be a resetting of his place in the firmament of critical opinion after having been written out of it by Pauline Kael over *Dirty Harry* (1971) and other films. She was on a roll since having championed and rescued *Bonnie and Clyde* (1967) and even tried briefly to work in late seventies Hollywood. Kael seemed fine with Sam Peckinpah's brand of "fascism," or at least she'd go on at length respectfully belaboring his artistry, spoon-feeding his aestheticized peckerwood violence to *New Yorker* tea-sippers. Kael's treatment of Eastwood and Siegel was merely derisive, even though Sam was another of Siegel's students, apprenticing on four Siegel features - he's dialogue director and plays the meter reader in Siegel's *Invasion of the Body Snatchers* (1956) - and when Siegel turned down a chance to bring radio's Marshal Dillon to television he recommended Peckinpah as a writer to Charles Marquis Warren and his first script credits are for early "*Gunsmoke*" episodes.

Marshall Fine in his Peckinppah bio, *Bloody Sam*, tells of Rudy Wurlitzer, screenwriter on *Pat Garrett and Billy the Kid* (1973), introducing Bob Dylan to Peckinpah when he needed a title song; Sam didn't know Dylan's music so he took him aside, sat him down with an acoustic and had him play the two songs he'd already written having read Wurlitzer's script. Peckinpah left the room, tears in his eyes muttering, "That son of a bitch. That cocksucker." Dylan hired, arrived at first day's shoot to find that the name on his chair read: "Bob Dillon"; the prop man had stumbled unknowingly onto the secret homonymic truth of Zimmerman's reference.

Paul Nelson may have been one of the first to understand what Clint Eastwood was accomplishing working through his own production company, and that Don Siegel was more important to this process than Sergio Leone. Paul was conversant with detective fiction and he understood genre filmmaking. I was watching Eastwood's films, and once back in Chicago I was reading Dave Kehr on these films and he too was hip to *Pink Cadillac*, *The Rookie*, et. al. The golden age of foreign film had, much like the British Invasion, lured elite opinion away from American traditions too déclassé for comfort. Insanity...

Eastwood liked Nelson but Paul was hitting that wall of his limitations and probably fretting about just what it was he wanted and might dare to seek. Just recently (Oct. 12, 2011) saw the obit for Fritz Manes, a producer credit from many an Eastwood film. Manes was a friend of Eastwood's since junior high, the obit said, but Clint cut him loose over leaving behind bad feelings with the U.S. military after receiving production assistance for *Heartbreak Ridge* (1986). Eastwood expected to go back to the military someday and they play for keeps too. Paul might've turned in an imperfect Eastwood piece (there's a two-page false start included in *Afterthought*), moved to Los Angeles and simply faked screenplays like everyone else out there. But he was apparently too idealistic about the Artist and his Work. All his known writing is criticism of others' creations. To create himself would require a loss of belief in an ideal of Art. He likely knew that even the best films are fifty per cent accident and the viewer has to make the leap, go with it, put it together.... The limitations of art (or the artist or the business of art) account for the durability of genre. It's not likely many of the greats of the 19th century novel operated much differently.

Manny Farber considered criticism important and difficult, "I can't think of a better thing for a person to do." That was easy for him to say, as he was always a respected painter and sculptor alongside his film criticism.

In fact, Robert Polito, in his Introduction to *Farber on Film* writes:

> "The painter Farber will be is forecast in his observations and descriptions of his favorite directors, actors, and film moments, but also (and vividly) in his writing style." (*Farber on Film*)

In this sense Paul left us hanging; his music criticism forecast nothing. Perhaps had some other magazine been an option he might have continued his long-form criticism, but circa 1982 when he quit *Rolling Stone*, *Esquire* was no longer that sort of magazine either.

Afterthought tells us that Paul had left a wife and son back in Minnesota long ago; Doris Nelson is credited as staff in the *LSR*. Paul told Lightbourne, "My father was kind of interesting before he married my mother, she kind of tamed him." Nelson appeared to some as haunted as he walked alone through Manhattan in later years, from his illegal sublet on the upper eastside to the video store in the Village and back. I didn't really know him, but I know how such elements would read in a screenplay because I know my Cornell Woolrich. But would the damned thing get made?

In July 1985 Eastwood finally appeared on the cover of *Rolling Stone* with a story by Tim Cahill. And Clint eventually found his Boswell in *Newsweek*'s Richard Schickel. But somehow I don't think Pauline Kael blanched as she might have. Kevin couldn't get either Dylan or Eastwood to throw him an interview, a memory, a blurb, or a syllable.... Satan won't shut up, but the Creator is silent, speaking only through His works.

(originally posted at *The New Vulgate*, No. 120)

The Grate Game: Tibet
This review of three books on Tibet was for the abortive web-mag we hoped to include at the merch site for O&O-Upland Records. Previously unpublished.

Orphans of the Cold War – America and the Tibetan Struggle for Survival, by John Kenneth Knaus
A Stranger in Tibet – The Adventures of a Wandering Zen Monk, by Scott Berry
Warriors of Tibet – The Story of Aten and the Khampas' Fight for the Freedom of their Country, by Jamyang Norbu

Kawaguchi Ekai entered Tibet on July 4, 1900 on a mission from Buddha. He was a Japanese monk and a bit of a crank. His sect did not meet his standards, which were very strict even by Japanese standards, though of course he couldn't know this until he got to earthy, forbidden Tibet. He intended to read and collect Tibetan translations of the Mahayana Buddhist scriptures which had been moved to Tibetan monasteries during the Islamic invasions of India. He disguised himself as a Chinese monk and began learning Tibetan in his two years of preparation in India.

Tibet was then an unclaimed prize in the Great Game played most intensely by Great Britain (through its empire outposts in India, Nepal, Sikkim, and Burma), Russia (through its Buddhist vassal Mongolia), and China, then struggling in the last days of the Manchu dynasty. The story in *A Stranger in Tibet* has the makings of a very funny absurdist tale of the paranoid machinations set off among great empires by a lone, disguised, persistent monk determined to realize his faith, in between fending off maidens desperate for a little good karma and a meal ticket that doesn't smell like a yak. Author Scott Berry doesn't write it up to accentuate this but he does appreciate it. However he spends too many words berating Kawaguchi's berating the Tibetans for moral and hygienic failures – no one bathes because clogged pores are all that keep you from freezing to death at 20,000 feet elevation. Whatever Kawaguchi's limitations as travel writer and ethnographer, more extensive quotations from the original sources would've made the book less dry. And what's a devout vegetarian, celibate, Japanese Buddhist pilgrim to think anyway of the purported Buddhist Shangri-la whose entire monkdom seems to be eating goat hamburgers while screwing peasant girls?

In any case Kawaguchi mellowed and did meet very devout lamas at various temples and monasteries, including the Panchen Lama (6th) and the Dalai Lama (13th), even though the penalty for entering Tibet without permission (impossible to get) was deportation if you were lucky, imprisonment, torture and death if not. As Berry stresses, "of all the foreign adventurers who had sneaked into Lhasa, Kawaguchi was the first sincere Buddhist traveling simply for the sake of his religion." He returned to Japan to a peculiarly Japanese reception, the Tokyo Geographical Society denounced him as a fraud. He soon returned to Tibet, this time as an invited guest of the Nepali prime minister Chandra Shamshere Jung Bahadur Rana, and the Panchen Lama.

The book is full of interesting color about Japan, East India, Nepal and Tibet at the turn of the century. It's also devoid of the western world's middle class white-wash of Tibet's grubby theocracy in its heyday, while being full of crazed ancillary characters of varied nationalities ripe for further research.

Warriors of Tibet is a short, simple, and very affecting memoir of a farmer from eastern Tibet (Kham) born in 1915, who became a Tibetan guerrilla-fighter and is now a government-in-exile apparat. In 1935 a Red Army detachment was repelled during four months fighting. Nomads of the north spoke a different dialect and often slept outdoors even in winter. The first soldiers of the new People's Republic of China entered Kanze one night in early 1950. Norbu was sent to the South-west School for National Minorities in Chengtu for a year in mid 1955. He writes,

> "Every week there was a general meeting where we were exhorted by the principal to save grain, kill flies, destroy sparrows, resist imperialism, remember comrade Norman Berthune, learn the correct handling of contradictions among the people and whatever else the Party communique was at that moment. We also had a criticism session every Sunday." (*Warriors of Tibet*)

Norbu writes about the Lolos who lived along the southern border of China and Tibet. They revolted in 1955.

> "They were a proud people and mean fighters, fond of weapons and strong drink. The men wore big turbans on their heads and bedecked themselves with ornaments made of coral conch shells and cowries.... The Lolos never surrendered and they never took prisoners. Many Chinese divisions were rushed to the area and thousands of soldiers died in the subsequent fighting. Finally, through sheer weight of numbers and superior arms the revolt

was crushed. The reprisals were savage... The extent of the massacres will most probably never be known. What is known is that the Lolos have ceased to exist as a people." (*Ibid.*)

Norbu himself fled occupied Tibet on the "18th day of the 8th moon of 1958" and fought his way to the border and crossed into Nepal on the "2nd moon of 1960."

Orphans of the Cold War is an excellent record of the American involvement with Tibet from World War II on, as the U.S. struggled to assemble its global portfolio of responsibilities from the broken European empires and against the new communist order. The book's story begins in earnest in the summer 1956 when, five years into the communist occupation Mao took off the gloves and Tibet erupted. Author Knaus is a retired career C.I.A. operations officer who worked on the Tibetan effort and, judging by the footnotes, was able to talk to nearly every Tibetan principal. He's also dug through boxlots of governmental archives to piece together a complicated story. Plus, there are over fifty photos, many from Tibetan collections, that freeze fabled moments such as the Dalai Lama and Panchen Lama's meeting with Mao, Zhou Enlai and Liu Shaoqui, and the Dalai Lama's flight from Lhasa four years later.

The peculiarities of Tibet and Tibetans were to preclude successful and prolonged guerrilla operations as planned and so the book's story is lacking in gunfire and recreations of engagements with the Chinese. It's strength is portraying the early years of Chinese occupation when Tibetans (and Knaus's sources) hoped the promises of freedom would be kept, and when they weren't the story shifts to the exile settings of his sources: India, Washington, Nepal, and Colorado. Here it becomes a story of the netherworld of state departments, diplomats, the White House, and the C.I.A. Britain is bitter it is no longer in the Great Game; India, now out from under Britain is obsessed under Nehru with leading a non-aligned third way and trying to lure Red China into joining India's leadership. Washington is glad to have a people in revolt against communism and asking it for guns and training but is loath to get fully behind Tibet's claim of independence for fear of offending the Nationalist Chinese now decamped to Taiwan who like the mainland communists believe Tibet falls within China's historical border. Surprisingly perhaps American policy makers in both parties across four administrations largely favored the guerrilla effort in Tibet with the predictable exception of the Kennedy administration's ambassador to India, John Kenneth Galbraith. Nepal hosts the guerrillas until Nixon cuts support, then Nepal's King turns on the Tibetans to curry favor with Beijing; even Russia reenters the game after their break with China. China invaded eastern India in 1962 which forced a bitter Nehru to now support Tibetan aims, and China fought the Russians along their eastern border in 1969.

But this tragedy was taking place inside Tibet. *Orphans of the Cold War* is a level-headed, somewhat wistful account of one phase of the attempt to resist the Chinese communists from outside. The Colorado-trained Tibetan guerrillas achieved some successes early, confirmed by documents seized during a raid which killed an assistant regimental commander. These documents also were the first indication of the destabilizing effect that the Great Leap Forward was having in China. This might have been a signal that China could be retaken – it had not yet exploded nuclear devices – but the Nationalists on Taiwan were not serious about that, and the Sino-Soviet split was not yet deep enough to have tempted our own mandarins. And so the Tibet operation was peripheral and limited by the open terrain, thin population, and the inability of the Tibetan fighters to re-orient themselves to the guerrilla life; many of the early fighters were killed as they ignored orders and hunkered down with their families and herds in tow.

Tibet slowly gained an international profile in New Delhi, Washington, New York, and Geneva through the fifties and sixties and finally, post-Tiananmen, the counter-cultural interest in China has swung to Tibet and books, television programs, and movies celebrate its culture. But back in the late forties, the Dalai Lama and his brother Gyalo Thondup had intended to open Tibetan society and break the feudal theocracy that is much romanticized today. Their first attempt failed. The normally fractious monasteries found common ground here and fended off reform, only to have the communists arrive to pull out these monasterial traditions root and stem. A democratic system might have made it less tempting for the Chinese to now game the succession procedures for the reincarnation of the Dalai Lama and Panchen Lama, but the monasterial system the Chinese found in place lent justification to their actions. The new young Panchen Lama (replacing his heroic predecessor who refused to be a Chinese puppet and spent 14 years in prison) is either in prison or dead and a Chinese-appointed imposter in his place; meanwhile Party hacks wait to replace the Dalai Lama.

The world had barely glimpsed some of the monasteries and temples before the Chinese smashed them to dust in the name of socialism – one of their smaller crimes against humanity, sad to say, but a very dramatic, one. To paraphrase a friend who used to say it of Stalin, whatever Mao's crimes in Tibet he can be considered the greatest anti-communist enemy of China given how many of his countrymen he killed.

Real Impolitik – Pat Buchanan in the Crossfire
This was done for the webmag that wasn't. All these election cycles later and both parties and the incipient next third party attempt continue to crib from Pat, currently the go-to reactionary for MSNBC's geniuses.

A *Republic, Not an Empire*, by Pat Buchanan

When CNN first put Pat Buchanan and Tom Braden's radio show in front of its cameras the guest would sit between Pat and Tom. What usually followed was a two-against-one argument as either Pat or Tom joined the guest to help defend his position for tactical or true ideological reasons. This needn't have been the case; you'd like to think that any position or politician ought to have to defend itself or himself against each philosophical premise. But the game of politics, and the gaming of the politics of the moment, do tend to debase discourse. And so they retooled "*Crossfire*" – replicating the ideological divide of the hosts by inviting two equally opposed guests. Only special guests got the center seat to themselves now, like when Pat Buchanan the candidate for president drops by. Buchanan's replacement was Robert Novak who actually provided better challenge to Pat's trade protectionism, where he's to the left of the Democrats.

Pat is currently after the Reform Party nomination and the third podium at the Great Debates. The Democratic and Republican nominees will be conspiring to keep the debates from being great by excluding that him. If Pat gets on that stage he will make the kind of noise that both parties fear. In the months since his new book, A *Republic, Not an Empire* has been published, idea-chewers from left and right and center have been having at Pat. This is good, though as on "*Crossfire*" the political needs of the respondents, whether politicians, reporters, academics or pundits, seem always to shunt critique onto a personalized siding that yields less publicly useful noise. The left tries to use him to define all Republicans even as he left the party, and the right uses him to define themselves as well, but both respond only to the media cartoon, not to the book or him. After coloring Buchanan a xenophobic, isolationist, racist, anti-Semitic crypto-Nazi they pause to consider if they aren't really treating a man of such noxious ideas so nicely because they've all known him for years and really like him. The *New York Daily News*' Sidney Zion refers to him as a "tramp," and "dirt under our feet," yet throughout the column routinely refers him to him as "Pat."

Post-WTO meltdown the Democrats and Republicans both have cause to increase the demonization of Buchanan: the Dems because they've just been caught between the pier and the boat trying to balance their alliance of environmentalists and unions with Wall Street, and the Republicans to head off any defections on the right's cultural issues. Unless Buchanan can be made radioactive he is perfectly positioned and perfectly skilled to split both parties down their middles. He is that man. And he might just be too well known to be demonized, though he certainly is a gremlin.

But what about the book? Last campaign Pat was beating the wrong drum with his *The Great Betrayal* joust at free trade and the exporting of jobs he claimed was occurring. Certainly it sounded tempting then when it was unclear what the vulnerabilities of Japan, Inc., and the People's Republic of China might be. Four years later and its clear that the intractable nature of their problems are due to the kind of protectionist rigging of their economies that Pat was advocating for us. Also, there is no Free Trade, per se, but the insistence that policymakers at least stay in sight of this ideal prevents the wholesale rampaging of sectarian and corporate interests having their way with policy (Think Ethanol Über Alles; Think too of the political paralysis in the face of these systemic corruptions in Germany and France as well, as once down that road the favored constituencies refuse to give back an inch no matter the cost to the whole).

This time, however, Pat is on to something big and more necessary to the debate. *A Republic, Not an Empire* asks the question of the moment: In a changed world should the responsibilities of the United States also change? Extending NATO eastward, and the empowerment of supra-national organizations are occurring with minimal debate. The WTO debacle in Seattle (like the earlier Test-ban treaty failure) is what happens when an administration no-one trusts tries to slip something past people and nations without debate. The advocates certainly don't want a loud debate, and in any case there probably can be none without a military crisis. Neither can there be one when the Republican and Democratic Parties both agree. (*The Wall Street Journal*'s editorial page believes the seemingly clumsy lead-up to WTO by the Clinton Commerce officials was designed to fail and so seal off the free trade question for Al Gore's benefit.) The Mediacracy pretends to despair over the Bush/Gore choice, but they don't really want an authentic debate or we'd have one, and neither does the electorate so the media gets away with their posturing. However, the electorate has an excuse; they have better things to do. The so-called professionals of Journalism – well, one more profession down the drain....

Luckily we have Pat who is up for this thankless task of opening a debate. He writes,

> "Europe's sick man of today is going to get well. When Russia does, it will proclaim its own Monroe Doctrine. And when that day comes, America will face a hellish dilemma: risk confrontation with a nuclear-armed Russia determined to recreate its old sphere of influence, or renege on solemn commitments and see Nato collapse." (*A Republic, Not an Empire*)

He argues that no American really believes that we will fight to defend Poland or Hungary, or Ukraine, or Latvia, and neither do the Russians. It is a bluff. And this is where Buchanan's history lesson yields important lessons long forgotten. After all, we are reminded, the British and French tried to bluff Germany by signing a defense pact with Poland after Hitler had taken Austria and parts of Czechoslovakia. They accomplished nothing for Poland except to issue a declaration of war on Germany upon the invasion. But England and France did not declare war on the Soviet Union, though it simultaneously invaded Poland from the east. Buchanan has it that Germany then turned upon the west and gave his real target, the Soviet Union, two years to prepare. It's speculation but Pat isn't the author of this theory; evidence abounds for it and historians have considered it for decades and will continue to.

He also recounts the "isolationist" FDR throughout the thirties, knocking back militarization requests and continuing the post WWI ship-building ratios of Wilson's peace which would handicap the U.S. - the only nation that would with certainty have to fight across two oceans. In fact, FDR was pushing as much socialism as this nation would stomach and as he deepened the depression he came to find what all socialists find: there is no international socialism at peace with the world, there is only national socialism on a war footing. This need for war to salvage what was increasingly a command economy was more important to Roosevelt than helping Britain, France, the Soviet Union, Nationalist China, the Jews of Europe, or anybody else. FDR needed the war but couldn't get Americans to agree for all the hell in Europe up to the date of December 6, 1941. By then Britain was not in danger of invasion as Hitler was nearly six months into the Russian campaign, and so despite the needs of FDR and the many Anglophiles and the few Communists in his administration America might very well have never entered the war. Attacks on Pat for countenancing not entering the war specifically to save Jews are premised on holding him to a higher standard than those who lead the Allies before and during the war . (This special standard is now being applied to Pius XII, "Hitler's Pope," as well.)

The Navy advised FDR against an oil embargo on Japan especially in light of their inability to get increased funding out of him and Congress (FDR had been Secretary of the Navy). The U.S. could read Japanese diplomatic and military codes as early as August 1940. The aircraft carriers were out of port. And author Robert Stinnett's new book, *Day of Deceit*, reproduces an October 1940 Naval Intelligence memo to FDR suggesting eight moves to force Japan to go to war against the U.S. If this is all true then FDR sweated out the four days it took for Japan's ally Germany to declare war on the U.S. Only then he was where he wanted to be, out of trouble and into the war.

Pat's parsing of how we got into WWII has been seized on by most of his attackers but it's just a part of his review of the American debate on military alliances and intervention overseas since the early Republic was torn by Anglophiles and Francophiles. Is this the same media and academia that dreams of catching the black hand of the politicians and military brass behind the most heinous conspiracies? Yes, but as lost professions they've all become gamers and the game ain't beanbag. They've turned the richness of our history into a convenient cartoon where they seem to work from a premise that says *The Greatest Generation* was such a great book and *Saving Private Ryan* such a great movie that any argument that we should have stayed out of the war that provided the glorious settings for them is an affront to two of our finest shoe-shiners, Toms Brokaw and Hanks. This is not serious and coupled as it is with calls for an improved debate it can get very hard to take unless one cultivates an appreciation for this scoundrel theater.

Pat drives home the importance of reconsidering our history and recognizing mistakes before we set off on global missionarying when he traces a "what if" outline of WWI: Without American loans and then troops, WWI ends in a stalemate; there is no Versaille; no American dead, possibly no Bolshevik coup, certainly no sulking bitter Germany, no Hitler, no Holocaust in Europe, no WWII, possibly no cold war. (Edward Luttwak, in his piece in the July/August issue of *Foreign Affairs*, "Give War a Chance," provides a contrasting but parallel revisitation of more recent American and International interventions in local wars; and once again it takes a special fearlessness to take up such thankless arguments.)

Those most important and egregious in their attempts to run Pat out of the debate are Bill Kristol (ex-Quayle aide, ABC's "This Week," *Weekly Standard*), Norman Podhoretz (*Wall Street Journal, Commentary, National Review*), Robert Dallek (Boston U., FDR biographer), Michael Lind (*Los Angeles*

Times), William Safire (New York Times), Andrew J. Bacevich (National Review, Boston U., Director Center for International Relations), John Judis (New York Times, New Republic), Joshua Muravchik (Commentary), Tucker Carlson (Talk, CNN), Mona Charen (synd., CNN), and Michael Kelly (New York Post). These brains provide reporters, TV journalists and news hosts with the cover to all ask the same pseudo-hardball question, "Just what kind of anti-Semite are you, Mr. Buchanan?" Buchanan is confronted with this diversion by TV hosts from Russert to Geraldo; even the lightweights get juiced up for him (Katie's never met a real live Nazi before). Safire, Kristol, and Podhoretz succeeded in pissing him off; otherwise, he takes most of this noise with good humor. The ex-conservative, now liberal Michael Lind ought to know better as he's in the midst of working his own new book, *Vietnam – The Necessary War*, which is asking an official culture that has made up its mind even more firmly, if only because they believe they remember that war, to rethink it based on revisiting the theories against the evidence which has now come in.

More interesting responses to Pat and his book have come from Charles Krauthammer (*Washington Post*), Nicholas von Hoffman (*New York Press*), George Szamuely (*New York Press*), Sean Wilentz (*New Republic*), Ramesh Ponnuru (*National Review*), Geoffrey Wheatcroft (*Wall Street Journal*), and Bruce Ramsey (*Liberty*) probably because they felt they should read the book and they have less pretense of being influential. Krauthammer's written one attack and one apprehensive appreciation of what Buchanan may pull off. Szamuely caught Podhoretz misrepresenting old Buchanan columns to fabricate evidence of anti-Semitism. Wheatcroft compares him to the European tradition of Catholic parties. Ponnuru focuses his critique on Pat's empowerment of the state to determine trade policy and compares him to Kevin Phillips, another old Nixon-hand populist. Wilentz (that double-dome freak from the Impeachment hearings panel of hystorians) tries to calm everyone by claiming Pat is not a Hitlerite, but a Francoist. Ramsey and von Hoffman like the book and *Liberty*'s headline for Ramsey's piece, "Pugnacious Peacenik" captures by indirection the looneyness that has greeted his book and candidacy. *The Nation*'s Monte Paulsen wrote up Pat and Bay Buchanan's permanent campaign's financial structure with helpless admiration, despite the editor's packaging of the story as if it were the expose of an ongoing criminal enterprise.

Pat is being consistently and pointedly defended by John McLaughlin, and both the left and right of "*Crossfire*," Bill Press and Robert Novak treated him respectfully, and the Cato Institute, a libertarian think tank, gave his foreign policy speech an enthusiastic hearing and the Q&A was no melee.

A Republic, Not an Empire begins with the leak of what came to be called the Wolfowitz memo to the *New York Times* in early 1992. Bush's Undersecretary of Defense had drawn up a post-cold war blueprint by which Nato war guarantees would extend east to the Baltics, and U.S. policy would be the prevention of regional domination by any nation sufficient to generate global power. 1992 was the election year and the Bush administration was ridiculed by Carter's Secretary of Defense Harold Brown, and Senators Kennedy and Biden as a "Pax Americana." But Biden and Kennedy both voted to expand Nato eastward just last year! Neither Party in the old sense exists anymore; much like the Reform Party, they are simply vehicles for the most active people in them. Both are pushed by the bureaucrats, academicians, journalists, and hacks who tie their wagons to that Party expecting a job on a stage worthy of their genius. Kennedy, Brown and Biden suggested they were outraged by the very idea, when in fact they were simply playing to the left while hoping the Republicans would succeed in foisting this new global role on the nation so that they could inherit these new sinecure postings to divy out under the next Democratic administration, which as it happened came very soon.

This game had to be put up with for fifty years in the Cold War world of an expansionist U.S.S.R. But today? Pat Buchanan has got the question of the hour to himself. Unbelievable, considering the media metastasizing going on. But he's game. In his preface he writes,

> "What was most heartening about that [1996] campaign was the respectful and extensive coverage my ideas received in the mainstream media." (*Ibid.*)

And if the Republicans and Democrats fail to head him off they stand to lose bigtime – epiphanous, revelational, mystagogic bigtime!

Rage to Serve – Hillaryland 10514

The Clinton administration was quite a feast for Sixtiesologists, especially those first two years when Hillary ran hog wild. This was written in 2000 as she ran for the Senate, but never published.

The First Partner - Hillary Rodham Clinton, by Joyce Milton
The Case Against Hillary, by Peggy Noonan
Hillary's Choice, by Gail Sheehy
The Seduction of Hillary Rodham, by David Brock
Hell to Pay, by Barbara Olson

In 1985 or so, Henry Rollins and Lydia Lunch performed at the Club Lingerie for the hipsters of Hollywood. The attendees lined up and went into a room one at a time only to find themselves verbally accosted and physically abused by these two scamps. The L.A. *Weekly*'s "La De Da" column the next week was full of outrage directed at La Lunch and El Rollins on behalf of friends of the editors. The performance was called, 'Help Us Hurt You.' And they lined up....

...and voted into office Bill and Hillary. (Al Gore only really got to assume the vice presidency from the point at which Hillary's healthcare task-farce catapulted Newt Gingrich into the Speaker's chair and her deep into Hillaryland). But the Clintons aren't self-possessed performance artists; they are, rather, a pair of homeless half-formed ids that together spark the only spasms that have animated the Democratic National Corpse since JFK got laid out.

But that's not good because today all parties of the Left are now essentially nihilist. As long as there existed the general expectation that historical evolution would progress toward centralized planned socialism the Democrats were at least true believers in their policies. Now that they no longer believe in their own political philosophy they are mere posturers – out of inertia, or fear, or self-interest. In Hillary's case it would appear to always have been self-interest, though a deeply sublimated, in-grown self-interest. How common this is on the Left is an open question as the Left's current quandary is a recent development. But it's certainly common in teachers union precincts. And trial lawyer environs. And in the media. And with others in the demi-mind economy. There may also be a gender aspect at work in Hillary's case – this kind of megalo-sublimation which yields a near perfect sealing off from doubt and reappraisal. This may be seen most clearly when this Empress of ours strode chin up into staterooms immediately after having been stripped bare so publicly. Hillary only transmits; Bill receives. In fact, what makes Bill such a poor public speechmaker is that he's too busy reading his audience as he speaks. He's classic as well.

Hillary Rodham had been a star in the Movement netherlands of the Democratic Party since she left the Republican Party of her childhood as a Wellesley undergrad. Her childhood was not like most, however, in that she paid more constant attention to politics. Most kids ape their parents as the presidential campaign begins to register with them through TV ads or via mock elections in history class. Only the creepiest age-traitors collude with the school administrators and run happily and seriously for student government positions. And that's our Hill (and Bill).

The permutations of their story are, if not quite Shakespeareian, at least richly telling of the soft post-war generation. The story might be traced in any of a number of narratives:

> The Psychological narrative:
> wherein young Hillary's response to her hardworking and challenging parents is a grandiose public, yet essentially personal, trumping of their modest, quintessentially American triumphs.

> The Social narrative:
> wherein the straight-laced Hillary inserts herself as the practical interface between the emotional radical youth and the staid political establishment, first in college, then law school, then in Black Panther defense work, then in the Legal Services Corporation, then Arkansas politics, and finally national politics.

> The Political narrative:
> wherein the ex-Goldwater Girl, Movement lawyer helps write the House Committee's expansive impeachment charter against Nixon, marries a Kennedy clone and lives to rue her own youthful implacability and her new party's criminalization of political differences via the Independent Counsel Statute.

> The Philosophical narrative:
> wherein the progressive Methodist interfaces with the New Left and feminism's Identity Politics and attempts to revivify the wel-

fare state and push it towards a therapeutic state – totalitarianism with a smothering mother's face.

The Class narrative:
wherein uppity children of the new upper middle class found that their appetite to forge a new criteria in which to best their parents (who had just mastered the fascists and rallied the free world against the communists) put them in alliance with a sullen Academia which had just been taken down several notches from its heyday in FDR's first two terms by the imperatives of war – the U.S. Army oversaw the brilliant physicists of the Manhattan Project, most every one of which was either a high-minded com-symp or U.N.-worldgovnik.

The Criminal narrative:
wherein the moral yet ambitious young woman who turns down the chance to buy the 1974 Congressional campaign for Bill because its wrong, is seduced by the chance to work her moralistic policies behind the mud-guard of her husband's henceforth amoral prosecution of his political career.

This is all certainly ripe enough material, but without a Shakespeare that's all it is. The chroniclers we had early on (Joe Klein, David Maraniss, Roger Morris) identified with the Clintons to such an extent that their body-english told the real story while they droned on and on about the supposed "larger story" of a broken system, as if the Clintons were no more problematic than the Doles, Bushes, Reagans, Carters, Nixons, etc., and as if the American system is broken when, in fact, it is all the other polities on the face of the earth that are unable to respond to their own intractable problems (high unemployment, expensive investment capital, punitive taxes, immobilizing regulatory regimes on business, protected inefficient sectors, corruption....). These nations often seem to progress against these self-generated problems only courtesy the competitive challenge they face from the American juggernaut.

The early approach to the Clintons by his biographers is not the approach of these later Hillary chroniclers because the various money stories of the 1996 re-election campaign make it clear that whatever the shape of our polity, taking money from everyone from Indian tribes (stiffing them on the casinos or lands they sought) to the Chinese military (giving them what they wanted!) is a personal corruption bordering on dessication. (If the Clintons were taken as seriously as they have insisted, they'd simply have to be charged with treason.)

The new prose attempts at telling Hillary's story (and there are dozens more Hillary books) are fired by the rich opportunities she herself presents. Most of the books lean on two important magazine pieces: Christopher Lasch's *Harper's* piece, 'Hillary Clinton, Child Saver,' which ran just before the 1992 election, and Michael Kelly's *NY Times Magazine* piece, 'Saint Hillary,' which ran May 23, 1993. Only Gail Sheehy, in her book *Hillary's Choice*, doesn't ref the Lasch piece, and she pointedly neglects to identify Kelly by name or as anything but "a young writer." Kelly had interviewed Hillary and got her to out herself as religious in motivation. Hillary must have hated the piece; Gail sure did.

Sheehy's book identifies with Hillary and is therefore precious about her insights and protective of her relationship with her subject. Her original reporting focuses on her own interviews with Hillary for *Vanity Fair*, and interviews with the denizens of Hillaryland (Betsey Wright, Jane Sherbourne, Bernard Nussbaum, Neel Lattimore, Harold Ickes, Susan Thomases). Sheehy's interviews with others from Hillary's life are all filtered through her 1970s Phil Donahue-style psycho-babble about "passages," "choices," "couple crossover," "the post-menopausal flaming fifties...." She does elicit inadvertent gal-pal confessions of bias from the likes of Martha Teichner (CBS reporter, ex-Wellesley classmate), and front row Hillary-watching from Don Jones, the dashing young Methodist minister pied piper – now there's a lost early sixties archetype! The best line in the book is attributed to an anonymous former press secretary of Bill's – likely Mike McCurry; when asked what Bill will be doing post-presidency answered, "He'll drive off that bridge when he comes to it."

Peggy Noonan is precious as well. She's responsible for some great speech-writing and some fine interpretive analysis in the *Wall Street Journal*, but her contribution here, *The Case Against Hillary Clinton*, is a fake book coasting on a publisher's advance and written to election year deadline. *George* magazine printed the absolute worst of the chapters, which almost put me off picking it up. But she is too good an observer to waste all of your time and money. She notes Bill's assuming JFK's posture from the Jamie Wyeth portrait that he passes every day in the White House as he walks from the helicopter to the White House. It's a posture Gary Hart had mimicked in his day. These acolytes studied JFK footage in the dark as if it were pornography. (Their breezy womanizing was/remains fully misogynistic because what they are actually doing in Sheehy-Donahue-terms is conducting a homoerotic relationship with Johnny-We-Hardly-Knew-Ye, only they keep finding themselves stuck to some bitch when they come down.)

Noonan doesn't go this far – she ain't Paglia – but she does hit a point or two home: "John Kennedy went to war; he fought for two years in the Pacific, came home, and, crippled with pain, went door-to-door in the triple-deckers of South Boston asking for votes as a veteran. Bill Clinton watched a war on TV and calls it his trauma. He watched the civil rights movement and calls it his proving ground." And this too:

> "I suspect we will be seeing more of a small and subtle habit Mrs. Clinton has developed in the past year or so. When she is asked a question that touches on what she considers a danger area, and to which she wants to give a 'no' response... she often nods her head up and down, as someone would when they're saying yes. When she is asked a danger-area question to which she wants to respond with a 'yes'... she often shakes her head side to side, as people do when they mean no. It is possible that this is an unconscious quirk, but I suspect it is deliberate, a way of taking the clarity out of a moment and leaching it of impact."
> (*The Case Against Hillary Clinton*)

This is actually an imitation of *ABC*'s very canny Diane Sawyer. (She's the wife of Mike Nichols, director of the film adaptation of Joe Klein's pre-novelization, *Primary Colors*, so, you know...)

As many have noted this year, Hillary seems intent on conducting her run for Senate without clarity or impact – as a First Lady mannequin saying little as she glides through campaign stops like the ghost of Princess Diana. Its campaigning-as-victory lap – what comes of running for what Harold Ickes termed, "redemption," instead of, oh say, to serve the public.

Barbara Olson, author of *Hell to Pay*, is one of the blonde pundettes that *Fox News* and *MSNBC* have used to chip away at *CNN* and its secondary market hirelings. They are an improvement but still disappointing. Olson's standing is based on her service as the chief investigative counsel for the House Government Reform and Oversight Committee, chaired by William Clinger (R.-Penn.), which looked into the FBI files and Travel Office firings scandals. Olson and her staff "wrote and rewrote the interrogatories for her to answer under oath and deposed her friends and loyal soldiers." She writes,

> "The members of my seasoned investigative staff would each tell

you they have never seen anyone better able to keep her stories, however improbable, straight. She was unflappable when presented with damning evidence and was adept at darting nimbly to a new interpretation that put that damning evidence in the best light." (*Hell to Pay*)

Olson begins with the false pregnancy of the 1996 re-election campaign. Actually it was Hillary's threat to adopt some almost poor bastard. Olson doesn't parse it deeply but Jane Schuman, a writer friend, explained to me why this Hillary gambit was so cold a political taunt. She launched it in a softball interview by *Time*'s Walter Isaacson: "I must say we're hoping to have another child." Really, why must you? Olson has it that it humanized Hillary who was Bill's principal negative but Jane considered it to be aimed directly at Elizabeth Dole who had no children and then in her fifties was never going to. You'd have to appreciate Hillary's personal hostility to any woman who would take her position, especially one who had actual independent professional accomplishments. Still, it can be breathtaking to consider the ease with which Hillary folds up and stows away her collapsible feminist principles for tactical self-interest in a mere symbolic contest with a true feminist pathfinder.

She was again using her daughter Chelsea for political gain, though this time by indirection. She and Bill claim to have never used Chelsea, even though she was a veritable prop in the weeks after the emission admission. Even that will be as nothing compared to what Chelsea will be asked to perform in the final weeks of this New York Senate campaign. She's skipping the fall semester to shadow mom during the fall campaign, and with Hillary trailing first Guiliani, and now Lazio, Chelsea the co-ed will be called upon to do precisely the opposite of what Hillary the college girl had done – she will be made to publicly validate her parents' worldview – certainly a new landmark in boomer hubris. Hillary's mother Dorothy Rodham may be the only person on earth who can fully appreciate this.

Barbara Olson's book is a breezy run through the story of Hillary and it leans heavily on published accounts. Hard to recommend when there are Brock's book, and Milton's book available. Olson's is another insta-book that owes its existence to the publishing world's politics rather than merit. Still it has the best cover photo of Hillary who seems to be caught whistling admiration for someone else's underhanded shiv thrust – same photo makes an appearance on the cover of Chistopher Hitchens' excellent pamphlet, *No One Left to Lie to*. Olson quotes two of the more egregious press toadies which are worth repeating: Martha Sherrill of the *Washington Post* on Hillary: "She has goals, but they appear to be so huge and far-off grand and noble things twinkling in the distance that it's hard to see what she sees," and Hard News Dan Rather, the Nixon-hater who yet salts his grave at every anniversary of the break-in or the resignation or his death, speaking to Bill via satellite before a CBS affiliates meeting, "If we could be one-hundredth as great as you and Hillary Rodham Clinton have been in the White House we'd take it right now and walk away winners." You are more than a winner Dan, so please... good-bye already.

After the New Left's disillusionment in the seventies, those who would not commit to the bilious, outsider life of the Left sold out in various ways. Most just turned the page once the draft, which had been their real concern, was over. Others crashed and burned as political and racial wet-dreams (Black Panthers, SDS, Weathermen, Red Guards, Red Army Faction, Japanese Red Army, Khmer Rouge, PFLP, Viet-Cong, Polisario...) dried up. They'd gotten what they'd wanted: Nixon pulled down, communist victory in Vietnam, the welfare state run riot, etc., but they turned around and the anti-draft legions were suddenly gone from the Movement. The millions more put to the people's sword across the third world meant precious little to them, but the New Left paradigms of the seventies (feminism, gay liberation, and ecology) did make the even the new commie regimes look as stodgy as Brezhnev and Mao shuffling through politburo ceremonies.

Sad to say, or thank God, much of the New Left was simple demographic-enabled herd instinct – the difficult years of adolescence writ large and expanded past the age of thirty. What really was happening in the world overseas, or even just off-campus, was of little true interest to any of them. It's actually the married-with-childrens who have such concerns. The sixties-to-seventies sequence of sexy radical totems was something like: Che, Ho, Mao, Allende, Newton, Carlos, Dohrn, Meinhof, Pol Pot, Ortega. (In Colombia, Peru, and Venezuela the radical leadership has been less personalized. Subcomandante Marcos has tried to resurrect the archetype in southern Mexico.) Today politicized consciousness in radical America has more to do with simply which coffee beans not to buy.

Hillary's choice of sell-out was law, but there'd be no funky ghetto store-front people's law office for her. She'd already interned the summer of 1972 with Robert Treuhaft, the Stalinist lawyer in Oakland married to Jessica Mitford, co-ordinating Black Panther defenses – a continuation of Hillary's Panther involvement while at Yale in New Haven. But while her heart was with the radicals, her head was determinedly focused on bourgeois goals. Or maybe it was her head with the radicals, and her heart with the bourgeois – it's hard to discern a heartbeat when the Left so thoroughly politicizes appeals to the heart in order to market class vengeance.

In perfect seventies curdled idealistic style, living the bourgeois life was the price they would have to pay for being serious, purposeful radicals, not the kind that just carped from outside (damned anarchists!). The Weathermen, and R.A.F. also couldn't afford to be seen in bohemian parts of town wearing anything downscale. Tactical considerations demanded they take on the coloration of the ruling class – how tragically ironically convenient.

Hillary was determinedly unchic and disinterested in creature comforts until the eighties which really was the decade of greed for her. She had been convinced that Bill's governorship of a small state with a part-time legislature was the best launching pad available to them, but as their incessant out-of-state politicking made it impossible for her to make enough money as a lawyer in Little Rock to set up themselves in the style they would demand, she focused on the inside deals available to any governor – gifted investment opportunities, sundry sweetheart deals, and board memberships (Wal-Mart, TCBY, Lafarge Corp., Bancorp.). Other liberals did not suspect that being on the board of Wal-Mart would not hurt you with organized labor, or that a Lafarge appointment would not hurt you with environmentalists... the chumps.

The best of these books is Joyce Milton's *The First Partner*. She is of Hillary's generation and admits to having been a supporter of hers from the beginning of Bill's campaign for the Democratic nomination. She wrote a children's book about Hillary (there were several of these!), though she has been a serious biographer of those with politically charged lives – Chaplin, Lindbergh, the Rosenbergs. Hillary ultimately disappointed Milton, though she nevertheless writes sympathetically as if personally understanding just what it was Hillary thought she was doing. I too (b.1955) remember the traps set for that cohort's herd instincts and am glad to have been just young and backward enough to have seen counter-culture trip-ups before being old enough to partake. That and *Mad* magazine's treatment of beatniks and hippies tempered my enthusiasm I suppose. But for those slightly older, once the demographic power of the baby boom made such schtick socially profitable, the die was cast. The original postwar iconoclasts of the fifties were cohortless and glad of it. This is why older cultural avatars are frequently so contemptuous of Bill and Hill, who came on the collegiate counter-culture scene when it was already an upper middle class sinecure.

Milton describes the period:

> "It was a time when disaffected young people felt great confidence in their ability to lead and when the older generation, conscience-stricken over its own shortcomings, was often more than ready to let them." (*The First Partner*)

She further considers that after the well-meaning college kids were run out of civil rights work, the nihilism began. Black power essentially painted the white race no less than the American polity itself as irredeemable. This defensive, cynical fantasy quickly made the jump to white radical culture where it caused a split. Most went off into late hippie/new age tangents which were very white with increasing Native American affectations. But a few were mesmerized by the specter of a black revolutionary vanguard. Jung youth! Instead of projecting patricidal energy into a perverse alliance with the Kremlin as the old Left had done, the New Left spiced it up by allying with and finally prostrating itself before the black man on the other side of town. This was in part picked up from British rock stars. Brit kids were crazy about American music, but black American music was perversely the safer interest for the better classes due to its distance. (There were more residual cultural and class issues with the white ex-colonials whose fathers had just come by and lead the vanquishing of the Jerrys.) British youth in its early attempt at a post-imperial culture made feints in the direction of "going native" but Britishness won out and they mostly merely exploited their music and fashion. White American college kids took the British pop culture as more sophisticated and though it seemed to direct them at black American music just as black power was in its ascendancy, young white Americans never had the same enthusiasm for black music; they seemed rather to want to maintain the shorter distance they knew.

Milton doesn't parse all of this but she does know her generation's backstory, both the official one that reflects glory onto all the right characters, and the actual backstory that is yet unwritten, merely felt. The Clintons have provoked the first stumbling efforts at investigating it since the Jewish neo-cons left the Left with the rise of black power. Milton is smart enough to begin with Bill's self-pitying allusion to Arthur Koestler's character in *Darkness at Noon* and catch that it is a more apt reference than he knows,

> "As a good revolutionary, Nicolai Rubashov has always believed that the end justifies the means. Now that he has become expendable, he is doomed by his own principles. Koestler, interestingly enough, describes Rubashov as entrapped by his habitual abuse of language, which he calls the 'grammatical fiction' – Rubashov's 'Truth' has been a lie all along." (*Ibid.*)

Milton also sharply notes of LBJ's Great Society programs, "there was nothing populist or radical about Johnson's program; it was strictly an elitist crusade. More than 14 presidential commissions made up of public policy experts labored in secret to produce Great Society legislation which promised to wipe out poverty in a decade." Sounds like a Goldwater Girl we all know.

Milton finds or makes important general observations and digs up specific items skillfully. Generally:

> "(Yale law) Professor Robert Bork... had long tried to challenge the assumptions of his mostly liberal students, but in 1969 all that changed. Students were so tightly wound that they reacted with tears and curses to his attempts to challenge them intellectually." (Ibid.)

And specificly, Hillary's lack of comprehension about just how sympathetic media figures like the *New York Times*' Howell Raines, and *CBS News*' Don Hewitt were towards them, even during the farcical firing of White House Chef Pierre Chambrin, and this first dust up over drugs and White House security:

> "Bill Clinton turned down requests from the *New York Times* for an interview with its health correspondent Dr. Lawrence Altman, and in December, 1992, his appointment with a heart specialist, Dr. Andrew Kumpuris, was omitted from his published daily schedule. In January 1993, just weeks after his inauguration, a package from Clinton's allergy specialist, Dr. Kelsy Caplinger, arrived at the White House containing a vial with a note identifying the contents as 'President Clinton's allergy medicine.' Dr. Burton Lee, who had been George Bush's official physician, refused to administer the medicine by injection without more information. 'I was not happy about how the serum came to us, delivered to the White House gate, no covering letter, no idea what was in the bottle or why it was mailed,' said Dr. Lee, who called the President's Little Rock physician, Dr. Susan Santa Cruz, to request his full medical records. Dr. Santa Cruz said she'd have to get Hillary's permission to release the records. Two hours later, Dr. Lee was fired." (Ibid.)

Consider Bill's refusal to release his medical records. His over the top sexual history and his telling Juanita Broaddrick after raping her not to worry that he was sterile, argues that the big medical secret is VD or Chelsea's paternity. The rampant cocaine use in his Little Rock environs argues for something like septoplasty to repair a coke-destroyed nose. Gary Aldrich's book, *Unlimited Access* portrays from the inside how White House security was destroyed with regard to traditional concerns of espionage, blackmail, narcotics, assassination, and replaced with a paranoid black hole where no information ever escaped. Instead polling data and political dirt and cash money and fixers and bribesmen streamed in.

Whatever the number of Clinton books out now, there will be forests of memoirs once Clinton is out of the White House; more if Gore and Hillary lose, slightly fewer if they are around to dangle jobs for silence. Each memoir will be bursting with the bile of post-traumatic-stress-disordered Clinton veterans now free to clear consciences and debts in a great gale of pretentious gossip.

The most anticipated bio of Hillary in its day (election year, 1996) was David Brock's *The Seduction of Hillary Rodham*. Brock was the most dogged reporter on the Clinton's trail and he was given the widest leeway by *The American Spectator*, most spectacularly in his January 1994 piece, "His Cheatin' Heart - Living With the Clintons," which was a critique of the press by example. He merely revisited the half-stories that the Clinton damage control officers had been able to shunt to the tabloids beginning with Gennifer Flowers, and then attempted to paint a portrait of who the man was as the Arkansas governor. The piece might have shamed the media establishment, if not the Democratic Party, but each refused to deal with reality until the inexorable court proceedings began to eat away their ability to ignore it all. Brock's earlier big splash was a *Spectator* piece of March 1992 called "The Real Anita Hill" which became a 1993 book of the same name.

Unfortunately for the Left, they believed Anita and thus set themselves up for the obliteration of their own credibility and the to-that-point successful ratcheting up of sexual harassment law. On the backs of John Tower, Bob Packwood, and Clarence Thomas the feminist Left seemingly extirpated the last legal inch of wiggle-room when it came to anything from kissing, tonguing, pinching, joking, and talking, to reading a *Playboy* in mixed company. Little did they know that Bill's sidewindin' lil' weed-wacker has a gift for filling holes, and over these last few years it's even filled the holes in their heads - witness Joe Eszterhas' memoir of Clinton-watching, *American Rhapsody*, wherein Joe's speed rambling continually sputters to a halt as he finds Clinton's cock sliding into his mouth. At least when it slips into CBS's Bob Schieffer's mouth he looks as if he finds it distasteful.

Based on Brock's dissection of Anita Hill and the Senate hearings process, his book on Hillary was expected to verily knock her out of the box. But Brock explains in the preface that even as he attempted to set up an interview with Hillary "I had come to believe that the Republican effort to make her the arch-villain of the Whitewater saga was wrong." Hillary had set many conservatives to climbing the walls, but as Brock's research confirmed, their suspicions were in large part correct. She was a radical and remains as radical as it is safe for her to be.

Brock's chapter on her years with the Legal Services Corporation is the most valuable part of his book, especially considering that the use of federally funded class action lawsuits as revolution by other means has since metastasized into a plague upon enterprise and governance. Legal Services began in 1965 as a Great Society program budgeted at $1million and "was run by professional activists whose idea of social justice meant litigating and lobbying to change laws, ...extending the welfare state, as well as Alinsky-style organizing of the poor into political pressure groups." It became an independent corporation in 1974 with a budget of $90 million. Republicans and conservative Democrats who understood the potential for federally funded obstructionism failed to pen in its mandate. In any case they did not understand that the rhetorical shift in favor of the radicals after 1968 meant that once activist lawyers pushed at even what limits there were, there would be no will to enforce them, especially after 1974 election of the Watergate congress. Hillary was appointed to the LSC board in December 1977 by Jimmy Carter and became chairwoman six months later. Brock writes,

> "Though less publicized than her links to the Children's Defense Fund, Hillary's service on the board of the Legal Services Corporation in Washington in the late 1970s thrust her onto the national scene. The publicly funded legal services movement was the perfect vehicle to accomplish the plans Hillary had broached with Saul Alinsky ten years before. She would now prove that the key to achieving real social progress was not Alinsky-style agitation but skillful bureaucratic manipulation from inside. This tactical difference with Alinsky is what made Hillary's radicalism much more effective, but also harder for the public to perceive."
> (*The Seduction of Hillary Rodham*)

By end of Hillary's tenure the budget was over $300 million. Brock also traces how during her tenure the LSC became allied with National Lawyers Guild, a commie front since 1937 which of course counted Robert Treuhaft, the lawyer she interned for, a member. Hillary organized and funded the poor to politic for Carter against Reagan in violation of the LSC's charter, and even ran an illegal rearguard action to draw their budget in advance to bank it outside the reach of the new regime, anticipating perhaps John Poindexter's "off the shelf" budget for aiding the Contras. She beat back a Reagan attempt to zero out the LSC and then left in 1982 to chair the New World Foundation where she helped fund the Christic Institute, CISPES, National Lawyers Guild, the Institute for Policy Studies and other commie-friendly operators until 1988. (Brock informs us that the NLG in their congratulatory note to the Clintons upon their election victory, explained that they had tried to help by not endorsing them or even discussing them.)

On the other hand Brock believes that Jerry Brown was wrong when he charged during the primary that Hillary had not brought any profit to the Rose Law firm. And he thinks the evidence suggests that Bill was the insider on the Whitewater and Madison Guarantee scams. Recently Brock was able to in effect defend his own research for this book under the approving eye of the *New York Times'* Howell Raines when he weighed in on the Hillary-called-Paul Fray-a-fucking-Jew-bastard blow-up. As Hillary is running for Senator of New York this charge made some noise. But as Brock had done his own interviews with Fray and his wife and they hadn't mentioned the Jew angle as being part of Hillary's red-in-the-face tirade, he suspects they've amped up old news for new circumstances. He may be wrong here; people move into the cold water of truth slowly and carefully when it concerns someone who has state power at his fingertips as Governor or President. And the Clintons have used Troopers and private investigators to harass and intimidate often as Brock well knows – he was one of the first reporters to establish their M.O.

I suspect Brock confirmed something but then decided against including in this book. I hazard a guess only because it seems to follow from the lay of the land. The right was disappointed in *The Seduction of Hillary Rodham* because it finds Hillary's radicalism to be religiously motivated and sincere, and it further seems to soften her culpabilities by blaming the political system for her seduction. I don't find the book soft on her at all; expectations of a smoking gun were just too high. But David Brock coming out of the closet soon after the book was published suggests to me that he found evidence of Hillary's long-rumored homosexuality, but in coming to terms with his own homosexuality decided not to run with hers. No doubt Brock feels he remains in no-man's land. His Anita Hill book and Troopergate story, which inadvertently launched Paula Jones on her quest for satisfaction, so to speak, made his name but cast him from polite journalistic society. The Hillary book was less explosive but he's one of the best reporters out there. I imagine he hopes for a Bush victory both personally and professionally. Brock'll sniff out that cocaine rumor as redemption.

But, whither Hillary? And what then is to be done about Bill? Their attacks on patriarchy were paternalistic; their attempts to shock the bourgeoisie were utterly middle class; their selfless devotion to public service was monumentally self-interested – the concern of a vampire for the survival of its host. Expect to never see their likes again.

If she wins she loses, because the Senate is an ice locker – look what it did to Al Gore. Rarely does anyone but a Governor get elected President anyway. If she loses, will she be gracious about it, or does she debase her currency finally and completely? Perhaps her one-time bête noire, now obvious parallel, Richard Nixon proved there is no final complete debasement. Gail Sheehy has reported in *Vanity Fair* that Hillary has had plastic surgery – another necessary bourgeois coloration. A loss to Lazio is less personal but more insulting than a loss to Giuliani. But it hardly matters to her who is in her way. She jumped at the chance that Joe Lieberman, Gore's vice president nominee, could help her out of her pro-PLO problems with the Jews of New York.

I don't trust the professional women of New York when they explain to pollsters that they don't intend to vote for Hillary because, a) she didn't leave Bill when he humiliated her, or b) she's not a New Yorker. I think Hillary has been very skilled at exploiting prideful feminine solidarity, and she and Bill have been entertaining in a period when it seemed safe to indulge in such. (Expect to see soon that it was not safe enough.) She might be elected simply because New Yorkers are embarrassed for her and fear a red-faced-anti-semitic concession speech, wherein finally, a second city Cub's fan's genetic hostility to the Yankees would ring out. Or they might find it too tempting to want to finally burst this little goody-two-shoes' bubble. Or maybe it's as simple as the fact that masochism is a feature of decadence – Help Us Hurt You.

My best advice is read the *New York Post* if you can.

The Complete Jack the Ripper, by Donald Rumblelow

Posterity Alert. This doozy was written for my own fanzine, Options R, *back in pdx, December, 1978. I was still a true believer in the independent D.I.Y. ideology just then forming.*

The Complete Jack the Ripper by Donald Rumblelow is a re-examination as of 1975 of five murder/mutilations that occurred in the Whitechapel area of London in 1888, and a recounting of the various theories proposed over the years trying to explain why and by whom they were committed. The introduction by Colin Wilson sketches the contemporary repercussions of these killings in Victorian England:

> "The Victorians were aware that something new and strange was happening. Of course they were accustomed to all kinds of violence, particularly in their slums, but this was the result of poverty and drunkenness.... All this was understandable. But these Ripper murders, with their nightmarish mutilations, simply went beyond normal comprehension. It was as if the killer wanted to shock the whole community, to fling the murders in its face like a hysterical insult.... [T]he reaction was more than shock; people were stunned and winded, as if by a blow. And a deep, instinctive disquiet stirred inside them." (*The Complete Jack the Ripper*)

And quotes George Bernard Shaw,

> "Less than a year ago the West End press was literally clamouring for the blood of the people – hounding Sir Charles Warren to thrash and muzzle the scum who dared to complain that they were starving... behaving, in short, as the propertied class always does behave when the workers throw it into a frenzy of terror by venturing to show their own teeth.
> Whilst we conventional social democrats were wasting our time in education, agitation, and organisation, some independant genius has taken the matter in hand." (*Ibid.*)

He makes the classic liberal point that crime arises from poverty and despair, but also makes in strong terms the Bakhuninist point that crime is of itself a revolutionary act. This should be qualified, tho, to the same extent that the particular criminal is inarticulate about his own motivations.

The extent of qualification is revealed by who is the target of the act. The prostitutes who were killed were poor and living hand to mouth, as were most people in the area and they were chosen arbitrarily. The Ripper was irrational. His disgust was not recognized by him for what it was. Instead of using his blade on those responsible for Victorian England, he unthinkingly (and safely) used it on those nearest him – those in the same boat.

This "process" whereby social elements (workers, poor, criminals, artists, writers) with allied interests (freedom from being used as economic and military resources by the ruling class) are split and turned in against each other in the single effective block to revolutionary change. This "process" is effective in most decades because of inherent human deficiencies in clearly grasping the abstract – in this case the abstract of power as it is used in the authoritarian world. It is only extreme circumstances such as were present in eastern and central Europe at the close of WWI that can even partially succeed in uniting these elements.

The working class and to a lesser extent the lumpen prole had developed a political conciousness in the last half of the 19th century and were beginning to flex their will. WWI had its important causes in both the end of first stage colonial expansion, and the need to smash the growing international revolutionary movement.

Enter punk....

Lest we forget, punk is/was anti-corporate music. Music of the people, if not actually popular music. It is revolutionary by the fact of its existence even if the sentiments expressed, lyric-wise, were/are not always an articulation of that fact. Thus it parallels the concept of crime as revolutionary activity.

So we have hundreds of bands in the UK, US, Canada, and France operating with a primarily underground system of distribution. There are two directions open to these bands: to concentrate on accumulating an audience and landing a contract with a major label, or, to make a point of not seeking or accepting such contracts and instead committing yourself to strengthening an alternate music scene.

Unfortunately, band after band jump at contracts which 1) limit their freedom in recording, packaging and booking, 2) incorporate them into the capitalist system they inherently do not fit into, and 3) defuse any threat once posed to the present order.

These bands and those that sign in the future gain very little in the deal. They escape the dirty work of releasing records, promotion and booking gigs. They value convenience over artistic autonomy and they rationalize about getting their message across to more people. They don't understand that the medium of their message (CBS, Virgin, EMI, etc.) undermines and ultimately invalidates that message. Revolution cannot be brought to you by RCA; Jefferson Airplane proved that. It is useless to bemoan the music industry indifference to our music. Its indifference is our proof of validity. It is not so indifferent tho to leave those more accessible bands, that could easily form a strong basis for an alternate system, to release their music independantly. New people should come to the music on its own terms. Arista should not be manipulating Patti Smith into mass acceptability. Patti of course doesn't care, but The Clash should know better. We need to consolidate our network so someday we can be in a position to kill the music industry in its sleep. Rock n Roll's been waiting for that day since 1958. BUY INDEPENDANT!

Sergei Eisenstein, by Ronald Bergan
I bought and read this for use in my upcoming film book. I had to pick up some new studies to augment the old standard title on Soviet cinema, Kino by Jay Leyda which seems to leave a worse taste every time I refer to it. This went up at New Vulgate, Aug. 19, 2009.

I've seen his films but didn't know much about him. Bergan tells Eisenstein's personal and professional stories well. Turns out his father Mikhail was a well known *art nouveau* architect and his work gives much of Riga, Latvia its turn-of-the-century character; he is better known there than his son. Bergan concludes that Sergei's father was hardly the bourgeois philistine his son made of him. Bergan guesses "his anger towards him was, in part, fuelled by his inability to express his anger towards that other 'fearsome and strict' father who was to control his life from then on." In 1918 Sergei joined the Red Army as an engineer while his father joined the Whites as an engineer, winding up exiled in Berlin two years later. Reason enough to rail against him publicly, officially.

Many anti-human currents ran through that era and so it isn't a simple matter of Eisenstein's style as "a cold-blooded montage maniac" as Bergan puts the stereotype he wants to dispel. Adam Smith, Charles Darwin, Karl Marx, Ivan Pavlov, Sigmund Freud and others were contributing schema to be naively misused politically and contribute to the twentieth century's all-time record body-count. Lenin's contribution was to use and abuse the recently established bourgeois institutions (just beginning to tread on the Tsar's prerogative) to weaken them from within and end them. This end of the culture, foretold by Dostoevsky, was then released in the cultural revolution that followed the political one.

Suddenly Russia was in love with machines, and speed, and drunk on the future. The resulting art was abstract, inhuman, and formalist. There was much contempt for the old regimes across the continent and art experiments were often cold and formal but for the glee with which they tore at earlier forms and foundations.

Bergan writes that Eisenstein as a boy hid his enthusiasm for the Circus clowns while echoing his father's study of the equestrians on display. In Russian the word for "clown" is "eccentric" and the influential FEKS (Factory of the Eccentric Actor) founded by the filmmakers Grigori Kozintsev and Leonid Trauberg brought certain formal concerns directly into a new political mainstream. Eisenstein explained that his first film, *The Strike* (1925), "brought collective and mass action onto the screen, in contrast to individualism and the 'triangle' drama of the bourgeois cinema." (Eisenstein may be referring to the Triangle Film Corporation which was formed by Griffith, Ince, and Sennett and did so much to hammer out Hollywood story structure that its name was used in Europe as shorthand.)

Eisenstein's professor had been Vsevolod Meyerhold whose theory of "bio-mechanics" involved "translating dramatic emotion into archetypal gestures, the abolition of individual characterizations, and the emphasis on the 'class kernel' of the dramatic presentation." And though Eisenstein himself was highly cultured, including knowledge of popular film currents from Italy, France, Germany and Hollywood, he was also of German Jewish derivation and a homosexual, and his nature fought to be circumspect. Maxim Gorky, the poet of rural Russia was now a commissar formulating what would be socialist-realism; in 1934 he'd declare, "Destroy homosexuality, and Fascism will disappear."

JAMES FOTOPOULOS.

Bergan is rightly quick to remind his reader that much of what Eisenstein said and wrote, even in his diaries, may have been for show to Stalin's KGB, or for use in vicious battles within the All-Union of Cinematographic Workers for the red Commissar's green light. Meyerhold's slogan was "October in the theatre!" In the mid-twenties the campaign was for "the Proletarianisation of the Screen!" Dziga Vertov's Kultkino studio's slogan was, "Only documentary facts! No illusions! Down with the actor and scenery! Long live the film of actuality!" Eisenstein, Alexandrov and Pudovkin denounced the realistic use of sound in film in 1928. Then in March 1928 the All-Union Party Conference on Cinema lowered the socialist-realism boom on the revolutionary aesthetics-era.

Eisenstein now spun from the commemorative, *October* (1928), to his *The General Line* (1929) by exclaiming in the declarative mode now suddenly turned reactionary, "The time has come to make films directly from a slogan." Unfortunately he began the film under one agricultural policy and on finishing Stalin ordered the Party to "liquidate the Kulaks as a class," and the film had to be re-written and partially re-shot and Eisenstein left reality even further for theory, though even that was not safe.

Eisenstein left for Europe and Hollywood where more films were started, none finished, and his return to the Soviet Union was as a penitent. He wrote insane, groveling celebrations of what Stalin had done to the arts for *Pravda* and then got to work on what were, perversely, his greatest films, *Alexander Nevsky* (1938), and *Ivan the Terrible* Pts I & II (1944-45). In the forced classicism of these historical bio-epics, the most turgid of genres, scored by Sergei Prokofiev, another prodigal radical now tamed and returned, Eisenstein ate his old critique of Kuleshev's Hollywoodism and used montage to build monumental narratives that moved their lead characters through a dramatic procession of striking tableau, subtly informed by all his own formal experimentalism had taught him about putting pieces of film together, and all the classicism he'd learned from his father. Eisenstein intended to be a theory-based free-associating genius-comedian, but his was another Russian tragedian's tragedy.

(originally posted at The New Vulgate, No. 7)

Warren Oates – A Wild Life, by Susan Compo
Oates seems hardly missed by Hollywood so this book is a surprise; turns out the
University of Kentucky wanted to honor a favorite son, though they do have a nice
line of film books. This went up at NV in August 2009.

Lately I've taken to explaining to young-uns that if they want to get a fix on the golden age of 1970s Hollywood they should forget about Scorsese and Altman and Coppola and just get a look at every film made by two actors, Clint Eastwood and Jeff Bridges. Sometimes I switch out Clint for Warren Oates since Eastwood did important work before and after too.

When I was last in L.A. and going through Book Soup, I was amazed to see a stack of a new hardcover biography of Warren Oates at the checkout counter. Who on today's earth was smart enough to produce that book?! Oates was from Kentucky and the University published this nice tracing of the kind of acting career which doesn't happen anymore. The author is a USC professor and though it's always got the information, it's written rather awkwardly on Oates' early years until he's in the swing of his film career when the telling improves.

That career included small parts in notable films like *Yellowstone Kelly* (1959), *The Rise and Fall of Legs Diamond* (1960), *Ride the High Country* (1962), *The Rounders* (1965), and *Major Dundee* (1965). Then there are some mysterious independent productions directed by Leslie Stevens that I'll have to track down, *Private Property* (1960), and *Hero's Island* (1962). But it's the Roger Corman production, *The Shooting* (1967), that picks up on what Oates had been developing guesting on virtually every television western and put him on his distinctive path. Still he followed that with a string of awkward studio productions before his seventies really begin in 1969 with *The Wild Bunch*.

Not everything that followed was excellent but these are the markers that chart his career from 1971 to 1978: *The Hired Hand, Two-Lane Blacktop, Kid Blue, Dillinger, Badlands, The White Dawn, Bring Me the Head of Alfredo Garcia, Cockfighter, Race With the Devil, 92 In the Shade,* and *China 9, Liberty 37*. What's striking about Susan Compo's narrative of this period is that Warren Oates basically, simply accepted what he was asked to do. His agent is mentioned in the sixties period when he's just migrated from New York and his stage and live television beginnings, but come the 1970s he seems to be asked to do parts in the most interesting films by people who know him personally. He was forty-two in 1970 and had become something of a psychedelic redneck, a lover not a fighter, a conservative anarchist, a prude in some ways who measured manhood first, before his career, by William Boyd and later by Ben Johnson who he came to know and did his best to hide his pot-smoking from.

Oates didn't see himself as a western man but he'd stumbled onto what he called "hip country" in his character on *Stoney Burke* (1962-63), the TV rodeo drama, where he was third-billed after Jack Lord and Bruce Dern. He played heavies and leads and curious combinations well-grounded in a reality that he kept in touch with moving around the country in an RV. Millie Perkins says, "Warren would have been great in silent films. There's something in him that was longing." Monte Hellman is quoted, "He pretended not to be an intellectual, he pretended to be just a very simple person. He was a very complex person and approached his role from thought and then as it became him, as he became the character, the emotions would take over. He would forget about all the thought." Oates said, "Actors aren't citizens, they're observers, the freest people in the world because of that. They're above politics."

He loved working with non-professionals whether they were Georgia crackers in *Cockfighter* or James Taylor and Dennis Wilson in *Two-Lane Blacktop*. On that road movie director Hellman moved the production down highways from Arizona to Tennessee, doling out just the scene to be shot that day so the actors didn't know where they were heading. Compo quotes a crewmember, "If it wasn't for Warren, we'd wonder if we were really making a movie."

She quotes Oates on his confidence in young directors, "You need a scorecard, but it's more exciting to work with the rising generation. At a time when major studios are afraid, young filmmakers are breaking old rules, making new ones. Which is why, I suppose, I throw in my lot with the Peter Fondas and the Mike Laughlins." He described himself, Jack Nicholson and Monte Hellman as "the tail end of the Beat Generation" characterized by "an enormous tenacity and individualism." It is interesting that the hippie era's leading men were slightly older 1950s characters. After Clint Eastwood and Charles Bronson "arrived" their presences warped the films they appeared in, whereas the less imposing Warren Oates played along within his films, which allowed their odd, subversive air to fill the movie theaters. These films are the best Hollywood representations of the counter-culture as it was in its true unfashioned adult sense.

That makes this book pretty important.

(originally posted at The New Vulgate, *No. 7)*

MEDIA.

Bring Me the Head of Lee Abrams
This was posted at The New Vulgate *on Oct. 20, 2010, after Abrams began to make noise at* The Tribune Co.

A few weeks ago Rebecca Mead wrote a *New Yorker* "Talk of the Town" bit about The Stooges where she got Iggy to explain how such modern classics as "Fun House" (1970) and "Raw Power" (1973) could have failed so completely in their days:

> "It's like this: I made some fucking great-sounding music that still sounds fucking great, and – to drop my intellect and just get emotional about it – a bunch of fat fucks and pricks wouldn't play my music anywhere where anybody could hear it, wouldn't sell it in a part of the store where it could be bought." (*New Yorker*)

I like to think that Iggy's "fat fucks" were led by Lee Abrams. (He doesn't mention the press but I'll add that I enjoy guessing that Jan Wenner is bringing up the rear in his parade of "pricks".)

In truth, Abrams was merely beginning in 1970. He joined Kent Burkhart, a radio programming power since the mid-fifties as an architect of the post-rock and roll Top 40 format. Burkhart was leveraging that mature consulting business into the booming, still freeform FM landscape. (FM was only just standard radio equipment in the late sixties after station-owners were forced to stop merely simulcasting on their FM sides.) But Lee Abrams the radio nerd stumbled into perhaps THE hippie-era goldmine. The singles market was giving ground to the album market; singles were suddenly a way to sell the more expensive albums. And with FM play in its early years one might not even need a hit single to sell albums; record stores once stocked pop music by chart position only, except for soundtracks, show tunes, and classical records; now hippies opening record stores were at first stocking records on some kind of cultural merit of all things. But radio station owners were generally straight older folks, conservative-modernist-entrepreneurs, and if they had to program for this wilder and wilder rock culture of the early seventies, they preferred to not need some troublesome company freak on the premises to do the programming. Having programming decisions phoned in was no-muss no-fuss, and soon no-rock and roll a'tall.

Burkhart-Abrams by the end of the seventies told a thousand radios stations what to play. The older AM side of their business did not manage by itself to destroy the Top 40 format. But as older listeners moved to FM, AM radio was left to kids and soon they no longer heard the likes of Jimi Hendrix Experience, Blue Cheer, or Bubble Puppy. Oddly, the freer FM band was easy for Abrams to destroy. As they'd abandoned AM for FM, the hippest ears could leave FM for the new 8-track and audiocassette formats in the car, while at home stacking LPs could give you music by the hour uncoupled from any radio culture. By my ear, FM and AM music radio was slowly strangled until by the end of 1973 one just stopped listening. *Wired* magazine had Abrams "winning 318 programming battles, while losing only 11." Perhaps there really were eleven good rock stations by the end of the seventies; it didn't seem like it. "It's really a war," Abrams told the mag about satellite radio in 2004. "We're out to bring music back to the people. We have this one opportunity to revolutionize radio, and if we blow it we should all be shot." What's this "we" shit, and where's my gun?

The Punk era culture began there then, with that 1973 death of music radio, but I believe the era itself was also an organic creation of that earlier living radio culture. As Iggy explained later about The Stooges' "Raw Power" album, "A year after I made it, that album was selling for 39 cents, and then two years after that, it was selling for about $39." (March 15, 1987, *Chicago Sun-Times*) It was as if broke kids haunting used record stores all bought that album in cut-out in 1974-75, then after their own bands hit vinyl with their self-released 45s, or Sire LPs, the album's price got bid up as an import. "Raw Power" was the initial template for punk rock before the Ramones' debut.

By then the Abrams's chokehold on airplay oxygen was destroying both music radio and the music itself. It needs remembering that the major labels at first did fine in terms of signing most of the more distinctive punk era bands (Patti Smith on Arista; The Dictators on Epic; The Ramones on Sire; Television on Elektra; Pere Ubu on Mercury; The Dickies on A&M...). When you see early photographs and videotape of seventies punk there are the requisite fashion plates with spiked and dyed hair, but there are more bearded hippies and long-haired girls attending than is remembered. There were still music people in the record industry; there were no longer any in the radio business. And soon the larger historied independent labels (A&M, Motown, Chrysalis...) were forced to leave for major distribution to maintain promotional clout as the Abrams centralizing effect played out through the greater music industry.

Radio didn't air the music so the first punk albums failed to sell and further adventurous signings ceased. SST released the equivalent of six or seven albums by Hüsker Dü or the Meat Puppets before they were signed by major labels; that's insane. How many bands even last that long? Midway through their SST careers the bands managed to get the ears of some of the erstwhile music press and that got us requests for their albums from the major labels. They claimed to dig the bands but as realistic, responsible A&R men, they knew they had to listen with Lee Abrams' ears and those were simply deaf to the era. Black Flag didn't want to run a record label, they wanted to sign to a major label in 1978! The New York offices signed most of the first punk bands but the LA offices knew the LA bands from that one non-Abrams station, *KROQ*, and from local press and the early doc, *The Decline of Western Civilization* (1980). The LA majors also saw that by 1981 The Germs, X, Black Flag, The Adolescents, and others were selling enough records in the greater SoCal market that if you extrapolated out to the rest of the country they'd be selling gold on their debut releases! But the major labels also knew that Lee Abrams was there in the doorway to stop that all from being conceivable.

Abrams was quite clear about the destruction he'd accomplished by 1980. He's apparently appeared on several Alan Parsons' albums, the nadir of engineered *musique concrète* that these numbers guys created while tripping on drugs left behind for musicians – it was pod music for pod people, "lifestylers" in the parlance of SST, the perfect wallpaper for that leather couch. Failing to reach Art, the engineers reached only design. Any doubts Lee might've had about shit-canning an entire next generation of rock bands were certainly relieved by every new issue of *Rolling Stone* magazine in those years (1975 - 1991). Unlike Lee, Jan hasn't come clean, though he is at least out-of-the-closet now, which probably calls for a revisionist book about the magazine and its effect, updating the Robert Sam Anson and Robert Draper books, neither of which really put the musical wood to Mr. Straight Arrow. And its what happened to music that matters. *Rolling Stone* followed up in the seventies on the New Journalism developed elsewhere in the sixties (*Esquire*, *Village Voice*, *New York*...), but it gave up on rock and roll.

As Abrams joined XM satellite radio in 2004 he was happy to acknowledge his crimes in the next context of all the miracles of Art he expected to achieve at XM. Unfortunately the hundreds of channels available allowed him to subdivide the surviving music further, and further isolate audience fragments. The bastard-child rock and roll that he initially found as a kid on sixties radio had humored R&B, garage rock, C&W, surf, rod, blue-beat, Sinatra, jug band, blues, acid rock, movie themes, folk, *et. al.* It was now dissected, drawn-and-quartered, pulled-apart racially, sonically, stylistically, classwise and other ways and then these have been further subdivided at XM and its former competitor *Sirius* and then beamed down from satellite with the destructive force of those SDI directed energy weapons, only those were theoretical. Good thinking Mr Laser Beam!

Had anyone wanted to make radio a contributor to our music culture once more instead of its tormentor it's easy enough to locate viable programming mix models from late sixties AM radio, or pre-Abrams early seventies FM radio – the airchecks are available even if the old radio station freaks' memories are shot. All those winners of the AOR game might have bought a station as many C&W stars once did and put its programming philosophy together with a musician's sense rather than the gonadal drive of coked-out fanboys.

However, the radio business is about advertising not music, and the resultant change in music could be noticed in the eighties and it was real. If you ask me, anyone starting a band after 1980 was handicapped by the lack of an immersive exposure to great music by good radio stations. Mediated America no longer allowed provincial folk cultures to develop deeply on the highly refined level they once achieved in Appalachia, Louisiana, the Mississippi Delta, the Piedmont, the border..., so this new airborne folk media was what we had to make do with after WWII. It was quite productive for awhile and great folk media synthesizers like Eddie Cochran, Dick Dale, Steppenwolf, Jimi Hendrix, The Doors, James Blood Ulmer, etc., made contributions as brilliant and nearly as organic as earlier, more rooted, less mediated folk synthesizers like Hank Williams, Muddy Waters, Bill Haley, Pop Staples, Elvis Presley, Chuck Berry.... But it was less sturdy and thereafter, if young kids got turned on to music in junior high and form a band by the end of high school, then the end of great music radio in the early seventies resulted in the end of great bands in the early eighties. The good bands thereafter, even if inspired by their immediate predecessors became more directly derivative, more conceptual and thinner in achievement. I'm thinking of bands like Social Distortion, Dream Syndicate, The Pixies, Eleventh Dream Day..., vs. those formed earlier such as The Germs, The Sleepers, The Wipers, Black Flag, The Minutemen... These unsigned and unheard casualties are far better known today than they were in their prime, and this too is culture damage charged to Lee Abrams, even though no small label releasing such records ever mailed him a copy.

By the late 1980s the slight demographic wind at their back and the slow advance of the new independent label economy through college radio stations, a smaller club circuit, and a new generation of music writer and editor yielded what passed for a watershed radio event where AOR and CHR (FM's Top 20 format) stations were suddenly forced to play what to them sounded absolutely foreign, Nirvana's breakthrough single. But by then the music culture of America was dumbed down to the level rather of a media culture; meaning Grunge was as the Twist and it evaporated. Our music culture's only been broken down further since then, of course.

Given all this, and the fact that I much prefer to listen to the radio than my record collection, I was interested when the new owner of the Tribune Company, Sam Zell, hired Randy Michaels and Lee Abrams to bring some new thinking from radio to the threatened newspaper business. Zell, a real estate mogul, had owned the Jacor radio chain where he met Michaels (Jacor was the last big competitor chain before Clear Channel bought it and began choking to death). The *Tribune* was our morning paper growing up and I knew of Colonel McCormick from family visits to his former estate, Cantigny, named for the town he took part in capturing from the Germans in WWI, earning his rank of Colonel. By the time I was reading the *Tribune* it was committed to living down the Colonel's legacy and playing catch-up to the *New York Times* and *Washington Post* by going after Nixon. It was also rejecting more than just McCormick's small government isolationism, it was joining the American newspaper zeitgeist which Mike Wolff called "orderly and genteel" in his semi-admiring portrait of Rupert Murdoch, *The Man Who Owns the News*. The Colonel died in 1955; that was the year Richard J. Daley became mayor. It's likely that Daley's performance in 1968 was more on their minds at the *Tribune*. What's true is that Daley was considered vulnerable before the '68 Convention but Chicagoans were never going to turn on him after it. But the *Tribune* was now a reflection of no one person. The Irish in the boardroom were no longer fighters.

The *Chicago Tribune* was founded by Joseph Medill, McCormick's grandfather. It was a leader in the industry as both a business, and as cultural organ. And McCormick was involved in everything from setting up the "Gasoline Alley" comic-strip to purchasing land, power and machinery to produce pulp for newsprint in Canada. McCormick and his papers (also the *NY Daily News*, *Washington Times-Herald*) walked point in the losing causes that the Tea Party have recently taken up, smaller government, no overseas military involvement. But he should also be better remembered by the newspaper business. Everyone knew who owned the *Chicago Tribune* in his day. And I don't think he'd have had his company owning newspapers coast-to-coast and then let Gannett found the *USA Today*, or owning the better part of a national TV network and then let Murdoch found the *Fox* network. The *Tribune* might have kept Murdoch, Gannett and the *WSJ* in their boxes by getting there first if they hadn't bought into the conventional wisdom about their own history. But they learned that conventional wisdom in j-school, perhaps even the Medill School of Journalism at Northwestern – destruction by duly degreed apparats everywhere you look.

Zell had taken the Tribune Co. private which was probably the thing to do as Wall Street considers newspapering a sunset industry and so valuations were down for the count. And that was at the peak of the real estate bubble, so now the resulting bankruptcy agreement is at risk which puts the deal itself in jeopardy. Today's old guard at the *Tribune* or in the Chicago media are full of bile for these radio sleazebags that Zell brought in, but they have no answers as the ships go down. They believe they love Chicago and its lore, they think they know about the old Front Page culture, the circulation wars, the press barons.... But their pseudo-appreciation for all that life back then is a Butterfly collector's appreciation of death. Back in 1983 when Ted Field forced his family (Marshall Field & Co.) to sell the *Sun-Times* so he could go into the destroyed record business (Interscope) with his wallet blazing, it was Rupert Murdoch who bought it and Mike Royko and others whose whole newspapering lives were set against the *Tribune* resigned and walked across the street and into the Tower the Colonel built. Royko even gave up the White Sox for the Cubs if you can believe that. But Murdoch failed at the *Sun-Times*, the Midwestern tabloid sensibility is/was not the London or Sydney or New York one, and he sold it to some local group and it's been resold and survives readably. However, the local attitude, Royko's included, won-the-day then as their predecessors won it against the Colonel.

Last week after the radio boys etiquette hit the *NYT*'s front page the new "genteel" j-school suburban bourgie ethos won out over smoking cigars and swearing and sexism and other juvenilia come over from radio minus the rock and roll charm. Combined with this local *faux*-Chicagological attitude, this won out against Chief Innovations Officer Lee Abrams, and this week they won again over Chief Executive Officer Randy Michaels, and soon maybe Sam Zell. And then what? The Colonel and Joe Patterson and Frank Carson and Walter Howey and Charles MacArthur and Hilding Johnson and Jake Lingle and the boys down below all want to know. I want to know and maybe Iggy does too.

Ten years ago Daley's wife in her drive to beautify the city had the newssheds of the city torn down and hauled away, including the world class shed in front of the old Central Library which some guy who believed in papers had just bought for a hundred grand from some guy who remembered when there were a dozen Chicago dailies and you couldn't tell the reporters from the criminals from the policemen from the politicians.

Media

There weren't enough parks on the lakefront for Daley himself so he tore up Meigs Field in the middle of the night, probably non-union guys. Now the city's safe for Lollapalooza no less.

(*originally posted at* The New Vulgate, *No. 68)*

The New Vulgate: Blog as Weekly Paper

Russ Forster resurrected his fanzine, 8-track Mind, for a special on blogging as an extension of the fanzine ethos, so I wrote this for him. It traces how a print-hound gave up on printing anything but books and learned to not hate the internet. The issue came out in Spring 2011.

I didn't want to be doing a blog per se, but I was sending out an occasional email with a string of items culled from what people send to me and what I read in the papers. Since high school I've always read the newspapers: *Tribune* in the morning and *Chicago Today* and *Aurora Beacon* in the afternoon, plus the weekly *Naperville Sun*. I'd even go through the Diocese weekly that my Grandma got. Now you don't really need the papers for news so much as for background features and analysis that help you make sense of the news you pick up from television or radio or online. The best papers for that are the national dailies, *New York Times*, *Wall Street Journal*, and *Financial Times*, though I pick up the local papers too when I travel. I go through the magazine racks thoroughly and Laramie is blessed with Grand Newsstands 1 & 2, plus a Hastings. In high school you think you're a critical reader but after reading papers for four decades you get to be a pretty good on-the-fly critical reader-editor.

 I moved to Wyoming in 1995 and David Lightbourne followed me the next year. No more *Trib*, *Sun-Times*, *Defender*, and *Reader*, instead we acclimated to the Denver papers, the *Casper Star-Tribune*, and the *Laramie Boomerang*. We were doing the Provisional video label and soon were also involved with the record labels O&O-Upland that my old SST-era pal Bill Stevenson (Descendents, Black Flag, All) was doing down the road in Fort Collins. Lightbourne did a great album called "Monkey Junk" for Upland. We didn't see the Napster thing coming but we were thinking of dressing up a merch site with some kind of magazine that would be filled with stuff Dave and I and anyone connected to the label wanted to throw in. Dave was going to call his column "The Antagonist," I remember that. I did get into culling stuff and writing a few pieces but the thing never got going. The internet helped kill the label before we could roll out our own internet magazine idea.

 At the time I was only using the computer to write screenplays – I bought notebook computers because I don't actually write at a desk. I didn't get online until the summer of 2001 when I bought a Dell that came with a modem. Then I could see how different publications and web-only start-ups and even individuals like Mike Watt were using the web and email. It was great to forage around the world for English language newspapers' sites. I also built up a list of friends and readers especially after republishing *Rock and the Pop Narcotic* in 2005. Soon after that I had to investigate the death of SST photographer Naomi Petersen and the result was an essay with photos that was too large for an email so I paid my book designer Snowy Range Graphics to design and host a site and that way I sent out just a link to it. That later became the book, *Enter Naomi*, but the essay site got me again thinking about doing some kind of publication with Lightbourne. Dave was by then only using the web for *ebay* purchases to round out his near complete collection of American folk and blues, but he was also using his tours to New York to connect up with and interview Paul Nelson and through him the rest of the *Little Sandy Review* crew, Jon Pankake, John Cohen, and Barry Hansen (aka, Dr. Demento). So I knew Dave would have an excellent piece about what was essentially the forgotten birth of the rock press in the form of a Minneapolis fanzine in 1960. We talked about doing a quarterly but it seemed barely realistic to think of doing an annual.

Meanwhile my book publishing activity got me a growing address book and the improvement of my *Wyoming.com* email software had me sending them out more regularly. I moved to Centennial which meant that I read papers online most days. I still print out articles to read later, especially on subjects I intend to write about at length someday. For exercise and to scout locations for a western I hike the nearby mountains and use a camera. These photographs are another element that I was already doing.

I guess I really gave up the idea of a hard copy publication when Tower Records went out of business. They'd been my biggest outlet when I first published *R&TPN* and I knew how important they'd been for Henry Rollins' book company, 2.13.61. It was hard to believe we could get into the mag racks at Borders or Barnes & Noble as dependably, and now even their survival is questionable. The difficulty that Jay Babcock had keeping *Arthur* magazine a print publication was another thing that got me thinking about the web.

I'd first met Chris Collins online; he's into photography and music, and reads military history and philosophy with an eye toward writing. He'd stopped by Laramie and got to know Dave and me. Being younger he was more computer savvy so I asked him at some point whether he thought we could use blog software to do a weekly posting of writing and photography. He checked out a few things and figured out what was possible, doing everything he can to keep the publication from looking like a blog. We'd released Russ' doc, *So Wrong They're Right* (1995), on videotape on our Provisional label and one of our last releases was the film *Zero* (1997) by James Fotopoulos. I've worked with James on a couple scripts and productions since then and he got involved in the weekly concept with graphics and occasional essays on film and video art.

I keep asking myself whether it's worth doing but *The New Vulgate* does gradually expand its readership and I am usually able to keep the work involved on my end to just Mondays and Tuesdays. We've had great written contributions over the electronic transom from good folks like Bart Bull in Paris, Carolyn Heinze in Paris, Spot in Austin, Steve Beeho in London, and photographs and art from others like Amy Annelle, Mike Watt, Spot, Lee Ranaldo, Grace Krilanovich, Alexandre Cohen, and Mike Vann Gray. So we'll keep doing it. With the recent deaths of friends like Naomi, and then Dave Lightbourne, Armando Acosta (Saint Vitus), and Frank Navetta (Descendents) I often feel like the official necrographer of the dim stars. I know the press can't be trusted in these matters. I used to submit pieces or send query letters or letters-to-the-editor here and there, but now I don't need to waste time doing that. I just throw it in the *NV* and figure I'll rework it for a book later.

What is most interesting to me about the form is that I can excerpt the best pieces I've read during the week and put them in some sort of thematic flow and then the reader can use that as a digest and pick however many of them seem worth reading at length and go to the complete piece. I think we do this a bit more conveniently than *Arts & Letters Daily*, or *Drudge* where you really have to go to the article to see if it's worth bothering with. We do it more like the old *Atlas World Press Review* which I subscribed to long ago. I don't like to comment on more than one or two of the pieces, mostly the dumb ones where I think I can point out some typical problem in media or political understanding. But sometimes those comments turn into free-standing essays with links. It's all supposed to be funny too. Other influences on the *NV* were the defunct *Winds of Change* blog that was very useful in the years after 9/11, and even Russ Smith's "Mugger" column back when the *NY Press* was too packed with stuff to ever finish reading the damn thing.

Of my own writing for the *NV* the pieces are of necessity first drafts and I know they could be improved, but my books will never get done if I allow myself to labor further over them. I've never written to a deadline so I have a morbid fascination with that aspect too. Mondays and Tuesdays are pretty wall-to-wall until I get my text off to Chris to go with any others we have for that week. Then I *google* for images to go with the articles and excerpts and Chris puts the feature images together from what James, I and whoever else has sent in.

Our most popular issues feature music topics and these get relayed around via other blogs. Recently an Elvis site re-posted Lightbourne's great eyewitness report of the 1957 Chicago concert he saw as a 14 year-old. We have a Comments option but there aren't often many of those, though there was a big response to my article about early San Francisco punk bands. We usually get one or two "follower" adds and email-list adds each week. We've only had one person ask to be taken off the list which is surprising in a way. I just hope no-one's thrown their computer across the room after reading us.

Rolling Stone, June 10 & 24, 1999
Never is this rag more bathetic than when it mounts the national podium to explain a youth issue. Their unconscionable drivel was occasioned by the Columbine High School massacre.

Life & Death at Columbine High School

"Guns and Violence," An Editorial by Jan Wenner
"Humiliation and Revenge," by Peter Wilkinson with Matt Hendrickson
"How They Got the Guns," by Erika Fortgang
"Columbine: Whose Fault Is It?" by Marilyn Manson

Since the respected journal of ideas and commentary, *Rolling Stone*, has decided to go off half-cocked firing both barrels in its sawed-off call for balls out gun control, presumably including some kind of involuntary retrieval of privately owned firearms once-upon-a-time legally purchased or won at church raffle, I thought some other just-as-respected journal of ideas and commentary should make fun of them.

Here are Wenner's points excavated from his 3000+ word opus (who edits Jan?):

1. We don't need a pointless debate about causes of violence.
2. Only the U.S. allows its citizens open access to guns.
3. The massacre was evil, a mystery, and there is no answer.
4. "Rock is too popular to blame."
5. The establishment loves Spielberg and his splatter film, *Saving Private Ryan*.
6. Rock and Movies need to defend Video-games or he'll impugn both of their motives.
7. We need "thoughtful community safety nets for adolescents."
8. Clinton is wimping out.
9. "The NRA's by-laws appear to have been blatantly rigged in favor of a small minority, a situation that warrants investigation."
10. "There is no making nice here; these are not nice people. Charlton Heston blah blah blah...."
11. "It is patent insanity to think that art causes violence."

Jan knows that the film industry, television, and the record industry are likely to steer the government's hounds toward the game industry, but he doesn't know that Art and Violence go way back together. And expecting this country to operate like his favorite European hot spots is patent leather insanity. The people who left Europe to found this country didn't come here for security; they came for freedom. They set up something called Constitutional Government. What the Constitution provided for was a system of representative government. That was a great achievement. But there had been elections before, the hard part was preventing this new state, its institutions, representatives and agents from degenerating into a new tyranny.

What was to keep a George Washington from saying, "If I could only extend and consolidate my power I might really make something of this Godforsaken place?" They in their wisdom knew that nothing would; the logic of the state is tyranny. So they split the power three ways and channeled it against itself, and then passed the first ten commandments – I mean, amendments, the Bill of Rights, to drive into the foundation of this state certain immovable stanchions as guarantee against the gravitational pull power has on inhumane human nature. The first of these puts speech beyond the control of the power of the state. This will protect Hollywood, the game industry, and Jan. The second recognizes a right to bear arms. This was a priority for the founding fathers as they sought to safeguard freedom from tyranny – we can't have one without two. Their success shouldn't lull us into assuming freedom is the natural state wherein we graduate as a nation into some kind of Scandinavian therapeutocracy. That might put art back into its pre-Enlightenment relationship to the Church, only this time to the church of high-minded social engineering. Radical. You'd hope the co-founder of *Rolling Stone* might have some sense of where the appetite for the pursuit of risk and volatility comes from in American culture and that it is worth protecting from contemporary Liberalism's reflex to tame and control. Ah, but if Jan's had anything to say about it, rock and roll grew up and graduated long ago.

And this Marilyn Manson! Aha! Nothing but a closeted good-government liberal. Unmasked at last. It only took a high school massacre and a real threat to his cashflow-padded drug/sex cocoon. Rock! Rock! Rock! as long as it's safe sex with trained behavior specialists and grief counselors standing by. Did he cancel those shows after the massacre out of "discretion and sensitivity" as Wenner insists, or as part of his claim that he "didn't want to contribute to these fame-seeking journalists and opportunists looking to fill their churches or to get elected because of their self-righteous finger-pointing."

"Self-righteous finger-pointing!?"

Marilyn then joins Jan and comes out for gun-control and against the NRA. Elsewhere Marilyn writes, "admittedly, I have assumed the role of Antichrist; I am the Nineties voice of individuality, and people tend to associate anyone who looks and behaves differently with illegal or immoral activity.... Rather than teaching a child what is moral and immoral, right and wrong, we first and foremost can establish what the laws that govern us are. You can always escape hell by not believing in it, but you cannot escape death and you cannot escape prison.... I'm a controversial artist, one who dares to have an opinion and bothers to create music and videos that challenge people's ideas in a world that is watered-down and hollow...." Hey man, thanks for bothering. But don't cancel shows the next time they have a chance to amount to something in criteria in which you claim to deal, Mr. Organization Man.

I better spell out something for this type of liberal perv: You cannot cheer on the regulators and control freaks in government without someday finding them outside your bedroom door debating not whether, but when to enter. The state and its courts are after tobacco, guns, pigs, apples, coffee, lawnmowers, SUVs, cars, drugs, pillows, five gallon buckets, et. al.; they are very, very busy, but they will get to you and yours by and by. They're rooting around in your theaters, your garage, your car, your office, your computer, your refrigerator, and what?! You expect them to stay out of your bedroom?! Well... are you decent? (Y-yes..., I mean, N-no!)

The founding federalists didn't design this state with efficiency in mind and they didn't design it so as to allow passions of the moment and sectarian geniuses to carry the day. Therefore, the continuing "pointless debate" has a greater point and will certainly continue. We all get paid by the word. No doubt why Publisher Jan wants to end the debate.

MTV's Adults-Only Juvenilia
As late arriving scavengers on the body of rock and roll, MTV's dingbat braintrust will never be as much fun to pillory as Abrams or Wenner, but that doesn't mean I can ignore them. This went up Jan. 26, 2011 at NV.

Life and Death are a single continuum. We at the crown of creation are allowed glimpses of that but do our best to forget it, especially we moderns busy as we are spinning our trivialized, hollowed out fictions, myths and legends. The primitives had their rituals for appeasing or fending off Death, but the modern age for all its sophistication – *because* of that sophistication – can use the drive to solve the particulars of the many varieties of deaths to forget about Death itself. The modern believes mostly in physics now, and yet hopes to earn the ability to ignore the physics that governs him in particular. For every advance here, there's unforeseen charges due there. Marshall McLuhan was mostly a physicist of communications, and even though academia was full of haters of broadcast media and low publications and movies, these others were so reflexive as to merely manifest those physical laws. It wasn't like McLuhan really dug TV, but perhaps as a truly elite intellect where he worried about what new media was doing to people, the merely elitist false intellect only grabbed for social profit by impuning the audiences for the media's programs.

Like that earlier disinterest in the coming media environment, there is little interest in tracing or deducing the physics that govern what happens beyond the newest new media which might be separating persons rather than connecting them. Certainly the former mass media of three television networks created mass audiences which could share a deeper culture than just baseball's World Series. I think often of Lester Bangs' summation of his 1977 Elvis Presley obit:

> "[W]e will never again agree on anything as we agreed on Elvis. So I won't bother saying good-bye to his corpse. I will say good-bye to you." (*Village Voice*)

Bangs was making a point about American culture rather than the efficacy of mass media (outside the south Elvis was first heard and seen via network television, then radio, then touring, then movies), but no longer do teenagers nor their parents set the cultural table for any but themselves. In the 1950s, pop had to make room for rock and roll, and Hollywood had to make room for Elvis. Today nobody outside the Disney channel demographic bubble even hears about some new pop-thrush until she's "grown up" and the prospect of another pop-tart immolation begins to interest so-called adults as well as the young fans, the youngest of whom are often the most outraged at the sight of their former favorite's sleepwalk into the media's sex/porn flame. For all the attention paid Britney Spears, Christina Aguilera, Lindsay Lohan, Miley Cyrus, Selena Gomez and others, there's a lost voice of those young fans, some now college girls or even fully adults and too embarrassed to recall until they are raising girls of their own.

What's in this spectacle for men is the prospect of a sudden permission to act as boys or animals. What's in this for women is where physics breaks down. No Fermi Lab or Hadron Collider can lift the dark energy that cloaks any truth or truths which pertain. Rape rules certain sad harems of Islam and sadder jungles of Congo, but men have such practical minds they learn nothing from the sparks of these collisions. The rest of Mankind begs no question of Womankind in hopes of a favor or two in that dark.

Luckily we have the *MTV* programming department particle accelerator just now beginning to focus all they've learned from their decades of reality programming and apply it to the fever dreams of screenwriters and directors fresh out of film school and a young cast ready to grind Larry Clark's m.o. into series television sausage as "Skins." David Carr writes as the light sparks, "'Skins' has a TV-MA rating and *MTV* has suggested in press releases that the show is 'specifically designed to be viewed by adults.'" Carr has written about music I think, so he knows that's laughable, no adult has watched *MTV* since they dropped rock and roll, although the channel has been the place on the dial where the true-lies traces are fleetingly visible ever since the talk shows touched bottom. Somebody black once said they didn't realize white people were just like niggers until they saw them paraded on "Maury Povich" in the bright light of a television studio. The n-word means a number of things but an old meaning to whites was accepted and sharpened in the urban ghetto to mean an id-like country creature lost in-the-moment, out-of-control in the city's 24-7 stimuli, a raping robbing fighting machine that runs until it either meets another of its kind or the po-lice. *MTV*'s cameras hope the hope of all pornographers, that the messed-up self-loathing exhibitionists they've cast will be productively messed-up self-loathing exhibitionists at the command, "Action!", and the most skilled cameramen with state-of-the-art steadicams and double-drive digicams won't miss a money-shot drip.

Author Harris Gaffin quotes pornographer Ron Hightower:

> "Being a director is like being a baby-sitter. Everybody's got a problem. Everybody comes into the business thinking sex is easy. Girls on the set change their mind, have flashbacks of home. They miss their mother.... I tend to be hard on the guys because they come in here with no respect for the industry.... I've seen girls freak out. They go through so many head trips."
> (*Hollywood Blue*)

That's hardcore of course, which for MTV remains in development, but still it's quite relevant. Carr continues about MTV:

> "Senior executives are now considering additional editing for coming episodes, but that's a little like trying to lock the door after a naked 17-year-old has already busted out and gone running down the street, which is precisely what one of the characters does in Episode 3 – with a pill-enhanced erection, no less." (*N.Y. Times*)

The cast of this show is apparently full of first-time actors and one wonders what is going on behind-the-scenes if a 17 year-old boy requires Viagra, even for a re-take.

Carr concludes conceding,

> "You could produce a show that clearly depicts what happens when kids do only what they want and exercise some poor judgment. There's already a very good one on MTV, by the way. It's called 'Teen Mom.'" (*Ibid.*)

Well now, really..., then let's move along to Carr's colleague, *Times* TV critic, Alessandra Stanley's piece, "...And Baby Makes Reality TV," which begins:

> "DEATH is scary, but it's not nearly as frightening as birth.... Motherhood, at least the way it is depicted on cable networks like MTV, TLC and even *FitTV*, is a menacing, grotesque fate that is mostly ill-timed. Procreation comes either way too soon, ruining the prom and summer beach plans of teenage girls on MTV shows like '16 and Pregnant' or 'Teen Mom 2,' or way too late." (*Ibid.*)

Sounds like MTV is doing its Lord's work pushing the Pill and the Procedure on the premise that children cannot otherwise stay modern.

The *New York Times* doesn't understand this victory they chide and disown in the culture pages, so abortion is treated separately in the metro pages by Ariel Kaminer in the "City Critic" column, "Abortion: Easy Access, Complex Everything Else":

> "This is officially the abortion capital of America. A health department report released last month proves it: about 40 percent of all pregnancies in the city end that way, an average of about 90,000 a year in recent years. No one is exactly celebrating the title. Archbishop Timothy M. Dolan and a group of multi-denominationally horrified clergy condemned the statistics this month. Even abortion rights advocates expressed some concern about the numbers, trying to change the conversation to a broader one on reproductive health." (*Ibid.*)

The sainted Provider quoted later in the piece doesn't give her name for obvious as well as covert reasons, but the *Times*' Sabrina Tavernise gives you another Provider's name in her story, "Squalid Abortion Clinic Escaped State Oversight":

> "It was always open late, way past the time the pizza place next door closed at midnight. The women who emerged from it – often poor blacks and Hispanics – appeared dazed and in pain, and sometimes left in ambulances. The doctor who ran the clinic, Kermit Gosnell, had been sued at least 15 times for malpractice. Two women died while under his care. But the dangerous practices went unnoticed, except by the women who experienced them. They were discovered entirely by accident, during a prescription drug raid by federal agents last February.... On Wednesday, the Philadelphia district attorney, Seth Williams, indicted Dr. Gosnell on eight counts of murder in the deaths of seven infants and a Bhutanese refugee who died after a late-term abortion in 2009. A grand jury report issued on the same day offered its own theory on why so little happened for so long. 'We think the reason no one acted is because the women in question were poor and of color,' the report said, 'and because the victims were infants without identities, and because the subject was the political football of abortion.'" (*Ibid.*)

Those agencies sound under-funded; yeah that's probably the problem, they desperately need sufficient funding. And that Doctor, he may have some kind of disorder. I sure hope he gets treatment, maybe the Health Department can help him out. But seriously, switch out those poor folks of color for some hot teen white-niggers and you got *MTV*'s next p.r. stunt if not smash hit. A new down low.

I don't want to sound like a Christian (more expedient to be Muslim about it) but there's a missing component to these four pieces, each actively dis-associated from the others by the editors of the *New York Times* on behalf of their modern readership barricaded behind a wall of metaphysical misunderstanding sustained against both Darwin's reality and Christ's truth by their daily *Times* and the drone of *NPR*. With each new micro-generation young women are further away from the wrongo precepts of sixties' Feminism, and yet there's a new version of female silence that oddly enough is now a tribute paid to those first feminists and all their bitter, swallowed regrets.

Again, physics applies, but requires a McLuhan and Bangs to comprehend. Welfare, The Pill, any grand step forward in the progress of mankind is first visited upon a society that was formed before it. They utilize the innovation close to the way conceived by the engineers, also formed before its introduction. But those younger who grow up with the breakthrough in place, leverage it and thus are changed, and those who follow them further reorient to the change and any wreckage wrought. There's a great work of philosophy to be written but it won't be. Women aren't often philosophically inclined or can't afford to pursue it, and extant philosophers have little to go on. Heidegger didn't sense it in Arendt because she wasn't modern either and neither had a clue they weren't, because earlier breakthroughs and breakdowns in Europe were contained in a class structure at least until America came back to stay in 1942.

It seems likely that American knowhow's next trick will be bio-engineering, something Mary Wollstonecraft Godwin Shelley wrote about as a teenager in her 1818 novel, *Frankenstein, or The Modern Prometheus*. Her parents were both philosophers, William Godwin and Mary Wollstonecraft. Her mother was at first claimed by the Feminists but they just don't seem comfortable with the past generally. It's easier to misinterpret the present. But bio-engineered humans... now there's a modern Prometheus. And probably not something to commence in the dark, girls.

(*originally posted at The New Vulgate, No. 82*)

Letter to the Editor, San Francisco Bay Guardian

Posterity Alert. Bruce Dancis made the mistake of writing his farewell to punk rock ("Goodbye Punk" Aug. 26, 1981) after reading about the early hardcore ruckus called slamdancing in the dailies. He got raked over the coals by Tim Yohannan and me several issues later. Tim asked the question, How can Bruce say goodbye when he was never really here in the first place? This was just as I was leaving Systematic and the bay area for SST and Los Angeles.

Why Bother, Bruce?
San Francisco Bay Guardian Sept. 23, 1981 Letters

Bruce: Let me offer you on behalf of punks and those who enjoy the music our sincerest apologies for having disturbed your sleep. We certainly never meant to. The music was never designed for media-slugs such as yourself. We understand that maybe at one point you may have appreciated the idea of the musical form as it stood in relation to AOR rock, and we sure do appreciate this appreciation of yours, long gone as it may be. But forgive me if I point out that that has nothing to do with music per se, and neither, I suggest, do your reasons behind your infatuation with black music. Naturally I will be misunderstood here because white rad/liberals such as yourself have for a long time felt it was necessary to suspend certain critical facilities when discussing black music. But I guess the idea of black music is so much more compatible with your intellectual/critical limitations than is a musical form based in young white energy and total disaffection with what is - this includes Reagan AND THIS INCLUDES YOU. Again, for the mongoloid, I reiterate that I am not casting aspersions on blacks or black music or whites or white music: I am talking about progressive mental cases who like music or dislike music for reasons non-musical.

    You might have a case for your argument had you paid even the slightest attention to the non-hardcore music and bands associated with the new music scene. You only review big bands - usually New York or London ones - at big clubs. If you have a healthy respect for stimulating new music where are your clippings on Minimal Man, Woundz, Slava Ranko, Tommy Tadlock, Esmerelda, Wilma, Negativland, Indoor Life, Bay of Pigs, Factrix? I guarantee you that none of them play that nasty fast puuuuuunk music. They are all Bay Area bands and could certainly use any press they can get, seeing as how they have the unfortunate luck of trying to find an audience for their art in the "big" city with the worst, least responsible, most anemic music press in the country.

Yes, yes I know there's no rad chic kudos or jetset international elbow rubbing in writing about these bands, much less the hardcore punk bands, but then it all boils down to why the writer is writing, doesn't it? I guess all the writers in the Bay Area just like the idea of writing, huh? Or rather the idea of being a writer.

What I don't get is why bother mentioning punk in the first place. If you're a music writer write about music, not the music the *Examiner* and *Chronicle* have decided to fodderize this week.

Time – The Antagonist's 'Obituary of the Year'

The Antagonist was Lightbourne's name for a section of our never-was web-mag seemingly designed to efficiently burn as many bridges as possible before they might unfairly collapse on their own under the pressure of real existing web data streams which paid them no mind.

Setting aside the question of whether there is any longer a place in the sun for any newsweekly, what has happened to *Time* is particularly sad. It used to be the fount of conventional wisdom alright, but at least it was that of an experienced journalistic elite with the ear of the political elite. Now it's as if some teenage hacker has broken in and taken over – only worse, it's a wannabe teenage hacker. So you get a "Notebook" full of doo-dad news assembled by ivy league journalism school victims pretending to be skatin' surfin' cyber-savvy whiz kids. Most of this drivel is now signed in *Time*. I miss the old *Time* where the reportage was unsigned in complete confidence that it would be taken as God's word as He was otherwise silent. But that stuff was edited and written by professionals. And professionals are now few and far between.

The most curious recent *Time* fiasco was its attempted handling of David Horowitz's new book, *Hating Whitey and Other Progressive Causes*. On August 30, regular columnist Jack E. White, sought to dispose of this most inconvenient critic of the left in a column titled, "A Real, Live Bigot." Horowitz is particularly inconvenient for those trying to sustain their radicalism by sleepwalking through the everyday evidence strewn around them that their ideas are fundamentally wrong. Horowitz was born red and was one of the few rigorous engines of the sixties American left. This same rigor now applied on the left as it remains in the academia and media must be quite uncomfortable. Horowitz is one of the best at delineating how vanity and hatred are served by the ostensibly selfless, social concern of the left. So they feel his heat as something unfair, and for Horowitz it is a little like shooting fish in a barrel.

So Mr. White, who is of course black, has been hired by the hip posturers at the new *Time* to be the one humorless voice of stock black outrage – if it doesn't fire from the pages of *Time* it would fire at them. Their wise-guy exertions come to a screeching halt at Jack's page, though even he tries, "So many racists, so little time!", at risk of tipping his hand – damn four flusher. So anyway, he calls David every name – well, the two names in the book – and concludes, "I think we'd all be better off if he'd just shut up." This triggered by DH's *salon.com* piece, "Guns don't kill black people, other blacks do," which characterized the NAACP's lawsuit against gun manufacturers as essentially a bait-and-switch at the black community's expense.

According to *Insight* magazine (Nov. 22), "*Time* magazine's editorial board apologized to Horowitz about the August 30 column denouncing him as a bigot." And then in the Nov. 22 issue of *Time* the apology appeared publicly in the form of a positive review of Horowitz's book by Lance Morrow. Certainly Morrow wouldn't be caught appreciating such a bigot in a signed *Time* piece unless he meant it, but it is phrased awkwardly as if written by an ombudsman, or a teacher attempting to explain Death to five-year olds. It's a minefield shooting fish in a barrel. "Shut up." Yes boss.

New Yorker Than Thou
Another salvaged bit of previously unseen Wyoming-based Manhattan mediacrit.

The *New Yorker* was once a precious flower, delicately ungrowing, merely displaying its perfection for the few worthies in town, and the ex-pats, wannabes and librarians scattered to the north, west and south. Editor William Shawn, in the seat for more than thirty years of high stasis had merely to continue rejecting anything too noisy and American, not to say too New Yorkish, or too anxious to levitate alongside the choir. That and covering up that it was printed in Chicago were his principal concerns.

So you see we're dealing with a New York *qua* New York idyll that is far New Yorker than reality could hope to approach – rarefication on a scale where cosmopolitanism transubstantiates to proud, impenetrable provincialism.

In the August *Harper's* a provincial dust-up is grist for Renata Adler, one of the high critics of the *New Yorker*'s past, now an in-country ex-pat, exiled for her tough-love memoir, *Gone: The Last Days of The New Yorker*. Her *Harper's* piece, "A Court of No Appeal – How One Obscure Sentence Upset the *New York Times*," is the story of unintentionally provoking that other cosmoprovincial Manhattan institution, *The New York Times*, into a meltdown that reveals its own recent alleged fall from grace. The single sentence at issue was in reference to a proposed Adler review of Judge John Sirica's 1979 memoir, *To Set the Record Straight*:

> "In the course of research, I had found that, contrary to what he wrote, and contrary to his reputation as a hero, Sirica was in fact a corrupt, incompetent, and dishonest figure, with a close connection to Senator Joseph McCarthy and clear ties to organized crime." (*Harper's*)

Adler writes in *Harper's* that she found "astonishing discrepancies and revelations" when she looked into claims made by Sirica:

> "I did some research, gave the matter thought, and decided not to review the book. I was sure newspaper or magazine journalists would pick up these anomalies and write about them. By the time

> I published my book about *The New Yorker*, I assumed other journalists had found and written about them. It turned out they had not – had, it seemed, no interest in these matters, apart from the recent questioning of my right to address them, even now." (*Ibid.*)

How's that for blithe offense-by-defense? She's out of the china shop and into a cab before the ware hits the floor; Manhattan style at its best.

Adler catches the *Times* defending matters forcibly settled by it, as well as the *Washington Post*, and *CBS News*. These news organizations even now compete to display the scalp of "the disgraced ex-president Richard Nixon," to quote Dan Rather, whenever the subject of Watergate comes up. The eight or nine pieces that the *Times* ran in a virtual deconstruction campaign against this sentence included pieces spread throughout the paper (Arts, Magazine, Business, Letters, Book Review, Editorial, Op Ed, and Week in Review) from January to April, 2000. Why?

Adler's *Harper's* piece runs through the evidence behind the sentence she gathered twenty years ago, the product of relatively straightforward spade-work. But sustaining a fiction takes enormous effort and continual maintenance, and when it's so obviously a self-serving fiction, it further requires a light touch. That the *Times*' touch was so heavy and clumsy is not taken personally by Adler (that is after all a compliment), but rather as a professional affront. She responds as if just discovered that the other New York publishing institution has imploded. (She was Bosley Crowther's replacement as the *Times*' film critic, 1968-9.)

Sirica's supposed heroism occurred in a period when the majority party was attempting to offload its racism and war-mongering onto the minority party. There are many lies from this period that yet comfort the Democrats and irk the Republicans. Sirica, like the segregationist Sen. Sam Ervin of North Carolina, was simply pressed into his righteous role by the immediate needs of the Democratic Party and the news media, then as ever peddling narratives simplified beyond all reality.

Adler's dissection of Sirica's memoir – a quickie unsophisticated jobber – seems a fair reading of what she quotes. Sirica was a typical early 20th Century product of Italian-American urban neighborhoods. His father wasn't a mobster, nor was he a law-abiding citizen. He let the mob use him as a front to run bowling alleys and barber shops where hootch was distributed during prohibition. Sirica himself was involved as a young boxer featured in illegal and often fixed matches. This much she pulls from the memoir itself. Further, Sirica's narrative strikes Adler as so convoluted as to suggest he had a mob-connected businessman's help to finally get past the bar exam and become a lawyer. This is the story of urban

America in those years – an iron triangle of the mob, the courts, and the local Democratic Party. Ovid Demaris' book, *Captive City*, about Chicago in the 1950s is a signal portrait of this largely extinct world.

Adler goes on in her *Harper's* piece to establish Sirica's bumbling dishonesty during the Watergate trials, but her focus is on New York, of course:

> "The documentation for it is ample. [*Times'* media correspondent, Felicity] Barringer, her 'sources,' and her colleagues could have found it if her agenda had really been journalism: the gathering, that is, and publishing of first-hand information." (*Ibid.*)

Felicity Barringer, wife of editorial board member Philip Taubman, being one of the *New York Times'* hounds on her trail, is caught out by Adler engaging in something more like advocacy history. She traces the defense of their long-running portrait of Sirica and then tries to explain the *Times'* devolution:

> "Partly because a relatively recent, complacent kind of sloth on the part of many reporters – sitting at a desk, phoning around, either repetitively badgering or, more commonly, passively receiving, quotes from anonymous, self-interested, possibly lying, or even nonexistent sources – tends to welcome, and to perpetuate, every sort of conventional wisdom and cliché. Partly because the *Times* is committed most profoundly to a certain notion of itself.... as a bureaucracy, a complacent, unchallenged, in some ways totalitarian institution convinced of its infallibility." (*Ibid.*)

Adler also caught the *Times* enforcing that imposed history – seven or eight Winston Smiths without a doubt among them because of course they phone out from the *Times*. Well this time they got a live one on the line. Poor New Yorkers.

Wired: The Geek Looks Up
Another unpublished attempt to prototype the O&O web-mag in 2000.

Bill Joy is cofounder and Chief Scientist of Sun Microsystems. He did important work on Java and Jini about which I know nothing. But I know something about people who wear all black and live in Aspen, Colorado....

He writes in "Why the Future Doesn't Need Us" (*Wired*, April 2000) that he's lost his faith in science and any kind of future for humanity due to the coming noxious convection of robotics, genetic engineering and nanotech. Thinking machines (robotics) designed on an atomic scale (nanotech) that can replicate themselves through software/genetic breakthroughs not really described has led Joy to despair.

Now, the man's evidently intelligent but the piece isn't smart. Fifteen footnotes in a magazine don't impress me when the writer leans so heavily on the high-minded canards of the academics who were ninnies at best throughout the cold war when the doomsayers last got down. He's read a lot of stuff but there's no thinking to synthesize it into something original. And in terms of history its kid's stuff. It's enough to make you fear for those who've had their heads to the monitor all their lives.

Virginia Postrel's critique of this piece in the June issue of *Reason* makes the case for the Future and Science and Humans in a quarter the time and rightly harps on Joy's willful gullibility on the desirability after WWII of placing nuclear weapons technology in the hands of the UN. For Joy to resurrect the high-minded/air-headed UN gambit as a model for today tech issues reveals a self-absorption and self-regard on a scale that transcends mere mortals – these be intelligentsia; ye shall know them by their double-domes and half-baked works. Those who did the thankless heavy-lifting dirty work of shepherding free (and slave) societies around the post-war shoals – both conventional and unconventional – were much lower sorts with reputations to match: Churchill, Truman, MacArthur, Marshall, Kennan, Dulles, Eisenhower, Nixon, Thatcher, Reagan, Wojtyla....

The letters that poured into *Wired* (printed three issues later) might seem to further confirm that the geekdom's comprehension of recent history is undigested and fully received, and from television and films at that! (What sites are they at on the web?!) I'm not even talking about the letter-writers' sober references to Gene Roddenberry and the Wizard of Oz.... Oppenheimer was not the Cold War's Christ-figure! He was wrong! About the commies, the UN, America, the West, human nature... have I forgotten anything? His self-regard demanded he be seen as high-minded, and so he could yield nothing to such neanderthals as the American public and their manservants in Washington. (The Institute for Advanced Study at Princeton, where Einstein, Veblen, Oppenheimer and others fed at the trough, was endowed by a department store magnate who was trying to turn "useless knowledge" into practical information - how mortifying for poor pure Oppie - scion of a wealthy merchant family, though he was.) Stalin was no threat to him that he could feel; not compared to Truman and Ike and that damn General Leslie Groves. He did his best to have us all incinerated or enslaved, but he looked good doing it and that's what's important.

Some of the letters-to-the-editor are from movement types not likely to have ever seen a copy of *Wired* before - Norman Lear isn't scared by Joy's cautionary tale, he's thrilled. It's all politics to him and his in Hollywood - now they just need to hire another tutor.

There were actually a few letters in defense of Science etc., that made it back to the editors, which is nice to see considering the mag is devoted to computer culture, if not computer science itself. My favorite letter is from a *Village Voice* staffer who cites the Amish as the model for us all, that we may elude Dr. Frankenstein's fate at the hand of his own monstrous creation. Well okay, but then let's not hear any crying about trying to get a decent bagel.

The sad truth is that these science critics are mere obstructionists. They aren't even interested in the solar or wind or tidal energy tech breakthroughs they claim to want. The last thing they want for humanity is that it get endless free clean energy. They are puritans. The neo-neolithics of the Northwest WTO protests are at least open to their own reality. The public deserves punishment at the hands of they-and-theirs; visualize world justice at the hands of this imagined meritocratic elite. From this reservoir of frustrated expertise comes this elite's totalitarian appetite. Even a Stalin had vicarious allies in every free western democracy because democracy is ever in this class's way.

Bill Joy and another *Wired* writer, Paulina Borsook, with her book, *Cyberselfish*, are dropping out of the silicon rat-race (somewhat too real a meritocracy perhaps) and they are noticing that the world of ideas as it exists in publishing and politics offers comfortable refuge from the immutables of silicon valley, but only if one takes up that class's critique of it. See you in the *Times*, Bill. Oh joy.

WORLD.

~

Brave New Class
This was my first significant piece done for The New Vulgate *in Aug. 12, 2009. I'd been thinking around the idea for several weeks.*

Most Americans regret the intractable contest of politics. As a young and idealistic nation we like to imagine there's a way beyond it. But the third ways – Thurmond, Wallace, Anderson, Larouche, Jackson, Weicker, Perot, Buchanan – have failed to attract and represent that discontent. The American political equilibrium is pretty sturdy; it involves the two parties, each a product of its own shotgun marriage. These then trade lead as they spin through their lop-sided waltz. No-one is going to applaud such an unsightly dance...

Before the founding of the United States there was actually less politics. In Kingdoms of yore politics amounted to subjects petitioning King, or noblemen positioning themselves within the Court. For peasants, politics amounted to certain local questions resolved by force, by marriage, or by deferring to an elder. The King's Court was too small to be considered a class, but new classes formed between the peasantry and the Court. Bankers, traders, innkeepers, landlords and merchants thrived as towns grew and transportation by river and sea expanded markets.

The Romans had executed Jesus Christ, but their empire was taken from within by His followers within three centuries. Thereafter the Kings of Christendom ruled by a sanctioning power vested in the Pope. The Divine Right of Kings was now observable, rather than merely asserted by some ambitious Duke or Baron. The Pope's embassies knit the now *Holy Roman Empire* together on a grand new level of politics. A few centuries more and this church-state power was ebbing to new centers of economic power. The theo-political doctrine of the King's two bodies was delineated such that his *body politic* interacted with new, non-royal institutions, while his *body natural* had to sustain the appearance of the paragon of Christian virtue. The King's regional representatives evolved from royal figures in themselves to purely administrative appointees and then to appointed members of consultative bodies. It was not yet democracy but the more wise the Royal House, the more successful its reign, the more its subjects commanded a voice in governance. As their nations weaned themselves from absolute rule the Holy Roman Empire dissolved and the Pope's power began a slow retreat from the political realm.

The push toward democracy was not quite from the People themselves, though. The People have more often been spoken for by a new class. A rhetorical and political bait-and-switch evolved from the classical Greek and Roman worlds, through the American, French, Mexican, and Russian Revolutions to the here and now where this deception remains the principal discord in representational politics in these now democratic republics. At times it can appear the bait-and-switch be politics itself, which might also help explain the people's distaste for it.

The failure of Communism demonstrated how easily the political party inspired by Marx turned his fundamental insight that economics drives history on its head as the Party once in power repressed economic forces. It also demonstrated that those market forces cannot be tamed by the political class without sending that economy into a regime-breaking death spiral.

At times a culture might prefer political tyranny to roiling economic growth – late Tsarist Russia's economy had the highest growth rate in Europe until WWI. And the Chinese in the early 20th Century may have felt that their commercial culture was so corrosive of national structure that it had led to colonization by European powers. Certainly the once innovative, dynamic Middle Kingdom was closed down long before, according to the needs of its administrative class – a neo-Confucian new class then coming into its own after 1433 when the last of its exploratory trade missions sailed. (Christopher Columbus was born in 1451.) By 1500, according to Kaoru Sugihara, China was on a labor intensive path while Europe was beginning on a capital-intensive path. China was then left behind beginning in 1750 according to Kenneth Pomeranz (*The Great Divergence*), and that would bring the British around the world to China's doorstep rather than the reverse.

The late Tom Butler, ex-lower east sider, ex-Santa Monica Synanon alumnus, ex-Trotskyite, one-time Laramie coffee-shop bon vivant, thought that the Khmer Rouge had finally proved Marxism-Leninism fraudulent, for once Pol Pot got through with Cambodia no frustrated Com-symp anywhere in the world could ever say of yet another failed revolution, "They just didn't go far enough." Philip Short writes that the years Pol Pot and his comrades spent studying in Paris meant that "the foreign intellectual legacy which would underpin the Cambodian revolution was first and foremost French." (*Pol Pot*) Though he does allow that Pol Pot was influenced by the Russian anarchist Prince Peter Kropotkin, whose study, *The Great Revolution*, counts its failings as 1) Robespierre was a moderate, and 2) it didn't go far enough. So it was the good serf-loving Prince – author as well of *Mutual Aid*, an attempted counter to the theory of natural selection – who put it in young Saloth Sâr's mind that the only revolutionary crime was to not go far enough.

My friend Tom was an optimist though, because right after the Cambodian cataclysm revolutionary parties in Central America and Africa were cheered on. For the least fussy each Communist revolution is a virgin birth, and the blood excused by an all-purpose black legend about Kings or strongmen or "so-called democracies."

Marx had thought economic forces would yield communism. But almost immediately after the Russian Revolution, the invisible hand forced Lenin into his New Economic Policy semi-privatization because even the full expropriation of the wealth of entire classes of royalty, manufacturers, merchants, speculators and land-owners bought only a one-time cash infusion which was quickly spent and then unreplenished by the new socialist economic structures that replaced them. The command economy quickly devolves into the game described by Russians decades later as "They pretend to pay us; we pretend to work."

The new class that Milovan Djilas discusses in his 1957 classic of Communist disillusionment was the political bureaucracy, which he counter-posed to the political party itself. "The party makes the class, but the class grows as a result and uses the party as a basis. The class grows stronger, while the party grows weaker." (*The New Class*) Djilas was not simply bemoaning the loss of the Party's idealism and initiative; he was an ex-Communist tracing what fundamental flaws had wrought under the guise of its idealism. He had been the Vice-President of Yugoslavia, then was expelled from the Communist Party and jailed in 1956.

Socialism weighed far more heavily on the people than had the royal families or even the Mongol horde. Was there ever King or Khan as invasive as Stalin, Hitler, Mao, Castro, Kim Il-Sung, Pol Pot, Mugabe? As Djilas put it, "The monarchy did not think quite as highly of itself as the Communists do of themselves, nor was it as absolute as they are." We assume otherwise today due to lingering propaganda from the revolutions driven home by the new class. The very idea of royalty, even as mere non-governing cultural institution as in Britain or Spain, is a mote in the eye of the new class. Even now the new class – these made-members of the meritocracy – gives evidence through its media of being deeply insulted by the *demos*, for they must submit their grand social-engineering plans for the approval of this rabble. The allergy cultivated to this indignity is only human nature, of course, but its negative affect is exacerbated by the new class's clambering into the less productive sectors: the arts, media, academia, and most expensively, law and government. Their products are not worthless, but they do exist at the sufferance of the wealth-creating hard economy. The new class senses this and has trouble with any response but denial. At that point they become a threat, real and imagined.

Contempt for the people in the name of the people is acted out again and again: in the ongoing formation of the EU in Brussels, in the last attempt to nationalize healthcare and this one, and in the bathetic brinksmanship over global warming where any doubts expressed over causality or the wisdom of loading costs onto the productive sectors become a new kind of treason akin to holocaust-denial. Such political behavior reveals this new class believes they on merit should have inherited the divine right of Kings.

Our world here is a product of the FDR presidency. The news media speaks of the Obama era following the Bush era, the Clinton era... but we still live in the FDR era. And the new class still dreams a thirties dream of corporatist fascism. Only Eisenhower had the standing to roll back the government involvement in the economy and culture that occurred over the course of Roosevelt's four terms. But he did not, and then Johnson and Nixon expanded from there, thinking to buy time for their efforts in Vietnam and the Cold War generally. It was thought that social security had bought the Democrats a generation of voters and that of course bore repeating. The Clinton's healthcare initiative failed because it looked too much like it was – a coup on a weakened profession, Medicine, by a fallen profession, Law. At most, there are two or three doctors in Congress; there are hundreds of lawyers, and in appointed positions and staffers, thousands...

What Hillary Clinton did pull off in her unwild youth was delineated best in David Brock's book, *The Seduction of Hillary Rodham*. Brock had his crisis of conscience and gonads while researching it, but the book is no simple hatchet job and his narrative about Hillary Clinton's tenure at the Legal Services Corporation in the chapter "Alinsky's Daughter" is one of the best portraits of these corporatist combines that once authorized take on a life of their own as planned:

> "The question of whether the federal government should provide free legal services to the poor has been bitterly contested since the government first began spending $1million a year on the program during the heyday of LBJ's Great Society in 1965. The LSC

became an independent corporation by an act of Congress in 1974 and was given an annual budget of $90 million. By the end of Hillary's tenure, that budget had ballooned to over $300 million a year.

In the view of Roger Cramton, the Cornell law professor and chairman of the LSC board under President Gerald Ford, the original Great Society legal services program set forth objectives far beyond the goals of traditional legal aid. Previously, legal aid had been thought of as helping low-income people apply for government benefits, deal with landlords, or fight for child support. The LBJ program was run by professional activists whose idea of social justice meant litigating and lobbying to change laws, and extending the welfare state, as well as Alinsky-style organizing of the poor into political pressure groups." (*The Seduction of Hillary Rodham*)

It was still the seventies and the radicalism of many involved was as yet unreconstructed, but the turning of a legal aid program for individual poor people into a vehicle for radical lawyers to fund class action lawsuits in all directions was theft in any decade. Theft that corporate America had to accept and consider as another tax to be passed along to their customers. The costs were baked in and remain invisible.

And Brock's tale is one of the few exhumations of the too-often unsuspected ulterior motives of the new class. Mass higher education has yielded more pretension than wisdom. This might not be so dangerous, but it does saddle the left with an unwanted higher burden of proof as everyone goes to college. When they – a cultural elite within a social elite – are not trusted implicitly by the object of their affection – the People – they get angry because they aren't actually smart enough to be able to explain themselves. They cannot now be trusted for they no longer believe in the Left's endgame, nor have most of them accepted the less pretentious short-term role of reforming and administering and checking the Republicans within constitutional bounds. This leaves them operating with no philosophical basis, but rather on a cynical political level straining at every constraint with only a hollow etiquette to cover what may drive them. Unfortunately for the left, the right whatever its own brand of confusion, generally believes in the American tradition and free market capitalism.

Another late friend of mine, musician and itinerant intellectual David Lightbourne, explained the idiocy one finds in academia and media as resulting from mass higher education on top of compulsory schooling which he believed "educates people beyond their intelligence." With this new and suddenly common affect, large numbers of nominally, notionally smart folks group-think within asserted empathetic manias. These manias now come of a Left project having given ground on economics and materialism. Rather than think openly and continually they quickly adopt useful ideas; these are more easily thrown in a fight. For example: The earth's climate is never really stable; it is always cycling through its variables. And the sun's intensity runs on its cycle. Anyone authentically educated knows how scientists express themselves and there's very little of that tone in the uniform deeply invested prejudices on exhibit, and notice the quick bending of our unfree corporatist industries to the ruling class's sudden mania which is called Science. My unlettered suspicion is that any warming causes cooling and that cooling triggers warming. Any other overarching physo-chemo-bio-dynamic and we would not have survived and thrived to be here arguing over Darwin and God.

The new class consciousness has these lawyers, sociologists, bureaucrats, professors of government, artists, counselors, welfare apparats, AmeriCorps hirelings, etc., favor any aggrandizement of state power (except military and policing functions) even if they personally do not directly benefit. The greater self-interest is difficult to see and it disappears utterly when viewed through the enlightenment bias of the last five hundred years of western history. I suspect we'll know when this new class feels fully in power by a tempering of its bias against military and policing power.

Wolfgang Schivelbusch's book, *Three New Deals*, is about thirties responses to the Depression in Italy, Germany and America. It begins by describing their stimulus programs of public works construction. Each country rejected architectural modernism for "Baroque monumentality" in its new government buildings. Schivelbusch quotes architectural historian John W. Reps calling it a "supreme irony" to have Washington, D.C., capitol of the foundational democracy import the style designed to sing praise to national socialist despots. I think it's a somewhat smaller irony, because the reason our democratic republic has a constitution is that the founders understood well that this new state would exhibit the same straining toward tyranny as any other.

Favorite images of members of our new class in their rage to serve include Vice President Gore in his Navigator, his manse, his jet, multitasking his way to a superhuman carbon imprint as he concocts to cover his convenience as Inconvenient, or Governor Jon Corzine being driven at ninety miles an hour through New Jersey traffic without wearing his seatbelt and barely surviving the wreck. His State Police's first impulse was to prosecute the citizen obeying the speed limit that the Governor's SUV ran up on. They'd like to clear American roads of the American people, put them all on rapid trans so they could speed through unobstructed on the People's business, just as the members of the Soviet politburo did through the once empty streets of Moscow. Victor Davis Hanson recently characterized the lives that Gore and *New York Times* columnist Tom Friedman, both environmental scolds, live as like "grandees of the 18th-century English countryside."

In politics there are certain near-term priorities that have nothing to do with political philosophy. But political philosophy provides a cover for anything and so most nations other than Britain count on a constitution as a kind of guardrail against on one hand public servants acting like sovereigns, or on the other, simple mob-fueled passions. The U.S. Constitution as interpreted by the Supreme Court stopped FDR from taking his *ad hoc* ideas even further when it ruled the National Recovery Act (NRA) unconstitutional. After his 1936 reelection an attempt to pack the court by adding seven new justices to the Supreme Court failed, but did reveal the scale of the administration's desperation to revive an economy that the state now had in its grip.

One suspects that above and beyond Roosevelt's determination to come to Britain's defense and vice president Wallace's to come to the Soviet Union's, the rationale for America's entry into WWII was at base economic. A war-time command economy is the logical end of socialism because once nationalized, overtly or by taxes and regulation, the productive and wealth-building sectors lose their competitive edge and begin to seek state favor instead. All become rent-seekers and focus on lobbying the powers that be. This was the American Left's contribution to our military-industrial complex, and yet they still charmingly believe it ironic that a Republican President and ex-General might famously warn against it. It also explains Wal-Mart's recent signing on to the national health-care initiative. The Wal-Mart board (which once included Hillary Clinton) knows that raising the cost of doing business serves a mature company by precluding the arrival of new competitors. Once the private sector shelters under government protection that becomes job one, and only a military threat to the state can supply motivation enough to maintain a productive edge.

Our new class wanted to stride the world stage with the European powers soon after the Civil War, and so Republican Teddy Roosevelt and Democrat Woodrow Wilson delivered it walk-on roles in the Spanish-American War and WWI. FDR ran for his third term on a peace platform in 1940 but soon ordered a halt to the sale of oil to Imperial Japan, which took this as an act of war. The Anglophile Roosevelt thought so little of the Japanese race that he imagined they'd only sink a ship or two in the South China Sea.

In the end, foreign affairs, the threats America faced in its first century and its burdens and adventures in the second, have always worked against the prime domestic agendas of both parties. The issues of slavery and state sovereignty were settled in the Civil War, but the continued disenfranchisement of the new black citizen did not immediately trigger a federal power grab. The Great Depression did; perhaps it was something we caught on our return to Europe in the Great War. Earlier panics and depressions had occurred in a less integrated world. By the early thirties the major trading nations exhibited greater international consciousness and they all made the wrong moves. Herbert Hoover was a progressive Republican who had supported Teddy Roosevelt's Bull Moose run, and he signed the Smoot-Hawley Tariff Act into law and raised the income tax close to forty points - Franklin Roosevelt was able to campaign against Hoover's socialism!

The various New Deal programs initiated then for the poor, the elderly, artists, veterans, farmers, etc., were bestowed at first on Americans whose expectations had been formed in earlier decades. But these programs re-engineered the expectations of those born into a compromised citizenship now circumscribed by these ongoing programs. They bought votes in their day, but votes don't stay bought because the programs stoke greater, magical expectations. Human nature quickly adapts to gifts, charity, welfare payments, etc. It's a wonder there is still a traditional American impulse left. Democrats and their media plus a fair number of Republicans fret that we are the only industrialized state without national healthcare as if it's a problem that the United States isn't like Europe. Well, we wouldn't be here if we thought Europe was the standard.

The state keeps hitting its head on the budgetary ceiling. There will never be enough revenue. The states with the highest tax rates are running the highest deficits currently. According to the *Wall Street Journal* the Center for Responsive Politics reports that 1,000 municipal, county and state governments paid over $20 million this spring to lobby the federal government for stimulus spending.

Massachusetts and California have tried to initiate universal healthcare coverage at the state level and are finding that it doesn't save money, it costs more. Now they hope to offload their programs onto some new federal plan. And further, writes Thomas Donlan:

> "A state commission last week recommended that Massachusetts end fee-for-service payments for health care. The new payment system... would mandate flat-rate per-capita payments to networks of doctors, hospitals and other providers. The networks would receive a payment for each member each month, regardless of the services performed." (July 27, 2009, *Barron's*)

If doctors are to become wage labor they will unionize and join that other fallen profession, Teachers, and compete only to avoid as much of their work as possible. (The teachers' professional association became a union in 1969.) As the baby boomers are just entering old-age they may believe this is how to get more for less but given the demands they will place on the health sciences this all seems foolhardy. For one thing research and medical progress will slow and they will have traded Fed-Ex healthcare for the Postal Service.

There is some balking within the Democratic caucus. Some fear the true-believers in their leadership and the White House could create a wholly-owned political nightmare. And they fear a bridge too far as well – one that might even trigger a roll-back of Medicare, Medicaid, and Social Security, all of which are unsustainable in their present forms. (In the current issue of *Fortune* Allan Sloan compares what's coming as Social Security begins to borrow in five years to make its pay-outs as one, two, many AIGs every year out.) Democrats might soon wish they'd settled for Bush's Social Security reform, as they often wish they'd settled for Nixon's health care initiative.

The new class talks often of greed and sustainability. Greed explains all behavior but their own, and they think of public monies as clean and private monies as filthy. The sustainability gambit seeks to give state policymakers a new veto over all private sector activity. Power is their game, though they often find substantial salaries and grant money to go with their positions, which unsurprisingly feature none of the personal liability they lard on to the private sector. They behave as if certain that the greed of those others is powerful enough to survive their best attempts to eradicate it. Therefore they take productivity for granted and cease to worry about what might be a necessary policy for optimum wealth creation. Even what might be necessary to, by taxation, fund their own social plans. They do not give this a second thought until they achieve political power, and then it's only those in the elective administrative positions. Here Djilas's observation that the bureaucracy is sturdier than the Party obtains.

Politicians cannot raise taxes without losing revenue. Can they cut benefits and get re-elected? Historically in America tax revenues as a percentage of economic activity remain in the mid-twenty percentile, no matter the rates; the only true variable is how large and how fast the economy is allowed to grow. Again, the more complex the taxation regimen becomes, the more time and cost is spent on compliance and this again is part and parcel of a system that aids large established businesses by making it more difficult for new competitors to grow. Here, Hillary's offhanded comment, defending her healthcare proposals, that she couldn't be responsible for every under-capitalized company is illustrative.

When the federal income tax rates came down in the early 1980s, the revenues that were collected by the lower rates went up due to increased economic activity. The Democrats in Congress seemed to ramp up spending so they could hide the fact of these increased collections under the resulting deficits. Perhaps the principle-of-the-thing – the state's claim to its citizens' earnings – outweighs even the state's most profitable tax philosophy if it be lower and flatter. This Democratic behavior dared a veto by President Reagan and he blinked perhaps with an eye toward the Cold War end-game. The Republican Congressional response seemed to be to shovel as much spending into the military before the Democrats had spent it all on social programs; they seemed to reason that if the Federal government was going into debt anyway it would be best to get some increased defense capacity for all the spending.

Politics in Washington is now quite often this kind of shadow play. Clive Crook in the *Financial Times* recently reminded his readers that the shape of healthcare in America is already the product of state control. There is only a vestigial fee-for-service option. Yet the failings of this level of state involvement will be used to rationalize further state takeover. The new class cannot lose. Ban drilling and then claim oil is running out. Charge a person or company with malfeasance and then claim their defensive action is proof of guilt. Regulate perverse incentives into a sector and then blame free market capitalism.

The auto industry was warped by its experience filling orders for the military during WWII and the Cold War, especially General Motors. Now it appears American carmakers will have to surrender the trucks, vans and SUVs where they lead, to compete on smaller vehicles where the Japanese and Koreans lead. And the state's recent rescue of GM and Chrysler punishes Ford by propping up their weak competitors. Ford is denied the reward the marketplace might have delivered it. And the purchase of GM will make the decades long process of opening up world markets in the WTO even more tortuous as protectionist regimes point to this action in defense of their own.

Rube Goldberg is their patron saint as they overlay new laws on old, new regulations on old; not to worry if they conflict, all will be adjudicated by them. Douglas McCollam describes what elite law-firms have been up to in the *Wall Street Journal*:

> "When times were good, lawyers earned enormous fees engineering mergers and takeovers. When things were bad, they earned enormous fees fending off angry shareholders and breaking up the

conglomerates that they had helped put together. When things turned really ugly, they made a fortune carving up the bankrupt carcasses of their former clients and toiling to keep top management out of federal prison. And when questioned whether they bore some measure of responsibility for the malfeasance that felled their erstwhile patrons, lawyers typically answered with a 'hey, we just work here' shrug." (July 30, 2009, *Wall Street Journal*)

When they begin to talk about lawyers' fees and liability caps like they talk about doctor's fees and approved treatments then we'll know that an even newer class is being born. Don't hold your breath. Law is now the language of social interaction; everything is a federal case, and repeatedly. It's a baked-in tax worse than the VAT about to be proposed.

Youth culture is in for a big surprise, because once health-care is government-issued, then everyone's health is the state's business. Big Bro, Big Sis, they know you want to smoke a little, drink a little... and they would like to allow it, because they like to think they're pretty hip themselves, left of center and all that, but you must understand.... It's simply no longer your choice to make. In June, California added marijuana smoke to its official list of known carcinogens. How does this square with the continuing drift toward legalization of pot? And how does that square with the drift toward criminalization of tobacco? Well, I guess it'll all be adjudicated.

The last "big idea" book influential in Democratic Party circles was Naomi Klein's 2007 book, *The Shock Doctrine*, which claimed to reveal the American right's m.o. of using catastrophes as opportunities for tearing down state safeguards and leaving Americans defenseless before a *laissez faire* capitalism unbound. It sounded to me like rather the Left's m.o. she was describing in some sort of projected guilt formation considering FDR's behavior during the Depression, and sure enough her book is now never spoken of at all; rather it's principle accusation is now officially the Rahm Emanuel doctrine. Elections have consequences.

In truth, the American economy has been subordinated to the federal government since WWII and the New Deal. Our allegedly savage jungle capitalism is nowhere near savage enough to pay for social security, never mind what's to come. Some smart mathematician will someday crunch the economic growth numbers and chart them over the years against deaths and injury by violence and disease. This will be the Blood Index and it will underline the importance of enterprise and growth, and perhaps the sustainability of government expansion. India and China understand this because their leaders, democrats and Communists, understand that they ride a tiger and a dragon, and if they fail to maintain growth the social dangers are grave on a truly awesome scale. Neither will indulge their thankfully microscopic new classes' wish to shut down smokestack industries and stop highway and automobile construction. And they must look at our new class's environmental embassies cross-eyed when they blithely demand that they quit burning coal and oil.

Here in Wyoming we have our own microscopic new class:

> "The Equality State Policy Center (ESPC) is encouraging lawmakers to reassess Wyoming's mineral severance taxes, which make up to 20 percent of the state's general fund along with another 12 percent in interest from the savings account.
>
> Sarah Gorin, an ESPC researcher, told the Wyoming News Service on Monday that the interest stream is unlikely to sustain the state if mining production declines and tax revenues disappear. 'We've felt for a long time that we're not saving enough against the future when these resources will be gone, or no longer marketable.'" (Aug. 4, 2009, *Laramie Boomerang*)

Our new class is not world class; they claim they just want for Wyoming what Alaska has, but its cover for their principle-of-the-thing – a state income tax. They cannot abide that our state does not have its hand in our pockets, though they've learned to never mention this. So it's more shadow play, even here on the wide-open high plains – look there goes Shane now. I like her phrase "or no longer marketable." They sure dream big about their brave new world.

(originally posted at The New Vulgate, No. 6)

Kalifornia unter Alles

Another NV piece, this one might've been more ambitious but I got tired of waiting to find time and dashed it off with what material I'd collected. My deadline was the election so this went up in late October 2010.

What with all the sharpening of fundamental issues to do with spending, taxing, economics, and the U.S. Constitution in these mid-term elections it's like the man in the street is talking metaphysics, or plate tectonics, when the news media and the two Parties expected to go again at guns or abortion or race. The Founders Top 10 are in motion due to issues involving the Fed, and Hayek and Bastiat are pushing Strauss and Schmitt from the Republican Party reading room. It's like Letterman's Dumb Guy understands something about Pension liabilities and wealth creation and how moral hazard finds better disguise with each step up the government ladder, that the Wise Guys do not. There were many missteps the de-centered ad hoc Tea Party might have made. Mistakes along the lines Ross Perot made, or talking conspiracies or race. To some extent what mistakes have been made were made so locally they did little damage.

The smartest commentator on American politics down to the county level, Michael Barone, recently pondered the Tea Party's outfoxing of the pros of both parties – they beat many Republican organizations in the primaries and look to beat the Democratic organizations next. I was driving through Nebraska last Wednesday when Rush Limbaugh was chiding Barone for his surprise that his own readers, who also overlap the viewers of *Fox News*, the readers of the *Wall Street Journal*, and listeners of Limbaugh himself, would be up to speed by now. Also recently, I saw a letter warning Tea Party folks that money coming into races via something called the Tea Party Express is old-line Republican money trying to co-opt them. They seem ready to resume a struggle with the Republican Party on Wednesday as they form leadership before January's next Congress brings them back up against the Democrats.

And then there's California... There the elections seem unsharpened by the Tea Party lexicon so evident elsewhere around the country. This despite California's clear lead in the fundamental unsustainability sweepstakes. The Milken Institute's new study, "Addressing California's Pension

Shortfalls" by Perry Wong and I-Ling Shen, offers no magic answers, just two obvious ones:

> "The first involves implementing feasible adjustments to the current defined benefit plans, such as increasing contributions, lowering pension benefits, and raising the retirement age. The second solution set is more fundamental: an overhaul of the current pension plan so that investment risks are not entirely borne by the employer but shared with state employees." (Milken Institute)

The Report's real drama is in its laying out the case that things are far worse than the Governor or the Assembly or editorial boards have admitted. The recent budget dance indicates that reality is still to be resisted in Cali. One of the study's charts, "Actuarial unfunded accrued liabilities" for the three state pension funds reveals that these grew outsized even in the teeth of the boom/bubble beginning in 2003 when money was still pouring into their coffers. These boom revenues went somewhere else. And now the boom is over; nothing was banked.

The uniquely California problem has to do with the Cali Dream within the American Dream. It is America out there, yes, only ideologized in that boomer manner of pretentious soft-sciences and debased Humanities. The entire game's been floated by the heavy industry in and around Los Angeles, and the mechanized agriculture of the San Joaquin Valley which operates on a scale hitherto unknown (Soviet agriculture don't count), with significant contributions from home construction. All of this earthy wealth creation put the gold in the Golden State, but is hidden away from the soft-headed culturati tracts. Industry is well south of Los Angeles's west-side, and agriculture due east of I-5 (the vineyards are west). The smaller inland economies of Northeast California and the deserts, which in other states might carry real clout, in California are jerked around helplessly by these large interests and the great population centers which give these Nevada-like, Utah-like, Oregon-like regions not a single thought outside of checking compliance with all state social mandates.

But it's in those isolated high rent tracts where the terms of discourse are approved and disseminated. Here, where everyone wants to live: the Westside, the beach, the canyons, San Francisco, coastal small town California – not to be confused with small town America. This is where they dream of taxing legalized marijuana or taxing the revenues of foreign corporations' overseas' earnings or taxing the Ports to within an inch of making Seattle the gateway to America.... Their conventional wisdom is that it's all Howard Jarvis's fault (his Proposition 13 of 1978 capped property taxes until sale). They must believe they could keep their own fancy digs were these beach houses and canyon cabins and cliffside manses and corner flats and high-rise condos taxed at their true merciless Golden State dreamy market value. Everything from Manhattan Beach to North Beach might easily look like Merced or Riverside, to an accountant anyway, were it not for Saint Howard. And surely Nevada and Utah would have filled up two decades quicker if that Cal Assembly had been able to tax away at people's homes.

   No doubt the referendum system is a problem with its atomizing of issues to an anti-philosophical, even anti-political level. But the referenda system was caused by an earlier breakdown of the political system no-one remembers. This election it's Prop 20 which seeks to banish the gerrymandering of safe districts in the Assembly that bears watching. But somehow the scale of California insures a critical mass of terminally disaffected

CHRIS COLLINS.

voters/tax payers/consumers/citizens no matter what the issue and these must be bought off with matching funds thus doubling/tripling/quadrupling proposed expenditures as many times over as there are contending groups. The economy is so large and invisible that the politicians and Parties have given up any discipline. Only now they've hit a wall they did not know existed.

The California indulgence is largely about releasing the inner being/ true self, not thinking hard about actuarial or constitutional issues. There's plenty of vote-buying using state revenues and spending. More in fact than you'd find in other states with similarly intractable budgetary problems. But in Illinois, New York, and New Jersey these purchases are grubby and smelly like corruption ought to be; they are the brokering of ethnic and class and business power. But in California all corruption is cleaned by the sunlight of pretension. Mass higher education does that to a culture. It's claimed that Cali's systems of universities and community colleges is the jewel of its postwar development; well, that depends. That

GRACE KRILANOVICH.

the system is one of former Speaker Willie Brown's achievements makes one suspicious. Certainly there's heavy duty work going on in the labs and affiliated research facilities of the hard science colleges, but even that is quite easily squandered when it's the Humanities schools' sensibility ordering them around on greenish wild goose chases. The pretense knows no bounds and so while the budget won't add up, all kinds of micro-legislation continue to authorize the creation of new boards to oversee pets, or plants, or motorcycles or air. Utterly unproductive indulgences displaying a contempt for wealth created by the hidden productive sectors.

Truckers used to tank up at the border to California to use as little of the special Cali blend of fuel as possible. They were just trying to save their engines from the damaging effects of California's mandated additives and didn't want to pay a premium for that corrosion on top of it. Lucky for them those additives soon proved carcinogenic and were outlawed by another of the state's fiefdoms. Never mind, call it hamster-wheel workfare for citizens or not. The state mandarins believe their make-work is better than real naturally occurring jobs. They now control a tangled mass of puppet strings whereby what economic actors want to do is frustrated while they are enticed to do what they do not want to do.

The next Silicon Valley may be unable to develop in California no matter its resources and the creative energy of its population. In any case it's already been decided in Sacramento what that next Silicon Valley will be.

Socially conscious government spending further crowds out naturally occurring folk patterns in a society and the trouble this causes then seems addressable only by more government intervention. This was the new class's magic formula for amassing power through government growth. And it is why today the Right is radical and the Left reactionary.

California is only just recently a net loser with regard to federal taxes taken and spending given. The older industrial states of the Midwest and Northeast have been losers since Pearl Harbor as the Feds used their wealth creation to fund development of the west for defensive purposes after the attack on Pearl Harbor. The nation's air force research, development and construction were moved to the west coast. Such spending was more wind in California's sails. But all that and more came to be leveraged beyond the near-term, and then beyond the far-term, so that even the return of economic growth will not refill the sails and move the state government toward fiscal equilibrium. And this election, which in California appears merely administrative in its concerns, may not change much. Except that things cannot go on as before.

The trigger for Cali's "dysfunction" as it's called, occurred neatly in 1980 when Republicans supplied the votes necessary to make Willie Brown Speaker of the Assembly (while two other Democrats fought a scorched-earth battle over the post). Brown, a born pol from east Texas was no utopian and hardly issue-driven even when it came to black issues, but in a sense he's the one who channeled the remaining eastern-like political battles into an everybody-wins game of utopian roulette paid for by round after round of increased taxes and fees. This couldn't last but it did because Brown was so free a pol – he moved in and around the corrupt and the idealists, swindling each out of what together they might oppose.

He shafted the Republicans over redistricting and so the one-time Republican-trending state of Reagan became a Democratic lock. Republican Governors could do nothing at best against the Assembly majority under Brown, more often he set up face-saving mechanisms that seemed to forestall tax increases while lining them up to be triggered by some next budgetary shortfall his deal making would insure. Even when Willie stumbled there were Republican Speakers he could rule through, he seems that nice a guy. Only a term limits referendum donnybrook got rid of Brown in 1995 and he left in such a way that he further poisoned the well.

Contrasting California's Brown with the colorless Illinois Speaker Michael Madigan, one would say Madigan is likely escaping culpability once again (under Governor-cover: the old Republicans in prison and Blagojevich circling) even though Madigan is still in the damn office!

Jerry Brown may be the one Democrat who could conceivably call the Tea Party's bluff on spending, but it's not as if Arnold Schwarzenegger didn't try. Perhaps in the state there will be some change in the makeup of the legislature, but change enough? There won't even be half the differ-

Los Angeles 1853

ence there will be in Washington. Why? Because they're all Californians! But Jerry Brown was already Governor and his father was a Governor too. Jerry was even a Jesuit seminarian for a year in the fifties. In the seventies as Governor he was another utopian Californian but though he opposed the Jarvis Prop he adjusted to it and the state was in surplus. But he ran for President in 1976 and 1980, and for Senator in 1982 so he seemed pretty anxious to get the hell out back then. The seventies were more boom for California but by the time Brown left the Governor's office the state had a then-unprecedentedly large budget deficit. Since then he's done real work as Mayor of Oakland and one hopes he reads the state's problems better than his opponent Meg Whitman, an older type of Republican candidate without even Schwarzenegger's capacity to throw a curve. Brown hasn't campaigned to indicate such however.

The *Wall Street Journal* just reported on baby steps in Pennsylvania and Kentucky to eliminate one chamber of their legislature. Nebraska went unicameral in 1937. Only Maine seems poised to follow; their House passed it but the Senate whistled suspiciously as it died there. Which reminds me that even the Chicago city council once had two Aldermen in each of the fifty wards. How did they ever dispatch half the grifters in city haul?! A *Chicago Tribune* editorial Monday called, "Somebody Nobody Sent" touts the city's Inspector General Joseph Ferguson's cost-cutting proposals which are a challenge to a council which according to the *Trib* "is warming up to rubber stamp Mayor Richard Daley's I'm-outta-here budget."

This week Britain and France provided an interesting contrast as they made motion to address their own recession/corruption crises. Alan Cowell wrote from Paris in the *New York Times*: "Faced with the prospect of a longer working life until a minimum retirement age of 62 (up from the current 60), a million French citizens took to the streets.... But, confronting government measures promising not only a longer working life but 19 percent cuts in public spending... the British barely seemed to blink." And in the *Financial Times* John Thornhill writes: "Whereas the French seem to regard austerity as an affront to their national identity, the British appear readier to embrace the challenge...." He also quotes Charles de Gaulle, "France cannot be France without grandeur."

These differing notes sounding from Europe, perhaps create harmonic pairs with the different sounding elections of California on one hand, and those in the rest of the country. Don't have to tell you which one harmonizes with France's.

Jerry Brown addendum

Doug Moe in *Brava* magazine, "Lost and Found Francis Ford Coppola," on Brown's last ditch 1980 Presidential primary campaign's live half-hour television special from Madison, Wisconsin that Coppola botched horribly on state-of-the-art video technology, sending up Brown's one time technocratic pretense and cinching Mike Royko's appellation, Governor Moonbeam in the electorate's mind. I remember that the live video images were overlayed and the images frayed badly and you could see through holes in Brown's face as he rambled on against the largest video screen of the day. Why isn't this on *youtube*?

(*originally posted at* The New Vulgate, *No. 69*)

Two Wisconsins

Once into the rhythm of the weekly blog the news and the coverage often presented opportunities toapply my own sense of the context and setting. This was posted at The New Vulgate on Feb. 23, 2011.

I lived in northern Wisconsin for a couple years in the mid-nineties and growing up we always vacationed up there like any normal Illinoisans and often had cause to visit relatives up there, and now a couple of my sisters live there. As close as Wisconsin is it isn't like Illinois, except for those smaller cities that retain heavy industry. Manitowoc and West Allis probably share a lot with Decatur and Peoria, and all those Midwest industrial towns pressured by globalization. But rural Illinois is more grain-based than Wisconsin's agricultural areas which are mostly involved in dairy production.

And then there's Madison – it's a fatal mistake to put the elite University in your state capitol. In Illinois, Champaign-Urbana is where the University of Illinois system is centered and it's exiled at sea in the waves of grain between Chicago and the capitol Springfield. The Illini can't lure the best prep stars away from Chicago and its poli-sci and liberal arts grads don't cluster around the state government for power and money. Springfield is just another minor burg lost in the cornfields of downstate Illinois. As it happens every Illinois grade school kid visits Springfield exactly once to walk through Abe Lincoln's house.

But where do you begin with Madison? It's like the droning low-horizon of Midwestern fortitude applied to the lifestyle goofball radicalism found in Boulder and Berkeley. Madisonites have some idea that the boredom of the Grange or Bob La Follette were virtues to take the edge off of the wackiness of wasting money on fair-trade creature comforts and hare-brained recycling programs that double-down on energy consumption while un-reusable paper and plastic piles up to the sky in tribute to their new improved puritanism.

Up near Minocqua I could listen to three different Public radio stations, one programmed classical music and came from Madison, another was all-civics-all-the-time and came from Madison, and one served the Ojibway from nearby Reserve. These bright signals no doubt cramped the style of the small town country and oldies stations. I listened mostly to the classical, but the "Drum" program of Indian singers was a weekly highlight from the reservation. I listened to the civics station when things were going on or when driving. They featured all the network programs plus "To the Best of Our Knowledge" which was their own political affairs show from Madison. There's always been a tactical Leninist use of boredom, which is actually how the Bolsheviks got their name: Lenin's minority used their "iron buttocks" to delay and lengthen meetings late into the night until anyone with a life had to leave, after which the vote was taken and that minority (the mensheviki) became the Bolsheviki and the majority (the bosheviki) became the Mensheviki as those losers are still known to history. Anyway, this is evidently how they run public radio too.

The uproar in Madison is hard to take serious for anyone who knows the town. It's their dream come true on one hand, another Bring-the-War-Home moment, where they feel certain that they were right after all to stay, and not leave for Boulder or Berkeley. However, the Left cohort of Madison can't relish the evidence that they've been paying to broadcast Public radio in triplicate to all rural corners of the state and have all those hunters, fishermen, and snowmobilers turn on them. The *New York Times* ran a portrait of a Janesville GM employee who's been up and down in his own union job to explain how the public-sector unions have lost solidarity with private union employees:

> "Among the top five employers here are the county, the schools and the city. And that was enough to make Mr. Hahan, a union man from a union town, a supporter of Gov. Scott Walker's sweeping proposal to cut the benefits and collective-bargaining rights of public workers in Wisconsin, a plan that has set off a firestorm of debate and protests at the state Capitol. He says he still believes in unions, but thinks those in the public sector lead to wasteful spending because of what he sees as lavish benefits and endless negotiations. 'Something needs to be done,' he said, 'and quickly.'" (*New York Times*)

Elsewhere, coverage that clouds the difference between public and private reminds one of the routine journalistic erasure of the distinction between legal and illegal immigration. Such reportage might seem unable to account for the crises in the states at all. It seems to me that if Wisconsin Governor Walker, or New Jersey Governor Christie wanted to really attack the civil service and teachers unions they would do what Illinois Governor Quinn was doing, just dig a deeper hole of debt to maintain contracts until any theoretical unsustainability proves itself pronto with a quickened default.

World

In Wisconsin these demonstrators, formerly concerned with violent rhetoric, are not opposing a corporation that they might drive out of business or off-shore. James Taranto at *WSJ.com*, has it that, "The privileged are revolting in Wisconsin." He notes the discordant Marxist analysis coming from Madison public servants, reviews how economist Paul Krugman and others don't admit the distinction, and quotes *Time*'s Joe Klein, "Public employees unions are organized against the might and greed... of the public?"

Mark Guarino in the *Christian Science Monitor* both notes the Governor's radical determination and its roots in a Wisconsin political tradition.

> "The urgency of his agenda just months after the election shows he is eager to take on not just Democrats, but also his own party, much in the tradition of former Gov. Tommy Thompson, whose battles for welfare reform and school choice in his state led the way for national policy changes. Governor Walker served in the state Assembly during the Thompson years. At that time, between 1993 and 2002, he flexed his conservative muscles by supporting welfare reform and a cap on state spending. In his campaign for the governor's office, he ran on a platform critical of state spending and in favor of rolling back state tax increases for small businesses and top earners. He also positioned himself against President Obama in refusing to build a high-speed rail line from Madison to Milwaukee, saying it would be too costly and end up unprofitable...." (*Christian Science-Monitor*)

Guarino even places him with Russ Feingold in Wisconsin's tradition of party mavericks.

The actual issues are both smaller and larger than the demonstrations might indicate. Steven Greenhouse writes in the *New York Times* about this "watershed moment" for Public-sector unions:

> "From Florida to California, many political leaders are seeking to cut the wages and benefits of public-sector workers to help balance strained budgets. But Mr. Walker is going far beyond that, seeking to definitively curb the power of government unions in his state. He sees public-employee unions as a bane to the taxpayer because they demand – and often win – generous health and pension plans that help push up taxes and drive budget deficits higher. To end that cycle, he wants to restrict the unions to bargaining over just one topic, base wages, while eliminating their ability to deal over health care, working hours and vacations." (*New York Times*)

You'd have to move on to the *Wall Street Journal* to understand why he would go so "far." Steven Malanga writes there:

> "Unions use that money not only to run their daily operations but to wage political campaigns in state capitals and city halls. Indeed, public-sector unions especially have become the nation's most aggressive advocates for higher taxes and spending. They sponsor tax-raising ballot initiatives and pay for advertising and lobbying campaigns to pressure politicians into voting for them. And they mount multimillion dollar campaigns to defeat efforts by governors and taxpayer groups to roll back taxes." (*Wall Street Journal*)

David Brooks writes in his *New York Times* column:

> "Private sector unions push against the interests of shareholders and management; public sector unions push against the interests of taxpayers. Private sector union members know that their employers could go out of business, so they have an incentive to mitigate their demands; public sector union members work for state monopolies and have no such interest. Private sector unions confront managers who have an incentive to push back against their demands. Public sector unions face managers who have an incentive to give into them for the sake of their own survival. Most important, public sector unions help choose those they negotiate with." (*New York Times*)

And in the end, one might say, as they succeed they simply give themselves raises and perks. (These "perks" often involve getting out of the classroom in under ten years to some administrative ghost-work when it comes to "teachers," but who knows, perhaps it is worth more money for bureaucrats to do less work.)

Back to that Janesville GM worker's understanding: He notes first that the county, the city, and the schools are three of the top five employers in his town. This means that the public/private balance is tilting toward these "insider" public-sector unions, and despite, or because of his own perilous job situation he understands this danger, that to service these contracts of a growing state workforce the private economy might be beggared and a crisis slide into disaster. The obliviousness of all those smart, "To the Best of Our Knowledge"-listening Madison know-at-alls is, one hopes, galvanizing efforts to reset an economic balance that was set in the postwar years when the American economy was the only one to survive intact and was not pressed by competitors as it is now. Those years of the 1950s thru the 1970s were the real moment of unipolarity was far as economics went because the Soviet Union couldn't actually produce anything by ICBMs, AK47s, tanks, MiGs, and Professors of now extinct sciences of History and Economics.

(originally posted at The New Vulgate, No. 86)

America in the Old Worlds
I wrote this in late 2002, perhaps for the no go website but I think I submitted it somewhere too. It was a response to the hyperpower critique of America and what 9/11 demonstrated. Much has happened in ten years, not least the unlearning of most of that.

Two years ago America got a sudden lesson in China's special sensitivities. Last year we got a crash course in Islam's eternal grievances. And recently Europe has been the plaintiff. The complaints, however, are not as advertised. These aren't discrete dust-ups that might settle if the U.S would only change policy on Taiwan, Jerusalem or bovine growth hormone. The complaints are both deeper and shallower than that. They are decadent swan songs of willful civilizational stasis, if not failure, in the face of what Jean-Jacques Servan-Schreiber was calling the American Challenge over thirty years ago. In mounting defenses against "American jungle capitalism" (a.k.a., globalization, Anglo-Saxon capitalism, *laissez-faire*, the free market, Anarchy, Empire...), these cultures routinely conflate their particular mortifications and general failures with the very essences of their civilizations. Thus, China would seem to become its sum historical victimization by foreign powers; Islam becomes its barricade against modernity; and Europe becomes its corrupt social peace. There are many in these cultures that dissent, or might were the penalty not severe, but a pattern has become clear.

The U.S. is a 226 year old polity, sometimes referred to as a mere teenager among nations, when in truth since WWII it has played the responsible, slow-burn adult in its relations with hypersensitive ancient civilizations. Robert J. Samuelson recently explained about the American advantage, "The disdain for history can be liberating. It focuses us on future opportunities and not past failures and resentments." (*Washington Post*, May 15, 2002) Americans are afforded today the luxury of any such disdain for history only because the founders of this nation wrote the Constitution with an acute awareness of the lessons of history and the limits of human nature. (This is where I would locate Jean Baudrillard's idea of the "radical empiricism" of America, which he contrasts with Europe's "utopian radicalism.") The resulting economic dynamism has largely subsumed aggressive energies into productive enterprise. It has also been subversive enough of immigrant and native folk patterns so that becoming a forward-looking American is far more certain for any immigrant's child than even the founders might have imagined.

America's standing in the world today is further rooted in its initial withdrawal from the Old World, afforded by accident of our geography. The great student of Chicago politics Milton Rakove noted that Irish-Americans were drafted into their historical role in urban American politics by the continental immigrants around them who, still trapped in their Old World feuds and languages, could agree only to trust the Irish, for they were peripheral neutrals in terms of the Old World, and English-speaking intercessors in terms of the New. America, then, has become this Peripheral Neutral writ large (not least back in Ireland itself). In historically immutable terms, there can be no trust between any two of Russia, China, France, Germany, India, Britain, Japan, etc., that isn't built upon a provisional alliance against a third nation, and they know this as clearly as the Chicago rabble knew it.

But because the world's policy debate-of-record is by elites in American terms, in English, and premised on influencing or critiquing American policy, this other-perspective is hidden under all the immaterial fulmination over the *hyperpower's* unilateral neo-imperialist bullying. Americans easily accept this overseas noise because they are a practical people, not arrogant idealists. Further they don't listen to it; they hardly know that what the Gore campaign uploaded into the world media hardware software code that locks all interpretation safely outside of reality. It works for Europe, for Russia, and is now mouthed by Saddam Hussein and Kim Jong-Il as they play for time in the U.N. It is true that when Bush proposed stepping back from all of the entangling treaties and agreements initiated over the Clinton years he was hitting international (including American) elites where they live, but it's also true that in the Street, where non-Davos man lives and works to improve his lot the conversations are fundamentally in sync with American intentions, whatever the vagaries of translation.

America's fictional heroes are generically flawed, scarred and unheralded as they go about their deeds, so an effective American president does not expect to be loved. Doubt and self-criticism are fully acknowledged in the vigorous American debate over proposed actions regarding dirty work dumped at America's door – these are part of the motor of this state. From France, but in America, Baudrillard wrote in 1986:

> "We remain unconvinced by the moral vision Americans have of themselves, but in this we are wrong. When they ask with such seriousness why other peoples detest them, we would be wrong to smile, for it is this same self-examination which makes possible

both the various 'Watergates' and the unrelenting exposure of corruption and their own society's faults in the cinema and the media, a freedom we might envy them, we who are the truly hypocritical societies, keeping our individual and public affairs concealed beneath the bourgeois affectations of secrecy and respectability." (*America*)

After 9/11 this leading *philosophe* responded to the event in isolation without opening the can of worms that is Islam as he had once opened the can of worms that is America. But this self-examination is not self-seeking. It is not used as cover to shunt aside trouble, in part because there is no greater power standing behind America, but also because Americans have become a practical, problem-solving people looking to apply themselves to such matters.

Other nations were built anew on discovered continents yet only one stands as the symbolic incarnation of socioeconomic modernity. And the U.S. is not merely Canada plus blacks, or Brazil minus subtitles. It is a carefully engineered polity that upon independence first erred on the side of decentralization with the Confederated States of America, and only then edged carefully to a more complete federalization as the United States of America. (This movement is the reverse motion of every other nation-state – they struggle to open up to a freedom that seems counterintuitive, while the U.S. has over its history gradually traded freedom for increased security.) The classical lines of American constitutional government have been warped regularly of course, most notably in response to the great wars: Civil War, World War I, World War II, and the Cold War, while The New Deal, the Great Society, and the Legal Services Corporation have also pushed the federal, state and municipal governments even further into American lives.

We have lost more than enough of our classical republic and the free space it left its citizens to warrant Pat Buchanan's warning/lament, *A Republic, Not an Empire*, but might it really have been otherwise? Not in this world. Not the way our political parties meet and circle in the center, devising joint rationales for a larger state that heads off supposed contending social catastrophes. And not with the relentless, accelerating integration of the world – something seen as very nearly *the* macro American product. The U.S. is probably the one nation on earth that could wall off its economy and withdraw into an isolationist Valhalla. It has the natural resources, the space, the native population and the immigrants to do it. The patriots who bid her do this were truly America Firsters. But WWII and Soviet expansion determined that America would see itself as thrust into Metternich's shoes, and no willed pretense that we were still running around our Eden in Daniel Boone's moccasins could be sustained. America might have let Hitler, Stalin, Mussolini, Tojo, and Mao sate themselves o'er there and profited quite handsomely or not at all; but the call the Old World has on U.S. policy, though necessarily diluted, nevertheless precludes indifference. There are Americans from every nation of the Old World with residual sympathies, plus there is the general sense among Americans that they are who they are precisely because their ancestors found such tyrannies intolerable. Conversely, the unusual resonance of the world response to 9/11 was in part recognition by the world of the stake they have in America. And perhaps as well, we know in our bones that the free market (merely an ideal but a useful north star for navigation) will in the end knit together mankind the world over the way it has done here.

The American Left opposed the foreign interventions of the Rightist Reagan and Bush administrations' 12 years, only to discover their own more righteous criteria led to even more military operations abroad during the Clinton administration's 8 years. Secretary of State Albright was either fretting about unspecified dangers of a uni-polar world (she had a Republican White House in mind) or chiding a reluctant U.S. military before endless police-action opportunities with the question, "Well why do we have this big military?"

Might the U.S. have passed on military intervention in Bosnia or Kosovo as it did in Rwanda? Hardly. It's now considered an unconscionable dereliction of our moral military duty to have not "done something" about Rwanda in 1996 if not already by 1994. But the naïve, feel-good, catastrophe in Somalia had just stung both the Bush and Clinton administrations. Apparently we got over the Somalia syndrome in a fraction of the time it took to get over the Vietnam syndrome. And Democrats were most vociferous in their post-9/11 judgment that the problem was we had left Afghanistan after the Soviet withdrawal, not that we had been there in the first place. And so this time it's agreed: we'll stay. Will this apply in Iraq? Colombia? Indonesia? Zimbabwe? When the Chinese start breaking bottles of Dragon Seal over the prows of their new blue-water fleet how will the U.S. respond when Vietnam and the Philippines invite its navy back to Cam Ranh and Subic bays?

Might we opt out of it all? The dueling rationales of what I'll call the political right and left – the mainstream divide – don't appear to leave room for that option. The idealistic right and left – Buchanan and Nader in the last election – insisting that there is an entirely different reality possible if we'd all just insist on it, barely count in the domestic realm where everyone is a citizen bound by the same laws. And they count not at all in international affairs where the leaders of other states – some elected, most not – come upon you as strangers in a wilderness (though all seem to wear Italian suits).

There's also the CNN-NGO effect, wherein news-video of sundry horrific injustice and the charged testimony of competing professional do-gooders send us into Ethiopia, Somalia or the Sahel. America seems inevitably culpable by action or omission, and once the world's better half-wits seize the moral high ground they spin to the magnetic north of American power and wealth and we intervene just the same. They'd prefer we lead with wealth transfers and U.N. personnel, but social breakdown or tyrannical subjugation tends to require more. It matters little that massive infusions of foodstuffs caused the collapse of agriculture in an Ethiopia, leading her farmers to abandon their fields for the city's shantytowns, upon which the desert has advanced on such untended fields in east Africa.

After the attacks on the World Trade Center and Pentagon, American military advisors spread through Latin America, Africa, Arabia, Central Asia, and East Asia because they alone are trusted. China's diplomatic gambit to counter American influence in Central Asia and seal off its restive Muslim province of Xinjiang, the Shanghai 5 (China, Russia, Kyrgyzstan, Tajikistan, Khazakstan, and later, Uzbekistan), was so much paper blown away after 9/11. But Russia and China both, forced to respond immediately to the attack on America, revealed their most honest assessment of American power – they trust it.

This is not to say they like it, or that they could ever admit so. But conventional Western wisdom expected they would object strenuously to the basing of American forces and advisors near their borders in Central Asia and they did not. Neither have they drawn additional troops to their borders to counter the Americans. (There were minor and temporary Chinese movements.) Instead Russia and China have further legitimized the American effort because it allowed each to repaint their own more controversial military operations in the Caucasus and Xinjiang in the universally respected colors of the American operation. But again, this doesn't mean that China, the one still-rising other-power today, would beg off seeking to impose a *Pax Cinesa* upon a world from which America withdrew; it just means their leadership fervently but silently hopes America does not, for in truth they do not secretly individually trust their own polity with such power. (Though formally, they do seek it.) For now China remains, as its Army Colonels Qiao Liang and Wang Xiangsui put it in a recent paper, "a junior student in international affairs... learning to be a global power." They contend that China is not up to speed in terms of the diplomatic response time demanded by the modern world and so after 9/11, "[f]aced with this emergency, S.C.O. members (formerly, The Shanghai 5) could not even come up with a common position. Instead, they declared their support for the U.S. anti-terrorist campaign individually." (*Asia Times,* 7.31.2002)

Necessarily Pakistan's response came more quickly, and India's followed aggressively lest they lose ground with America to their hated neighbor. As *Stratfor*'s analysis has it: "Since the start of the U.S.-led war against terrorism, China's position in Central Asia has rapidly waned as several countries have opened their doors to the United States. Now India is trying to ride in on the U.S. coattails and establish a position in an area vital to its security and energy interests." (*Stratfor.com,* Aug. 9, 2002)

Despite the reflexive re-calculations of self-interest by these nations, the deeper truth, suspected after witnessing the U.S.'s behavior after the falls of Eastern Europe and the Soviet Union, was now revealed suddenly post-9/11: They trust American power.

So what, then, is all this complaining about? When it is about the Kyoto Agreement, or the ABM treaty, or S.D.I., or the International Criminal Court (I.C.C.), or globalization, what is it really about? And what is the drive to herd the nations of Europe into a superstate union about?

When it's "about" the spy plane, it's really about political advantage *outside* American terms (and generally outside the English language as well). It's about China in its struggle with its island neighbors in the Pacific, in its struggle with India along the Himalayas and now in Central Asia, in its struggle with Taiwan, Russia, South Korea and Japan too, but more fundamentally it's about China in its struggle with itself as it attempts to escape its stasis, the vulnerability and the convulsive violence of its past, to reach a politically stable Chinese modernity.

In the Middle-East it's about temporal states and enterprises desperate to fend off the one challenge they cannot survive, that from their own faith which, to date, simply cedes no standing to any state or business outside the Mosque. The behavior of the Palestinian Authority, Iraq, Iran, the Taliban, the Saudis, Syria, Algeria, Libya, etc., only seems senseless in ahistorical future-focused American terms. In terms of the closed world they inhabit and fear leaving, they behave in the only way open to them. Unlike the Chinese or Europeans, Muslims do not see a version of modernity for themselves. And the dynamism of the West now precludes for the Islamic world a Reformation on their own terms; unfortunately for their core cultural pride, we are their Reformation. Iran under the Shah, and Lebanon were attempts at modernity and thus drew the wrath of the faithful. And Israel continues to draw assaults from within the Umma that manage to be both hysterical, like movie Indians after pioneers, and reflexive, like antibodies after bacterium.

When the U.S.S.R. collapsed, the mujahedeen believed that it was their achievement, and the Muslim world generally misunderstood it too. They then dared believe the West itself might fall if pushed. Only a severely cloistered culture might think so. But the Russians had decided they no longer needed the communist pretense which once assuaged its brutality by feeding Russians' wounded pride with dreams of leading humanity into a socialist modernity only they truly saw. Instead, the Russians, seeing East Asians demonstrate that capitalism was not a rigged Western scheme, and seeing that the Mongols and Germans were not poised to return, and that the Americans were opening up to accelerating social, technological, and economic changes, simply decided they wished to be "a normal country." The Party leadership, long lapsed in its faith, saw on Tiananmen Square in 1989, soon after Gorbachev had attended the state funeral of Hu Yaobang, what would be required to sustain the dead system in power and blanched. The Russians have been through several rough phases already and there will be more, but Russia is a different nation after a dozen years – one no longer fighting off its own potential in submission to an archaic orthodoxy.

The severity of the secular-military authority in Turkey may now be seen more clearly for what it has been: a willed Reformation within a single Muslim nation-state, the one that remained of the Ottoman Empire when it collapsed after World War I. Mustafa Kemal Ataturk, a General-turned-President, staunched the bleeding of Ottoman territory to the victorious European powers, and then commenced his Reformation. Ataturk ended the Caliphate in 1924 and disestablished Islam in 1928. Women were enfranchised in 1934. A Latin alphabet replaced Arabic script and a European legal system replaced the Islamic one. Pre-9/11 it seemed hypersensitive and illiberal of the Turkish parliament to prohibit the wearing of scarves by women deputies, but now perhaps we see instead that they are steeled against a totalitarian Islamist mindset whereby in any voluntary system those women who choose not to cover invite attack were *any* women allowed to cover their hair.

The development of the modern corporation in the Islamic world was derailed by the Quran's detailed inheritance laws, which limit development of large-scale capital-intensive enterprise to the shortest lifespan of any single partner (Prof. Timur Kuran via Virginia Postrel, *New York Times*, Nov. 10, 2002). The level of detail in the Quran thus precludes a faith-observant modernity. Without a Reformation, the logic of Islam is totalitarian and, more to our concern, Muslims in the West are left to understand their own emigration as the seeding of the lands of the Infidel for an enlarged Ummah. With no internal modernizing dynamic, they are left in all their numbers fundamentalists, latent fundamentalists or covert atheists. Judaism and Christianity have small fundamentalist sects, but even these are reconciled to playing their role in pluralistic, modern societies. Whereas the small liberal circles within the Ummah cannot yet stand up to the stasis of Islam. This was demonstrated most clearly in Iran where the (Marxist) Tudeh Party and middle class university students managed to pull down the Shah only to lose their revolution to the logic of the Quran: rule by Mullahs.

Bat Yeor, an Egyptian Jewess writing from London, reminds us that Christians, Jews, and others in the Islamic world are *dhimmi*, which is to say non-citizens without possession of even what few rights are held by the Islamic faithful. She blames the Muslim elite for concealing this doctrine (alive in Sudan, Nigeria, Iran, Pakistan, Indonesia, and now felt in the West via the impact the terrorists are having on daily life), and she blames the West for its "collective cowardice" in forgetting it a hundred years ago so as to more easily sustain its economic, and geostrategic interests through the colonial period, the world wars, and the Cold War. (*National Review*, Aug. 9, 2002) Today this cover-up is further encouraged by the Western elite's doctrine of multi-culturalism, which to date still appears to trump other elite doctrines such as feminism, civil libertarianism, and pacifism.

In the meantime regimes across the Islamic world shake in fear of the West, and their own young, and their women, thus reinforcing the logic of Sharia, which alone offers refuge from the challenge of modernity, as well as relief from their own corrupt satrapies. In the formulation of Moroccan sociologist Fatema Mernissi from her book, *Islam and Democracy – Fear of the Modern World,*

> "The Muslim man had to be alert, on the defensive, with one eye on the hudud (boundary) that hemmed in the women, the other on the frontiers of the empire. What happens when the two boundaries give way, and both at the same time?"

She continues,

> "Democracy... is not as new as the imams proclaim. What it is is repressed. Democracy in this sense is not foreign to the Muslim East; it is an infected wound that the East has been carrying for centuries.... The West is frightening because it obliges the Muslims to exhume the bodies of all the opponents, both religious and profane, intellectuals and obscure artisans, who were massacred by the

caliphs, all those who were condemned like the Sufis and the philosophers, because, the palace said, they talked about foreign ideas from Greece, India, and ancient Persia." (*Islam and Democracy*)

It is the unique tragedy of the Islamic world that to choose any measure of modernity is so easily demagogued as surrender to the West or Christendom or Zionism or Satan.

Lebanon was once a beautiful country - an imperfect, ethnically gerrymandered democracy, but modern with promise. What was Lebanon's destruction "about"? Well... what stops Palestinians from taking their West Bank and turning it into an international business hub, a banking capitol? Their movement has been a Marxian-nationalist one, rather than a religious one - many in their leadership are nominally Christian. Israel is a high tax state; the Quran forbids charging interest thus complicating banking in the rigidly Islamic states around them; and Beirut, once the banking capital of the Arab world, is history. It would seem there is one unending world of opportunity surrounding these lucky Palestinians.

Such a scenario is prevented, not so much by the true history of the Palestinians as by the lies they tell themselves. They have lost faith in themselves and they are impractical. So they focus instead on a blind, blundering stratagem against "Amreeka" and its puppet "the Zionist Entity" (despite the fact that they too trust American power - they consider it naïve, even!).

Now the nationalist Palestinians are losing control of their movement to the Jihadis in the pay of Iran and Saudi Arabia. And Islam's influence encourages the destruction of any sign of modernity in its midst for such beacons no matter how dim illuminate things and choices beyond the Quran's Great List, and beyond their nationalist tyrannies - things and choices that all people want, even the faithful of Islam.... That's what the destruction of Lebanon was about.

The Chechens are another nominally Islamic nationality with even clearer grievances than the Palestinians but similarly left flogging a cause lost to the Jihad. When Tsar Alexander II annexed Chechnya in 1859 it had been an independent "island" for decades, surrounded by Russia and its earlier annexations, Dagestan and Georgia. Chechens ignored the new Soviet regime after 1920, but were subject to repeated punitive campaigns, to disarm in 1925, and to force collectivization in 1930. Then, during WWII, after the Soviets lost the Caucuses for several months to the Nazis, Stalin ordered Beria to deport the Chechens, among many others, to Central Asia and Siberia. Nicolas Werth writes that it took "194 convoys of 64 trucks for the deportation on 23-28 February 1944 of 521,247 Chechens and Ingush." (*The Black Book of Communism*) What Chechens survived the trek and the dozen years in exile, began to return to Chechnya in the late fifties only to find Russians in their houses.

In late 1991, just before the dissolution of the U.S.S.R., the Chechens declared independence. The new Russian Republic ignored the declaration until it sought to stop the loss of formerly Soviet territory at the boundaries of the Russian Federation. The new Chechen President, retired Soviet air force General Dzokhar Dudayev, raised a Chechen army and it shocked a Russian column sent blithely into downtown Grozny to reassert Russian rule. But after the slaughter and an agreement that booted the question of independence down the road, who showed up but the mujahedeen fighters victorious in Afghanistan determined to the Muslims of the Caucuses. In this period of tacit independence the mujahedeen launched deadly and pointless attacks into Russian Dagestan, while in the chaos of liberated Chechnya the ancient bandit culture of mountain clans reasserted itself, kidnapping any foreigners they found: reporters, U.N. aid workers, construction teams, friends of Chechnya.... Whether Chechens were responsible for the apartment bombings in Russian cities in 1999, their mujahedeen pals have proven themselves just as likely the culprits. The new Russian President Putin was thereby handed an opportunity to define himself and his nation. And woe unto Chechnya. The recent seizure of 700 hostages in a Moscow theater just further debases the sad, lost cause of Chechen nationalism.

Stephen Schwartz, an author who went to the Balkans in 1990 never having heard the term Wahhabi, reports that as desperate for help as Muslims were in Bosnia-Hercegovina, Kosovo, Macedonia, Montenegro, Serbia, and Albania, they were quickly very suspicious of the Saudis and their Wahhabi pressure upon traditional Balkan Islam. Schwartz later found similar stories in Chechnya, Uzbekistan, and Tajikistan. "Chechens, Bosnians, and Albanians are all condemned by Wahhabism to death for the alleged crime of 'grave-worship,' i.e. honoring and praying for intercession by Islamic saints." Schwartz is sympathetic to the claim of Uzbekistan President Islam Karimov, much criticized in the West for human rights violations, that only Wahhabis are being repressed rather than the Sufi-derived "folk-Islam" of the Uzbeks. In a recent speech in support of his book, *The Two Faces of Islam: The House of Sa'ud from Tradition to Terror*, Schwartz noted an interesting parallel:

> "I have flattered myself in saying that I learned about Wahhabism the way George Orwell learned about Stalinism. Orwell did not go to Moscow; he went to Barcelona, where he witnessed the nefarious

activities of the Soviet secret police. I did not go to Riyadh to study Wahhabism; I witnessed the attempt of Wahhabi-Saudi agents to take over Balkan Islam." (Stephen Schwartz)

Srdja Trifkovic parses The Tradition, a formal blueprint for Islamic government, based on the Quran, written in the 11th Century by Abu Ala Al-Mawardi, and places it in the context of what had been happening to Christians in the Byzantine Empire, and what has happened since to dhimmi living under that Tradition. He too finds a parallel to last century's totalitarian threat:

> "Recent attempts by Islamic apologists to assure the West that only the 'spiritual' definition of Jihad really applies amount to distorting history.... The author quite correctly admits that 'in Qura'anic terms, peace does not only mean absence of war, it is also a positive state of security in which one is free from anxiety or fear.' He does not specify, however, that this state of security is only available in Dar el-Islam, once Islam defeats its enemies and conquers their lands. This is exactly the same definition of 'peace' as that used by the Soviet empire... it is the objective, but it is fully attainable only after the defeat of 'imperialism as the final stage of capitalism' and the triumph of the vanguard of the proletariat in the whole world.
>
> What matters to non-Muslims today, and to non-Communists 60 years ago, is not the metaphysical meaning of 'Peace" within the community of believers, but the consequences of their definition for the rest of us...." (*National Review*, June 5, 2002)

Trifkovic goes on to note that modern Christians "outlawed Crusading" and calls on Muslims to do same regarding Jihad.

Muslims who have framed their lives within modernity will not be able to live in a modern Islamic society until they are able to create institutions capable of facing down their fundamentalists. That a group of Middle Eastern intellectuals would produce an unvarnished assessment of the Islamic world such as the recent U.N.-commissioned Arab Human Development Report is a positive sign. Its authors soft-pedal much of the data, seeming to focus on the positives of Bahrain or Morocco, but in several summary sidebars the urgency can be felt, as in Jordanian Senator Leila Sharaf's:

> "The essence of the modern state, which we have failed to estab-

lish to date, is what has come to be termed 'good governance'....
It is no longer possible to delay the establishment of the pluralistic, democratic state in our Arab world because we need the benefits that such a state provides – good governance...."
(*U.N. Arab Human Development Report*)

Perhaps the neo-cons are right and occupied Japan and Germany are useful models for an approach to Iraq. Certainly a righted Muslim nation that could conduct elections and routinize its civic order around all those U.N. human rights charters and declarations the present corrupt tyrannies of the Islamic didn't hesitate to sign (the U.N. report has a chart showing which Arab nations have signed onto which covenant) would be a worthy experiment and a positive pressure on the rest. If the modernist minority can dramatize its demands and survive they will surely find that a majority of those in the street, Muslim men and women, want to live in "a normal country."

And then there is the French mode of pro forma complaint, whereby say, once NATO is set up in Paris 1949 largely for its defense (West Germany is occupied; Britain safely across the channel), France refuses to place its forces under NATO's command and then finally withdraws! It is a thing of beauty to have others do your dirty work, but to then step away and object to how they do it – *très sublime!* Psychology aside, what this accomplished for De Gaulle's France, still a pompous colonial power, was to allow her to posture sympathetically before the Soviet empire, the third world, and Mao's China free of the baggage of NATO and *Le Défi Américan*. For when a great power *must* do dirty work in the international commons, Macchiavelli would surely advise any secondary power to make that great power pay a price lest it amass credit for the further use of its power. By a similar dynamic any I.C.C. would certainly specialize in pulling American soldiers and policy-makers into the dock, so as to allow American power to do the dirty work but then erase any credit for the job done.

A couple weeks after 9/11 Yale Professor Lamin Sanneh made a curious and unique point in the *New York Times* suggesting that America might better disarm Islamic zealots by less zealously separating church and state at home – the American Challenge as seen from Mecca, then, is an atheistic, hence Satanic, threat rather than a challenge-by-example from among the friendly neighborhood people of the Book. No doubt the professor speaks for those Muslims who have emigrated to the 21st Century without contemplating certain contradictions that may have slipped into their luggage. Better, maybe, to stress the cost of modernity itself to America. Modernity is not American, of course, though as an energetic nation of immigrants we have most completely interfaced with it on its pitiless terms. Immigrants have come to America one by one to improve the prospects for themselves and their children, yet one by one they regret losing their children to America. Watching their children swim away into the deep sea of American possibility is heartbreaking for the first generation immigrant on an existential scale as first the language of the old country, then the culture, then the frame of reference, and finally the backstory of the family itself dissipate until that immigrant in his old age knows that all he knows will end with him.

Even a native-born American in his thirties typically finds that his childhood home or neighborhood is already gone with the winds of our restlessly dynamic economy. (The very likelihood that an adult American has lived in a succession of homes since childhood is a measure of the cost modernity asks.) But the motion and energy of our modern savage jungle capitalism tempers alienation and reaction with hope and "the pursuit of happiness." Why, when there are so many American possibilities, would one obsess on hating a neighbor and nurse that grudge into a lifelong death-match? Many a century-old flat in American cities has been a way station for a succession of German-, Irish-, Italian-, Polish-, African-, and Mexican-American families on their way from "quiet lives of desperation" to somewhat louder, more enjoyable American lives.

The North's victory ended the American Civil War in 1865 in a way that the Turks' victory over the Serbs in Kosovo in 1389 will never end. After Tito and after communism the Southern Slavs had a choice: Race each other to the good life, or try to settle ancient grievances once and for all. They chose to re-fight their Antietam; it wasn't unanimous, but neither did Milosevic force it on them.

China, confident of its centrality as the Middle Kingdom, chose administrative stability centuries ago, thus locking down its roiling mercantile energies just as the fractious West embarked on its "capital-intensive, energy-intensive, land-gobbling 'European Miracle,'" as author Kenneth Pomeranz refers to it in his book, *The Great Divergence*. He soft-pedals the evidence of divergence itself (as per Western, modern multicultural etiquette), finally discounting cultural factors entirely for geography to explain whatever it is that may or may not have diverged.

Today the Chinese communists open up a once utterly closed down economy and seem to understand this process is a prerequisite for national security and implicitly as well for a stable Chinese modernity. The Party seems even to want some measure of democratic assent for their mandate of heaven. The Chinese people, meanwhile, gravitate in dramatic numbers to Christianity, the believers numbers approaching a hundred million in a decade from the small underground church that somehow survived Maoism. These Chinese seem to understand their society's need for some new basis of civic trust to replace the old Maoist code and the older clan-based one. To freely associate with each other as citizens of a modern state they will have to trust each other as if they were one clan, rather than mere strangers – "marks" they expect to never see again. These developments are cause for optimism, but consider the difficulty Americans have maintaining the transparency and efficiency of their market structures, and extrapolate this to a country where the exchanges are as new as the companies listed. And everyone involved – shareholders, directors, boardmembers, regulators, banks – must learn every lesson from scratch.

What is not cause for optimism is that this is happening in a China with an unhealthy fixation on what they consider their national humiliation. Wang Jian, Secretary General of the Economic Planning Commission, Beijing, summarized geopolitical fundamentals in his recent paper, "US-China-EU: An Exercise in Asymmetry":

> "Looking into the 15 years ahead, after a rough calculation, the total population of Japan, Hong Kong, South Korea, Taiwan, mainland China, plus the Russian Far East... is about 1.7 billion, and GDP is $25 trillion. With the expansion of the European Union, its population will reach 500 million, its GDP $21 trillion; in NAFTA, the population is 400 million, and GDP about $19 trillion. Therefore, the world structure after the Cold War is a pattern of 'a world in three', and the largest economic zone is the West Pacific Economic Zone. In light of this, we should find a new starting point to study China's strategy."
> (Heartland/*Asia Times*, July 5, 2002)

As dry as the piece reads, its implications may be quite wet. The Chinese, like the Arabs, are a race, rather than a nation. They will invite enormous tragedy and retard their move into modernity if they continue to covet in part or whole lands once ruled by ancient dynasties. Most maps printed in China feature as China parts of Siberia, Mongolia, Tajikistan, Vietnam, Taiwan, Tibet, Nepal, Sikkim, Bhutan, Kashmir, India, the Sengkakus, the Paracels, and the Spratlys.

The Russians were slaves (Slavs), the French peasants, the English yeoman, and the Americans freemen; each culture bears the marks of its history and choices. But modernity did not begin in America and it exists outside American terms. If the American debate recognized that, perhaps the issues that confront these ancient civilizations would not be so loaded with the prospect of conceding to our teenage country that which they can never concede. Recent good news for most of the world is that as Islam fails and projects its failure out onto the infidels, we are reminded of just what we have achieved and what we must defend.

Arab Explanationalism

The breakthrough in Tunisia became an Arab Spring which caught the Turks, the Iranians, President Obama, the EU and others as they were attempting to build new relationships with these regimes premised on the idea that Bush was wrong, there would be no change in that part of the world. Most were nimble enough, but not so the specialists of Arab Studies departments safely in the West. Posted at NV in April, 2011.

At this hinge moment in the history of the Middle East there's a steady stream of discordantly irrelevant concern on the part of some Arab intellectuals, re what this all means for the west's Orientalist paradigms as understood and policed by the academic orphans of the late Professor Edward Said. One would think they might drop such needlepoint and rush to whatever nation they are in exile from, to pitch in and help make of their home country some place worth staying in. But rather these folks are obsessed with what these revolutions, however they turn out, might mean to their enemies cross campus, cross-town, or across the Potomac. In *Bookforum*, Hussein Ibish, senior research fellow at the American Task Force on Palestine, contributes to such instantly dated self-abnegation with, "Under Western Lies – The popular uprisings in Arab nations should bury some long-standing Orientalist myths," which proudly notes all the many Said and Foucault investigations and demonstrations of how the "Western imagination conjured the Arab street into being." Ibish continues:

> "Such traditional attitudes have routinely received new glosses in the Orientalist literature on what is purported to be a closed and rigidly change-averse 'Arab mind.' This body of work usually bears the appearance of dispassionate cultural inquiry – but its authors are expressing essentially medieval anxieties about the mortal threat that Arab or Muslim power presents to the West."
> (*Bookforum*, Apr-May 2011)

At *Qantara.de*, a Germany-based site focused on "dialogue with the Islamic world," a portrait of the Algerian novelist Maissa Bey traces her ideas on the prospects for democracy based on what she saw in Algeria during the decade of terror that began with the 1991 coup that prevented the Islamist party winner of Algeria's first election from taking office. Bey appreciates her country's caution today but tells Martina Sabra, "The Algerians now know that Islamism is not the answer. This is a realisation that puts us a stage ahead of other revolutions in the Arab world." Sabra writes that Bey considers Europe's relations with Arab dictatorships "preposterous" and then the piece goes off onto this much more comforting tangent:

> "It is really bizarre that Europe is only now wakening up. I find this absolutely intolerable... As an Algerian citizen, I can tell you that we didn't need any *Wikileaks* to tell us what was going on. Everybody knew that the Arab leaders were illegally amassing large fortunes for themselves and allowing their people to suffer. How can it be that this Europe, that so prides itself on its ideals of human rights and liberty, kept so quiet for so long, and only opened its mouth after the people themselves had risen? ...We intellectuals expect nothing more from Europe." (*Qantara.de*, Apr 1, 2011)

That'll be the day. An academic might say she's upset because Europe treated Algeria as if it had agency of its own. I might say she's upset that George Bush didn't invade her country. (I noted early instances of this weird preoccupation in *NV* 89.)

Algeria is particularly interesting in that its successful guerrilla war for independence from France meant that its agency was actually hard-earned. In fact, this authentic triumph over a European colonial power may have lead its own leadership class of heroic veterans to be so unyielding to its own people. Surely this is not how they imagined they'd rule when they dreamed of a post-French Algeria.

Gideon Rachman in the *Financial Times* puts it, "It's 1989, but we are the Russians." Being a properly sensitive modern western European Rachman immediately shores up Arab agency vis-à-vis the old east European slave nations:

> "The good news is that this is the Arab 1989. The bad news is that we are the Soviet Union. An exaggeration? Certainly. But there is enough truth in the analogy to explain why both the US and the European Union are uneasy about revolutions that - on one level - promote core western values, such as democracy and individual rights. Much of the corrupt and autocratic order that is wobbling so badly in the Middle East was western-backed. The sponsorship was nowhere near as brutal or as overt as the Soviet repression of eastern Europe. And there have always been anti-western regimes, such as Iran and Syria...."
> (*Financial Times*, Apr 4, 2011)

Western-backed, client states, allies, colonies, puppet regimes, little brown brothers, apes, pigs....

France certainly could have granted Algeria its independence more helpfully but you know they were having a bad century. The British might have left border-drawing to some local Sultan or King to come up with but you've heard the *BBC*, the Brits are just a little too interested in the world to leave it alone. However, to hear the Iraq and Afghanistan efforts routinely called after that colonial era, or now have them ignored so as to allow calls for more airpower in some other godforsaken corner of the Ummah invites derision.

It seems as if only Christopher Hitchens is boorish enough to as he puts it, advance "the quaint belief that the removal of two of the worst regimes in the region – the Taliban and the Iraqi Baath Party – did not have nothing to do with the subsequent democracy 'wave'..." He writes this in his *Slate* critique of Karzai's amplifying the recent response to an obscure Quran burning to a murderous level, and he compares this to his earlier responsible response to an alleged Quran desecration at Guantanamo. Hitchens notes what he calls "the same old dreary formula: self-righteous frenzy married to a neurotic need to take offense." Certainly this pays locally there, in some way we cannot control. But that such pays here we really ought to try to control. Islam after all sat out reformation, renaissance and revolution. As a result it is a civilization now experiencing a challenge from a fully-formed modernity as if it were a cold bath. And worse, the threatening figure of the West is now reinforced by the rising Far East.

All the bloody battles fought over centuries to remove the Church from western governance were part of a necessary process. One which has barely begun for the removing of the Mosque from the palace or parliament. There is a great reactionary temptation for the Arab or Muslim intelligentsia to hide its need of the West's modernity by focusing on the West's failings, which are there, of course, but after reformation, renaissance and revolution, mistakes become part of the machinery of progress.

The Said folks managed to conquer the university departments, but they found there isn't much one can do from an American university, especially after al-Qaeda succeeded in vaulting the Arab world's powerful weakness onto our plate. (China had been first on our plate on Sept. 10th.) 9/11 brought many of the best minds in the West – academics, journalists, do-it-yourself wise-asses, and dramatic plain-talking refugee-writers like Ayaan Hirsi Ali and Bat Ye'or – treading all over their hallowed conquered discipline. They won their tenured positions quite easily with their ethnic trump-card bluff because western academia was in a decadent phase of radical dementia: deconstruction, identity politics, etc. Turns out they don't like attention from outside the academy. And even their once submissive academy is tightening up a bit, under pressure from Chinese economic and intellectual and cultural success.

All Said really wanted was for Arab studies departments in the West to be staffed by Arabs. Unlike Women's studies and African-American studies programs, which were brand new and staffed with women and blacks, Arab studies were time-honored departments that focused on language and history and were staffed with doddering old obsessives creeping around musty collections of ancient manuscripts and dusty relics in what was then an academic graveyard. Suddenly these quiet old professors were rudely pushed aside by race-baiting Palestinian activists full to the brim with self-esteem.

Bad enough I suppose, but given the slow sinking-in-on-itself of Arab civilization since it failed to enter Europe at Vienna and Andalusia, even the refugee Arab intellectuals who've been able to clamber into the wonderland of American and European university or western governmental bureaucracy life seem unable to redirect their attention at this moment. They've measured their achievement since the Munich Olympics by how successfully they manage to make Arab problems our concern, as that is far easier than getting down to work in their own lands. The gerontocratic condition of their old world culture made this understandable, but now there is a break in history and that weight might lift and what do they first think of?

They seem to be trying to prove something as small as that they understand their people better than we do. Who cares? This is not something that was the first order of business for the Japanese, Hong Kong, Singapore, the South Koreans, the Taiwanese, the Thai, the Chinese, and the Indians. They made their peace with the world and got down to work bettering their lots. If Arabs do not do this, it will have little to do with what any American or European thinks or says or does; that is their fear I guess. And no doubt they can find many colleagues in academia encouraging them to not to try. But we can hardly be faulted for noting what takes place or fails to take place from this point on. Someone has to pay attention.

(originally posted at The New Vulgate, No. 92)

Egypt, and Step on It!
Written for the New Vulgate *as the Arab Spring stand-off in Cairo took over cable-news coverage. Posted on Feb. 9, 2011.*

It took someone named Crook to get down to some reality about what the President, or the US, or the West, or Anderson Cooper should do about Egypt. In his *Financial Times* column, "Stop carping at a wise wariness," Clive Crook summarizes the two opposing critical positions which demand either Western support for Mubarak-our-ally or the forces-of-change-in-the-street, then writes:

> "On two things, though, most critics agree. The right course of action for the US was (and still is) apparent; and Mr Obama's decisions, when he finally makes some, will drive the outcome. The last 10 days of fervid debate among US foreign policy experts have circled around these premises. Both are delusional. This thinking puts US choices at the centre of everything, so you might call it a distinctively American delusion. Surprisingly, this too would be a mistake. The same notions – that the choices are clear, and that decisions in Washington will influence more than tangentially what happens in Cairo – hold sway abroad as well. Many who would usually question the US instinct to take charge suddenly want it to...." (*Financial Times*)

What he's describing is something like courtiers and anti-courtiers colliding yet sparking darkness rather than light. I suspect that darkness is useful somehow in the day-to-day of the careers involved, and not just these TV Anchors – Anderson Cooper isn't the only one who deserves ten punches to the head. Frank Rich's Sunday *New York Times* column, "Wallflowers at the Revolution," infers we should be more involved except when he complains we were famously too involved; that's rich. The dissonance accounts for the strange passivity of his column's meaninglessness. (Note to self: Check Rich's past columns. Response to self: Do I have to?) Frank ain't risking a single punch to the head so instead he's upset at his TV again:

> "We can't get enough of revolution video – even if, some nights, Middle West blizzards take precedence over Middle East battles on the networks' evening news. But more often than not we have little or no context for what we're watching. That's the legacy of years of self-censored, superficial, provincial and at times Islamophobic coverage of the Arab world in a large swath of American news media." (*New York Times*)

David Remnick in the *New Yorker* prefers to re-fight the last war even though he lost it:

> "In November, 2003, eight months after the U.S.-led invasion of Iraq began, George W. Bush seemed to break with years of realist orthodoxy, saying, 'Are the peoples of the Middle East somehow beyond the reach of liberty? Are millions of men and women and children condemned by history or culture to live in despotism? Are they alone never to know freedom and never even to have a choice in the matter?' Meanwhile, Bush was pressing the Egyptians not so much to democratize their politics as to rent their torture chambers." (*New Yorker*)

Touché, maybe..., or maybe not. Did the U.S.S.R. fall in the Sinai, or Tehran, or Gdansk, or Kabul, or Managua, or merely inside the Kremlin?

With no Court and no King, history becomes everyone's stories massed and there is no author. Who cares about that! Give us Tales of Great Men and their concubines. Our great journalists, analysts and academicians need a white whale to measure themselves against. They've lurched from Reagan to Bush to... Palin, all the while dreaming they are stopping incipient American fascism like they did with Nixon or Humphrey or somebody..., meanwhile Mubarak's been in Cairo all this time, if that's this story.

This lack of whale was the prime disadvantage the doctrine of Anarchism has always had in communicating through history. People might ask, How do you survive invasions by the Sovereign next door, or of his unhappy desperate millions?, but what the folk really didn't understand might've been, Who will we blame?, or Do I have to attend regular meetings? One doesn't really get an endorphin kick from replacing the Tsar with merely a free people if you're in the story-telling business, and it can take a long time for a race-culture, even one as mixed as the Russians, to give up on grand world-historical religio-national missions.

I grew up fascinated enough with the Boris Badenov Bolsheviks to figure out that what they really capitalized on was the people's instinct for fealty – too many simply begged to have history written in their blood. And the Mensheviks and Tolstoyans and others couldn't manage to convincingly explain what-all people might achieve for themselves were they to declare themselves as other than The People: raw material for some genius. I pretty much stopped reading up on Anarchy after reading an interesting piece by Bob Hertz called "A Different Kind of Anarchism" (*The Match!*, April-May, 1976). Over the unruly issues of rape, revenge, a trial, rehabilitation, honor, justice, etc., Hertz indirectly scolds fellow Anarchists for their idealistic expectation of harmony come freedom. From there it seemed clear to me that different cultures get as much freedom as they, in total, wish. And in that sense, Anarchy does prevail everywhere, excepting where one distinct culture rules another.

Americans tolerate more freedom than most, but often nose around ideas of giving up a measure of freedom for security. There are plenty of countries that provide more security. America, meaning the United States, is the breakthrough model nevertheless, given the governing syndromes of the old worlds. Often around the world the average people are very interested in America, whereas elites with a franchise or concession to defend in a less free state are wary of its influence. The early Bolsheviks eyed America as a threat, though they understood that its capitalism, if not its revolution, had been necessary by their own theory. But the American dynamic that followed as it settled the west and processed millions of immigrants opting out of more stable European and Asian lands, scrambled classes and that made Marxists nervous, even though the theory *emphasizes* the destruction capitalism will wreak on old time-honored feudal and folk ways. Once those are destroyed by capitalism *then* communism was to arrive. Lenin and Mao didn't want to wait so they commenced their own destroying *sans* much creation. Still their ability to control vast nations impressed third world strongmen, whether ex-colonial administrators or ex-guerrillas.

Mubarak and his predecessor Sadat were military men, products of Nasser's nationalism. Nasser took a lot of risks and mostly failed. Sadat cleaned up after him and was killed by an Islamist group for signing a peace with Israel. Mubarak cleaned up after him and was more colorless and oppressive. After decades of the good works of OPEC and the PLO, the Islamic world finally achieved the coveted Problem #1 status in the first world with the 9/11 attacks. If that wasn't enough, attacks in London, Madrid, Bali, Moscow, and elsewhere bound the second world to the first; Russia and China even joined as cover for ongoing operations in their Muslim nether regions, Chechnya and Xinjiang. Al Qaeda, remember, had given up on attacking the regimes in Egypt and Saudi Arabia, concluding that they were impregnable, backed as they were by America. This was a conclusion probably deduced under the influence of *BBC* kvetching. But as Crook also writes, "The US did not keep Mr Mubarak in power. Dictators in other Arab countries received less support, or no support, or actual US opposition: they lasted too."

Post-colonial developments in Iran, Saudi Arabia, Lebanon, Syria, Iraq, and Turkey have changed in turn what has followed elsewhere. That Syria leveled the city of Hama to stop a Muslim Brotherhood revolt in 1982 and that its military is home now and not in Lebanon makes it harder for unrest to manifest. This week's call for a demonstration failed in Damascus. That Turkey has opened its economy and gradually accommodated rule by an Islamic party also changes what seems possible for a Muslim nation.

Landon Thomas in the *New York Times* notes that Mubarak came to power in 1981 while Turkey was under military rule,

> "But while Mr. Mubarak, a military man himself, banked upon authoritarian rule, paying only lip service to democratic institutions and running rigged elections, the general behind the Turkish coup, Kenan Evren, moved to withdraw from politics. The constitution he imposed left the military considerable scope to meddle in political affairs, but it allowed civilian institutions to bloom. On the economic front Egypt maintained state control, with many restrictions on foreign trade and domestic competition. By contrast, Turkey, which hopes to join the European Union, has opened up its economy and unleashed a dynamic private sector. Today, with similarly sized populations of about 80 million, Turkey has an economy that is nearly four times the size of Egypt's." (*New York Times*)

One surprising detail in coverage of the current unrest is that Egypt's economy has been growing at 6%. This is better than one might assume from casual reading of pre-crisis middle-east reporting. The Mubarak regime must have been yielding some state control over the economy for this much growth to occur. But 6% is likely all the growth that can be allowed by the reigning insider groups and rentiers who cling to the state and feel they can only lose ground against any new competitors. The easy use of new communications technology by the young demonstrators must really frighten these interests; they surely sense they could never compete with the ambition and skills on display in the street.

The *Wall Street Journal* reports that "outside of agriculture, 70% of Egyptian workers work for the government," and further, that according to an IMF report, this "has inflated the graduates' wage expectations, put a premium on diplomas over useful skills and diverted talented workers from what might have been more dynamic private-sector enterprises." That reminds me of Chicago where some of my immigrant tenant-neighbors dreamed of landing a job with the city – better pay for less work. And once inside the government one wants stability.

Just about any country can decide it wants to grow at double digits, but more often it is stability that is prized. After all, many of the most frustrated and ambitious Europeans left for America, followed by same from Asia, Latin America, and Africa, leaving greater concentrations of security-prizing populations behind. When the countries of eastern Europe were freed, Slovakia seemed uncertain. It looked like it might secede from Czechoslovakia to join Russia's CIS club for homesick prison-nations. But they didn't; they did secede and they wasted about a decade, but then simply decided after one election or another to begin to grow at or near double-digits; Slovakia has no interest in the CIS now.

Were Egypt to decide to open up its economy now, even if done in a lame-duck Mubarak period, capital from the Gulf states and Turkey would certainly be invested. And more would come from high-growth China and India and Brazil, and from slow-growth Europe and Japan and America. It's no mystery, but then Egypt, old unchanging Cairo, would become as a new place and its culture would change. Istanbul and Ankara are changed; Baghdad is changed; perhaps Tehran will be soon. Men, especially the older men of these semi-feudal cultures, have something to lose but it sounds like Egyptians have reached a new consensus.

As for democracy and Islam, here's Egyptian-American sociologist and Mubarak critic Saad Eddin Ibrahim's sense of where this Egyptian regime fits in the recent history of the mid-east from his interview at *Qantara.de*:

> "This so-called 'Islamic exceptionalism' theory is wrong because 75 per cent of Muslims are actually ruled by democratically elected governments (Indonesia, Malaysia, Bangladesh, Albania ... not forgetting India with its 165 million Muslims).... Egypt was a democracy for almost 100 years until the Nasser Revolution of 1952, which brought to an end the Egyptian and Arab liberal age. I argue that the cause of this end was the establishment of the state of Israel.... The defeated Arab armies returned home looking for a scapegoat for their defeat in the first Arab-Israeli war.... [O]nly three months after the signing of the armistice treaty with Israel, there was the first coup d'état in Syria, followed by those in Egypt and Iraq." (*Qantara.de*)

The other important changes in the mid-east landscape are post- (or pre-) revolutionary Iran, and post-Saddam Iraq. Iran quickly and absurdly claimed the Arab street for an aftershock of its own revolution of 1979. That too started as a secular-Communist street revolt, but it was taken over in the eighties by the clerisy that has become its own defensive counterrevolution. Reuel Gerecht writes in the *New York Times* about what relevance Iran and Iraq may have for Egypt:

> "What we are likely to see in Egypt is not a repeat of Iran, where fundamentalists took undisputed power, but a repeat of Iraq, where Sunni religious parties did well initially but started to fade, divide and evolve as the powerful Sunni preference for laymen of no particular religious distinction comes to the foreground. Sunni Islam has no clerical hierarchy of the holy – it's tailor-made for nasty arguments among men who dispute one another's authority to know the righteous path. If the Brotherhood can be corralled by a democratic system, the global effect may not be insignificant." (*New York Times*)

Gerecht anticipates the sadly unheroic reality of democracy-attained, however much heroism may be required to establish it. Like Baghdad, Cairo was a first city, with its own urban culture that predates Islam and any other monotheism by millennia. It is a capitol and with everyone watching these events it seems the regime has already made the principle concession despite its early dirty tricks at the prison and in the street. But the hard-won post-cold war developmental consensus continues to play out and melt the last pre-modern national cultures. Oddly, there may be no Tiananmen-style massacre in Cairo because of China's economic achievement since.

(*originally posted at The New Vulgate, No. 84*)

The Tea Party vs. The Metagaming of the System
This was posted at the NV just before the 2010 mid-term elections (Oct. 13, 2010). Now Occupy Wall Street demonstrations are bracketed with the Arab Spring, when all they were was Tea Party envy.

The best thing about the Tea Party is that it's stealthy as it makes headlines. Even those in-the-know do not know who they are or what they want. Experts seem so invested in this rolling consensus of theirs, the one that has it that we are behind Europe in social development and that history moves in one direction toward, I suppose, Sweden pre-1989.

You might expect a Brit to pocket the tribute the American elite pays the old world as Gideon Rachman does in the *Financial Times* this week, but he really mightn't oughtn't phrase it so: "The Tea Party movement that is stirring up US politics means different things to different people... To many foreigners and American liberals, the Tea Party does indeed seem like a crazy mix of wild conspiracy theories... and impractical nostalgia for an era of distant and minimal government." To "Foreigners and American liberals" says a lot right there methinks, wot?

It's something of a hangover of the postwar civil rights era. All kinds of scoundrels run to steal fire from the civil rights struggle including the entire baby boomer superstructure; they somehow remember their interest in hearing the Temptations do "Cloud Nine" on 'The Ed Sullivan Show' as them risking their just-healed fontanelles to Bull Connor's billy-club. Blacks freed themselves in postwar America with some help from churchmen and -women, not student radicals or hippies. All that smoking violence was America learning things. Even then that was nothing compared to the European violence just ended. We're seeing now what was not learned over there for all that. As the old world considers itself advanced they relished the American street-fighting and took it to mean what they enjoyed believing: Americans may be rich but they are like animals.

The real story in Europe is that they still cannot quite get along with their neighbors never mind immigrants from elsewhere. Lately in the news, some Muslim jihadis captured in Afghanistan are being referred to simply as "Germans" – doesn't really work does it? Europe, even roped-together in the EU, is still a collection of discrete race-nations in a way that America is not. Perhaps we're going to find out whether they can break that impulse and each-and-in-total become a new bastard-breed born of loose stock like us. Their history argues not, and respectable opinion over there seems to approach those who have decided they do not have it in them to be as Americans, as if indeed they were Tea Party manque.

Here, though, among English-speaking ex-colonials and the many Others, race is more like a golden oldie, hummed enthusiastically by Taylor Caldwell or Howell Raines to rescue some part of their family, or the south, or their own white-ass from some judgment day of their imagining – maybe before the ICC in The Hague. The idea that the Tea Party is racist or racially-formed is a conceit of those barricaded inside the public power structure, near the top of the our hierarchy of servants, yet still believing themselves to be committing blows against someone else's empire. I've written before about this brave new class; Vaclav Havel has written about young American Academicians who toured the East Bloc, commiserating with political prisoners and dissidents, comparing their own American lives in the belly of the beast, with theirs in the prison nations' prisons. These tourists' assumptions being something along the line that Havel's situation under the boot of Communism was caused by American resistance to said ineluctable fate.

Socialism was too much a product of the Romantic era to ever be grounded in even a science as wobbly as economics. But the new class loved his idea of the march of time, one-way history, the inevitability of the triumph of socialism. They were never too sure about the withering away of that state but trusted that might be well after their rule. All this pertains, even as the principle metaphor of our age has been built out of the old one-way Ma Bell, pay-the-bill or be ex-communicated phone system. Everything now is an always-on local call between one and as many others anywhere as anyone likes. And Sweden was taking cues from a society that licensed typewriters.

Some of such nonsense is pure etiquette, a kind of misdirection play whereby the meritocratic elite assumes egalitarian coloration when outside the family – something like the ruse a Soviet academician might have pulled as he bowed and scraped before ex-peasant commissars. As mere etiquette their questions are disingenuous. They don't want to know who the Tea Party is, though they fear it is signaling the formation of the long-rumored third party, only not the one of *their* dreams.

Sean Wilentz, fresh from Dylanizing like a foreigner or a Democrat, roots around Glen Beck's bookshelf in the *New Yorker* this week and then goes off on a wild goose chase through John Birch Society history as if that's relevant. Along the way Wilentz absolves not just Teddy Roosevelt and Woodrow Wilson but also Richard Nixon, Ronald Reagan and George W. Bush of any taints of extremisms anyone might want to make, all in the exercise of demonstrating to *New Yorker* readers that they needn't check into any of this revisionism. Go back to sleep, fair liberal (or foreigner).

I'd suggest keeping one's eye *off* the ball for a bit in the next few months to see what the Libertarian Party makes of winning an argument in the down-and-dirty of real-existing-democracy. In some ways it's the Democratic Party that has won a number of these discrete arguments but they and their partisans in the news media wouldn't quite know what face to make if they thought they won an argument, and in video it's all about the reaction-shot. They prefer to pretend they lost in the face of withering racist reactionary resistance, but survived to sip fair-trade coffee another day. They dream of pulling off an in-your-face victory that leaves nothing in its wake – so satisfying, so self-defeating in the long run, this cult of the progressive outrider misunderstood in his own time and country and media.

Matt Bai in the *New York Times* posits that the larger and larger independent voter is simply swinging back and forth against the sitting Party. This may be the third unseating in a row of the President's Party two years into a first term, which Bai writes is something...

> "that has never happened before in the country's tumultuous political history. This suggests that however much the issues of the moment may seem to be defining these elections, there are some deeper forces at work, too." (*New York Times*)

"Deeper," meaning shallower – nothing to do with taking another look at the beginnings of the welfare state under the Roosevelts or Wilson, despite its sustainability being under sustained attack from within – the claimants, the rent-seekers, litigants, pensioners, all of those and us who want the state to invest in us or pay us off, and from fascist math itself simply refusing to add up or multiply the loaves.

Alan Brinkley in the *NYT Book Review* goes at some of the new books seeking to maintain the Tea Party's stealth-shield, and again there seems to be an ideo-historical backstop at the size of government now among polite opinion – this size today is simply ground zero for next year's enlarged and improved government; it fails more so it grows more to do a better job failing. Brinkley assures us all that "The reality of the creation of the Constitution is a far cry from the idea that it instituted immutable limits to what government could do." He the Historian at Columbia then dismisses stated concerns since they are new and not historical. He the Historian ought to remember the way things move: first through this-or-that attempt at doing, and this-or-that witnessed by others whose follow-up attempt will be altered based on what the leaden powers that be successfully fend off. Learning occurs, and some may continue defending Jimmy Carter or Woodrow Wilson but the non-Historian electorate is fine with dropping Hoover, Nixon, or Bush. And if you can only do one thing you'll only get one term. Brinkley fancies himself as part of a new meritocratic royalty so naturally he resists the U.S. Constitution which was put in place precisely to halt every first impulse of either royal or mob prerogative.

It seems to me that the Tea Party has committed to the Republican Party, but only if they can rehab it now. Otherwise they'd have filed to run as third parties by now; instead it has been sitting Republicans beaten in their own primaries that are left to run as independents. The Tea Partyers want the Republican Party to stop competing with the Democratic Party on spending, to stop gaming the system to win elections. Such promises of spending are the sales-pitch of the Democrats since Wilson. Only the Democrats conflicted, foreignized souls and the sense of traditional Americans that the economy is more than a cookie-jar for the government that kept Republicans competitive, for they could never outbid the Dems. Only Nixon and DeLay ever even tried. But the competition for ministering to voters through spending devolved into an overarching strategic game of locking federal spending into endless out-years of commitments of future revenues to favored expenditures – social spending for Dems vs. military spending for Repubs. This metagaming of the system was a stealth final straw. Those pols invested in this game cannot look up to regard it, they might lose an edge and a long night of fascism or communism, national socialism or international socialism commence.

David Brooks asks a good question, "Why are important projects now unaffordable?" Assuming agreement on what is important, "Many of us would be happy to live with a bigger version of 1950s government: one that ran surpluses and was dexterous enough to tackle long-term problems as they arose. But we don't have that government. We have an immobile government that is desperately overcommitted in all the wrong ways." But what is the failure, guns or butter? The Tea Party is saying both. They have changed their mind on what they call the Neo-con War on Terror but the left won't accept this as their victory; they keep seeing gun-nuts in the woods or the desert. On this and other issues, they much prefer to fight a class war.

Only the most unexpected angles allow the straights who write for major metropolitan dailies to offer a fresh insight into an outgroup. Lee Siegel, also in the *NYTBR* contrives somehow for whatever reason to compare the Tea Party to the Beats. It's the recent film, *Howl* (2010), that triggers it, and especially the filmmakers' Hollywood-like impositions on what is known to be true about this formerly underground subject:

> "Hollywood loves self-righteously to portray now-unchallenged liberal causes under siege, even though in this case the cause of free speech was vindicated when the presiding judge ruled that 'Howl' [the poem] was a work of 'redeeming social importance' and that Ferlinghetti [the publisher] was innocent. What the movie should have spun out into its own subplot was the fact – never mentioned in the film – that the judge, W. J. Clayton Horn, was a conservative jurist locally renowned for his Sunday-school Bible classes. Horn might well have been as much an outsider in San Francisco's sophisticated social circles as Ferlinghetti and Ginsberg were in the eyes of the law. It takes an outsider to know an outsider. Or perhaps Horn had a glimpse of the future. The eventual assimilation of Beat hedonism ensured that by the end of the millennium, white middle-class Christians like him would themselves be marginalized – at least by the dominant culture – as the 'silent majority.' When the Tea Party came along, however, the silent majority started to get its voice back. Liberals could well be drawn nostalgically to the Beats nowadays because all the countercultural energy belongs to the other side." (*New York Times*)

Siegel goes on to revisit the Beats contempt for the liberals who in their comfort "accepted the government's role in organizing their lives." Not bad for something in the *Times* in an election year where so much is at stake, etc.

In the end the thinnest strand of bohemian conservatism is sustained by the individual points at which some few culturati come to understand that they love American culture for its peculiarly but duly constituted Author. And so they depart the rush to Europeanize them both. As for all this fear alleged, only two years ago the "coup" was on the other foot, and America was to be taken back or else a move to Europe. Unfortunately for them they won and stayed.

(*originally posted at The New Vulgate, No. 67*)

The Framers vs. The Farmers – Bust the Corn Trust!
This was written in the run-up to the Healthcare bill passage. It seemed that the Times op-ed in question was a politically naïve and prideful boast of strategic thinking, but some things are written to juice the "most emailed" list. Posted at NV Sept. 16, 2009.

Last Thursday Michael Pollan, author of a book called, *In Defense of Food*, spun through a likely scenario that follows any new healthcare bill in the *New York Times*. He optimistically writes, "even if we get a health care bill that does little more than require insurers to cover everyone on the same basis, it could put us on that course." That course he celebrates is the enlistment of Big Insurance in campaigns against soda pop and "America's fast-food diet."

As Pollan sees it "Agribusiness" is producing cheap food and charging social and environmental costs to the future. His anticipated enlisting of the Insurance industry in the social engineering to follow from President Obama's healthcare reforms is of course one of the main threads of opposition to it. The resistance understands that the text of any legislation is just the beginning, and they probably appreciate this confirmation. Especially as it is a reversal of weeks of news analyses and fact-checks pretending otherwise. Pollan thinks we can't afford the Man's corporate death-burger, but can we afford the New Man's Sustainability surcharge?

Young Americans – new to their political ideas – are the first to wonder why we can't have national health-care and, as I wrote in NV #6, they will be among the first to find out what behavioral autonomy they will surrender in the attempt to make it achievable. The behavior of the young and the care for the elderly are the only savings-give in these brave new proposals. It is also likely that cost pressures due to the advances of medicine will lessen as state-control slows down research and medical progress.

I lived on First Street in Laramie overlooking the main Union Pacific east-west rail-line for a decade. It was an interesting perspective on world activity to look out the window, with the Snowy Range forty miles beyond (where I now live), and see the relative strengths of the coal industry, the auto industry, the military, construction, and agriculture roaring past. In the build-up for the Iraq war there was a blip of heavy traffic of tanks and military vehicles on flatbeds heading east. Most of them were already painted for the desert but every once in awhile there'd be a green vehicle painted for the forests of Europe. Otherwise the winner by my eyeball study of UP train traffic in those years was surely agriculture, specifically Cargill and ADM, most specifically: High Fructose Corn Syrup. Tanker train after tanker train of the goop.

But what Pollan calls Agribusiness is really the kind of state-directed enterprise he favors – he simply wants *his* agenda served rather than somebody else's. I expect he favors Mayor Bloomberg's health campaign as well; there is apparently no fear of jumping the gun and scaring off the prospective subject population. Peta is trying to banish the horse-drawn carriages as well. Such a cosmopolitan world capitol! And they only just got decent Chicago hotdogs and Mexican food around town!

The Corn Trust is the product of yeoman farmers seeking stability ever since the Panic of 1857. This they sought through Grange socialism, New Deal nationalism, Cold War internationalism, and anything else they could wield against the serendipity of weather and grain prices. The futures markets in Chicago were the laboratories for new securities and investment tools and price hedges. These were first designed to ward off the chronic boom-and-bust cycle of farming on the unfolding American scale in a roiling economy laying railroad track in all directions.

The farm states are not so powerful in the House of Representatives, but in the Senate, North Dakota's two votes are the equal of California's. And since Jimmy Carter used the Iowa Caucuses to upset the 1976 Democratic primaries and win the nomination and White House this corn-belt contest has become a Corn Trust veto on all such issues. There was talk in a number of states of jumping ahead of Iowa but when they wimped out the chance to stop burning 150 BTUs of energy to create 100 BTUs of Corn-Ethanol ended. Instead, the Iowa question remains, What am I bid?

We have High Fructose Corn Syrup in about all of our processed food. Why? To engineer a guaranteed price for too much product. The Federal government continues to fund research at farm-belt Ag schools to find new applications for corn product. The Sugar Trust was too successful in keeping the price of cane sugar up and this opened the door to corn syrup mayhem. It isn't just the Cuban-Americans in Florida that keep America anti-Castro, it's also the Sugar Trust's fear of Cuban cane sugar driving down prices.

Wal-Mart recently began importing Coca-Cola from Mexico where it's still bottled in the original formula using cane sugar rather than corn syrup. Can you imagine the expansion of the bottling plant capacity in Mexico necessary to fill the order from Wal-Mart? Can you imagine the palm-greasing it took in Atlanta, and Washington, and Arkansas, and Mexico to effect this sale?! Could be it was palm oil.

Pollan is only a UC Berkeley Professor of Journalism so one can hardly be surprised to hear him relish the day soon-come when the health insurance industry begins "buying seats on those agriculture committees and demanding that the next bill be written with the interests of the public health more firmly in mind." The left loves social engineering so much they favor the prerogatives of public corruption over private freedom and the probity it might ask of them. One hopes the counter to this would have the new localist small-scale organic-or-merely-healthy agriculture out there demanding equal consideration if not actually a level, free market playing field as they compete with state-favored behemoths. Pollan will by then represent his own problem and free-market cranks at the *Wall Street Journal*, the *Investors Business Daily* and *Reason* will become the health-food producers best editorial allies.

Pollan might read Sunday's *New York Times* cautionary dissent by Tyler Cowen, "Where Politics Don't Belong," which is a quick run-through of how Washington exacerbated the banking-financial-mortgage crises, with an eye toward warning off what he sees as the final crisis resulting when Obama uses the same deal-making m.o. on health care reform which will break the government itself:

> "We have made a grave mistake in politicizing the economy so deeply, and should back away now. In health care, the Obama administration should drop its medical sector deals and try to sell a reform plan - in whatever form Mr. Obama chooses - on its own merits. That's not only good for health care, but also good for the American polity. And in the longer run, that will be good for banking, too." (*New York Times*)

Cowen - a Professor of Economics and the author of some of the more disinterested and therefore stirring books and essays on globalization and what follows from it - is a bit cavalier about whatever an Obama might propose outside of his deal-making pol guise, because frankly there's nothing but this guise. Like Pollan the President recognizes nothing "on merit," just the game of the deal. As JFK and Bill Clinton did, Obama considers ideological sedition the mark of a grown-up. Only the Supreme Court might have stopped this politicization of the economy. As long as we officially celebrate an expansive reading of the Commerce Clause we will have petty constituent service and favor-dealing metastasizing beyond the productive economy's ability to pay the freight.

(*originally posted at The New Vulgate, No. 11*)

The American Alloy - Model, Export, Ideal...

Opinion had swung against the War in Iraq over lies about some truth that didn't matter anyway regarding Iran. Politics isn't enough. This was written the first week of the Arab Spring, mid-January 2011.

Ivory Coast joins Zimbabwe and Cambodia as nations presided over by the losers of their elections. Perhaps Iran belongs here too, Russia not quite as Putin is violating only the spirit of its election law. With his KGB bonafides he was uniquely positioned to step down and provide a George Washington-like new model for how to leave power in semi-democratic Russia. The orderly leaving of power is the most important technical lesson a polity must learn, which is why it is so destructive to allow idealists or mere opponents to prosecute an ex-president anywhere. They don't need to be literally above the law, but it is certainly best in the long run that they be so in practice. Or any leader is foolish to leave willingly.

The electorate itself is often imperfect and drifts into fealty, strapping in for long-term subject-like relationship with a President-for-life. And they often have good apparent reason to choose a security-based tyranny. Fully *stolen* elections are often related to a poverty culture's lack of interest in risk. Still the machinery of fixed elections can often not survive what are called wave elections here. This was People Power in the Philippines; Marcos had fixed elections fair and square but when it was clear the election machinery made him vulnerable he seized power militarily, only to lose it ordering the shooting of one man. Something like this happened in Ukraine as well with the so-called Orange Revolution that vaulted the "loser" Viktor Yushchenko over the "winner" Viktor Yanukovych, but then it un-happened under the pressure from neighboring Russia whose patience is an improvement over the original assassination attempt on Yushchenko that had in part triggered that wave election.

Elsewhere traditional, pre-feudal clan-based gerontocratic patterns survive and lend legitimacy to Egypt's Mubarak or Belarus' Lukashenko, or Kazakhstan's Nazarbayev, or Uzbekistan's Karimov. Then there's Thailand where a watershed populist election-winner was deposed constitutionally, then put back in power more emphatically by the electorate before finally (?) being unseated by the King via the Army. And Venezuela, where a static class structure led its rural majority to elect a failed ex-military coup-leader, and Nepal where Prachanda's Maoists came out of the hills to strong-arm the nominal ruling party after a wayward Prince erased the Royal line with a machine-gun. It can be hard to generalize, not so much about the desirability of encouraging democracy but about how it might be received here or there, wherever the Americans or the EU or UN or the Vatican or some NGO or union are pushing it. How could they know, when many indigenous constituencies calling for democracy do not themselves know what may come of it? Often these constituencies are frustrated elite groups with one foot in Europe or North America already via education. In any case, even the most advanced, largely single race nations of Europe only truly settled into mundane democratic means after the two world wars nearly decimated population and place. It's a lot to ask of Egypt or Nigeria to expect them to get to it more smoothly. America's ongoing loose, de-centered and unsettled reshuffling of power and people lets off steam constantly – the injustices and tragedies and crimes are smaller and more localized and have been more quickly addressed, however inadequately – this is all relative. (I'm no idealist.)

Often troubled polities are caught between feudal patterns whereby wealth is held as land in the form of fincas or plantations or ranches which keep one extended family wealthy, but depend on peonage if not slavery. (Industrial wealth creation and the movement of rural population to cities for work in factories broke up that residual pattern in America too, though literature and Hollywood kept the romance of the old South alive for a century or more.) What development is possible in a feudal mode moves along clan lines, rather than being open to applicants on a meritocratic basis and so classes can become separate cultures and even races.

A big question as America industrialized, modernized, developed in the late 19th and early 20th centuries was, How can a working class whose wages are depressed by the stream of new factory laborers from the farms, and then depressed again by new arrivals from Ireland, Italy, and Poland, and then further depressed by the exodus of blacks from the South, how can this increasingly impoverished proletariat afford to buy the products they produce? The people who asked that question had an answer in mind, of course, and they mentored graduates who today still counsel despair and centralization. It is a mark of American history that these brainy folks remain frustrated. In many other countries those ideas are not frustrated. Feudal patterns gave way to centralizations that were red or brown or green but which merely allowed their great question-asking answer-knowing class to starve and murder more people than purple ever imagined could be desirable.

The wrecked west European powers in 1946 were open to new ideas and the American model began to be identified as an improved variant of the old models. But what Americans had developed by accident of economic and technological dynamism was not just a manufacturing capacity, but a new polity. Many immigrants had actually come to America intending to purify their old world beliefs. But here they found a liquid base of Natives and those early Anglos, Franks and Spaniards who had gone native. The United States of America is the real dream of *Mexico* whereas the Estados Unidos Mexicanos, though full of mestizos has never allowed industrialization to modernize feudal Spanish land grant patterns and forge a Mexican alloy. The lords survived the revolution in Mexico, and the classes stayed racial and simply made small room for Mestizos between the Indios and the Euros, with work in the U.S. as a release-valve for social pressure.

Given the old Protestant paranoia regarding the Vatican and its Catholics, it was an enormous risk taken by America to allow millions of Irish, Italians, German and Polish Catholics into the country. In terms of race relations with the newly freed blacks these Catholics, coming in blind to the issue of slavery surely set back race relations even in 19th century terms. And not deporting blacks *en masse* back to Africa or to the Caribbean was another fateful choice too little appreciated. There is a lot of talk of various and sundry American genocides on campuses but that talk never actually accounts for the reality that eliminationist policies might well have been pursued had white Americans still been merely their unaltered European selves. No, America was simply not going to be as France or Germany. And the settling and industrialization of the country meant that its human mix wouldn't be merely the multi-cultural Great Britain either. Rather it made this new populace alloy into a new people creating a new culture and polity.

Obviously America remains the model. Many poor countries can learn a lot from China just as they could learn from Japan, South Korea, Singapore, etc. But none of those countries can model for a country that is multi-racial and full of immigrants and different faiths and is looking to live together and become one people. The Chinese are prosecuting a demographic culture war on their conquered peoples in Tibet and Turkestan in the bald way that only a culture with none of America's experiential knowhow might. The Han may think they are settling their west as America settled its, but Americans went more and more native as they went west. The Han have virtually zero interest or respect for the culture of their peripheral neighbors. There was always a deep American interest in native tribes and blacks and it gradually developed into respect.

Just last week in Tunisia the self-immolation of an unemployed college graduate who was not allowed to sell vegetables and fruit on the street for lack of a license or the cash to pay a bribe triggered the government's fall. His un-Muslim, rather Buddhist gesture tells us this was not an Islamist act. But on top of the *Wikileaks* cables of 2008 and 2009 where American diplomats expressed shock and detailed the decadent corruption of the ruling family it unleashed a people's revolt. There are reports of similar self-immolations across Arab countries in the days since. These static fixed economies filled with clan-based property owners and rent-seekers have no need for young people with or without skills.

The temptation for proud peoples, especially their western-educated elites, is to obsess not on whether Tunisia can become democratic, but rather on impuning America (or France) for "backing" the Ben Ali regime. Mohammed Hussainy, called "director of the Identity Center in Amman, Jordan" focuses bitterly on this in a short piece at *openDemocracy* called "Messages from Tunisia," which starts out calling the uprising a popular revolt and looking optimistically for its replication across the Arab region, but then settles into his first concern, the maintenance of his personal legend, disguising his lust for the West by berating it:

> "Tunisia has also highlighted the double-standards adopted by most democratic states, particularly the Europeans and the United States. Having been involved in occupying Iraq under the pretext that they wanted to help the Iraqi people against the dictatorship of Saddam Hussein, the US and many European nations refrained from advancing democracy and maintained a foggy attitude vis-à-vis what has been taking place in Tunisia. They have failed to justify their support for Bin Ali's regime – which is but one example that those democratic states are supporting non-democratic regimes in order to preserve their own vested interests." (*OpenDemocracy*)

I understand it's easy to become a target in that part of the world, but post-Edward Said, it may also be that he's bucking for a chair at Columbia. These pro-democracy, anti-Western postures are very common there too.

On Tuesday Francis Fukuyama, once somewhat in favor of the Iraq war (that bit of history is certainly over) writes in an op-ed in the *Financial Times* called "US democracy has little to teach China":

> "Democracy's strengths are often most evident in times of adversity. However, if the democratic, market-oriented model is to prevail, Americans need to own up to their own mistakes and misconceptions. Washington's foreign policy during the past

> decade was too militarised and unilateral, succeeding only in generating a self-defeating anti-Americanism. In economic policy, Reaganism long outlived its initial successes, producing only budget deficits, thoughtless tax-cutting and inadequate financial regulation. These problems are to some extent being acknowledged and addressed. But there is a deeper problem with the American model that is nowhere close to being solved. China adapts quickly, making difficult decisions and implementing them effectively. Americans pride themselves on constitutional checks and balances, based on a political culture that distrusts centralised government. This system has ensured individual liberty and a vibrant private sector, but it has now become polarised and ideologically rigid." (*Financial Times*)

Now it's likely he did not write his own headline and I doubt even "Reaganism" is a term he would use, but notice his oddly disguised reference to the Ron Paul/Tea Party push to cut spending and retract military commitments to our borders. *His points exactly!* Though he is apparently ashamed to see them in action out in the real world of the American polity, and after all he wants his piece published somewhere, you know, legit.

Fukuyama is a smart man and took needless grief over being correct that the Hegelian-Marxoid End of History was upon us with the collapse of communism. Perhaps he should have called it the End of Historicity, but then he has to live on campus, albeit Stanford. In truth it was long clear that communism was failing but it was a measure of Academe's compromise to it that their eyes were averted as much as possible. Francis is a slight polite Japanese-American, whereas Christopher Hitchens is a boozy, chain-smoking ex-leftist English-Jewish-American. Hitchens' cancer battle hasn't slowed him much. His latest column concludes with his own non-revisionist take on the Iraq war, the real one that he still supports with conviction rooted in his formerly leftist solidarity with the Kurds, eternally trapped between Iraq, Iran, Syria, and Turkey. At *Slate* Hitchens writes:

> "Go back to the first days of the coalition presence in Baghdad. The Iraqi people had not been directly consulted about anything for several decades. But the new authorities promised a constitution and elections, and they unshackled the press and television. Might it not have been interesting to see what happened? To test this promise and, where it was wanting, to demonstrate against it and petition for the redress of grievance? The population never had a chance to try this novelty. It was a matter of days before

> experienced killers and bombers were hard at work, without so much as a leaflet being distributed. And our own willingness to rationalize such behavior on the part of Muslims allowed us to call professional assassins by the name of *insurgent* and to write that they were defending 'Muslim soil.'" (*Slate*)

There were months of underground Baathist provocations against the Shi'a until with the arrival of jihadis all hell did break loose, but the actual overturning of the Saddam regime went quickly. The Mohammed Hussainy-types refer to such authoritarian regimes as Western-backed and presume we have some magic power to isolate them out of existence after which the naturally-occurring democracy and industry of the people will simply manifest. They don't approve of what America and its allies did in Iraq, or what the CIA did in Iran in the fifties. They cannot approve, no matter how fervently they wish for some cavalry to arrive. There were all manner of isolating embargos applied to Saddam's Iraq and the Ayatollahs' Iran, after all, to little affect.

None of this is America's job *per se*. Our people left all them old worlds for cause. But let's remember, it was thought we had learned that we should not have left Afghanistan, and before that it was thought we had learned that we should have gone into Rwanda to stop genocide, and before that it was thought we had learned that democracy could be transplanted into ruined Japan and Germany and South Korea and Taiwan and Eastern Europe and Latin America and Indonesia... But back in our uni-polar heyday – the 1990s! – when all right-thinking people (including France) worried about American power, what was left unstated was that that fear was not about neo-colonialism or an American tyranny, but rather about the chaos our model entails and unleashes inside of any society that opens itself to the market, immigration, democratic rules of order, and transparent governance. America since WWII has seemed a Goliath, and as Wilt Chamberlain famously said, "Nobody loves Goliath." Though let's recall the rest of Wilt's story – *he laid ten thousand women!*

America has been more Tasmanian devil than Goliath which is why all these Davids keep missing the point and get scratched to bits in the whirlwind that follows the following of our model. This was the premise of Amy Chua's book, *World on Fire: How Exporting Free Market Democracy Breeds Ethnic Hatred and Global Instability*, which toured the world trolling for hot spots made hotter by capitalism and democracy. That's counseling despair in my book, and akin to saying that all the blood, sweat, tears, and injustice of early America just wasn't worth it. No passage is possible. When her own life is proof otherwise.

It's in all that ignored un-theoretical practical American experience where the secret to our special providence lies (that special providence, reputedly a Bismarck coinage, is the secret to why we're alleged to be hated by that burning world). Chua is safely on the mommy beat now but judging by reviews she might have called her new book, *Mommy on Fire*. That book seems to indicate that like most liberals she publicly advocates a soft touch for outsiders yet follows every time-honored tyrannical drill to get her own up to speed to rule over the indulged Other.

But even Europe seems it may fail to master our model. Europeans are living for themselves and living for today, and with plummeting populations they are making up the difference with immigrants from north Africa, these apparently expected to be content serving food and emptying the bedpans of their betters even if managing to gain full citizenship. And further, Europeans don't seem to remember the bloody battle their ancestors waged to drive the Vatican from governance. They treat the Islam of these immigrants as if it has less not more designs on power.

The *New York Times* referred Monday to Tunisia as a putative "first Arab democracy," and this is a paper with a bureau in Baghdad dutifully reporting the machinations of a crazy quilt of representatives in a tri-confessional republic. The *Times* does this out of undue concern for Washington politics; they needed Al Qaeda-in-Mesopotamia, as they term it, to make the cost high enough for the US to not repeat what first seemed easy enough in Iraq, in Iran or North Korea. That's a legit position, it's hardly our job to do these things. But nobody knows nothing, after all, which qualifies anyone's confidence in their best guess whether they know it or not, especially the *New York Times*.

Still, there's no honor in not doing them either. Kurt Vonnegut once said of the men who dropped the bombs on Nagasaki and Hiroshima that they might have become in essence the fathers of all those people had they just flown past and let them all live. Allowing the House of Kim or the Ayatollahs to do their worst when a button-push could erase their asses is also an indirect culpability in their crimes. This is what Hussainy is saying despite himself. And despite our noblest intentions and selfishest motives nobody doesn't understand why America plays for time with these worst of nations, the ones that believe that exposing one's culture to the modernizing dynamic is surrendering to America, and appear to believe that nuclear weapons are required to defend their 19th or 8th century ideals. But if these dramas play out as worst-case scenarios more than just conventional Iraq War opinion will change.

(*originally posted at The New Vulgate, No. 81*)

Metaphysics of Boomer Materialism: Death Panel redux
It's a tragedy when a young person dies, but it's going to be truly harrowing when the baby-boomers aging youth culture dies. Post at the New Vulgate *on Jan. 5, 2011.*

Several threads in the news are being left unknit together by editors for the probable purpose of avoiding the conclusion that Sarah Palin's coinage was just as loaded a term as what is coming will require. Or maybe the editors being aging boomers yet hauling the dead weight of their youth culture paradigm uphill just remain unwilling to face facts on a deeper non-tactical level. I've written before that all the hipster young, lighting each other's cigarettes or bongs or buying beer for even younger friends as they do, have been voting and symping to make themselves criminals, because once healthcare is nationalized every citizen's health is everyone else's business – "everyone else" as in the Feds, the Narcs, the Man. As it happens apparently the Man himself still smokes. That's a special crime in my book, like a member of the tax-writing committee not paying his taxes. Perhaps President Obama and Congressman Rangel together with ex-Governor Palin and the Tea Party will help unravel this looming granola tyranny.

Here's how the *Wall Street Journal* editorial, "Death Panels Revisited," describes what happened accidentally on purpose through no fault of Big Tobacco:

> "On Sunday, Robert Pear reported in the *New York Times* that Medicare will now pay for voluntary end-of-life counseling as part of seniors' annual physicals. A similar provision was originally included in ObamaCare, but Democrats stripped it out amid the death panel furor. Now Medicare will enact the same policy through regulation. We hadn't heard about this development until Mr. Pear's story, but evidently Medicare tried to prevent the change from becoming public knowledge. The provision is buried in thousands of Federal Register pages setting Medicare's hospital and physician price controls for 2011 and concludes that such consultations count as a form of preventative care. The office of Oregon Democrat Earl Blumenauer, the author of the original rider who then lobbied Medicare to cover the service,

sent an email to supporters cheering this 'victory' but asked that they not tell anyone for fear of perpetuating 'the Death Panel myth.'" (*Wall Street Journal*)

What that all means is not that somebody finally read those thousands of pages of the ObamaCare rules and regs – no those reams still sit around DC in unread towering piles, insulting the murdered and mulched trees that died to produce them. The *New York Times* reporter simply got his hands on Blumenauer's e-mail! The *Times*' follow-up editorial very carefully parsed their own news so's not to be accused of concurring with a Palinism they already wrote reams of coverage denouncing, which were read by me at least. Didn't work though, here's MediaMatters' hysterical charge:

> "The *Times* never indicates that 'death panels' was a lie – PolitiFact's 2009 lie of the year, in fact. The closest it comes is a passage deep inside the article that refers to claims by Sarah Palin and John Boehner that the proposal would 'encourage euthanasia' as 'unsubstantiated.' Printing a politician's lie without making clear that it is a lie simply encourages politicians to lie." (*MediaMatters*)

All the good shit is buried by editors, ain't it? Jamison Foser might be all of 22 thinking that the *Times* is covering for Sarah. But let's hear it for the plywood or whatever that wall separating the *Times*' editorial romper-room from the reporters' cubicles is made of; those trees died for a purpose, a necessary evil, or a necessary fiction.

Out in California the *Los Angeles Times* takes the 700+ laws that kicked in on New Years at face value thus making each and every one good news! "New laws aim to make Californians healthier and safer." As a result folks that might've died naturally at seventy-five in the recent benighted past will soon be reaching triple digits and practically unable to die without state assistance; see: Preventive care.

Another loose thread elsewhere in the papers comes from a friendly visitor to that romper-room. Susan Jacoby an "unsparing chronicler of unreason" has been stamping out religion her whole professional life, and she wrote a personal-political op-ed column in the *New York Times* last week called "Real Life Among the Old Old," in which she abuses her own familial emotions to feed ideological compulsion thusly:

> "I can see that the '90 is the new 50' crowd might object to my thinking more about worst-case scenarios than best-case ones.

But if the best-case scenario emerges and I become one of those exceptional 'ageless' old people so lauded by the media, I won't have a problem. I can also take it if fate hands me a passionate late-in-life love affair, a financial bonanza or the energy to write more books in the next 25 years than I have in the past 25. What I expect, though – if I do live as long as the other women in my family – is nothing less than an unremitting struggle, ideally laced with moments of grace. On that day by the riverbank – the last time we saw each other – Gran cast a lingering glance over the water and said, 'It's good to know that the beauty of the world will go on without me.' If I can say that, in full knowledge of my rapidly approaching extinction, I will consider my life a success – even though I will have failed, as everyone ultimately does, to defy old age." (*New York Times*)

By all means, let's counsel Gran on her range of end-of-life options, because now that the government is on the hook for healthcare it is death that must be sold. Jacoby clearly looks forward to strapping her Ahab ass to her own personal white whale, but a moral hazard is a moral hazard even laundered by big-D Democrats and delivered by unbelieving bureaucrats or outright automation. I wonder whether there might be a civic form of Last Rites described in those unread pages where an old old citizen might be forced to confess, say, cigarette-smoking, etc., and whether some sub-clause in those unread reams might demand in such case a timely end, or happy release, or even the coveted mercy killing *coup de grâce flambeau*. Or maybe it's up to, you know, some panel of experts or something.

Two double-dome philosophers, Hubert Dreyfus from Berkeley and Sean Dorrance Kelly from Harvard, have gotten good notices for their new book, *All Things Shining*. As the book's described it brings to mind another of these un-knit yarn threads I'm talking about, although here it's more the general boomer generation's vague not-quite-metaphysics of mere existence if not life. David Brooks' column, "The Arena Culture," compliments the book as it ranges outside the heretofore unsuspectedly narrow confines of philosophy and writes:

> "[T]heir book is important for the way it illuminates life today and for the controversial advice it offers on how to live. Dreyfus and Kelly start with Vico's old idea that each age has its own lens through which people see the world. In the Middle Ages, for example, 'people could not help but experience themselves as determined or created by God.' They assumed that God's plans encompassed their lives the way we assume the laws of physics do.

> For the past hundred years or so, we have lived in a secular age. That does not mean that people aren't religious. It means there is no shared set of values we all absorb as preconscious assumptions. In our world, individuals have to find or create their own meaning. This, Dreyfus and Kelly argue, has led to a pervasive sadness. Individuals are usually not capable of creating their own lives from the ground up. So modern life is marked by frequent feelings of indecision and anxiety. People often lack the foundations upon which to make the most important choices."
> (*New York Times*)

Unusually for academics, their big idea seems to be that sports are filling in for this void of meaning and providing much needed shining. That might explain how sports ain't no gym-rats' tawdry diversion any more, coming from some sour-smelling stadium into your home on some snowy UHF channel. Back in the overly political years of the sixties-seventies, boomerdom seemed to drop sports after growing up in thrall to Mickey Mantle and such. They later sort of backed into sports interest again, first with basketball in solidarity with Dr. J's afro, if not UNLV's Runnin' Criminals. I think the Detroit Pistons were the first NBA team to start five black players at the end of the seventies; such cultural racism was still a live issue at least in terms of marketing departments. Then the boomers even got back into baseball as a way of saying, "Sorry about the NVA flag, our cockamamie political ideas are as American as apple pie after all." After that it was the NFL, TV shows, and a good cigar.

But here too, anomie, meaninglessness, the void, the Western Conference quarterfinals, etc., are all of interest to members of the old Youthquake as they try to fob off the costs of their more likely endless endcare on everyone else, i.e., the Federal government, just before they face facts. They likely want us to think they want to be free to plan their own living will, or death, but they have no such plan. They show complete confidence generally in their ability to manipulate matters and micromanage even the government that can't say no to itself. They expect to wind up planning everyone else's death. And the minute you've done the responsible thing, they'll rip the I.V. from their arm and go racing down Broadway in their hovercraft.

I imagine they'll be bring up gun control again at some point. Probably have to.

(*originally posted at The New Vulgate, No. 79*)

Hipsterama Heterodox

Christmas 2011 brought the hipster car commercial – she buys him a Lexus – and Samsung's wanton attack on creatives lining up for iPads. But Santa Claus himself? Squaresville. Posted at NV Nov. 10, 2010.

Mark Greif's piece from *N+1* is adapted, presumably abridged somewhat, in *New York* magazine. It's still called, "What Was the Hipster?", and it attempts to answer that question via its "sociological investigation." Perhaps the original version which is credited to the editors of *N+1* rather than Greif, answers the questions this version begs; I haven't seen it. But here there's only one study referenced, an ethnography of Wicker Park by a sociologist named Richard Lloyd, claiming that he...

> "...documented how what he called 'neo-bohemia' unwittingly turned into something else: the seedbed for post-1999 hipsterism. Lloyd showed how a culture of aspiring artists who worked day jobs in bars and coffee shops could unintentionally provide a milieu for new, late capitalist commerce in design, marketing, and web development. The neo-bohemian neighborhoods, near to the explosion of new wealth in city financial centers, became amusement districts for a new class of rich young people. The indie bohemians (denigrated as slackers) encountered the flannel-clad proto-businessmen and dot-com paper millionaires (denigrated as yuppies), and something unanticipated came of this friction." (*New York*)

I think Classicals called this the Spontaneous Generation theory back when its adherents were sure that if you just threw a bunch of seeds, hay, refuse, and wood scraps into a large sealed container, mice would surely pop into being. Good to know some old superstitions survive all that critical theory crossfire on campus.

Again, maybe the editors or Dr. Lloyd don't throw around nonsense terminology so freely but since this version in *New York* magazine – a pre-eminent organ of late capitalist consumer-choice via its regular rankings of all the city offers – contains not a single mention of Liberal Arts colleges or Art Schools which are proven reactants in today's cultural hells-broth it is hard to take the essay seriously. The editors and the scientist of soshe may be loathe to implicate any factor that might snare themselves, but if they won't include themselves in their study then it's just another hipster gambit, and all the proof I require to conclude their own fine adaptive skill in higher edumucation. (They needn't mention Film Schools, the culpability of those in all this is well known.) Personally I was a bit slow; I didn't drop out until my second year at Univ. of Denver.

After I'd spent ten years on the west coast involved with a bunch of like-minded drop-outs or never-wents who made music or tried to sell it or write about it, I moved to an area of Chicago that seemed to have no name. I had very little money to show for those ten years in the music business so I couldn't afford anything in any part of the city I looked at for months until I guessed it might be interesting to be just west of the Kennedy Expressway and my patient realtor found an area south of Bucktown and north of Ukrainian Village that was less than half the going price of those neighborhoods. On some neighborhood maps I saw later it was called East Wicker Park – I was on Pierce Ave near North & Ashland from 1987 until 1995.

In the year I worked on my building I'd eat breakfast at the Huddle House and then for dinner get a burrito at Tacos Mexico or a hot dog at Duk's. Once done rehabbing the building and resuming work on *R&TPN* I began to explore the area west to the Milwaukee-Damen-North six-corner. I found I could pick up the *Wall Street Journal* and *New York Times* at the L station so I'd often break my fast at Sophie's Busy Bee on Damen, or Friar's which was in the low wide triangular Flat Iron building and opened onto both North and Milwaukee. This intersection was the center of the area, rather than the Park itself. The mansions around Wicker Park had been rehabbed in the seventies and the Flat Iron building started filling with painters and artists beginning in the late seventies if I remember right. According to Mark Greif this all rather begins in the nineties – Nirvana must be the reigning post-postmod backstop before which nothing of interest occurred. He seeks to rescue the nineties from "post-1999 hipsterism" and explore any inadvertent culpability.

Now let's take our eye off the ball, as I often recommend, and think instead about all the homosexuals in or around the arts on the west coast back before golden age of Greif's Grunge, way back in the seventies and early eighties. I don't recall a single one-of-'em ever expressing an interest in getting married. Unless I miss my guess today's marriage-minded homosexuals – descendents (?!) of risk-addicted sexual outlaws – could be a profitable analogue to this discussion. What kind of subculture is this marriage-mania from? Again, are these descendents of that first subculture bohemia in the Romany ghetto of Paris of the early 1800s?! And also, did they attend college?

It seemed to me that the bands that formed after the 1970s were more often formed in college and these, though inspired by music of the drop-out music ghettos of the sixties and seventies, did not intend to live unheard in exile from the music industry as those had. If their music wasn't as fun and free-thinking as sixties frat-rock was, it was because of changes in the schools. Everything became pretentious and arty rather than musical and rooted. Culture studies were mostly new programs and perhaps it's a coincidence that once kids are studying rock and roll and film and pulp and cartoons in college all of these once-vital popular arts began to fail.

There seems to be a cut-out blind that keeps the impact of mass default college education from factoring into any studies other than of income. I'm sure all God's graduates perform their jobs much better than do the degreed rockers so why the averted eyes?

As Greif has it,

> "The hipster is that person, overlapping with the intentional dropout or the unintentionally declassed individual – the neo-bohemian, the vegan or bicyclist or skatepunk, the would-be blue-collar or postracial twentysomething, the starving artist or graduate student – who in fact aligns himself both with rebel subculture and with the dominant class, and thus opens up a poisonous conduit between the two." (New York)

It's like an overblown version of that long 1992 thunk-piece by Samuel Nathan Schiffman that appears quickly after Nirvana's platinum break-through in *Maximum RocknRoll*:

> "If MTV wants to attempt to legitimize former hard-core forms of rebellion such as slamming, moshing, hair-dyeing, leather jackets, Doc Martens, Converse sneakers, flannel shirts, ponytails, skinheads, flight jackets, dreadlocks, Misfits shirts, swearing, let society have our cultural trappings. If they mosh, we'll all pogo. If they wear leather, we'll all wear cotton. They can take our styles, but they can't take our souls." (*Maximum RocknRoll*)

From my positions at Systematic and then SST it didn't seem that *MRnR* ever chose soul over style, not that it was great music's real problem. Back in NV68 I observed radio programmer Lee Abrams' indirect but massive contribution to the destruction of rock and roll as it was coming out of the sixties, and I wrote fairly efficiently about postwar music-cultural techtonics:

> "If you ask me anyone starting a band after 1980 was handicapped by the lack of an immersive exposure to great music by good radio stations. Mediated America no longer allowed provincial folk cultures to develop deeply on the highly refined level they once achieved in Appalachia, Louisiana, the Mississippi Delta, the Piedmont, the border..., so this new airborne folk media was what we had to make do with after WWII. It was quite productive for awhile and great folk media synthesizers like Eddie Cochran, Dick Dale, Steppenwolf, Jimi Hendrix, The Doors, James Blood Ulmer..., made contributions as brilliant and nearly as organic as earlier, more rooted, less mediated folk synthesizers like Hank Williams, Muddy Waters, Bill Haley, Elvis Presley, Chuck Berry.... But it was less sturdy and thereafter, if young kids got turned on to music in junior high and form a band by the end of high school, then the end of great music radio in the early seventies resulted in the end of great bands in the early eighties." (*New Vulgate*)

When you're talking art, sociology goes to the back of the bus. In fact, unless it gets its act together it really should be thrown *from* the bus as it gets up to speed.

David Brooks in a column this week about other aspects of live cultures vs. dead ones, he notes this about creative types:

> "Howard Gardner of Harvard once put together a composite picture of the extraordinarily creative person: She comes from a little place somewhat removed from the center of power and influence. As an adolescent, she feels herself outgrowing her own small circle. She moves to a metropolis and finds a group of people who share her passions and interests. She gets involved with a team to create something amazing." (*New York Times*)

Another Goddamned academic – two of 'em in facts. Thirty years ago, I'd've said her choice of pronoun was an ideological imposition on the truth of the arts. But as Art has moved away from Nature it finds itself in a weightless cultural cul-de-sac which is safer and safer as it withdraws from gazing upon cruel cold nature, and instead goes myopic with allegedly sophisticated games of one-upsmanship in an artificial marketplace whose rewards are bestowed on those who best disguise the absurdity and inflate her audience's self-regard. Women like safety so they do well in schools now that they must prepare to support themselves. Unfortunately by the time they filled universities Humanities missions had been broken. But nature will catch up to them. It's the men that are the real concern here.

The arts in America today often put me in mind of Edward Abbey's construction from his book, *Desert Solitaire*; I've quoted it here before so I'll just note that it posits Civilization as the river, and Culture as the dam. People, even the Abbey-ite EarthFirsters, don't realize the extent they prefer the dam, but they are sure other people do. Greif's use of the past tense is unwarranted of course – it sure ain't as simple as a passing fad. But there are Americans living outside of the great pasteurization process. They are immigrants, or rural, or overseas or in the military. And maybe there's a self-starter or two in Silverlake or Wicker Park or Brooklyn, etc., but enough to form a band?

(originally posted at The New Vulgate, No. 71)

Racism as Set-aside for White Americans
This is an early New Vulgate piece (July 15, 2009) and was triggered like many of them by intensive news coverage that reveals a blind-spot in the way the news-media looks at the world.

Something about the reporting from Urumqi lines up with what I've noticed generally about news coverage of conflicts overseas: There's no racism involved. No matter the bodycount. The newsmedia reserves the term "Racism" for America. It doesn't seem to matter what the Han think of the Hui, the Mongols, the Uighurs or the Tibetans, or how heavily they sit on their cultural or national aspirations, or how many of them they kill. Ethnic tensions? Well they're to be expected. You can claim that the Hutu and the Tutsi in Rwanda aren't racist for what that'll get you. But the Chinese, as contemporary citizens of a classical civilization, do have the cultural arrogance – a wounded one at that – that can lead to what you'd have to call racism. But it's not called that by the American and British press because I suppose that in and of itself could be considered racist by the lights of, oddly enough, post-colonial studies. And though western reports don't echo the Chinese press's blaming of exiled Muslim terrorists, the *New York Times*, *Wall Street Journal* and others did dutifully ID as the Dalai Lama-of-East Turkestan, Rebiya Kadeer, a mother of eleven who in her spare time became the richest woman in China by doing laundry.

    The best known Chinese cultural export, the film *Crouching Tiger, Hidden Dragon* (2000), tracks with the outlines of old Hollywood cross-race romances – the Manchu princess kills herself at the end, leaving her lover – a Xinjiang bandit likely a Hui or Uighur – to grieve. The western twist, courtesy of James Schamus and Ang Lee, is to have the "high race" character sacrifice herself, although in the original novel she only fakes her death. In the classical Hollywood narrative it was the character of "lower race" who died to save the "higher race" lover who was left to fully relish the painful burden of his nobility reflected in the low lover's submission to it. China is as racially complex as India, Africa, and Micronesia; the Han have largely subsumed the Manchu though not entirely and the film must diddle this relationship in some way we in America do not comprehend, even if we suspect there is something wrong with her suicide in dramatic terms.

Today there is motion in Chinese culture and the new middle class has an interest in travel, and touring their empire's ethnic minorities. But there is still a hair trigger xenophobia that is stoked by the state as often as it is suppressed. My sister has studied, worked, and traveled in China since 1986, and her Han friends in Shanghai and Beijing couldn't comprehend her interest in seeing Tibet or Xinjiang – she made it to Xinjiang but Tibet was closed to individual travel. The Han consider those people and regions "dirty." Her Fudan U. roommate moved to the U.S. and after fifteen years here she now understands such interest.

The original trigger for the Xinjiang violence was the supposed rape of a Han woman by a Uighur man. That certainly sounds familiar to Americans as the classic pretext of a riot or a lynching. The Chinese media found the woman and she claimed she merely stepped into a room occupied by Uighur men and let out an involuntary cry and left – I bet that sounds familiar to black men in America – but the Han men who heard her shout did beat several of those Uighur men to death.

Monday's *Financial Times* reports on India's fear "that Beijing is extending its power to control shipping lanes in the Indian Ocean and Arabian Sea – waves that it prefers to rule." Like Russia, China is just not a good neighbor; Russia lost many of its internal colonies when the Soviet Union collapsed, but China still possesses its internal colonies, and covets Taiwan and, if certain Chinese academic cartographic historiography is to be accepted, North Korea and parts of Mongolia and Siberia as well. These were never part of any Han empire, which is why it is necessary for the Han to first absorb the Manchu as a race, then any and all territories of its empire's high water mark.

Iranians are the inheritors of a similarly classical civilization, what was once called the Persian Empire. And yet Iranians make up barely half their population; other groups include Azeris, Arabs, Turkmen, Baluchis, and Kurds. Perhaps there exists ethnic tension here too. The reporting about Iran's election which turned into street demonstrations and repression, doesn't broach the subject. One is left to wonder whether the split is rural/urban as in Thailand and Italy, or tribal as in Kenya and Congo, or merely historical as in Ukraine? Or is it something unique to Iran? If so that might be because sophisticated Tehran is largely Shi'a which is a pre-modern blood-line vision of Islam's clerisy, in contrast to the clerical meritocracy of Sunni Islam. I foresee further trouble.

In Ukraine, the east has been so Russified that those votes might just as soon vote to secede and join Russia. And so the dynamic there has the eastern vote stymieing western votes for integration with Europe and NATO. The Orange revolution was achieved by round-the-clock street demonstrations which succeeded in reversing an election apparently stolen by Viktor Yanukovych with the connivance of Putin and the FSB who apparently recommended vote-fraud when they failed in their bid to poison his opponent, Viktor Yushchenko. I thought that first handshake between Putin and Yushchenko after the reversed election was great theater, Yushchenko with his face scarred by the potion; I imagine Putin was doped up on a very specific antidote from the FSB medicine cabinet.

The violence that followed the election in Kenya was initiated by the Luo tribe whose candidate Raila Odinga had the election stolen by the sitting President, Mwai Kibaki from the Kikuyu tribe. The theft was obvious and in dramatic disconnect with the parliamentary results that favored Odinga's party. The Luo were left with having to lump it, or dramatize that the cost to the Kikuyu would be high, even if it would be paid largely by themselves. This violence might be said to have been in necessary defense of democracy. It succeeded in forcing Odinga into a coalition government, but those who got him half his victory will now be named by Kofi Annan to be prosecuted by the International Criminal Court. Good thinking by the all tangled-up post-colonial Right-Thinking folks at your U.N. Everywhere outside America one can look but one won't find anything called racism, other than in Israel, oddly a nation formed by victims of racism.

Saturday's *Wall Street Journal* describes "China's Ethnic Fault Lines" and how the regime cooks the official statistical breakdown, claiming that 91% of China's population is Han – the rest split between 55 minority groups. Dru Gladney writes, "The supposedly homogenous Han speak eight mutually unintelligible languages..." Linguistically speaking, China is a Europe, rather than a single country. Europe was held together by Rome and the Pope until wrenching wars tore the empire apart, and then with the collapse of the Soviet Union evolutionary changes began to pull the nations back into supranational formation. But the EU overreaches when it does anything more than streamline trade. Its technocratic center in Brussels is not politically accountable and so gets into trouble in country after country as it grabs for state-like prerogatives, and extreme ones at that. China does reveal evidence of its latent "Warring States" constituent pieces when Beijing steps in whenever local provincial corruption gets exposed by horrific disasters such as the Aids-tainted blood scandal, earthquakes, poisoned baby formula, mine explosions, etc. Neither fealty to Emperor nor fear of Mongol Khan holds this supranational entity together anymore. The Party seems to be encouraging religion, especially Christianity, as Islam is tied to Xinjiang, and Buddhism is tied to Tibet and the now outlawed Falun Gong. The Party must see Christianity as a proven asset to social equanimity; they sure aren't getting that from the *New York Times* or the *BBC*.

When it looked like Iraq was going to fly apart I thought that maybe the realists guessed right when they advised investing nothing in democratization projects, even when they seem to serve our national interests. But a nuclear arms race in the Islamic world might be something worth avoiding at any cost, especially given the currency that martyrdom possesses in that culture. Additionally Al Gore claims our number one concern is global warming and any nuclear exchange between or betwixt Shi'a, Sunni, Jew, Hindu, and/or Chi-com might raise temperatures another 0.114°C in good ol' Tennessee we may are being called upon to stop it now.

The United States in any case is put on the hook for these calamities by elements of the left and right, as well as by the news media. Both *CNN* and Michael Jackson pulled us into Ethiopia, Eritrea and Somalia in 1985 though they were each Soviet bloc basket-cases. I'm agnostic on American involvement in these rescues and wars, but it's no surprise that it is us on the hook. We are the peripheral neutral; the only possible trusted arbiter. Britain, France, Russia, India, China, are all distrusted by neighbors or ex-colonies. This American privilege is resented and so a kind of anti-American bluff is touted loudly, but it isn't real, or to the point anyway. France's third-way was vaporized at the fall of the Soviet Union so they began to speak of the American *hyper-puissance*. That was only the geo-political surface of their unease. Underneath that was France's frightening realization that America had got its act together on race! All the proud European nations that had to accept American aid for decades after WWII, took a not-so-covert satisfaction in the brutal racism of America. It lent comforting support to the civilizing cover they had once used for their imperial adventures. The news through the fifties and sixties seemed to confirm Soviet propaganda which trumpeted incidents of American racism in the south and in northern cities as proof of the terminal sickness at the heart of America.

But the dynamism of the American economy, where new players and new sectors rise quickly to challenge or eliminate seeming behemoths (ITT, IBM, GM...), has a cultural analog as well. The achievements of black individuals sink roots and get marketed and their examples mainstream quickly. The old Irish-American everyman of Hollywood films has morphed suddenly into a black-American everyman. The integration of the military services and team sports probably did the most in the way of racial progress in the modern era, and then the history of American music in the twentieth century is another parallel train of accommodation. The American left credits the Supreme Court above all as if progress was all top-down from the point of 1954. But there wasn't that much more work to be done after four hundred plus years of living together, or at least next to each other, in the new world. Perhaps the heavy immigration of the late nineteenth and early twentieth century actually retarded racial progress as the country accepted large numbers of Catholics and Jews from Ireland and Eastern and Southern Europe. It took these new Americans of recent European heritage fifty years to even accept European intermarriage! My parents' marriage was a form of rebellion for each of them and their parents (his Italian immigrants, hers German-American) took it for that I'm sure, despite both families being Catholic. The American economy's growth and its shift westward also helped transform apparent zero-sum competitive pressures within the polyglot working class.

When I moved back to Chicago from L.A. in 1986 I watched and read the local news including the venerable black daily, *The Defender*. I also listened to Lu Palmer's radio show on *WVON*. Palmer, more than any one individual had convinced Harold Washington to run for Mayor. Once in office Washington had to distance himself from Palmer and other activists because he wanted to administer City Hall as something more than a black machine. Palmer used to reject the circumlocution "African-American" for his own construction, "I am an African in America." This he'd pronounce calmly in the most patient voice imaginable. When one of these activists went 'round-the-bend over the Jews, Washington distanced himself further from these street pols of the south-side. Palmer explained over the radio that he couldn't tell whether there was hate in the heart of Steve Cokely but he could stand by his brother. Cokely lost his job in the city administration as I recall and began to dress more and more "African."

I saw Palmer get off the bus outside of the Huddle House diner at North & Ashland one morning. Rostenkowski's ward was now majority Hispanic and the Washington forces (The Reformers) were working to take it from the Vrdolyak-29 (The Regulars) and finally get control of City Hall. (It was damn hard to avoid being registered to vote in Chicago back then; I had to duck the Regulars, the Reformers and the Mafia.) I asked him if he was Lu Palmer, and he looked over and saw me wearing a Blackhawks sweatshirt and answered "Yes" guardedly as if he expected God-knows-what to follow. I said, "You do a good show." He nodded and smiled in relief and said, "Thank you."

Today in America, racism suffers a kind of inflation, because there is so little of it. This inflation will be on display this week as the Sotomayor nomination hearings begin. The racism she and her backers will talk about wouldn't raise an eyebrow outside our borders where they still dream of final solutions, redrawn borders, and what Thomas Sowell calls cosmic justice. Here now, thankfully, it's a question of etiquette or respect. Meanwhile it's become clear to the French that they now are where America was decades ago, and they do not have a way for immigrants to become Frenchmen and women. It's true of the rest of European nations as well. And they hate us for that, and though they were all for Barrack Obama last year, they hated us all over for electing him President. We've set the bar quite high.

The newsmedia in this country is conflicted, and as they take their cues from the *BBC*, the *Economist*, and *NPR* they aren't likely to figure it out anytime soon. It takes Dorothy Rabinowitz of the *Wall Street Journal* to say something as called-for as, "We must face the truth about ourselves, no matter how pleasant."

(*originally posted at* The New Vulgate, *No. 2*)

Clinton Legacy Found!
This is probably not the tone to take writing about politics and the world but six years into the Clinton administration I'd claim it was understandable. I don't think I submitted it anywhere, but between screenplays I was trying out essay strategies.

Clinton would like to be Left, but it's not his priority. First he wants to feel good. And this ain't so easy with that bitch Hillary around. Bill gets reminded first thing in the morning what a drag the Left can be - well, most mornings anyway. So in between launchings of the White House rolling pin and reams of Navy-worthy cursing Hillary sets the policy he would like to be for. Of this ridiculous totalitarian fantasia wherein we are all reduced to "chuldren" only one issue can not be sold out by Bill - Abortion. This is Hillary's G-spot - that red button right there. No! Don't touch it! Women's freedom was born of the Pill and abortion goes the "logic." And you thought womyn hated being patronized.

Only the most pointillist Leftists (visibly speaking, say, Alexander Cockburn, Christopher Hitchens, Noam Chomsky) threaten to even countenance the idea of holding Bill accountable for doing fun stuff like bombing and lying and raping and killing. But then, even they are no longer true believers so they have no reason to cling to the former party of the Popular Front which is too busy loving presidential power to hate injustice, in any case.

It hasn't been since Lyndon Johnson that the Democrats have really been able to stride the world stage as anything but junior Senators or junketing Congressmen - talk about your ugly Americans. (Carter was a party outsider which was why Ted Kennedy challenged him, though when pressed Teddy himself didn't seem to know that.) But since 1992 the likes of Federico Peña, Hazel O'Leary, Henry Cisneros, Joycelyn Elders, Alexis Herman, Janet Reno, Warren Christopher, Laura Tyson, Togo West Jr., Robert Reich, Webster Hubbell, Bruce Babbitt, Strobe Talbott, Les Aspin, Ira Magaziner, Donna Shalala, David Kessler, Richard Holbrooke, Madeleine Albright, Carol Browner, Ron Brown, Bill Lann Lee, et. al., have paraded in their French-cut Futurist finest through global-this and global-that conferences grabbing at perqs and power while their actual bureaucratic fiefdoms wobble like 1990 Moscow. But they sure look like America! This first generation of sixties-dented student gov-types were handed the keys to a colossus built through the enormous uphill efforts of generations of Americans. All they could think of to do was run downhill squealing ecstatically as they inadvertently commenced the unraveling.

The Persian Gulf war, whatever its absolute merits, earned something concrete for America in a world where the Soviet East was deciding whether to go down fighting or not, and the Chi-coms were debating post-Tiananmen whether to reform or repress or attempt both. The demonstrated abilities of American equipment and personnel earned America and the West political capital, and foreclosed on any dream of a socialist vanquishing of capitalism. This has now all been spent, and worse.

There were about a dozen military actions during the Reagan and Bush twelve years; there has been almost four dozen in less than seven years of Clinton. And he picks his fights perversely, carefully avoiding any prospect of *real politik* profit; he intends to spend capital in the age-old high-minded quest of the Wilsonians to build a world government – Oh what a wonderful stage that would make! This fantasy appeals to a bitter American elite cheated, they feel, out of their destiny to redesign our society and redirect our resources. The U.S. has the most to lose to these multilateralist pipe dreams and our elite hurry to the gaming tables of Europe and Asia to lose it. They wince at the dealers in embarrassment of the power they represent (belly of the beast, you know), while they preen over the ostensibly selfless example they waste on the postmoderns of Europe or the pre-moderns of the third world. Our elite are right to feel cheated, of course, because democracy works against merely theoretical expertise. America is not run by its elite professions or it's Academy; it rather quarantines them while exalting the process of free people bettering themselves. We may foolishly recognize Liberal Arts expertise, but we actually reward the skills coming out of the science buildings and business schools.

And so, whither Bill Clinton? He'd like to be Left, and stay Left, like Hillary. But after the initial radical indulgences (gays in the military, healthcare nationalization) led to Speaker Newt Gingrich and the Republican Congress, and his personal indulgences led to impeachment and a lowering of the bar to "service" by his generational allies into the dirt to accommodate him, he's running downhill too fast to stay on his feet. So he is stopping and turning around. And after the world-gov pretensions have been stripped bare in the Balkans (they are good for something), and after taking money from the Chinese military, waving them through our research labs, selling them the hardware and allowing them to steal the software and the data (the Legacy codes!) to perfect their ICBM technology and MIRV their missiles, there is only one avenue left open to him and any hope the Democrats have of securing the presidency for Al Gore: Hawk Avenue. Al's already tuning up on the campaign trail, circulating photos of himself in uniform carrying an M-16 and declaring, "I'm a Vietnam veteran – one of the lucky ones." And the reflexive ridicule once dumped on SDI (Reagan's kookie Star Wars delusion!) has already spun 'round in environs like *New Republic*, *Washington Monthly*, and *CBS*. This, amazingly, is trumping the Left's concern over the U.S. as sole superpower, or what some Frank has dubbed, The Hyperpower. Our own Secretary of State Madeline Albright wishes out loud for a counter-power to America's "frightening dominance," in Bob Woodward's words. (It's all beginning to make sense!)

Hawk Avenue is defense spending on a scale necessary to re-widen the strategic, tactical and technological advantage. It's the Strategic Defense Initiative (SDI), it's the Theater High-Altitude Area Defense system (THAAD), it's heavier military spending on people, weapons, research, overseas bases, intelligence, and it's revamped security relationships with the Philippines, Japan, Taiwan, South Korea, Vietnam, India, Pakistan, and Russia:

- The Philippines has upgraded its defense relationship with the U.S., reversing the sentiment that turned American forces out of Subic Bay and Clark Air base.

- Japan's post-war constitution imposed on them by Douglas MacArthur forswore military action; this was accepted by the Japanese who'd lost faith in their military, but if the American defense umbrella seems full of holes they will not be polite about re-militarizing.

- Taiwan's electorate having reached democracy first, may next vote for independence which the Chi-coms would rightly take as a challenge to their heavenly mandate.

- South Korea's former dissident-prisoner president has been forced by missile-happy North Korea and economic circumstances to forego a promised radical redefinition of the American-Korean relationship.

- Vietnam is an ancient enemy of China's and they are fighting over islands now, and Vietnam was alarmed at the eviction of American forces from the Philippines and events may find them inviting American forces back to Cam Ranh Bay.

- India's strategic partner had been the Soviet Union against China and China's ally Pakistan. India and Pakistan are now both nuclear equipped and still they skirmish over a cease-fire line in Kashmir which they both claim. India and China both have claims on the other's territory as well, and India has all but seized Nepal, Sikkim, and Bhutan for use as buffer states along Tibet, which is occupied by China, though it's government-in-exile headed by the Dalai Lama operates from India.

- Russia finally climbed back down off of the ledge communism had put it on, and this was enormous comeuppance for its national pride. The bombing of Serbia is swinging the debate in Russia back to the unreconstructed premodern Slavophiles. Russia was only willing to reduce its nuclear stockpile while the Chinese sat there with twelve missiles and no carriers.

Jimmy Carter ramped up military spending in 1979 after his soft-headed gambits exploded in his face in Iran and Afghanistan, but it was too late to save him from anything but being our finest ex-President. Ronald Reagan wasn't even considered electable, is how bad Carter blew it. Clinton has that all memorized. The new militarization is about the Spratlys, the Paracels, the Yalu River, Quemoy and Matsu. It's hoping the Japs can remilitarize without going bonkers; it's hoping the Russians can use a Chinese missile challenge to get their act together without taking it on the road. It's the Draft!

Our boy Bill has danced through life leaving everyone around him – especially his allies and enablers – covered in mud, blood and sperm. He danced his way out of the old draft and will leave us with a new draft, though it will be dressed up with communitarian pretense, a la the Civilian Conservation Corp. He danced his way through money, sex, defense, election, cover-up scandals. He dashed his allies' (and Hillary's) hopes on issues from sexual harassment, campaign finance, welfare, social security, public schools, church-state relations, affirmative action, human rights, etc., and now the crowning glory of his betrayal of the Left: a re-militarization of American culture. There's no-one left to lie to, and there's no more secrets to protect. We are at a ground zero of sorts struggling to avoid being placed at a true ground zero. It's now safe to say that the sixties are truly over.

At the 1992 Presidential Inaugural when the White House was handed to a Democrat for the first time since 1976 some of the party's Hollywood backers come to DC to reflect in someone else's glory for a change and they began boo-ing when the jets flew over in formation. Actorvist Ron Silver was heard to counter the boo-ing with, "No, it's okay; they're our planes now." In power now since 1992 the Left has had occasion to exercise muscles that had atrophied. In defense of their power they've found things to cheer in a bull market, in tax cuts, a military success, a B-2 stealth bomber, hell even a B-1B. This is the principal positive result of the Clinton presidency in terms of the greater political culture. Whether it's positive enough for a net gain will be determined by whether the Clinton Legacy turns out to be a deployed missile defense and a revamped Asian defense structure, or whether it is merely hundreds of MIRVed Chinese missiles targeted accurately on the cities and forces of every nation ringing the Middle Kingdom – that is, the world.

So. Viet-nam
I wrote this for the Vulgate *posted Aug. 26, 2009, utilizing reading about the Vietnam War I'd begun a few years earlier for a book yet undone.*

The *New York Times* is edited to steer debate by devising the terms of debate. Their columnists are hired for their skill in Belling the Cat – said cat forever after sounding in shapes from the *Times'* editorial board. This often yields labored attempts at pictographic constructions both vivid and cloudy (Geo-Green?) Sunday's weak soup was "L.B.J. All the Way?" (title changed online to: "Could Afghanistan Become Obama's Vietnam?") by Peter Baker. Certainly Jr.'s steely masthead-minds do not mean to harm President Obama's chances in Afghanistan, they are mostly looking out for their own reputation. The piece has so many qualifiers that it disqualifies its own point ("To be sure, such historical analogies are overly simplistic, and fatally flawed..."), but they may tout it as a prediction should there be some meltdown. It is meant as well to steer the President himself. I'd bell this cat as "the weak force" in the cosmology of *New York Times* analysis. (I didn't catch what the hope-heads at *NPR* made of this but I think we can assume that they are very concerned.)

As in Vietnam the Democrats have cornered themselves. Their commitments in both theaters were mere campaign feints. JFK may have meant it but his brothers led LBJ on, and then turned on him in order to return a Kennedy to the White House at all costs. It never happened but had it, such a Kennedy, Bobby or Teddy, would've pursued policies the opposite of brother John.

This is all forgotten. So one must ask, Which Vietnam is Peter Baker talking about: the actual country fought over in the cold war with real blood, sweat and tears? Or the flashing idiomorph *"Vietnam"* of the *Times'* and others' rhetorical investment?

JFK had run to the right of then-Vice President Nixon and in Vietnam he initiated an attempt to bring the war to the North. This story is told in a book called *The Secret War Against Hanoi*, by Richard H. Shultz, Jr. Shultz tells how the Kennedy White House tried to foment resistance inside North Vietnam a la Hungary '56. The CIA had learned from Hungary that Communist states were essentially "denied territory" and resisted involvement in the President's plan and once Kennedy was assassinated

Johnson suspended but didn't kill the program. It became some strange kind of useless theater, though even then it managed to trigger some amount of paranoid self-abuse on the part of the North.

JFK had settled for a bogus U.N.-brokered neutralization of Laos, which our military observed but North Vietnam did not. It organized its supply lines around the DMZ through Laos and down into Cambodia, which came to be called the Ho Chi Minh Trail. The story of this strategic blunder is told in *The Key to Failure – Laos & the Vietnam War*, by Norman B. Hannah. He writes:

> "It could be said that the neutralization of Laos... was the major strategic decision we made with respect to Indochina from 1961 until we departed in 1973. All else was either geared to it or was incremental, barnacled encrustation. That so little attention is devoted to Laos in studies of the Vietnam war and to the role of the 1962 Geneva Accords is more than an intellectual curiosity. It is a profound enigma...." (*The Key to Failure*)

Well, it might be the boomers' then juvenile hormonal political investment in the many canards that live on in our hearts about the fifties and sixties, the Kennedys and Nixon, require such averting of eyes – entire politicultural identities have been built on them. Hannah, then Deputy Chief of the American embassy in Afghanistan, writes earnestly, "*We had to stop the aggression through Laos or we had to stop defending South Vietnam,*" (his italics). In his book, published in 1987, Hannah recounts his comparison of Afghanistan to Laos in a 1962 meeting with Kennedy's "special representative" Averell Harriman. Hannah has Harriman concerned only about slipping a fast one by his own country's Congress to please international opinion and boot Laos down the road via a fake "neutralization." The CIA ran its own rather useless theater in Laos, casting Hmong in their plays.

I have a lot of Vietnam history on my shelves yet to read but of what I have I'd also recommend as correctives to the prevailing fantasy "Vietnam," these:

> Michael Lind's *Vietnam – The Necessary War*, which dissects the contending strategies and theories quite clearly and thoroughly and concludes that the Cold War was fought in Vietnam and Korea, Africa and Latin America, because yet another European war was inconceivable all around.

Lewis Sorley's *A Better War*, which the author explains was triggered by the suspicious fact that Neil Sheehan's *A Bright Shining Lie* "devotes 725 pages to events through Tet 1968 and only 65 pages to the rest of the war, even though John Paul Vann, the nominal subject of his book, lived and served in Vietnam for four years after the Tet Offensive." Sorley discovers why the newsmedia's standard history of the war ignores everything after.

Nayan Chanda's *Brother Enemy – The War After The War*, for the story of what happened next to the peoples o'er there with emphasis on the maneuvers among the communist powers.

B.G. Burkett & Glenna Whitley's *Stolen Valor*, for the stories of what happened and didn't happen next to men over here – those who served and those who didn't but claimed they had.

Another suspicious void in the later discourse has been the lack of any discussion of the Korean War's bearing on any Vietnam metaphor. South Korea was after all, even at its roughest years of military dictatorship, a far freer place than North Korea and once it became a democracy and a first world economic power there should have been a revised look back at Vietnam – we now know by the example of Vietnamese-Americans that the Republic of South Vietnam could have made it as well. Only Lind makes much of South Korea's success as possibly analogous.

One more book key to lifting the veil on all this is James Piereson's *Camelot and the Cultural Revolution*, which makes the case that it was John F. Kennedy's assassination itself that "shattered American liberalism." In his reading, Jackie and the keepers of the Kennedy flame immediately began to bend the JFK story away from the truth, "He didn't even have the satisfaction of being killed for civil rights. It had to be some silly little communist. It even robs his death of any meaning." (quoted from *Jackie After Jack* by Christopher Andersen) Piereson writes about the *New York Times*' James Reston's coverage in the aftermath:

> "The fact that the assassin was actually a communist did not enter into the equation or alter Reston's judgments as to who was ultimately responsible for the crime, even though an extensive report on Oswald and his communist affiliations appeared in Reston's

own newspaper adjacent to his article. He seems to have reached an instinctive conclusion about the cause of the event without any reference to the actual identity of the assassin."
(*Camelot and the Cultural Revolution*)

Piereson also notes that Arthur Schlesinger's thousand-page history of the Kennedy administration does not mention Oswald by name though Schlesinger "allocated several paragraphs to a description of Dallas's hate-filled atmosphere." Thus the *Times* aids Camelot's court in laundering the assassination until the right takes the blame for a leftist's act. Then JFK's own pressing of the Cold War in Vietnam, Cuba, Berlin... turns into just another cover for the false theater of defense policy thereafter in the Democratic Party.

As for Afghanistan, whether it is the promising-but-besieged democracy it seems or not, we were told by the Democrats that it was the good war. The Iraq War became the bad war once they'd changed their mind on it in an echo of their party's Vietnam syndrome. (Actually, historically, the Iraq War will more likely be seen as the second battle of the Gulf War.) Further complicating policy matters, we were told that the Clinton Administration should have intervened in Rwanda! President Clinton, the reigning statesman of his party has apologized for not having done so. Whether the U.S. should have or shouldn't have is debatable; I'm agnostic on these questions. However, we should not throw away American lives on moralistic gestures; America should profit from these costly actions, whether that profit be defensive as in Cold War calculus in Vietnam or the War-on-Terror calculus in Afghanistan. These are all wars of choice for America; so too WWI, WWII, Korea, Vietnam, *et. al.* That's our special providence, our luck and perhaps burden. We do not live under jeopardy as, say the Poles do. Perhaps we owe something to Poland therefore. I don't know; I can't do the math.

What I do know is that the Democrats have supported wars in Vietnam and Iraq and Afghanistan, and then had schizophrenic meltdowns. Their crime against the Republic of South Vietnam was not repeated elsewhere because the baby boomers' generation-wide teen tantrum could occur only once. We can be thankful for small things. President Obama is sending 21,000 more troops to Afghanistan...

(*originally posted at* The New Vulgate, *No. 8*)

Pinochet in Winter – Last Act for the Hero
This outrage came to me as I followed the heroes of international law chase down the single finest dictator the world has ever seen. God knows if I submitted it anywhere.

By the time the recently published 800 page *Black Book of Communism*, gets to Latin America (pg. 647) the sober accounting of the cost of Communism has reached an estimated 90 million human dead. And this figure merely hints at the scale of the Terror that earned the Party room to commit its delusional program – delusional because the whole thing was at essence a closed rationalization for the killing and Terror itself. These were actual humans we must remind ourselves: some were artists, some workers, some nomads, some ne'er-do-wells, some academics, some Party members, some played guitar, some played soccer with their children....

The pall cast over the survivors will have a long half-life. The internationalists, the fellow travelers, useful idiots, fifth columnists, dupes, spies, and high-minded posturers that ran interference for that system have been de-pantsed in the last decade, and there remain more fraternal socialist secret archives to be opened. (The sixties activists may rue having to outlive the antediluvian Viet regime, but it'll be good for them.) However, that communist specter has not stopped our contemporary version of the socially delusional. They believe in Castro, or if pressed that he is as decent as that rotten Cuban heritage or all-purpose American culpability will allow. They also believe Allende was "our" best hope and that's why he was stopped. They believe the North Vietnamese would have been very kindly if only we hadn't picked a fight with them. They believe Subcommandante Marcos is the last best hope for mankind (only Dude, no smoking!).

But they don't really believe all this. Some of them, the realist-fantasists, used to gaze longingly at Yugoslavia as the Third Way. (An unnoted illustration of God's: contempo Third Wayfarers Tony Blair and Bill Clinton were given to bury that embarrassing fantasy.) In truth, they do not care what comes after their putsch. They are not that serious; they are mere gamers – only, rather than tactical players, they are more spectators with all the outsized emotional rooting interest, but no actual stake. The better for irresponsible idealism.

That "Part V., The Third World" in the *Black Book* features only Cuba,

Nicaragua, and Peru from Latin America is due largely to Augusto Pinochet Ugarte, his fellow generals in the Chilean defense forces, and three former presidents of Chile. They and the instinct for self-defense of the classes scheduled for liquidation as Socialist Allende lost control to the Movement of the Revolutionary Left (Maoist), made Chile an exception and possibly the mortal fulcrum of Communism's life-span.

Salvador Allende Gossens placed first with 36% in a three way presidential race in 1970. His Popular Unity coalition included the Communist Party, Allende's more extreme Socialist Party, and the Radical Party. This threw the contest to the Chamber of Deputies where the Christian Democrats of outgoing President Eduardo Frei agreed to support Allende over the second place rightist candidate after he signed a pledge to respect the democratic institutions – a pledge Allende later explained to French Communist groupie Regis Debray as "a tactical necessity." (Frei had been elected with CIA help in 1964 on a third-way platform which alienated the Right by expropriating farmland for peasant co-ops.) It was a close three-way split in the electorate with each candidate polling in the thirty percentiles. But Allende took his total as a mandate for nationalization of mining, banks, and factories (the nationalization of the copper mines was approved unanimously in the legislature and the copper industry remains nationalized with 10% of its revenue tithed to the Military). Allende also raised wages by fiat and accelerated land reform. This quickly drove Frei and the Christian Democrats to the right, and Allende found that his own followers, now augmented with Cuban and Soviet operatives and the free-floating leftwing adventurers from the Free World, could not be satisfied. He had humored the hip, young Movement of the Revolutionary Left (Maoist) and now they were promising death to their class enemies.

Factory production fell as managers were replaced by workers committees, and then stopped as the workers went on strike. Leading into the election year for deputies, Allende spent and raised wages until inflation was 300%. The early unity in the Left coalition split over the spoils. With the Christian Democrats now in the opposition *majority*, Allende's ministers ruled illegally by decree. Allende pleaded for the strikes to end. Foreign trade plummeted and rationing was introduced for those without the correct party affiliations.

Allende and the Christian Democrats and the Military circled each other to find a compromise in the final months before the coup, but by then no-one trusted anyone. Allende hadn't won a majority in the Chamber of Deputies, but the opposition didn't have the votes to impeach him. On August 22 a majority of deputies declared the government was acting in violation of the constitution and called on the military to seize power.

Senator Carlos Altamirano, secretary general of the Socialist Party, stopped fomenting mutiny in the armed forces long enough to threaten the right with an internationally supplied urban guerrilla force. This force existed in numbers estimated at 15,000 but they fled abroad, or into embassies, or went underground, and the coup of September 11, 1973 went easier than the military had expected.

The post-coup battle for justification has been lost, however. Here in the world of ideas there is an international guerrilla force of overwhelming numbers. No matter the resolute manner in which this unique dictatorship rationally reconstructed the economy and social policy in ways that kept its growth rate at thrice the rest of Latin America while government staffing plunged from 650,000 to 158,000 and infant mortality fell by three-quarters. In real existing socialism, such stats would be worth millions of dead in any Marxist nation's omlette, but here they don't buy a measly 3,000 commies. Russian General Alexander Lebed visited Chile soon after the fall of the Soviet Union to learn about the Chilean model and Pinochet's experience. When asked by western reporters, What about the executed and the disappeared? He asked how many had been killed. When told over three thousand, Lebed made a dismissive "ppffft" sound and said that was nothing. Perhaps this ex-Soviet General truly knows the value of a communist life. (James R. Whelan, *Wall Street Journal* 10.30.98: "The Rettig Commission – named by the first post-military government to investigate human rights abuses and headed by a former Allende minister – counted a total of 2,279 dead and missing on both sides. The first three months of fighting claimed 1,261 of the victims.")

Jean-Paul Sartre did not visit Chile as he did Peru and Portugal and anywhere else leftist military coups raised hopes for his vision of a divine tyranny. But there is no divine tyranny, the best hope is a grubby republican democracy of mean ambition philosophically, but based in a sober assessment of human nature. This rubs intellectuals and academics and poets and artists and all manner of pretentious megalomaniacs the wrong way, because it tells them their expertise is limited and may prosperously be ignored. They may not kill over this directly, but they will certainly cheer on that party or guerrilla army or system which is up for the killing – though history fairly yells at them they will be next to die themselves. For Ariel Dorfman, an adviser to Allende once upon a time and novelist, there is no talk of Allende, it is all Pinochet because Pinochet rescued them from their own culpability for Chile circa 1973. Describing his play, he writes after Pinochet was arrested in London,

> "I imagined a woman, Paulina, who believes she recognizes the man who raped and tortured her during the dictatorship and, aware that the newly elected democratic government of her country cannot punish him, decides to tie the man up and judge him in her beach house. I let Paulina loose on that doctor, let her say to him the things I would have said, so many of us would have shouted from the rooftops in Chile if we had not suffocated our hope, if we had not been afraid that this would destabilize our transition, if we had not been sure that if we went too far in our demands, the military would come back and punish us yet one more time for daring to rebel." (*L.A. Times*, 10.28.98)

Aside from being self-absorbed and peurile, the premise is dishonest by omission. Ariel, poor suffering aesthete, is doomed to a world of lies and foreclosed comprehension because he cannot let the question change from, Who killed two thousand of his pals? His false emotion (for The People) masks his cold materialist use of actual people in the no-rules rhetorical battle against ideas. It's literally sophmoric, and yet the piece is titled, "Have Chileans Become Strong Enough to Grow Up?" Grow up and reject their father, then Christ, then Chilean history, then Pinochet, and yeah, let's call it a political philosophy – a very subtle insular one so no smart class enemies can catch us up in it.

The Chilean Reaction was the elite, the institutions, and the lumpen deciding they would not go to the gallows knowingly at that late date in the history of communist atrocity. For the Allende fan-club this must be made to seem mad and unforgiveable.

Marc Cooper, a young translator for Allende once upon a time writes in *The Nation* (March 23, 1998):

> "Chile was not the prelude to my generation's accomplishments. Rather, it was our political high-water mark. The Chilean military coup of 1973 was merely overture to the massacres in East Timor and in the Khmer Rouge's Cambodia, the Argentine dirty war, the scorched-earth campaigns in Guatemala and El Salvador, the C.I.A.-orchestrated contra destabilization of Nicaragua, the rise of Thatcherism in Europe, the Reagan/Bush counterrevolution in the United States." (*The Nation*)

This is to him bad news and tossing in East Timor and Cambodia is designed to infer he's learned hard lessons. But his contempt for modern Chile seems mostly based on the sight of miniskirts, Nikes, and privatized social security. That is, it is an aesthetic judgment not connected to what is best for most individuals and all together, but rooted in the revolutionary's failure to author said society. Cooper continues, "Chile is perhaps the one place on earth where idolatry of the market has most deeply penetrated." The market subverts those who know what's best for us and they can't let it go. They are the idolators. They love only themselves, but they've buried this deeply in their psyche, and they have to keep jabbering on about The People and The Poor and The Workers lest they risk personal crack-up.

1973 was the high-water mark for that post-war demographic boom and more sophists were being stamped out of liberal arts programs than ever. Then suddenly they found themselves ignored as "the masses," or "the kids," dropped back into society as the draft ended and they grew up.

This is in America. We have little dust-up flash-backs over resurfacing Weather-girls, and the odd, very odd, Lori Berenson (first girl on her block to get down with Peruvian terrorists!), and Jennifer Harbury (I married a guerrilla!). In Europe the socialist dreams lives on. Spain evolved fairly smoothly from the Franco dictatorship to a democracy in the late seventies and early eighties. This was accomplished in some part by accepting or pretending to accept that the Franco years were, if not necessary, than at least understandable and forgivable and not the worst that might be imagined coming out of those deadly years. But a Spanish lawyer and polisci prof, Joan Garces, who was an aide to Allende, working with Spanish prosecutors, Manuel Garcia Castellon, and Baltasar Garzon, also socialists, have been working diligently to prevent Chile from following a similar evolution. Why? Why are they not trying to haul eighty year old Francoists into court? Or ninety year old Stalinist killers of the Spanish Republic? Is this some strange form of imperial projection?

And why so few criminal trials of ex-government officials in Hungary, Russia, Bulgaria, Poland, the former East Germany, etc.? Far more than three thousand killings took place in these nations and I'll be tactless enough to mention that the deaths earned nothing but further degradation. The worldgovniks speculate over who will follow the Pinochet precedent, but it is never followed, even though it's the only way any nickel-and-dime African or Latin American dictator could justify himself. All the little Hitlers of all the other national socialisms are on pensions or tenured. The day the British authorities decided to adjudicate the Spanish extradition request and held Pinochet, ultimately for 16 months, Castro happened to be in Portugal for the Iberian summit. He canceled the rest of his stay and abruptly returned to Havana. But he needn't have worried. As long as he keeps McDonald's and Nike out of Cuba he remains a hero to the Left even in their darkest winter.

Pinochet had no intention to lead a coup. The Chilean military has almost no history of them, unlike the rest of Latin America. But there he was at the crisis point in his nation's history and it was left to him whether to allow Allende & Co. to defend their abuse of the constitution by invoking its proscriptions against the society they were intended to safeguard. And it was not as if these jackals hadn't advertised what they intended. By 1973 most of those 90million murders had been committed by parties with the same names spouting internationalist class war. Allende was at the founding of the Socialist Party in 1933; it was not a virgin birth.

It is the anomalous success of the Pinochet years that attracts unending attacks from the Left, and it's not simply all of Allende's surviving allies. The clear example the Pinochet regime held up on economic policy was not lost on the undeveloped world. After Japan, South Korea and Taiwan began to prove that capitalism was not a rigged system for the benefit of Western white men, Pinochet's Chile was the clincher – a real world experiment conducted under the dispassionate guidance of economist Milton Friedman. If you sat in India or Arabia or Indonesia, why give your ear to the Soviet advisor or the communist organizer after 1980? The Left lost the ears of the third world in this period. They must wish Pinochet could be killed everyday forever for the damage he's done their cause.

Heroic tales are never as they are represented by our poisoned intelligentsia. They simply can't abide representations of men of action – being pencil-necked critics of others' works. They would have it that heroism is simplistic and regressive, a construct for oppression. But any story or film intended for those above comic books is inevitably much more realistic and darker than this straw man academia clings to. The hero dares to challenge fate. If he survives, he does not pretend it cost him nothing. And those around him, even those he saved, feel uneasy in his presence. He remains in part a physical threat, but more importantly a moral challenge they suspect they cannot meet.

Before Pinochet was held in Britain, *The New Yorker* did a profile of him titled, "Autumn of the Tyrant." In it, reporter Jon Lee Anderson quotes Augusto Pinochet Ugarte, "'I've always been a very studious man, not an outstanding student, but I read a lot, especially history. And history teaches you that dictators never end up well.' He said this with an ironic smile." (*New Yorker*, October 19, 1998)

Sports.

~

Dad's Pirates vs. The Yankees, Game 7, 1960

I wrote this after Christmas 2010 for the New Vulgate. *I've since bought the DVD of the game for Dad and we'll have to sit down and watch it again soon, this time without the constant Bob Kostas interruptions.*

Dad is 83 and his Alzheimer's occasionally makes you wonder, Is this now the true person with all the past and politesse stripped away? Or is the real person, born Delio Pacifico Carducci in Sarnano Italy in 1927, gone? It's not entirely either way, but sometimes you see something that isn't the person you've known your whole life.

It's interesting what Dad does remember. He remembers most of his kids most of the time, and he seems to know that the youngest ones running around the house on occasion are his grandkids, but other than with Mom, every relationship seems tenuous. As the eldest son of an immigrant he had it particularly tough in that unique American way. My Grandfather Secundo thought sports were wasted energy that might be spent in the mines or landscaping, or around the house. He did his own handiwork, made his own wine and beer, grew his own vegetables and grapes. He was sure everything was fixed in American sports the way it all was in Italy. As a soldier in the Trieste area in WWI he found himself and others' lives treated so cavalierly by the Italian officer corps that he began to plan to leave. Once in America the culture shock lead him to put in Dad's mind that being Italian was going to be used against him his entire life here. Secundo never quite learned English. Dad entered first grade without any English. The Nuns told him, "We don't have any Delios here," and changed his name to Donald and he picked English up quickly.

Dad still does remember certain burned-in experiences, both positive and negative. Secundo worked in America for several years before returning to Sarnano to bring his wife and son to America. Dad still remembers his earliest memory – the porpoises following alongside the ship; he was three years old. Secundo worked with his older brother in the mines of West Virginia, Kentucky, and eastern Pennsylvania. They carted coal and materiel around in horse-drawn wagons until moving up to working with explosives. Primo was killed in an accident and so Secundo and family left coal country for Bradford in northwest Penn. The family came to include three boys and a girl.

Today, Dad can usually tell the story of getting into a fight out front of his new house with a neighbor kid who was Irish. He searches for words but still tells it well. Basically the Irish kid was picking on the new kid and both mothers came out on their porches. Dad remembers his Mother calling out, "Dalio, don'ta you fight," while the Irish kid's Mother was yelling "Tommy, you whip that little dago!" Dad also tells the story of making the basketball team at St. Bernard's High School in Bradford, and having the star player, the coach's son, a white kid, admire Dad's "blinding speed." Clearly an early validation that meant a lot to him.

When I spent six months in Naperville last year to see if we could avoid the use of caretakers for him, he told me these stories often. I'd try to tease out a few new details each time: On the boat over they were in common steerage; from the porch his Mother was using her rough English in the futile hope of taming the Irish. She would have used Italian to talk to her son.

DAD AND HIS MOTHER, 1931 PASSPORT.

Dad had to quit the basketball team when winter came as he had to wake pre-dawn to shovel snow for his father. Secundo was then a groundskeeper for wealthy families in Bradford, mostly from local oil strikes and the Zippo lighter company. This was not something he did for spending money. He was soon working his way through college at St. Bonaventure and Pitt, then through medical school at Loyola, and then interning at Oak Park Hospital where he met Mom who was a nurse who'd grown up in Chicago. He had his residency at Merced County Hospital in California where I was born. We moved back to the Chicago area in 1956 and settled in Naperville the next year where Dad looked around at all the Germans and wondered if they'd allow an Italian to touch them. But it worked out great; they had nine kids, and Dad is well remembered and often out at a restaurant he is approached by former patients, so many he often couldn't remember their names even before he developed Alzheimer's. Mom worked at the office often enough in later years as my brother took over the practice to remember many of them though.

About five years ago, when his memory was still sharp, my sister had her husband set up a videocamera and they taped Dad talking about his early life. After about a half hour Mom joined him and they talked about how they met and got married. They did this for us since in our busy lives it's hard to keep any of the family's past straight. We visited Sarnano in 1991 with Dad and his American-born siblings and got to see the house he was born in. An ox was now in the basement the young family had occupied. We met some of his cousins who showed us the small patch of rocky hillside the family still farmed. Another cousin, a slight, high-spirited widow wearing black told us in Italian that she remembered when Dad was a baby crawling on the floor and she had worried he might be stepped on. My sister asked how recently her husband had died and found he'd died over ten years earlier.

Sometimes Mom or my sisters have to reassure Dad that he has no worries financially; that immigrant kid's fearful drive can still surface. As strict an upbringing we had in small town Naperville we now know better the immigrant pressures Dad had to face, and if he'd given in and moved his wife and us back to his hometown we'd have really understood! While I was back at my parents' we'd walk about a mile every morning along the Riverwalk to the coffeeshop and then walk back. As the winter progressed the walk got harder for him. He'd want to stop and rest and that became impossible in the cold. One time as we walked he said he felt like he was in a dream. Maybe the daily impression the walk made on what remained of his memory made it seem endless. When my brother came into town we went down a couple times to see the Blackhawks play. Dad isn't the biggest hockey fan but he enjoyed the spectacle

SECONDO CARDUCCI, MY PARENTS WEDDING, 1954.

at the United Center, but the second game it wasn't until we walked out of the concourse and down to our seats that he raised his hands and said, "We were just here!" That was good to hear from him. He settled in for another exciting game of ice hockey. I lost him for a few minutes as we got stuck in the urinal lines between periods and he casually took cuts and got out ahead of me. People were very understanding. His physical slowing down and intermittent Alzheimer's paranoia made caretakers and an antidepressant necessary, so I moved back to Wyoming last spring.

In November I linked here to an interesting story about the discovery of a complete 16mm kinescope of Game 7 of the 1960 World Series when the Pirates beat the Yankees on Bill Mazeroski's 9th inning home run – the only time a World Series ended that way. Bing Crosby was part owner of the team which played at Forbes Field in those years. Crosby, the article related was too nervous to watch the final deciding game. The series was tied and the Yankees had crushed the Pirates three times while Pittsburgh had barely won three close games. Just before he stepped on a plane to Paris Crosby decided to have an assistant film the game just in case the unimaginable happened. The game is one of the only full baseball games filmed before the 1965 introduction of videotape.

My Dad would've understand Crosby's anxiety. He often listened to Bob Prince call the Pirates games on *KDKA* in the car at night, or up in his room when reception permitted once games got important late in the season. My brothers and I followed the Cubs on *WGN AM* and *WGN TV* with the much friendlier Jack Brickhouse announcing. Hearing Bob Prince announce strike-outs, base-hits, double-plays and even home-runs like they were nothing in that even, tobacco-cured voice made it seem to us like the Pirates were a grown-ups' team that played late at night and the Cubs were for kids playing in daylight – even the pitch of the crowd-noise was higher at Wrigley. Prince would drone on over the ionosphere's interference while

ROBERTO CLEMENTE, GAME 7, KINESCOPE, MLBN.

Dad would groan or shout at each development like he was suffering the torments of the damned.

Home for Christmas I checked the *MLB* channel at my parents and found the Game 7 special was on and got Dad to watch. My Mom and sister were in too. The spectacle of the game itself on a flawlessly filmed print was interesting enough. Mom marveled at how thin the players looked and how well-dressed the fans were. Forbes Field looked great with its outfield ivy, the see-through fencing behind home plate, and the box seats jutting out in short right and left field. The telecast standards of that day were interesting too. There were very few close-ups, no replays that I recall, and just the names of the players put on the screen as they came to bat. And it was "Bob Clemente." I didn't hear Prince say it that way, he called the first half of the game, but I did hear Mel Allen call him "Bob" during the second half. There was no second color man, each announcer – Prince the Pirates man and Allen the Yankees man – called half the game solo.

DAD IN THE HOUSE HE WAS BORN, SARNANO, ITALY, 1991.

Dad was riveted to the game as he watched the 1960 Pirates line-up of excellent but far less famous players. For the Pirates it was Dick Groat, Roberto Clemente, Vern Law, Rocky Nelson..., for the Yankees it was Yogi Berra, Mickey Mantle, Roger Maris, Bill Skowron....

They broke into the game every couple innings to have Bob Kostas interview surviving players and Dad was interested in that too, though not many of the players survive. We'd ask Dad if he remembered the game, or that player, Bob Prince, etc., and he'd answer yes but wouldn't be distracted from watching. He would have been just four years into building his medical practice as a doctor in Naperville, then a small town at the end of the southwest suburban commuter line. He would have made some time to see that game even if only checking a small set at the hospital or office. He said he remembered seeing the game and I tend to believe him. You don't play the Yankees in the World Series every day, though the Pirates did make a habit of winning the World Series in the late sixties and early seventies, amazing for an underdog team with limited resources. They had the first scouts combing the Caribbean for great Latin players of which Clemente was paramount. He died in a plane crash running supplies to help after an earthquake in Nicaragua but the team continued to win with a black-Caribbean style. While I was in Berkeley in the early 1980s I was able to report to Dad that based on the number of Pirates caps in Oakland they had become the national team of black America. He got a kick out of that. But today he isn't responsive to his Pittsburgh teams. He'll watch a game and respond to some of the plays but has no rooting interest anymore.

DAD AND MOM, FALL 2011

But that one game, the one that promised to be too excruciating to watch for even Bing Crosby and ended with a home-run by Bill Mazeroski to break the tie in the 9th and win the World Series for Pittsburgh, proved a memory stronger than Alzheimer's. Nice to know that something is.

(originally posted at The New Vulgate, No. 78)

Chicago Blackhawks, Stanley Cup 2010

I would've been content to watch the finals on television since the games wouldn't take place in the old Chicago Stadium, but my brother scored the tickets to game 5 so I was glad to drive back for a few days. The team was fun to watch all year. I wrote this after I was back in Wyoming and posted it June 16, 2010.

Even when Chicago was by convention referred to as the Second City it was the largest coherent city that was not cobbled together like New York for pride of first-place or Los Angeles which annexed south for a port and north for tax base. Those cities rumble with secession efforts from time to time, but Chicago abides, though not without changes and despite being topographically as inadequate as it is geographically ideal – the city was basically raised up out of swamp onto a concrete substructure to allow for non-disease-ridden living and the construction of skyscrapers. It lost a million citizens from its early seventies' 3+ million peak. As I've noted before, Houston has been the true Second City to Chicago in recent years if one is talking about cultural places that hang together as cities.

Hockey is to Chicago sports as Chicago is to its coastal betters. That is, under-appreciated, often forgotten and finding itself back in its old default status, bracketed with wrestling and roller derby. But people forget as well that basketball and football, especially in their professional leagues, were also cheap, gym-rat diversions. My dad followed his college teams, Pitt basketball and football, and St. Bonaventure basketball, plus the Pirates. Eventually the Steelers convinced him to follow pro football. The only Chicago team he got into was the Bulls. Back when we were following the college-like Dick Motta Bulls of Jerry Sloan-Norm Van Lier-Bob Love-Tom Boerwinkle-Chet Walker he told me that conventional sentiment among sports fans in the forties and fifties was that no-one would ever really take professional sports seriously, other than baseball. As late as the seventies professional basketball was a rather tawdry affair, especially the majority of the games between non-contending teams. Television and its money and the players' unions fight for more of it, and the owners' fight to find more money forged a desperate glamour from decades of tawdry locker room crud collected doing duty for b-ball, hockey, wrestling, boxing....

In the beginning the Chicago Blackhawks were founded by Major Frederic McLaughlin, a coffee magnate in the twenties known for his

Manor House Coffee brand. McLaughlin bought the Portland Rosebuds of a regional league and moved them from Oregon to Chicago and named them the Blackhawks, after Chief Black Hawk who'd been the last free Indian Chief in Illinois and was defeated by troops which included both Abe Lincoln and Jefferson Davis. The current team ownership, the Wirtz family, came in from Detroit in the mid-thirties as they collected indoor arenas and other real estate in the Midwest at Depression-era prices.

Originally, the players' services were owned outright and they were paid little and most worked off-season jobs. This allowed tickets to be cheap enough that these teams survived the thirties on gate receipts. The NHL was an ongoing concern from the mid-twenties as it came together out of regional leagues in the northeast, the upper midwest, and the northwest, plus of course Canada. While the Wirtz family dealt real estate and liquor they didn't control their principal tenant, the Blackhawks, until 1954. They ran the team and the Stadium as if it was still the thirties.

The *NHLTV* channel was running year by year Stanley Cup summaries and replaying old game telecasts recently and I caught Toronto vs. Chicago April 15, 1967, a semi-final Game 5 at the Chicago Stadium. For all its tawdry grubbiness the game was quite refined in its presentation compared to today's game's high-test melodrama, borrowed mostly from professional wrestling and action movies. The Stadium ice circa 1967 had nothing on it but the red-line, the blue-lines, the face-off circles, the goal lines and two small Blackhawk logos. The boards were white; there were no sponsors' logos anywhere until the NHL began to sell league-wide sponsorships. Before then advertising on the boards was a minor-league or small market expansion team characteristic. The old scoreboard is an unreadable deco mess of clock faces. The pipe organ was supposed to be the largest, loudest ever made and its steam boilers were across the street and it took about four seconds for a note to sound. And the television production itself is likewise minimal. The announcer, probably Dan Kelly, is fine. There are rudimentary replays of goals and great saves, and even a slow motion replay that the kinescope can't quite reproduce. The Stadium crowd doesn't sound so different but it sounds older and more male. And the occasional flashes of the audience behind the benches reveal no logo clothing or jerseys, but suits still, and fedoras. It's no small credit to Arthur Wirtz and his son William who took over in 1983 that this austere thirties flavor was only slowly modernized and was still largely extant until the Stadium itself was dismantled in 1995.

My dad took my brothers and me to our first game sometime in this period, probably before 1965. We sat back in a corner of the mezzanine well under the first balcony. We didn't go often but we got into the Stadium once or twice a year to see the Blackhawks or the Bulls who'd launched in 1966 as an expansion team. For basketball you could walk right down and take one of the good seats, there were so few people attending games in the years before the Dick Motta teams of the early seventies.

We went to see the White Sox once, and more often the Cubs, who always played during the day in Wrigley Field and whose announcer, Jack Brickhouse, seemed pitched to kids. The Cubs audience sound was high pitched – younger and more female; the Sox's crowd was a low-pitched noise and they played at night in not-so-friendly Comiskey Park. Brickhouse's second was Lloyd Pettit. He wasn't a distinctive baseball announc-

CHICAGO STADIUM, 1995; PHOTO: JOE CARDUCCI.

er but he came to set the standard for hockey. And because the Wirtzes did not televise the home games, one listened to Pettit a lot during their competitive stretch of 1969 thru 1974 when they made the finals twice, losing both times. Pettit married into the Bradley family and moved to Milwaukee where he built the Bradley Center and tried to bring an NHL franchise to town – the Wirtz family stopped him. By the time Pettit was gone so was Bobby Hull as the WHA lured several high profile but underpaid NHL stars away to cities hungry for professional hockey. Free agency, expansion, European players, and mandatory helmets ended that world of old-time hockey. (See Harold Barkley's book of photography, *Hockey's Original 6*, for a portrait of what looks positively otherworldly now.)

Chicago was pronounced "America's Greatest City" in a 1985 issue of *The New Republic* and it seems even that late it was the traces of thirties Chicago that the author was touting. Those plus the pall of pessimism that the Slavs lent the city. There is something to that; the city is, or was, very Catholic but underneath the Irish and Italian sensibilities lies the Eastern Catholicism of Poles, Lithuanians and Croats that tilts toward the Orthodox in Ukrainian, Serbian, and Greek neighborhoods. Chicago filled up with the foreign-born and with blacks and also whites from down south. It's amazing anyone could understand each other. The Democratic Party machine was organized by Anton Cermak but the Irish came to be the political interlocutors among the others. Not to say the Daleys have been particularly fluent speakers of English but they are quite eloquent in speaking politics with and for these populations.

That Slavic sensibility works its way through the Blackhawks story more-so than even the star-crossed-when-not-fully-cursed White Sox or Cubs stories. And that's because hockey itself barely has its chin above the grown-ups' table where the MLB, NFL, and NBA feast. The daily papers and local news and *ESPN* all display the reflexive disrespect the sport gets, even though the expansion teams are now established and often Cup-winners and there's been a parade of astonishing talent from Gretzky to Lemieux to Lindros that no-one questioned. But the hammerheads on *ESPN* know nothing about ice hockey per se and somehow they profit by belaboring arcane football and basketball trivia. With baseball it's understandable I suppose, but I suspect the NFL is perfect for the sports-media rabble because the game is just once a week and that gives the local reporters six days of fulmination over the last game and the next. It's overblown civic fandom feeding on marketing.

Still, unless I missed something I don't believe that even that professional Chicagoan on Saturday's *NPR* program even mentioned the Stanley Cup story. Went straight to the World Cup, i.e. Soccer, you know, futbol, comprende? Professional Murdoch critics have been sniping over stray Brit turns-of-phrase in his *Wall Street Journal*, but given *NPR*'s *Beeb*-fallout I wasn't buying it until last Friday's and the *Weekend Journal*'s two-day flood of articles and graphics about the World Cup, with no mention of the only trophy anyone really cares about. There is only one Stanley Cup and the winners do not keep it; they get their name etched on it and it's passed on to next season's winner. What explains such misplaced priorities? Must be some unfathomable Limey-Cheesehead issue from back in the Commonwealth days. But that doesn't explain the *Drudge Report*'s soccer obsession. Is this the metric system constituency revealing itself?

But this year it's working for Hockey. A strike/lock-out ended the season only five years ago and in Chicago where the team was doing well it seemed Cubs-like in its serendipity. Bill Wirtz was in his cranky pre-death phase and angry fans dropped their season tickets by the thousands. The minor league Chicago Wolves set up shop in 1994 the last year of the Stadium and played decent human-scale hockey in Rosemont in the northwest suburbs and built its base on disaffected fans, often featuring former Blackhawks like Al Secord, Troy Murray and Chris Chelios. But Game 6 of the Stanley Cup finals last Wednesday in Philadelphia was the highest rated network hockey game since 1974 and the days of *NBC*'s Peter the Puck; still the share was barely to the level of the worst the NBA finals or the Superbowl have ever done. The game I attended wasn't as dominant outside of the two cities and Canada due to the NBA and NHL both insisting on prime-time, so the Chicago show at the United Center wasn't seen as widely. The United Center show isn't what the old Stadium show was (see the Gulf War-era NHL All-Star Game anthem for a taste of that) but it was loud in there. They lined the top with reflectors when the original structure didn't sound anywhere near as loud as the much smaller, solid brick Stadium had been. The ice is standard size now too. If you ask me only the food is better.

Ben Bentley, once the PA announcer at the Stadium and former boxing promoter and all around thirties-type gym rat, exclaimed once in the decades-long dog days of Chicago sports, "If you could only win in this town!" Bentley knew that all those Chicagoans walking around their bungalows in an East European fog would near jump out of their skin if their identification-investment in the local teams actually paid off in a championship. A big part of the Blackhawks diehards are from the first ring of working class suburbs within Cook County. The last year of the Stadium's existence, 1994-5, was the year Lightbourne moved back to Chicago. My brothers and I had season tickets but I bought two in the second balcony so Dave could get a last look at the place. Up there it was all young adults from Berwyn, Cicero, Maywood and the like. Couples in groups sneaking a smoke reveling in the glory of their tawdry low-rung sport – their secret: the Blackhawks at the Chicago Stadium. You can see today's version of these Bohunk girls running after the busses at the Victory Parade last Friday in the *Trib*'s video. Patrick Kane could lose a limb to one of these girls if he's not careful.

The city is quite changed from Bentley's day. That lost million make for large chunks of Denver, Phoenix, Las Vegas and other places. I used to go to see the L.A. Kings in the early eighties and most of the original six visiting teams had their cheering sections but the Blackhawks fans turning out in Los Angeles could be quite present, almost like what you hear in St. Louis or Milwaukee baseball stadiums when the Cubs visit. I saw those Kings games on Rick Van Santen's or Kelley Thornton's tickets. They'd have Richard Meltzer or Raymond Pettibon or Mike Watt or others to the Lakers or Kings games. We weren't on the floor by Jack Nicholson or Dyan Cannon but there's no doubt we were the coolest bunch in the Forum. The camera never settled on Mike Watt, but it's on Flea all the time now. Rick's uncle was Ralph Backstrom, a Cup-winner for Montreal and an ex-Blackhawk and back then the University of Denver hockey coach. The Blackhawks could barely stay with the Edmonton Oilers in those years, but who could? They managed to get into the finals in 1991 but were swept by the Pittsburgh Penguins. When my dad would be relishing another Steelers championship or Pirates World Series, I'd remind him of how good the Penguins were and he'd smile and say "That's right, the mighty Penguins!" We were in Sarnano, Italy visiting the town where he was born during the 1991 finals so just one brother got to use our tickets and witness the nightmare.

My brother Mark lives near Las Vegas and he found us tickets this time that somehow came from a stash Tony Esposito had (that made it less painful to pay $800 apiece). Mark then flew back home Saturday and writes, "I went to the Hard Rock Sunday with my Hawks jersey on and couldn't get far without unending high-fives, fists, and lots of yelling 'Hawks'...sent chills up my spine, and I still can't believe all the years watching culminating in the Cup win and over 2 million at the parade after expecting 350,000 per the press. My sports life aspirations are fulfilled!" One of Mark's quirks is his conviction that one shouldn't shout when everyone else is shouting, but should pick a moment when the arena is quiet, and then yell! In the old days he might wait a whole period for a quiet spot to yell out "Koharski you suck!" and it worked, he'd get a good chunk of the crowd laughing in assent and you knew that referee Koharski heard it too. This time Mark's son heard his dad's voice in the background on television when he shouted from one aisle over at the announcers doing a pre-game report. We thought at first it couldn't be possible he heard him until we remembered that poor TV crew light up in the still empty arena; Mark yelled at them because it was quiet and they were there.

If the Blackhawks' youthful core can be kept together under the pressure of the new salary cap, we'll see if any of them actually needs to win the way Michael Jordan needed to win. Even if not quite, they have a good chance to win a couple more in the forseeable future. Certainly Bobby Hull and Stan Mikita can caution them how they'd expected their 1961 Cup win to be repeated given how good the team was and how young they'd been. Jeremy Roenick was emotional on *NBC*'s post-game wrap because he'd been a Blackhawk and a fan favorite and never got his name on the Cup; Bobby Hull was emotional because he never got back on it and in the end regretted leaving the city. Wirtz retired Hull's jersey in 1983 and that seemed a watershed moment that you can watch at *Youtube*, but Hull was not invited back until William, "Dollar" Bill Wirtz had passed from the scene. His son Rocky Wirtz now has the place crawling with ex-Blackhawks and the good feelings are everywhere in Chicago and chunks of Vegas, Denver, Phoenix and Los Angeles. The thirties were hard-core.

*

It seems quite common for teams that reach the finals to be made up of pieces put together by some GM or coach who has recently been fired. Professional sports is a pitiless business but somehow players must be able to lead themselves on as if they fully identify with their new team and new city and they mean everything to them. They must call up more energy than human nature normally allows. And then they must play generously and intelligently as a team; something easier to do in college or high school where the bonds and loyalties are more personal. In an NBA final feature on coach Phil Jackson and what he learned playing for the Knicks they played a clip of then-Knicks coach Red Holzman saying, "You can't replace team-play with ability or anything else."

For the Blackhawks it was Dale Tallon who was fired earlier this championship season. A player with the club, then the color man paired with play-by-play announcer Pat Foley, he finally became General Manager. After a thirty year affiliation with the team he had to watch his signees win the Cup from his current job as GM of the Florida Panthers. Dale tells Adam Jahns in the *Sun-Times* that he took many calls from the team throughout the night of the victory. Rocky Wirtz replaced the insider Tallon for the hockey know-nothing John McDonough simply to try to steal some marketing magic from the Chicago Cubs where McDonough had been team president. But the Cubs don't really contend, and the marketing magic has been Wrigley Field which perhaps the new owner can be trusted to protect, but the old owner, the Tribune Company, wanted to replace. If the Cubs ever do that then they will really require marketing genius to fill whatever might replace it.

I like the Dale Tallon grace-note from October 7, 2007 as he memorialized the just-passed William Wirtz on the United Center scoreboard over the boos of the fans. I thought Rocky might give some indication of his conflicted emotions over seemingly showing up his dad so quickly but he didn't let on. Rocky's grandfather Arthur had run things and won the earlier championships, Bill ran the club only from 1983 until his death in 2007.

Life Against Dementia

*

Driving into greater Chicagoland Saturday morning, the day before Game 5, I was listening to Herb Kent, the Cool Gent, on Chicago's *WVAZ*, and he was playing great old tunes I'd never heard before but rather than back-announce them he took a call from I'd guess a middle-aged black woman and in the small talk that preceded whatever she was calling about, Herb asked her what she'd be doing on the weekend and she answered, "Oh you know, just getting ready for the big game." And Herb Kent, the King of the Dusties, audibly double-takes asking, "You doin' the Blackhawks?!" She sure was and I bet Pronger and Hartnell were hated with style at her place. *Sun-Times* columnist Richard Roeper wrote a rather routine provocation-of-a-column noting the pallor of the Blackhawks audience. He got what he wanted, a second column filled with Blackhawk testimonials-of-color. He quotes Kendra Dinkins: "There may be few of us, but not as few as you think... I think there are far more minorities cheering at home, in the bars, decorating their office spaces, and talking trash to their Philly friends than you think! GO HAWKS!!!"

Throughout the NHL playoffs the statue of Michael Jordan in front of the United Center was wearing a Blackhawks jersey. There was probably something on the Picasso and on the Lions out front of the Art Institute. So it wasn't a big surprise when to the sound of Tom Petty's "Learning to Fly" over the PA Jordan himself in a Hawks jersey stepped out to the front of his center ice first balcony skybox and waved to the crowd during Game 5. His image was up on the scoreboard suddenly and one had to scan around to find exactly where he was in the building. The audience first cheered at the video image but once they located his actuality in the building waving to the full house the cheers became fuller and warmer. I thought all those Berwyn-Maywood diehards were really grateful to share their secret and have it consecrated by the biggest winner this loser city ever got handed. According to the papers Jordan dined at Gibson's after the game with Charles Barkley and Chris Chelios.

Possibly in a related development, there was a photo of the Rev. Jesse L. Jackson hoisting the Stanley Cup somewhere online.

*

The *Daily Herald* reports on the Cup tour continuing at Wrigley at the Crosstown Classic Sunday night, featuring a nice photo of all three teams, Cubs, Sox, Hawks, together around the Stanley Cup on the pitcher's mound. I assume that Jay Leno did his best to end Cup fever on Monday night when the Blackhawks showed up with it. But still to come, the hoisting of the Cup by President Barack Obama at the Chicago White House.

*

Quote of the Finals –

Chris Pronger: "I'm day to day with hurt feelings."

(originally posted at The New Vulgate, No. 50)

Winter Sports Wrap, 1997-98

This appeared in July 1998 in the third and final issue of The Provisional M.O., *a company newsletter-catalogue put out during the years the videotape company was functioning.*

Even the third week of June is too early to have to be done with the NBA and NHL. This year the hockey finals followed basketball due to the Olympics. That won't happen again, unfortunately. I've always savored the last few turns of the hockey season before the ice is melted down. This year the ice beneath the Bulls was long melted thanks to the Blackhawks' pratfall – missing the post-season for the first time since the six team league of the sixties. But the Redwings, Sabres, Stars, and Capitols were carving up the ice nicely before summer rudely shoved them all aside.

The Redwings as suspected took the cup. They've been a slow-starting dynasty because all those Russians had to learn that the Stanley Cup is important. Now they seem capable of the self-fueling victory push epitomized by the Bulls. The Konstantinov tragedy from last season when he was paralyzed in a limo wreck six days after that cup win seems to have grounded the team. And the maestro Scotty Bowman needs just a bit of help from outside forces to deliver what is the eighth time his name and his team's names are etched onto the only trophy that means anything. (He won a ninth as director of player personnel.)

There is obviously a lot of jazz-like improvisation in modern basketball, but it's actually hockey where improvisation rules. Not only is there the flow of play, there is also the matching of lines and players that goes on between the coaches on the fly. Player substitution is easy to see and comprehend in basketball, whereas in hockey the changes go on during play with each coach looking for an opportunity to shape the match-ups. Only the spectators seated behind the benches can truly see the game, both the action on the ice and the strategic movement of players pulled off and sent in. The home coach has the last change at stoppages of play, so he counters the visiting coach. From there they each try to hit the other with a faster or more physical set of players, or they try to match their defensive specialists with the opponents' best scoring line, and the coaches try to spring their scorers fresh onto a tired line looking to return to the bench. Late in the game they may try to spring a third or fourth line that's been rested on the number one line that's pulled heavy minutes. Hockey = Jazz. And the coaches are the soloists playing the players in groups of two and three and even mixing and matching linemates and defensive tandems on the fly. Not bad for a bunch of Canadians; I think Pittsburgh had a hand in formalizing it as well.

Coaches are still overwhelmingly Canadian; players are less and less so. The Redwings are so Russian that rearguarders like the CBC's Don Cherry have lost their bearings regarding the sport itself. The early seventies WHA expansion was necessary and exposed the limitations of the NHL game – great as it was. (They should've done anything penalty-wise to keep helmets out of the game.) It was no accident that after the NHL responded to the WHA challenge and expanded itself, and subsequently incorporated the strongest of the WHA franchises, there followed twenty plus years dominated by expansion team Stanley Cup champions. Only the Montreal Canadians of the original six seemed able to continually contend. Instead it was the new ideas and new blood of the Philadelphia Flyers, New York Islanders, Edmonton Oilers, and Calgary Flames that carried the day. In the last few years it's been the Pittsburgh Penguins, New Jersey Devils, Colorado Avalanche, and finally the losingest old franchises the New York Rangers, and Detroit Redwings. The Rangers cherry-picked the Oilers better than the Los Angeles Kings had done, but the Redwings are built for dynasty despite their early failures. After the Finns, Swedes, and Czechs of the seventies and eighties have come the post-Soviet Russians of this decade and the original six are no longer rearguarding Canadian nationalists. The NHL is now a world league of professional athletes.

In the NBA, contrary to most understanding, there are only three and a half teams: the Chicago Bulls, the Utah Jazz, the Indiana Pacers, and the New York Knicks when they're on defense. The rest of the league is full of ball-hogging shoe salesmen. As the elders of these teams retire in the next few years the league and the sports press may attribute the inevitable downturn to Michael Jordan's absence but it will be because the team sport of basketball is no longer played. It is one thing to watch a poorly played 7-5 hockey game – each goal is still relatively eventful; it's another thing to watch a poorly played 124-111 basketball game. Nike, Fila, Reebok, and Addidas have already stopped payment to virtually all shoe-perstars. *NBC*'s ratings were record-breakers for this year's finals in the expectation that this was the end of the Bull's dynasty and that perhaps the Jazz, coming off of their manhandling of the Lakers, could actually beat them in the rematch.

Unfortunately for the NBA, *NBC* sports-boy Bob Kostas got to pour his cyclamate syrup all over the six game event – Forget Mumia, Free Marv Albert! If Dennis Rodman didn't have the network wired with ex-Pistons (Isaiah Thomas, John Salley) Kostas might have gotten away with character-assassination. And what a character! At the Grant Park celebration Rodman claimed he'd never get married again but if he had to he'd marry the twelve dudes standing next to him; now that smells like team spirit, and I don't mean Michael Jordan cologne.

Indiana coach Larry Bird nearly beat the Bulls in the semi-finals by suckering Jordan into trying to beat them single-handed. Bulls assistant coach Tex Winter has identified the triangle offense's weakness as Jordan's singular talent and the temptation he has to attack double- and triple-teams instead of swinging the ball to the other side. And Jordan has long personalized the Bulls' mastery over neighboring "junior" franchises in Indiana and Cleveland. Phil Jackson professed to "discover" his bench in game five but the Bulls despite their ultimate victory in seven over Indiana and six over Utah, still looked uncannily Knick-like in their offensive sluggishness. Steve Kerr played twenty-four minutes in the last game with Utah and took zero shots. Luckily he's upped his defensive game, eh coach?

After the Bulls' Grant Park celebration the Redwings finished their sweep of the Capitols. I watched the long post-game trophy presentations and cigar-lighting and Konstantinov-wheeling out at the bar next door on Laramie's front street. It started snowing outside and the trains rumbling through were covered with the heavier snows falling at higher elevations outside town. Two and a half months until training camps. I hate summer.

Songs.

~

Jesus and Tequila

Watching D. laze around SST while Black Flag was out on tour gave me an idea for a D. Boon country album to be called "Hard Workin' Man." I wrote three songs for it, as I was listening a lot to KLAC and getting a sense of what was what in C&W. When The Minutemen decided to make their next album a double this got drafted to fill the "Chaff" side.

I had a girl, she loved what she saw
She loved me so good, she made her daddy mad.
My woman cried, she's dead to me now.
My woman ran off and I can't deny it.

My life is Jesus and tequila.
I'm satisfied, I can't deny it.

I had a job, it paid me good
I could have my fun and tip the preacher too.
My boss yelled, he's dead to me now.
My boss kicked me out and I can't deny it.

My life is Jesus and tequila.
I'm satisfied, I can't deny it.

Don't give away your love.
Don't give away your sweat.
Because a girl can't know you
And a boss can't forget.

Remember Jesus and tequila.
You're satisfied. You can't deny it.

Better to Die
This was the second lyric written for D. Boon in 1983. He played me a rough acoustic strummed demo but never finished it. I gave the words to Angst and they played it live but never recorded it.

I was five years from her and I felt each one
Drag me further and further from what could've been a home.
I go from the hotel to the motel
From flophouse to whorehouse
From coffee to whiskey, again and again.

Time may dry the tears but it won't heal the pain.
Sometimes I think it's better to die than to have to face the shame,
Better to die than to sit here and cry
Better to die than to sit here and try to stare the morning down.

I was ten years from her and the jobs'd never last
So I'd cheat on the side and lie about my past.
I went from the car to the bar
To the store for some more
From thinking to drinking, again and again.

Wine may cheat the mirrors but it won't heal the pain
Sometimes I think it's better to die than to have to face the shame,
Better to die than...

Well I'm fifteen years from her and five in this pen
It took a man's life to find me a home again.
I go from the shower to the yard
From my cell-door to the wall
From solitary to chapel, again and again.

Crime may hide the fears but it won't heal the pain
Sometimes I think it's better to die than to have the face the shame
Better to die than to sit here and cry
Better to die than to sit here and try to stare the morning down.

Chinese Firedrill

Mike Watt was letting Ed do all the singing in Firehose, and even during the Minutemen I'd encourage him to keep singing. So I wrote this one thinking it would sound good in his voice. Instead it wound up coming out of Frank Black's mouth on Mike's first "solo" album.

If your watch is wound to run, it will.
If your time is due to come, it will.
But if it ain't, you lose your chance to choose.
Another day breaks, maybe I will too.

Living this life is like trying to learn Latin
In a Chinese firedrill.

If your clock is set to go, it will.
If your cock is like to crow, it will.
But if it ain't, you lose your chance to choose.
Another day breaks, maybe I will too.

Living this life is like trying to learn Latin
In a Chinese firedrill.

CARTOONS.

~

Oregon Organism cartoons

Jim Chasse was the youngest of the Portland punks and maybe the only one everybody liked. This is before PDX was... well, whatever it is now; there were only about 30 punk rockers of any stripe in the town. Jim was ditching school and I gather he was later diagnosed as schizophrenic, but he was just a nice kid interested in music and art. A group of us got into Greg Sage's pickup truck and went out to visit Jim when he was committed to a sanitarium for a while. He was so glad to see us all. Decades later he was killed on the street in 2006 by three sad green cops ordered to keep a high-end neighborhood beautified; there is a lot about it online and a film coming. Before he was in The Psychedelic Unknowns and other bands he did a fanzine called The Oregon Organism that came out pretty regularly for a couple years. I was at Renaissance Records and he often stopped by with his pages; he published the first review of The Wipers and it was accompanied by his drawing of the band. I was happy to contribute; The Organism had spirit. I wrote about records for our catalogs so instead I drew up cartoons if I had an idea.

Life Against Dementia

OVER: JOE CARDUCCI

Interviews.

~

Interview by Eduardo Ramos, Feb. 2008

This excerpt is from an email interview that was translated into Portuguese and posted at a Brazilian site.

ER – Sorry if the questions have no connection between them and might look random, but I need to start from somewhere. When you started to work with independent music, there were no rules, no knowledge about how to run things... You learned on a daily basis way how to make it happen. What's your view about how independent labels today are just called independent because they're not linked with the majors (though often in the end they are), do you think that the spirit of new discoveries in terms of music and forward thinking are gone?

JC – I have a friend, the musician Dave Lightbourne, who is focused on '20s and '30s blues. He is often objecting to stuff he reads about delta bluesmen and southern folk musicians of that era, because people assume it was all discovered by folklorist Alan Lomax when most of them had recorded for major labels a decade or more earlier. Majors like RCA-Victor (Bluebird), Decca (Champion), and CBS (Columbia, ARC, Okeh, Vocalion) often were assembled out of independents like Aeolian (Vocalion), Star Piano (Gennett-Champion), Columbia (ARC, Okeh), and the Wisconsin Chair Co.'s Paramount. A Brunswick-Balke (Brunswick, ARC, Vocalion) had the muscle of a major with its bowling/billiards manufacturing and distribution. And the majors had paid the artists, whereas Lomax expected them to record for free.

In 1940 the professional musicians union pulled all ASCAP-published songs from radio for ten months to protect what had been a world of live music that employed thousands of small and large orchestras. The radio industry launched their own music publishing rights company, BMI, so as to play records over the radio without having to pay what it considered prohibitive royalties. BMI began to sign up songs that were available, those written mainly by non-professional musicians in traditional folk scenes like blues, country, and polka, etc. ASCAP soon settled with radio but their tin pan alley pop economy was rocked by the sudden airplay that American folk forms had received. And that sudden radio exposure of blues, country, and then rock and roll led to all the famous small independent labels that built up the rock music economy once postwar rationing of shellac and plastic ended: King, Chess, Sun, et. al.

So I would say that there is no clear aesthetic difference between the major record labels and independent labels. At different times the majors was where it was at in

American music. In the (modern) era, the switch of focus to LPs from singles is part of what gave the British bands an advantage over the still single-focused American bands. To simplify, it's as if the Brits were all art-bands, the Americans all garage bands. But the money made from LP sales turned the American majors and larger independents from clumsy back-footed giants trying anything to catch up to the hippie music boom (67-72) to powerful, bottom-line driven, platinum-seeking marketing machines. And so when the Ramones and the rest showed up they were blocked because the game of selling millions of albums had to be protected (Fleetwood Mac, the Eagles, Peter Frampton, Journey...). Radio's disinterest reinforced disinterest of labels, publications, and venues. The Ramones began to look for gigs in 1975 and it took until 1991 for a punk rock hit to force its way onto radio and magazine covers. For ten years now one can hear Ramones songs over the PA at sporting events, so what was that all about? Punk was commercial all along.

ER – Nowadays you're more involved with writing. You own your publishing house. After years working with music, how was the transition? It seems that the book industry is not facing this huge crisis as the music industry is facing.

JC – I do think publications will also disappear into electronic devices; it's just likely to take longest for books. I put out the first edition of Rock and the Pop Narcotic in 1991 and I was surprised how honest and earnest stand-alone independent bookstores were in sending you a purchase order by mail and sending you a check once they received the book. I was used to independent record stores bouncing checks because the shop owner had grabbed all the cash out of the drawer to buy cocaine. Tower Records was also expanding then and building up book sections so they made it much easier too. Now many independent bookstores as well as Tower are gone and I will see whether I can interest the big chains in my books.

ER – In the past it was clear that touring was the most effective way to spread music. Nowadays people count less and less on the revenues from records and rely more and more on touring. Do you think that in the end, it's almost like a "Devo" thing, that the music business of today seems more and more like the music business of the 50's? Where touring is the way to make things happen and make money?

JC – *There are certain parallels to earlier days. There is so much hobby music made by people at home with their computers now; they don't intend to quit their jobs and go on tour. That could be seen to be like the parlor music the middle class family would make, or the church music or back porch music families made before the modern media began to overwhelm the folk forms. In the mid-70s bars did not allow bands to play original music. Ten years earlier they had all kinds of garage, surf, R&B, dance* bands but the late '60s boom had sent the business into ballrooms and then arenas, and the bars then only wanted professional cover bands. It took ten years (1975-85) to really change that. Black Flag did most of that heavy lifting. Unfortunately, we Americans are now so far from the traditional roots of our black/white musical tree that today's young kids can't be counted on to draw from high quality music as kids once did simply because it was in the air. At times as a kid I only wanted to hear the Standells, Steppenwolf, the Who, or Black Sabbath, but I was forced to listen to a lot of other stuff while waiting for them on radio or TV. Kids can find anything online but do they? Kids need to be educated about music by radio programmers and A&R men who know music. And these don't exist anymore....

Interview by Andrew Williams, late 2002

This is an excerpt from a phoner that was published in Alarm magazine, Jan.-March 2003, in the middle of the O&O-Upland Records effort with Bill Stevenson and his tribe of musicians in Fort Collins.

AW: Okay, during the 80s you were responsible for directing one of the most important and successful independent labels in history, and then it slowly fell apart. Was that an impetus for you to join Owned and Operated? Are you trying to start over and do it again?

JC: Well, I went out to Los Angeles to do film work. I didn't have any work, but I quit college and went out there to try to be a screenwriter, and the film business was just changing. I got out there and Jaws and Rocky and Star Wars all just opened. So that was closing up on me, and I wasn't good enough yet either as a screenwriter, but punk rock was just opening up, and the first issue of Slash Magazine came out when I was in Hollywood and the first Germs single and the Sex Pistols song and the Ramones were on KROQ out there. So I just sort of drifted into it because I wasn't ready to get anything going in film, and we started a record distribution company up in Portland called Systematic, and we had a connection to Rough Trade and all those English independent labels.

I used to... if I saw a band like Black Flag or the B-52s or anybody that had an independent single release, I'd write them and get a sample, and then buy it if I thought we could sell it. So, we built that up and then moved to Berkeley, and I went down to SST because I thought those guys were working at it harder than anybody else. You know my favorite band when I was in Berkeley was Flipper, but you know they were not going to work very hard, so for me, I still wanted to be a writer. I didn't want to waste my time in the music business, but I would continue doing it if I thought I could learn something from it and have some kind of impact. So, the Minutemen and Saccharine Trust and the Stains came up to San Francisco with Black Flag once, so I got a sense of what they were into beyond their own stuff, and I wanted to get back down to L.A. for my own reasons, so that's how I got in there. When I left, there was a certain..., you know, the cycle of the original group of bands that were friends from the South Bay area was dissipating. Black Flag broke up, or it was clear they were going to break up when I left, and D. Boon had been killed, and Hüsker Dü got signed to Warner Brothers, and I wanted to spend full time writing again. So I enjoyed it. I might have stayed... And the O&O thing came together because I happened to move

Interviews

to Laramie, which is close to where All happened to move, which is Fort Collins. And they got a studio together, and the record label came out of the studio because they recorded some bands they really liked, and they couldn't get the tapes released. They would try to help a band get on to a label and couldn't do it, so they started contemplating that. And since I was up here, they talked to me about whether I wanted to get involved and sort of set up a strategy for how we would do it and what we would do.

And everything's different now of course, so all of our experience is only indirectly of any value. You know when you're making a mistake to stop making the mistake a little quicker than maybe other people do, but there's no real plan to get back in the record business. I wrote a book after I left SST, and I wrote it in the frame of mind that I was not going to be back in the business, so I didn't worry about making enemies talking about the press and radio, so I think I shouldn't have done that if I was going to get back in the record business.

AW: Well it proved a much more honest look at rock music.

JC: Well, I always thought in terms of... what I liked when I was a kid was on the top of the charts. I mean it wasn't the only thing there, but if you liked Blue Cheer or Steppenwolf or the Rolling Stones or the Who, that stuff got to the top ten and you heard it on the radio, saw it on television. So when you'd see Flipper or Black Flag or the Wipers or the Sleepers you thought, "Man these guys were born in the wrong time because they're not even going to be on college radio." At first it was that bad. So, I wrote the book mostly as a way of forcing that generation of bands into the history of rock and roll because I didn't think the people writing about music would include them. They didn't sell any records.

AW: Yea, I was going to bring up the point that there have been a lot of books recently written about the L.A. and early hardcore scenes, books like Our Band Could Be Your Life, by Michael Azerrad, American Hardcore, by Steve Blush, Dance of Days, by Mark Anderson. Writers have called this a kind of cultural exhuming, because all literature previously written on punk has pretty much stopped at 1979, denying 80s hardcore and punk the importance many people feel it deserves. As someone who's written about rock and roll, and as someone who was there at the time, how do you feel about this new rock literature that's coming out?

JC: Yeah, I read most of American Hardcore, and all of Our Band Could Be Your Life. The latest books are about L.A., about the Germs and stuff. I haven't read those, but I just thought that American Hardcore was too locked into the idea that every city of any note had a scene worthy of attention, like I mentioned about Chicago, what was there was kind of derivative of English styles, and the bands that existed all *gravitated towards Joy Division or Gang of Four or something. And when I moved around, what I saw in the South Bay scene in L.A., in particular, not so much Hollywood, but where the Minutemen and Saccharine and Saint Vitus and Black Flag and the Descendents and Red Cross were... those bands weren't nervous about doing the right thing or being cool. They had complete confidence in what they wanted to do, in knowing what they wanted to do and then doing it 100%, instead of thinking, "Well, now there's this cowpunk thing and we should maybe do this and not wear those clothes anymore." And so, I think in American Hardcore he wastes a lot of paper and doesn't spend as much time where it's warranted by the music. And Our Band Could Be Your Life is a little more college rock. He could have written about the Descendents and the Wipers instead of the Replacements and Beat Happening and Mission of Burma, which are a little more of a college phenomenon, and that didn't exist in the beginning. I mean he covered some bands that were there a long time ago, but they were sort of anomalies. The real great stuff done in that period was done by people who were dropouts. They may have finished high school, but they got a guitar and got a cheap apartment or crashed in somebody's basement and focused on that, not on getting a happening lifestyle together. That all sort of came later....*

AW: Do you think rock has any meaningful place to go from here?

JC: Yeah. When I think about what I know from when I was younger, in retrospect, when FM radio got formatted in about 73, that's when it stopped being underground radio and became big business; that is what made it extremely hard to listen to the radio because suddenly you couldn't hear anything good on the radio, and the Ramones and a whole generation of bands started reacting to that and just really a year or two, you know, Television and the Ramones started in 74-5 and that was the time of the worst radio, and MTV wasn't around yet, so there was nothing on TV to speak of. Midnight Special was on and I guess In Concert on ABC, and they were a little behind the curve, so you actually could see better music on television than you could hear on the radio because they were still playing arena bands from years earlier. But it got to where things got so bad, it opened the door for an opportunity, but you know you think about it, I'm talking about 1974, well it took until 1991 for Nirvana to get on hit radio. You know, bands don't last that long.

You can't be optimistic about any one band, I would say. Like right now there's good music coming from even around the mainstream from the White Stripes and the Hives, and Queens of the Stone Age, and maybe a few other bands are kind of testing radio out, and they get a little bit, but is any of them going to sell five million albums and change the chessboard? I don't think those bands are going to do it, and that means at the moment, nothing will change radically. Until people gravitate towards good word-of-mouth kind of music....

We decided to do the O&O tour because, we put Wretch Like Me in front of other people's hands, you know, Honest Don's or Fat's or Epitaph's bands that are selling

Interviews

ten or thirty or fifty thousand albums, and so Wretch is on those shows, and they're just blowing those bands off the stage because they're a powerhouse band, and they're into Black Flag – I mean, they remember it. They saw, and they have that kind of commitment to starting the energy going and pushing it all the way, and they're good enough players that they don't screw the music up, and the audiences just sat there. To me it told me that we have to start all over, and make our own audience. So, the idea of putting all of our bands together, which we consider the best bands that are out there. I mean I've seen some bands that are really good, but our bands can go out together and work together, so the gig doesn't take eight hours to conclude; they all hit their marks and make it work because sometimes a four band bill can be a long ordeal. People don't want to go on early, that sort of thing.

So, anyway, that's our approach right now, just focus on putting the good music together and try to draw attention to it, and you just have faith that the people who are there will tell people that it was the best gig they've been to, and that that will slowly build momentum in the old fashioned way, word of mouth. We're media inundated, we're drowning in media, but it's like we're in the Middle Ages in Rock and Roll because it's all word of mouth. No one trusts radio; no one trusts anything. You hear one song you like, you buy the record, it's got ten shitty songs after the one you like because it's a fake band, and you can burn people once or twice, but... See I'm not young enough to know how the file-sharing thing is going to affect everything... do kids hear new music that way....

AW: Do you think if the Black Flag/Unicorn deal happened it could have affected the mainstream and radio?

JC: You know, it's hard to picture really. I think the record would have been a success if the Unicorn-MCA system had been in place. Primarily because they played everywhere they could possibly play. Even if it wasn't in a real rock club, if it was just somebody setting them up at their house. So, they would be playing in states like Oklahoma or Montana and all over the place, and you have to do that if a major like MCA was going to put records into Musicland stores and shopping malls and stuff like that. It wouldn't have worked for anybody but probably Black Flag and maybe the Dead Kennedys because the appeal to kids in high school in those years.... You know we wouldn't have been able to throw the Minutemen through the same system or something like that because they weren't touring at that point, and they were too much for a high school kid who was really looking for an adrenaline rush. They didn't want something that experimental....

Interview by Rob O'Connor, 1992
This excerpt is from the first lengthy interview I did after the initial publication of R&TPN. It was a phoner published in issue #3 of an interesting short-lived fanzine called Throat Culture.

Rob: Reading the book – and this is just my interpretation and I've asked others but no one else I now has read the whole thing, generally because they find it very hard going. Not that they don't like it but it's dense. There are a lot of ideas and they have to read slowly, but what they have gotten out of it and what I have gotten out of it is that it's a real fan's devotion to it, which I think is how we all come to the music originally, out of a fan's appreciation. And I guess one of the unusual things about the book is that even after you've gone through all the years being in the business you still retain that fan's devotion. You spot certain bands at what you consider to be their sell out or change from the original goal, but you still seem to have the same goal, even though you've obviously moved on away from that.

Joe: *Yeah, yeah, as a writer, I'm not interested in doing something that's not essential. In films, or in music there are authentic attempts and everything else in terms of spoofs or ironic treatments, anti-heroic hero films, all the stuff spins off the primary attempt that is sincere and authentic and straight and that doesn't mean that things aren't funny. I mean, the Ramones are the perfect case. They were very funny, but I think that the rock critics were primed to misrepresent the Ramones because to them the Ramones' love of the music didn't matter, what mattered was that it seemed like they were making fun of everything, that they couldn't play and yet they were playing...*

Rob: Sort of like the first post-modern band then.

Joe: *Yeah, but my point is that they weren't that. If they had been that, if they had been trying to be that, they wouldn't have been important, they just wouldn't have moved anybody. Their first album is musically problematic because they really were that primitive. But the second album is really very powerful. I like the second, third and fourth albums, and I don't think they would've got to that if their first album signified that they were making fun of rock music.*
   If I'm writing about bands that are current, I would say that a band that has a guileless or straight approach is likely to believe in what they're doing more than the band that is trying to appear all drugged-out or trying to be jokey or funny or trashy.

Interviews

A band like that may be really good and I value a lot of those bands, but I think on a fundamental level they are working in the wake of other people and the tendency is that they don't last as long because they don't have the clarity of belief in what they're doing. They're passing through.

Rob: Do you really think that rock critics have that sort of effect on what people buy, the way people perceive things?

Joe: No, but we're in a weird situation in the late 80s and the 90s. Most people in the record buying demographics, they don't know anything about the 60s so the only place they find out about the 60s, outside of buying the records themselves, to find out specifics they have to read those rock critics. And it becomes more and more important only because the hits that were perennials from the 60s are going to keep bringing people back to those myths that are mostly bullshit. I don't know what the most serious of them all is – maybe that all drugs are useful, or that we can all live in a commune, whatever those things are. But I knew nobody else was working on anything like it, and that it was important, so I thought I could do something that would state the case for the music, regardless of which little part of the aesthetic it was in. Commercial metal or underground metal or punk rock or underground rock. I tried to first get a useful definition of the music.

Rob: One thing about rock music is that, as you point out, it's usually a lot easier for people to identify with a particular singer, that the singer tends to suddenly become separate from the band in a lot of ways because of all the attention put on that person and yet it seems that people tend to, okay, I always thought a good example of this would be the Rolling Stones. It's almost like everyone relates to somebody different in the band, like there's somebody for everybody and while the music is what, umm..., I don't even know what comes first; whether people first like the idea of the Rolling Stones or the music. Obviously the music at some point had to be good in order to build the legend the way it is but the thing is that people are still very drawn into a Keith Richards or even a Charlie Watts.

Joe: I don't think I spent enough sentences on the Stones in the book but what's interesting about Keith Richards is that he's in a sense the ultimate druggie but he also has one of the purest interests in the music and the same is true with Watts probably. He's such a retiring personality, you don't hear from him, but he did that solo thing not too long ago and that seems to indicate that he's got his own slant. I would say the reason the band has existed for so long is that it's gotta be those two. Mick Jagger is not taken that seriously and hasn't been for quite a while. I mean, he's a star so nobody argues when MTV throws the videos right on but his last attempt at a solo tour didn't pan out. I wouldn't go out of my way to insult them. You can compare them to a lot of people from that era and say they're way ahead of the game just on talent or class or whatever.

Rob: The one part of the book I really have to commend you on and the chapter I want to focus on the most is the one about rock critics. Because your quotes from black musicians on the influences of country music in their work is the most ignored thing –

Joe: Part of it was the time I guess but... I don't know if they don't like America, but they don't trust it. They would write reviews of music with the racial idea that they might be able to prevent lynching by their record reviews and that implied a history of one way rip-off or borrowing. You know, if they like the band it was borrowing, if they hated them it was a rip-off. Musical people are not like that. Those critics put off Led Zeppelin and Black Sabbath because they thought that that sound and that effect was achieved technologically; they didn't hear the rhythm section, they don't understand that music starts with the drums and those two bands, especially Zeppelin, they couldn't have played traditional blues –

Rob: Oh it would've been boring as hell –

Joe: – secondhand with a drummer like that. Bonham's take on the rhythm changed the whole impression of motion or impact....

Rob: I think it's just a matter of everything getting too big. When you find you can sell 15 million records of something, you start to get weird ideas in your head.

Joe: I know I belabored the SST situation in the book but I was certain that we ranked. We ranked with a half dozen labels that were important as labels and we didn't sell shit compared to the others, but I think we had as big an impact. When we started people thought punk rock was over with and the only non-major label stuff college radio was playing was I.R.S. –

Rob: Right, ahgh god, yeah –

Joe: You know, people don't remember that and that's to a certain extent what SST erased. Now the stuff that major labels are signing are bands that were at Black Flag gigs, not at Romeo Void gigs. I mean, who are those bands? That scene is always around, the college pop thing, but that's how bad things were; and the Dead Kennedys, they were their own thing whereas what you can do with a label that a band can't do single-handedly is that you can almost throw a bunch of dots on the paper for people to connect and draw the aesthetic. I think most people did that. There were a few people who bought almost anything we put out and they knew Black Flag was the label and they would come up to them after their gigs all over the country and ask them about the various things and see how, in their minds, they connected Saint Vitus to the Minutemen. What was the aesthetic commonality? And I was wondering that myself. But SST should not be in the situation it's in. They took on everything they wanted as an expression of their own taste and I would never have done that. The market doesn't understand that. All the market does is say, "okay, this not what SST delivers anymore therefore I won't order these until I find out from a third source that it's great."

Rob: Yeah but doesn't that limit what SST can do because then it becomes a be-all end-all?

Joe: It was a label where you had Black Flag, the Minutemen, Saccharine Trust, Saint Vitus, Hüsker Dü, Meat Puppets. We had all these corners staked out and yet they were all bands. They played live in the studio, they toured and what I'm saying is that I would have had no qualms about making a sub-label –

Rob: I see, okay –

Joe: – because, besides communication with the audience, it's also respecting the, uh... I can't say it was the conscious aesthetic at the beginning of the label because I don't know exactly what Chuck and Greg were thinking... all I know is that they're individualists of the same sort that ran Sun and Stax and they've gone too far in too many directions at once and they're scrambling and that's a shame because it could've been handled. As Sub-Pop and all these 7 inch-underground-limited edition whatever, as the underground goes up its own asshole and everyone who's cut it with a pop sense gets signed by a major, most of these major signings will be dropped and a few will make money but really, we're two or three years away from 1975. That kind of played-out, leveled-out, watered-down feel from which we begin to look for the new Ramones.

Rob: Do you think it will be anything that's ever gonna sound like that?

Joe: You look at the differences between Black Sabbath and the Ramones and, much quicker, between the Ramones, Motörhead and Black Flag. That Trumvirate all occured really within three years. In Motörhead, it's the bass player with the musical imagination and he's better or worse depending on who's around him because he's not the lead player. He's got a great guitar player now and their last album was great. I never would've guessed that Motörhead at this stage would be so good, but their last two albums are probably their best records. And the guy was in Hawkwind before! He looks like a burn-out but he doesn't play like one at all. So, that's the thing, you can't anticipate how the same three instruments are gonna combine because it's gonna be the people....

Interview by Kevin Unsell, March 1986

Kevin lived in Naperville and when he heard my sister's name asked her if she was related to the guy who produced the Minutemen's "Project: Mersh" EP. We met next time I was in town, and this is an excerpt from my first interview which appeared in Non-Stop Banter, Mar./Apr. 1986, just as I left SST.

Kevin: What do you know about D. Boon's death?

Joe: *I was in Naperville for the holidays when it happened. He and his girlfriend were on their way to her parents' house for Christmas and it was close to four in the morning. So it's hard to say what happened. Apparently, the axle broke on the van. It was the van they toured in, D. Boon owned it. The broken axle took them off the road... and they rolled down an embankment. Jeannine is D.'s girlfriend's sister and she worked our mail order. She is paralyzed, so once she's out of the hospital she'll be in a wheelchair and we're gonna try to get her working on our computer system. You know, try to get her something she can do without any problem.*

Kevin: What is the fate of the Minutemen now?

Joe: *Well, they're... Mike and George are gonna play together and they're trying out guitar players. They're gonna call it something else but they'll still be playing together. I'm sure the band will sound quite a bit different because they're not gonna get a guitar player with the same background. D. Boon and Mike Watt had the same background, in particular, what they listened to as kids. It's hard to say...*

Kevin: It's a terrible thing.

Joe: *...what will happen to with them in the future.*

Kevin: How did you come up with the title to the acoustic piece on "3-Way Tie" ("Hittin' the Bong")?

Joe: *Well, that was just a little joke on D. Boon. He was always losing weight and always quitting smoking pot and...*

Kevin: Always trying to...

Joe: Yeah, but he's always doing it, too. Working with the Minutemen is always fun because they're really plastic. You can play around and encourage them to play around with their image. They're really self-deprecating to the point of... you get sick of it.

Kevin: Yeah, I like their pictures on "3 Way Tie (for Last)." They all have big smiles and George Hurley is giving the finger and Watt has People magazine with Bob Dylan with his arm around Madonna. You can tell that it is a big, fun joke.

Joe: Well, that's the thing. That's what D. Boon's death should tell you. You only live once...

Kevin: Right.

Joe: ...So why do it conservatively? You have to leave something that was the real thing. D. Boon did that....

Kevin: How has radio changed recently and how will it change?

Joe: Recently, radio has found a new... uh... equilibrium. The formats like AOR, Top-40, and CHR are still strong. The difficult thing is to find a station in a big market and find someone in there willing to try something new... if it doesn't fly, it's not because there is a conspiracy. But at least you tried. It's like trying to find somebody who wants to wing it and try something bold but people don't like to do that in business. WXRT has been very slow to incorporate anything new into what they do because they get complaints from their regular listeners.

Kevin: If you listen to XRT now it seems they've gone gung-ho for R.E.M. and Talking Heads over the past year.

Joe: Yeah, that's interesting. I'm a little surprised that Hüsker Dü and Meat Puppets aren't following R.E.M. on the radio.

Kevin: One last question, what does the future hold for rock and roll?

Joe: I don't know.

Interview addenda...

There are also a number of interviews that are available to read or listen to online:

1999 by Randy Gelling at *Perfect Sound Forever*
furious.com/perfect

2006 by Drew Katsikas at *The High Hat*
thehighhat.com

2008 by Andrew Earles at *Paste*
pastemagazine.com

2008 by Erin Yanke at *KBOO*
kboo.fm

2008 by Tony Rettman at *Swing Set*
swingsetmagazine.com

2011 by Matt Smith-Lahrman
smithlahrman.blogspot.com

also,

2008 WFMU John Allen program guest, History of L.A. Punk
wfmu.org

also by Joe Carducci

Rock and the Pop Narcotic - Testament for the Electric Church
Enter Naomi - SST, L.A. and All That...
Wyoming Stories: Yeung Girl, The Winter Hand, Homo Vampyrus
Stone Male - Requiem for the Living Picture *(available Spring 2013)*

also from Redoubt Press

redoubtpress.com
nightheronbooks.com

Reactions -

Enter Naomi

"One of 2007's finest reads on music."
Mike Wolf / *Time Out New York*

"As heartfelt memoir and micro-history of a genuinely inspirational, faraway time/place, *Enter Naomi*'s unfuckingbeatable."
M. Rowster / *Pig State Recon*

"Carducci makes a strong case that the 1980s were the last gasp of an American working class cultural movement called rock and roll. Enter Naomi is one of the exquisite corpses left over from the lost war."
Kevan Harris / *Dusted*

Rock and the Pop Narcotic

"This is not some opinionated critic's favorite-100-albums book. It's a coherent analysis by an informed musical sensibility."
Deena Weinstein / *Illinois Entertainer*

"This is the real shit."
Sean Carney / *U.S. Rocker*

"Demanding, a-trivial and universe-defining."
Byron Coley / *Forced Exposure*

"It is the Moby Dick of rock-crit – nothing else I've read comes close."
James Parker / *The Idler*

Joe Carducci
Rock and the Pop Narcotic
Testament for the Electric Church

Joe Carducci
Enter Naomi
SST. L.A. and All That...

Joe Carducci
Wyoming Stories
Young Girl . The Winter Hand . Homo Vampyrus

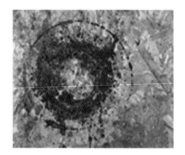

Joe Carducci
Stone Male
Requiem for the Living Picture

MICHELLE CARDUCCI